The Gay Archipelago

The Gay Archipelago

SEXUALITY AND NATION IN INDONESIA

Tom Boellstorff

PRINCETON UNIVERSITY PRESS

PRINCETON AND OXFORD

Copyright © 2005 by Princeton University Press
Published by Princeton University Press, 41 William Street,
Princeton, New Jersey 08540
In the United Kingdom: Princeton University Press,
3 Market Place, Woodstock, Oxfordshire OX20 1SY

LIBRARY OF CONGRESS CATALOGING-IN-PUBLICATION DATA

Boellstorff, Tom, 1969–
The gay archipelago : sexuality and nation in Indonesia / Tom Boellstorff.
p. cm.
Includes bibliographical references and index.
ISBN 0–691–12333–0 (hardcover : alk. paper)—
ISBN 0–691–12334–9 (pbk. : alk. paper)
1. Gay men—Indonesia—Identity. 2. Lesbians—Indonesia—Identity.
3. Gay men—Indonesia—Social conditions. 4. Lesbians—Indonesia—
Social conditions. 5. Gender identity—Indonesia. 6. Homosexuality—
Political aspects—Indonesia. I. Title.
HQ76.3.I5B64 2005
306.76′6′09598—dc22   200500187

British Library Cataloging-in-Publication Data is available.

This book has been composed in Sabon

Printed on acid-free paper. ∞

pup.princeton.edu

Printed in the United States of America

10 9 8 7 6 5 4 3 2 1

FOR BILL AND DÉDÉ

Contents

Illustrations

TABLES

Acknowledgments

THERE IS NO WAY I can do justice to all that I have been given. While for reasons of confidentiality I name none of my Indonesian interlocutors besides Dédé Oetomo, it is they who have made this book possible. Through all my time in Indonesia, all my mistakes and confusions and moments of insight, they have patiently taught me about their worlds. They have protected me, entertained me, and given me gifts beyond measure.

I dedicate this book to Bill Maurer and leave it at that. His generosity, good humor, and unfailing support made this book possible, and the intellectual and emotional debt is too great to enumerate. I also dedicate this book to Dédé Oetomo. He has been my greatest teacher, and I stand in awe of his intellect, courage, and grace. My debt to him can never be repaid, only honored.

Lawrence Cohen was my partner during the first phases of this project. His kindness, brilliance, and facility with the written word remain an inspiration. He will see himself on every page.

My mother, Neva Cozine, stood up for me early and often. She taught me how to cherish safety as well as take risks. Her advocacy for gay and lesbian rights in Nebraska and beyond has been inspiring; her ability to reinvent herself through life, a model I keep with me always. My father, John Boellstorff, taught me to persevere. My sister, Darcy Boellstorff, has been with me through it all. My stepfather, Daryl Hansen, has been a constant source of support and good cheer. Ruth Boellstorff, my grandmother, taught me how to find strength in every moment. Lisa Maurer and Maureen Kelly have been comrades in arms.

At Stanford University I found a group of colleagues who helped me frame this project in an anthropological light and continue to shape my intellectual growth. These include Katherine Coll, George Collier, Jane Collier, Carol Delaney, Paula Ebron, Akhil Gupta, Purnima Mankekar, Renato Rosaldo, and, above all, my dissertation advisor Sylvia Yanagisako.

Through the years I have been lucky to have many colleagues whose insights have helped shape this book. These include Anne Allison, Dennis Altman, Leena Avonius, Geremie Barmé, Evelyn Blackwood, Pheng Cheah, Jean Comaroff, Robert Corber, Tony Crook, Deborah Elliston, Shelly Errington, Judith Farquhar, James Ferguson, Thamora Fishel,

Katherine Gibson, Byron Good, Sharyn Graham, Stefan Helmreich, Terrence Hull, Peter Jackson, Iris Jean-Klein, Margaret Jolly, Carla Jones, Bruce Knauft, William Leap, Liisa Malkki, Hirokazu Miyazaki, David Murray, Diane Nelson, Don Nonini, Pat Norman, William O'Barr, Aihwa Ong, James Peacock, Charles Piot, Janice Radway, Vincente Rafael, Adam Reed, Annelise Riles, Kathryn Robinson, Lisa Rofel, Louisa Schein, Patricia Spyer, Mary Steedly, Anna Tsing, Margaret Weiner, Robyn Wiegman, and Saskia Wieringa.

I have benefited from the work and intellectual engagement of a community of scholars at Irvine, including Victoria Bernal, Mike Burton, Teresa Caldeira, Leo Chavez, Susan Coutin, Susan Greenhalgh, Inderpal Grewal, Karen Leonard, Michael Montoya, Kaushik Sunder Rajan, and Mei Zhan. Two dear friends in Long Beach, Brian Ulaszewski and Gina Wallar, offered me crucial emotional support. Tom Douglas helped keep me sane.

My participation in the "Queer Locations" group at the University of California Humanities Research Institute from January to June 2004 provided an important venue for revising this text. My thanks to Alicia Arrizon, Roderick A. Ferguson, Judith Halberstam, Glen Mimura, Chandan Reddy, Jennifer Terry, and Karen Tongson, as well as David Theo Goldberg.

My engagement with scholars in Indonesia has contributed significantly to my thinking. These include Mamoto Gultom, Irwan M. Hidayana, Nurul Ilmi Idrus, Marcel Latuihamallo, John H. McGlynn, Tuti Parwati Merati, Abby Ruddick, Pinky Saptandari, Yunita T. Winarto, and Danny Yatim.

Four colleagues read the first draft of this book in its entirety and offered extremely generous and helpful comments: Margaret Jolly, Johan Lindquist, Martin Manalansan, and Dédé Oetomo. I owe you one. Gilbert Herdt provided encouragement when it was needed the most.

At Princeton University Press, Mary Murrell saw this book begin and Fred Appel saw it through to its completion. My deepest thanks to them, as well as to Jennifer Nippins, Anita O'Brien, Debbie Tegarden, and my indexer, J. Naomi Linzer.

Support for research in Indonesia has been provided by the Social Science Research Council; National Science Foundation; Department of Social and Cultural Anthropology at Stanford University; Morrison Institute for Population and Resource Studies; Ford Foundation; Center for Asian Studies and Academic Senate Council on Research, Computing, and Library Resources at the University of California, Irvine; and Center for the Teaching of Malay and Indonesian.

Parts of chapters 1 and 4 were developed from "The Perfect Path: Gay Men, Marriage, Indonesia," *GLQ: A Journal of Gay and Lesbian Studies*

5(4):475–510. Parts of chapter 2 were developed from "Ethnolocality," *The Asia Pacific Journal of Anthropology* 3(1) (2002):24–48. Parts of chapters 1, 3, 4, and 6 were developed from "Dubbing Culture: Indonesian *Gay* and *Lesbi* Subjectivities and Ethnography in an Already Globalized World," *American Ethnologist* 30(2) (2003):225–242. Parts of chapter 4 were developed from "Zines and Zones of Desire: Mass Mediated Love, National Romance, and Sexual Citizenship in *Gay* Indonesia," *Journal of Asian Studies* 63(2) (2004):367–402.

Note on Indonesian Terms and Italicization

ALL NON-ENGLISH TERMS are Indonesian unless otherwise noted. Following standard practice, I italicize Indonesian terms on first use only, except for the following three terms: *gay, lesbi,* and *normal.* I italicize these throughout due to their similarity to English terms. I follow standard Indonesian orthography except that when writing *gay* language terms the front unrounded vowel /é/ (spelled "e" in Indonesian, along with the schwa) is written as "é" for clarity. Indonesian usually marks plurals by reduplication (*buku*, "book"; *buku-buku*, "books") or not at all if clear from context (*dua buku*, "two books"). I use English plural markers on Indonesian terms; for example, warias, tempat ngebers. All translations are my own unless noted otherwise.

PART ONE

The Indonesian Subject

CHAPTER ONE

Introduction

To You Who Have Opened This Book

If you have opened this book hoping for a traveler's tale in gay Indonesia, you may be disappointed. Yet I hope you will do more than skip ahead to the stories I tell. While I love a good story as much as anyone else, I also realize that we live in a time where the numbing reduction of debate to sound bites reflects a deep-seated hostility to asking the hard questions. Some readers may find this book refreshingly free of jargon; others may find it full of jargon. While it's difficult to please everyone, I have tried to write the most accessible book I can while remaining true to the following conviction: we are most human when we reflect upon the ways of thinking that constitute the very stuff of which our lives are made.

This book is written primarily to be read by cultural anthropologists—not the folks who dig up bones or reassemble ancient pottery, but those who hang out with contemporary peoples to learn about their ways of thinking and living. However, even if you are not typically interested in the theories of contemporary cultural anthropology (I just call this "anthropology" in this book), I hope you might find that wrestling with the intellectual issues I bring up can be as rewarding as good stories and can provide a better understanding of gay and lesbian life. For instance, while discussing the kinds of sex gay men have with each other in Indonesia might seem important (and I do discuss this), it turns out to be just as important to discuss how we in the West decide when two things are "different" or "the same."

Although this is not a short book, it represents only about half of the material I have published thus far on the gay archipelago. Additional articles analyze dimensions of gay and lesbian life touched upon only briefly in this book, reinforcing many points I make (the key articles are Boellstorff 1999, 2002, 2004a, 2004b, 2004c, 2004d, 2004e). I indicate where these additional articles might be useful.

Every word of this book is written knowing that it may someday be translated into Indonesian. For such a future Indonesian audience, my hopes are the same as for my English-speaking audience: an appreciation for the lives of gay and lesbian Indonesians, and an appreciation for the value of stepping back from tantalizing impressions of the everyday to ask how human social relations come to be, are sustained, and change over time. The title "The Gay Archipelago" is obviously not meant to imply that all Indonesians are gay, but that there is a gay archipelago that lies amidst the national archipelago. My use of "archipelago" in this book has no relation to the notion of "the gulag archipelago" used by Aleksandr Solzhenitsyn with reference to the former Soviet Union (Solzhenitsyn 1973)—a use of "archipelago" indexing a different form of state power, and a history of which my Indonesian interlocutors were unaware.

I do not recommend policies or provide solutions in this book. Solutions are important, but the rush to solutions can be part of the problem. Solutions are helpful, but in an important way they are boring: they close doors and silence debates. While I care about finding answers and often work as an activist, for this book I am more interested in asking new questions, questions that could point toward new visions of social justice.

TERMS OF DISCUSSION

In a classic essay, Clifford Geertz identified the goal of anthropology as "a continuous dialectical tacking between the most local of local detail and the most global of global structure in such a way as to bring them into simultaneous view" (1983:68). Nowadays, however, details can be global—and structure local—as much as the other way around. In the same essay Geertz wrote about the situation in his field site—near Surabaya, one of the primary field sites of this book—by saying it was characterized in the 1950s by a "curious mixture of borrowed fragments of modernity and exhausted relics of tradition" (60). In the contemporary moment, however, neither cultural transformation nor ethnographic interpretation can be understood as "continuous dialectical tacking" or "curious mixtures." New understandings of imbrication and transfer are needed. Geertz, like myself, was writing of Indonesia, a nation that has long served as an important laboratory for social theory in anthropology. Indonesia can now highlight changing forms of social life in an era of globalization.

For some time now Westerners have tended to think they live in a world that is already globalized. From the perspective of *The Lexus and the Olive Tree* (Friedman 2000) or *Empire* (Hardt and Negri 2001) to the global war on terror, there seems to be no corner of the Earth that remains untouched, as if the most "isolated native" drinks Coca-Cola or knows of those who do. The idea that those whom anthropologists studied were ever truly isolated was a fantasy (after all, anthropologists were there to study them). However, the trope of distance and otherness persists not just in anthropology but in the social sciences and beyond. It encodes a set of assumptions about the production of knowledge (knowledge is knowledge of *difference*) and the nature of human being (culture is, in the end, *local*).

In this book I offer *dubbing culture* as a metaphor for conceptualizing contemporary globalizing processes, ethnographic practice in an already globalized world, and the homologies between these projects of interpretation and reconfiguration. Where "writing culture" called attention to the possibility of a reflexive anthropology that decentered ethnographic authority (Clifford and Marcus 1986), "dubbing culture" suggests a postreflexive anthropology that decenters the ethnographic project itself. "Dubbing" undermines the empiric of ethnography, predicated as it is on the authentic. The term "dubbing culture" is my own invention, but it draws upon a late 1990s controversy in Indonesia where the dubbing of Western television shows was banned on the grounds that if Westerners appeared to speak Indonesian in the mass media, Indonesians would no longer be able to tell where their culture ends and authentic Indonesian culture begins.

Surfing the boundary between emic and etic, I use this term to investigate the surprising resonances between the dubbing controversy and how some Indonesians come to think of themselves in terms of the Indonesian words *gay* and *lesbi*. More generally, "dubbing culture" provides a rubric for rethinking globalization without relying on biogenetic (and, arguably, heteronormative) metaphors like hybridity, creolization, and diaspora, which imply prior unities and originary points of dispersion. In dubbing culture, two elements are held together in productive tension without the expectation that they will resolve into one—just as it is known from the outset that the speaker's lips will never be in synch with the spoken word in a dubbed film. "Dubbing culture" is queer: with dubbing, there can never be a "faithful" translation. It is like the relationship between voice and image in a dubbed film or television show: each element articulates a different language, yet they are entangled into a meaningful unit. It is a relationship more intimate than dialogue, but more distinct than monologue. While I intend the concept of dubbing culture to be broadly relevant, it is particularly salient with regard to gay and lesbian Indonesians because their sexualities are so self-evidently novel—in comparison to, say, "heterosexuality" in Indonesia or the West, which is no less a product of the times but is often misrecognized as natural, eternal, and unchanging.

This book is about gay and lesbian lives in Indonesia—the fourth most populous nation after India, China, and the United States—and what these lives imply for overlapping fields of inquiry including queer theory, Southeast Asia studies, mass media studies, globalization studies, postcolonial theory, and anthropology. Yet this book is an ethnography of sexual "subject positions," not persons per se, and is only occasionally about the Indonesian gay and lesbian political "movement," which is important but not indicative of how gay and lesbian lives are typically lived. I am interested in the social categories *gay* and *lesbi* not just because they are remarkable but because to Western eyes they can appear so mundane. I explore how these social categories have come into being, how they transform ostensibly Western concepts of homosexuality, and how they are taken up and lived in the Indonesian context. My data come largely from individual lives, and throughout I discuss the agency, freedom, and choice in how Indonesians negotiate their subjectivities within systems of power. Yet these systems of power create the preconditions for "agency" in the first place—a term that (alongside "freedom," "choice," and "negotiate") reveals more about Western ideologies of the autonomous self than the lived dynamics of selfhood. Too often discussions of agency assume structures of power against individual "negotiation," losing sight of how agency is also a transindividual social fact. A postreflexive anthropology must destabilize the figure of the preculturally agentive person that robs the ethnographic enterprise of its ability to investigate the relationship between the social and the subjective.

As someone originally trained as a linguist, I find anxieties over agency quite odd. I can, at will and as often as I please, create a well-formed sentence never before produced in the history of the English language—"I saw a black cat look strangely at an excited mouse near Redondo Avenue." Yet I cannot invent new grammars at will; my speech takes place within a horizon of language. Similarly, my agency is produced through (not "constrained by") culture. The linguistic metaphor has proven useful in addressing issues of postcoloniality: "a key question in the world of postcolonial scholarship will be the following. The problem of capitalist modernity cannot any longer be seen simply as a sociological problem of historical transition . . . but as a problem of translation, as well" (Chakrabarty 2000:17; see also Liu 1999). Dubbing, a translation that revels in its inevitable failure (moving lips that will *never* match the sounds of speech), opens up new ways to conceptualize relationships of similitude and difference when new incommensurabilities make "the stakes of translation seem high" (Povinelli 2002:321).

This book's starting point is the apparent puzzle of Indonesians who use the terms *gay* and *lesbi* in at least some contexts of their lives, yet consider these to be "authentically Indonesian" (*asli Indonesia*) ways of being. Under conditions ranging from grudging tolerance to open bigotry—but characterized above all by a society that does not know they exist—Indonesians reach halfway across the world to appropriate these terms, transforming them through practices of daily life to interpret apparently "local" experiences. It is *always* clear to Indonesians of any ethnic or religious background that the terms *gay* and *lesbi* do not originate in locality or tradition.

However, in contrast to stereotypes of the elite, cosmopolitan homosexual, most gay and lesbian Indonesians are not rich or even middle class. Few of them speak English or have traveled outside Indonesia. Rarely have they had sex with, or even encountered, a gay or lesbian Westerner. Most have never seen Western lesbian or gay publications, nor have they read published materials produced by other gay and lesbian Indonesians. While concepts have moved to and from what is now called Indonesia for millennia, this has typically been enabled by linkages to institutional structures, as in the cases of world religions (Islam, Christianity, Hinduism, Buddhism), colonialism, capitalism, and nationalism. But no religious authority, state bureaucracy, or transnational corporation intentionally globalizes *gay* and *lesbi*: in this case concepts appear to move in the absence of an institutional framework. Importantly, what they move to is the nation-state of Indonesia, rather than specific islands or ethnic groups. *Gay* and *lesbi* are national in character; this is why national belonging appears alongside globalization as a focus of my analysis. For gay and lesbian Indonesians *understand their social worlds in national rather than simply global terms*—in surprising but often implicit accordance with the government's "archipelago concept," which represents Indonesia as an archipelago of diversity in unity. They dub this nationalist discourse in unexpected ways. This is why I use the term "cultural logics" (of being a gay or lesbian Indonesian) more often than "discourses," since discourses are typically understood to be intentionally produced by powerful institutions.

Thus, alongside the concept of dubbing culture, a key theoretical intervention of this book is to think through the implications of *archipelagic subjectivities and socialities*, which do not hew to continental imaginaries of clear borders embracing contiguous territories. The archipelago metaphor permits understanding selfhood and sociality as not possessing sharp external boundaries, yet characterized by islands of difference. I examine how *gay* and *lesbi* are founded on rhetorics of national belonging based upon the figure of the heterosexual nuclear family—paradoxical as that may seem from the vantage point of Western homosexualities (and scholarship on the nexus of ethnicity, race, class, gender, and sexuality). How is one to understand senses of selfhood that connect and confound traditional social scientific levels of analysis (and, arguably, lived experience in the West) such as local, regional, national, and global?

This book examines a wide range of sexualities and genders, many of which have different names in different parts of Indonesia or even within one area. As a result I employ several terminological conventions. These conventions are a campy sendup of social scientific obsessions with finding the "right words" to label "things" assumed to exist in the social world independent of the observer. For instance, from this point onward I consistently italicize the Indonesian terms *gay* and *lesbi* to indicate they are distinct from English "gay" and "lesbian." I also italicize *normal*, an Indonesian term that refers to dominant understandings of modern sexuality. I wish to underscore that while *gay* and *lesbi* Indonesians reterritorialize the concepts "gay" and "lesbian," the terms have their own history and dynamics: they are not just "gay" and "lesbian" with a foreign accent. In italicizing these terms I use a graphic device to hold them at arm's length, defamiliarizing them while highlighting that they are lived concepts, not just analytical conveniences.

This is important because many a work in sexuality and gender studies congratulates itself for, and frets about, "discovering" that terms like homosexual, lesbian, gay, or even sexuality and gender, cannot explain non-Western contexts. This concern (which "dubbing culture" will destabilize) has a long history, which Geertz can again summarize for us:

> The history of anthropology has in large part consisted in taking concepts put together in the West ("religion," "family," "class," "state"), trying to apply them in non-Western contexts, finding that they fit there rather badly at best, laboring to rework them so that they fit rather better, and then discovering in the end that, however reworked, many of the problems they pose—the nature of belief, the foundations of obligation, the inequality of life chances, the legitimacy of domination—remain clearly recognizable, quite alive. (C. Geertz 1990:77)

Claiming that concepts like "homosexual," "sexuality," and "gender" fail to explain non-Western realities misleadingly implies that the concepts are adequate in the West. It confuses modes of argumentation, mistaking interpretive frameworks for authoritative typologies. It also makes it difficult to examine how what Geertz terms "concepts put together in the West" are increasingly "put together" in non-Western contexts prior to the ethnographic encounter. Ethnographic objects that collapse the emic/etic distinction force crucial questions regarding globalization, similitude, and difference.

For this reason I am interested in intersectional theories of sexuality; that is, theories of sexuality that understand sexuality to be formed at the conjuncture of multiple cultural logics. This interest in intersectionality arises from my understanding of *gay* and *lesbi* Indonesians, but it also arises from a sensitivity to my position as a gay white man: my own cultural background predisposes me to see sexuality as a singular domain and "coming out" as movement along a single dimension. I would argue that the very idea of sexuality requires a disavowal of other domains, particularly gender and race—indeed, that the drawing of a line around a subset of human experience and calling it "sexuality" is a foundational moment permitting the exclusion of gender and race. I therefore see a danger in the very idea of "sexual culture," which encodes an assumption that sexuality has an independent cultural logic, rather than existing at the intersection of multiple discourses. The theoretical architecture I develop in this book is concerned with disrupting these tendencies of the category "sexuality."

In this book the category "*lesbi* women" includes not only feminine women but masculine women who in some cases think of themselves as women with men's souls. Both feminine and masculine *lesbi* women sometimes call themselves *lesbi*, but there are other terms.[1] In much of Indonesia, including parts of Java and Sumatra, *lesbi* women use *cewek* (which in colloquial Indonesian means "female") as a term for feminine *lesbi* women (Blackwood 1999). In this book I use *cewek* as a catch-all term for feminine *lesbi* women anywhere in Indonesia. Masculine *lesbi* women are known by a range of names, including *hunter* in southern Sulawesi and parts of Java, *cowok* (male) in parts of Sumatra, the Bugis term *calalai'* in southern Sulawesi, and *butchie* and *sentul* in parts of Java. Across Indonesia these persons are also known as *tomboi* (occasionally spelled *tomboy* or *thomboy*); in this book I use *tomboi* as a catch-all term for masculine *lesbi* women regardless of whether the person in question uses *tomboi*, *hunter*, or *lesbi* or does not have a name for their sexual and gendered subjectivity. I use *lesbi* as an overarching term.[2] I refer to male-to-female transvestites (best known by the term *banci*) as *warias*, the term they prefer. In the past I have referred to both warias and tombois as s/he (the Indonesian third-person singular pronoun *dia* is gender neutral). While such novel pronouns can be useful, I have come to believe that they are too exoticizing and reflect a theory of language in which "words" and "things" ideally have a one-to-one correspondence. As a result, in this book I refer to warias as "she" and tombois as "he," knowing, as they do, that social gender is productively imprecise.

I use the term "the West" ironically, with the understanding that "I refer to the effects of hegemonic representations of the Western self rather than its subjugated traditions" (Gupta 1998:36). "West" should be read as if always within scare quotes. For instance, the idea of "gay and lesbian Westerners" refers to dominant Western discourses of homosexuality, precisely the ones that would seem to be most capable of globalizing, and intentionally does not account for the great diversity in sexual and gendered regimes in the West. For *gay* and *lesbi* Indonesians, the United States is typically the West's exemplar, but the West can include Australia and even Japan. That Westernness has a long history of slippage in the archipelago is indicated by the fact that the Indonesian term for "west," *barat*, comes from the Sanskrit and now Hindi word for India (*bharat*), the West's "Orient."

SUBJECTIVITY AND SEXUALITY

In this book I eschew the identity-behavior binarism in favor of a language of *subject positions* (extant social categories of selfhood) and *subjectivities* (the various senses of self—erotics, assumptions about one's life course, and so forth—that obtain when occupying a subject position, whether partially or completely, temporarily or permanently). Focusing on subject positions and subjectivities turns attention to the total social fact of *gay* and *lesbi* selfhood. This is a basically Foucauldian framework that draws from the epistemological break between volumes 1 and 2 of *The History of Sexuality* (1978, 1985), wherein Foucault shifted from an emphasis on the "systems of power" inciting sexuality to "the practices by which individuals were led to focus their attention on themselves, to decipher, recognize, and acknowledge themselves as subjects of desire, bringing into play between themselves a certain relationship that allows them to discover, in desire, the truth of their being" (1985:4–5).

I do not think that the notion of identity is useless, just that with regard to the topics of this book it is a poor fit. I think of "subject position" as a rough translation of *jiwa*, which means "soul" but often has a collective meaning: *lesbi* women will sometimes say "*lesbi* have the same jiwa"; warias will sometimes say they "have the same jiwa"; or *lesbi* women and *gay* men will sometimes say they share a jiwa. I think of "subjectivity" as a rough translation of *pribadi* or *jati diri*, both of which mean approximately "self-conception"; a *gay* man once distinguished pribadi from jiwa by saying that "every person possesses their own pribadi." *Identitas* has a much more experience-distant, bureaucratic ring for most Indonesians: one *gay* man defined *identitas* as "biodata: name, address, and so on."

This framework of subject positions and subjectivities is how I flesh out a social constructionist theory of sexuality. My understanding of the human condition is that it is not possible to have subjectivities without subject positions. Phrases like "biological *basis*" or "biological *foundation*" for sexuality are misleading. Language again provides a convenient example. There is undoubtedly a biological human capacity to acquire language, and language universals (for instance, plurality). However, no one speaks "Language": people speak Chinese, English, or Indonesian, cultural and historical entities for which no gene will ever be found. The biological capacity for language is not ontologically prior to these historically and culturally contextual practices of speaking. We have been biologically designed not to be biologically designed, to be "incomplete or unfinished animals who complete or finish ourselves through culture—and not through culture in general but through highly particular forms of it" (C. Geertz 1973:49). The million dollar question, then, is this: Is being male or female, gay or straight, more like "Chinese" or "Language"? The scientific evidence supports the contention that social facts like sexuality and gender are more like "Chinese" than "Language," and thus that claims of a biological "basis" for sexuality or gender engage in a category mistake, confusing an analytical category for an experiential one. Sexualities (*gay*, *lesbi*, gay, lesbian, straight, bisexual, a "man who has sex with men"), indeed all subject positions, are like English or Chinese, not "Language"—products of history and culture.

Subject positions can be occupied in myriad ways ("teenager," for instance, can be occupied antagonistically as a rebel, or normatively as a "good student"). Construing subject positions as multiply inhabitable provides a way to conceptualize agency without interpreting the metaphor of social construction volitionally—deploying verbs of concerted, self-aware action like "negotiation" to posit a sexual self that stands outside culture.

This is primarily a study of "sexuality," however problematized. I often use phrases like "gender and sexuality" to highlight how for *gay* and *lesbi* Indonesians, gender and sexuality are mutually defining. Yet on some level this is redundant, since sexuality is always defined in terms of gender, nation, race, class, and a host of other social categories. I thus respectfully disagree with my colleagues who claim that the analytical distinction between gender and sexuality (most famously set out in Rubin 1984) is flawed because it is not possible to conceptually separate gender and sexuality. First, it is obviously possible to separate them in certain contexts, and this is not simply a product of academic debates or globalization (as the distinction between *gay* and *waria* in Indonesia indicates). Second, a division between gender and race, or sexuality and race, or race and class, and so on ad infinitum, is also not conceptually possible on some level, yet on another level it is not only possible but enormously useful on theoretical and political grounds. In the end, everything is connected to everything, but this insight is of limited use. The danger lies not in conceptually separating cultural domains, but in ontologizing such separations so that the foundationally intersectional character of social life, and social inequality, becomes obscured.

Throughout this book I employ a relational analysis with regard to gender and sexuality. I focus on *gay* men but also address *lesbi* women, male-to-female transvestites (*warias*), female-to-male transgenders (*tombois*), and so-called traditional homosexualities and transgenderisms. Male transvestites are well known to the Indonesian public, often by the rather derogatory terms *banci* or *béncong*. They are visible in Indonesian society to a degree that has no parallel in the West, and that continually surprises

Western visitors. Yet this visibility does not translate directly into acceptance: warias are acknowledged, but to a great extent acknowledged as inferior. I will at various points describe waria life as it shapes the *gay* and *lesbi* subject positions (see Boellstorff 2004b for a more detailed discussion of warias).

Like *gay* men, *lesbi* women can be found throughout Indonesia. In fact, there appears to have been greater mass media coverage of *lesbi* women than *gay* men when these subject positions began appearing on the national scene in the early 1980s, but this is probably an artifact of the greater scrutiny placed on women's sexuality more generally. As in the case of *gay* men, *lesbi* women can come from any class position. Since they usually come to their sexual subjectivities through mainstream mass media, as *gay* men do, it is not necessary that they be members of feminist organizations, have a high level of education, or live in the capital of Jakarta. There are many other similarities between *gay* men and *lesbi* women. Both usually describe their desires in terms of a desire for the same, and both the *gay* and *lesbi* subject positions are found nationwide. Historically, *gay* and *lesbi* appear to have taken form more or less together, as gendered analogues, suggesting the (sometimes fulfilled) possibility of socializing between *gay* men and *lesbi* women.

Although the bulk of my fieldwork has been among *gay* men and warias, I have spent a good deal of time with *lesbi* Indonesians. This presents me with a dilemma. I wish to particularize my discussion when it could be misunderstood as falsely universalizing to the experiences of *lesbi* women. Yet I also do not wish to footnote my *lesbi* material (Braidotti 1997); such a move would be not only methodologically suspect (given the importance of gender relationality) but politically unsound, given that *lesbi* Indonesians often identify isolation as an important issue. This dilemma is not simply due to the fact that as a man, spending time with women was more difficult: no researcher ever has equal access to all social groups within a particular field site. My path of compromise is to weave together my material on *gay* men and *lesbi* women, paying attention to points of both similarity and divergence and calibrating my work with existing scholarship on *lesbi* women. When my interpretations apply only to *gay* men, I refer only to them. When speaking of *gay* and *lesbi* Indonesians together, I always use "*gay* and *lesbi*" (rather than alternating between "*gay* and *lesbi*" and "*lesbi* and *gay*") to underscore that I have more data on *gay* men than *lesbi* women. This is also why this book is entitled *The Gay Archipelago* rather than *The Gay and Lesbi Archipelago*. This relational rather than monogendered approach is not a dreaded concession but a theoretical necessity: "the tendency to ignore imbalances in order to permit a grasp of women's lives has led too many scholars to forget that men and women ultimately live together in the world and, so, that we will never understand the lives that women lead without relating them to men" (Rosaldo 1980:396).

FIRST PRELUDE: INDEPENDENCE DAY

Indonesia celebrates its Independence Day every August 17, but to my knowledge the first time *gay* men celebrated Independence Day in their own world was in Surabaya on this night: Independence Day's eve, August 16, 2004. I have come to a place *gay* men call "*Pattaya*." It is named after the famed tourist beach in Thailand, a place most *gay* men have never seen but that is rumored to be full of gay men.[3] Pattaya in Thailand is a beach, but in Surabaya—Indonesia's second largest city—Pattaya is a dark, narrow lane running along one side of the Brantas River, near a small dam right in the center of town, near a shopping mall, a major hotel, and a train station. Some of the city's poor live along the sides of the lane in wood shacks, often without electricity, while others fish in the fetid waters of the river. On many nights over a hundred *gay* men stroll along the dark lane, hanging out and talking with friends while perched on the back of parked motorcycles, or (in the darkest "center" of Pattaya) stealing kisses from a lover.

This night I have come to the best-lit portion of Pattaya at 10:30 P.M., where the most "opened" *gay* men tend to congregate. There are about forty *gay* men and a handful of warias hanging out. Several men take a blue tarp and set it out on the pavement, and a few moments later a taxi makes its way precariously down the lane, which is only slightly wider than the taxi itself. A *gay* man exits the taxi with food: yellow rice sculpted into a little mountain, fish, chicken, vegetables—foods of a celebratory feast (*slametan*). A few nights ago 5,000 rupiah (about 50 cents) was gathered from each *gay* man at Pattaya to pay for this food.

Now we all sit down on the tarp, surrounding the food, and are silent as one of the participants begins to speak:

Okelah teman-teman, semua, selamat datang kembali ke Pattaya . . . Malam ini kita kumpul-kumpulnya dengan maksud, yaitu untuk merayakan kemerdekaan pada besok . . . bukan untuk sendiri-sendiri . . . tapi kita maksud bahwa kita ada di tengah masyarakat . . . kita double, ya.

Okay friends, all of us, welcome back to Pattaya . . . This night we gather together in order to celebrate our independence [day] tomorrow . . . not for ourselves . . . but we mean that we are in the midst of society . . . we are double, yes.

Then we close our eyes as someone else leads us in prayer: "let us pray for the souls of the heroes who have fallen for us." For these moments of prayer and remembrance, for the sake of Independence Day, *gay* men try to bring together what they call "the *gay* world" and "the *normal* world." And in this intersection, this failed intersection, they articulate the idea that their lives are "double."

Yet the linkages between being *gay* and the Indonesian nation go back much further than August 16, 2004.

Setting: Makassar, capital of South Sulawesi province on the island of Sulawesi (Celebes). *Place*: the waterfront. *Time*: August 17, 2000, Indonesia's fifty-fifth anniversary. Two years ago, the downfall of the dictator Soeharto had brought new possibilities and dangers.

It is in this uncertain context that the citizens of Makassar now celebrate Independence Day afternoon. The city of over a million people sits along Sulawesi's western coastline, looking out toward Borneo two hundred miles away. On this day the city has closed off the road running along the waterfront and set up a raised stage on one end; the normally traffic-filled street has become a walkway for hundreds. It is hot, and by midafternoon everyone is wilted. From the stage comes an announcement about a boat race; the speaker is a Dutch man who has been living in Makassar for some time. Afterwards a "traditional" drumming group performs. The music throbs in the humid air, but only a few Indonesians sit on the blistering pavement in front of the stage. Most crouch at the edge of the road taking shelter underneath makeshift tents, sipping cool sodas and trying to bear the heat.

That, however, is about to change, as the drummers end their performance and an Indonesian emcee takes the stage. He says: "Now, on this anniversary of our independence, we present to you a skit about AIDS by the group 'Sulawesi Style.'" A pregnant pause, and suddenly American teen pop sensation Britney Spears' international hit "Baby One More Time" fills the air. Fifteen members of Sulawesi Style take the stage wearing junior high school uniforms; they will soon present a skit in which a substitute teacher explains AIDS to her students. In this opening number, however, they dance in formation. These dancers are *gay* men, but for this performance about half are in drag. Karim, one of the most charismatic, moves quickly to the catwalk in front of the stage. His long black wig flowing in the ocean breeze, Karim struts toward the audience, hips marking the beat, lip-synching Britney flawlessly with arms outstretched, as if to take in the multitudes watching him. Multitudes? Where a few tired eyes watched the drummers minutes earlier, hundreds now pack the street to watch Sulawesi Style's performance. The heat is forgotten as adults, teenagers, even small kids scream with delight, pointing at the

Figure 1–1. An Independence Day performance. Author's photograph.

drag performers and dancing along; mothers in Muslim headscarves clap along, pushing their kids closer to the stage to see. The street has become a big party and Karim is the center, standing over the crowd in all his drag glory.

I climb the stairs next to the stage to snap the picture reproduced as figure 1–1: the masses of onlookers smiling in approval, Karim at the end of the catwalk, one leg crossed in front of the other as he sashays to the edge, framed against a shining blue sky meeting shining blue sea. Stepping down from the stage, I happen to walk by the Dutch man who introduced the boat races. Understandably he assumes I am a tourist who has wandered into the crowd; I guess this is why he feels compelled to pull me aside and inform me that "Here, it's not like with our culture. Here transvestites are magicians and healers." Of course, these are not transvestites, magicians, or healers, but *gay* men who hang out in the shopping mall and dress most of the time in jeans and tee-shirts. What challenges me this Independence Day is not difference but similitude: *gay* men lip-synching an American pop star. The audience believes this is just a show; they are not "accepting *gay* men." Yet I cannot imagine a Fourth of July where devoutly religious families would find this to be great entertainment for

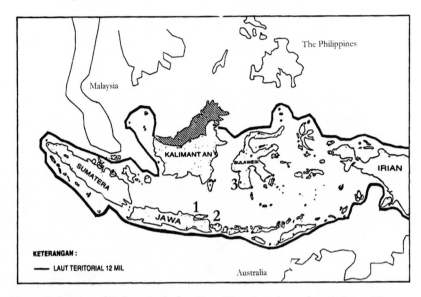

Figure 1–2. Map of Indonesia (before East Timor's independence). Most Western maps of Indonesia do not include the external border defined by the archipelago concept (black line). Numbers indicate the location of (1) the city of Surabaya, (2) the island of Bali, and (3) the city of Makassar. Lembaga Ketahanan Nasional (1995:17).

a holiday afternoon, where men in drag help to recall the independence of a nation in a state of crisis and change.

LOCATIONS

This book's archipelagic analysis will challenge the concept of boundary, which "is one of the least subtle in the social science literature" (Strathern 1996:520). The boundary determining which islands are part of Indonesia is not a geographic given: like constellations, archipelagos are networks, constituted through lines of connection. Indonesia occupies the world's largest archipelago, stretching over 3,977 miles (fig. 1–2). It is comprised of about 17,000 islands, about 6,000 of which are inhabited. (Note that all images of the archipelago in this book include East Timor as part of Indonesia; my fieldwork took place before and after East Timor's independence, but the archipelago concept began to be promulgated before East Timor's independence in 2002.) With about 230 million inhabitants and 670 ethnic groups, approximately nine-tenths of whom follow Islam, Indonesia is home to more Muslims than any other nation. Lying across trade routes that for centuries have linked East Asia with the Indian subcontinent, the Arab world, and Europe, this archipelago is anything but remote.

The imagined boundary delineating Indonesia does not correspond to any "traditional" polity or culture: it is inherited from the colonial encounter. The Dutch were the dominant power in this region from the 1600s until ousted by the Japanese at the beginning of World War II. The Dutch discouraged knowledge of their language beyond civil and domestic servants, and at independence less than 2 percent of Indonesians spoke Dutch (Anderson 1990:138, 197; Groeneboer 1998:1; Siegel 1997:13). In place of a European language, the Dutch communicated primarily through Malay, an Austronesian language that had been used for centuries in island Southeast Asia as a trade language. By the 1920s, nationalist groups had formed in the colony. While a few framed themselves in ethnic terms (such as *Jong Java* or "the young Javanese"), by the time of the "Youth Pledge" of 1928 nationalist sentiments were predicated on the assumption that independence was to be for the citizens of the archipelago, sharing a new quasi-ethnicity—indeed, an ethnocitizenship—as Indonesian; speaking Malay, renamed "Indonesian," as the national tongue.

Indonesia knew only two presidents during its first half-century as an independent nation. The first, Sukarno, worked for over twenty years to hold the young nation together in the context of communist and Islamic mass movements, conflicts in the military, and regional separatism. Getting citizens of the new nation to think of themselves as Indonesians first, and members of ethnic groups second, became a central goal of the postcolonial state. Sukarno's forceful anti-Western rhetoric and role in the formation of the Non-Aligned Movement helped sustain his rule until economic and political paralysis culminated in the bloody events of 1965–67, when an attempted coup and the murder of six generals provided a pretext for then-Major General Soeharto to seize power and eliminate the Indonesian Communist Party: it is estimated that over half a million people died.

Sukarno's rule was followed by the so-called New Order of Soeharto, which lasted until 1998. During this time, the period in which the *gay* and *lesbi* subject positions took form, development (*pembangunan*) replaced revolution (*revolusi*) as state keyword. The idea of national integration was intensified and redeployed through state ideologies, including the archipelago concept (*wawasan nusantara*) and family principle (*azas kekeluargaan*). Corruption and resistance to authoritarianism, as well as the social misery caused by the 1997–98 Asian financial crisis, forced Soeharto to step down in May 1998. The post-Soeharto "era of reform" (*era reformasi*) has seen unprecedented press freedoms and a resurgence of civil society. It has also seen a new visibility for political Islam, a rise in separatist movements, and the reframing of national governance in terms of regional autonomy (*otonomi daerah*), with a corresponding "rise of the local" (Aspinall and Fealy 2003:2) that would appear to renaturalize anthropology's own methodological and ontological emphasis on locality. Nonetheless, nationalism remains deeply felt by most Indonesians.

A central goal of this book is to examine how *gay* and *lesbi* subjectivities are linked to discourses of the nation. On one level this might seem obvious, since the concepts *gay* and *lesbi* are not accepted by local culture, but this is insufficient, since they are not accepted by national culture either. In contemporary Indonesia the concepts *gay* and *lesbi* remain poorly understood by most *normal* Indonesians, with the links between sexuality and nation largely obscured (S. Wieringa 2002:2). How can state ideology shape *gay* and *lesbi* sexualities the state never intended to incite?

In his famous 1871 definition, Tylor identified culture as "that complex whole which includes knowledge, belief, art, morals, law, custom, and any other capabilities and habits acquired by man as a member of society" (Tylor 1958 [1871]:1). While later thinkers have questioned Tylor's assumption that culture is a whole, what I find curious is his displacement of the question of belonging from culture to society. Tylor sees culture as acquired by "members of society" but does not ask how "societies" are bounded so that one person acquires one culture; another person, another. Recognized membership in society appears a priori. From the beginnings of anthropology, recognition has stood as precondition for culture, and the completion of recognition is belonging.

Given nationalism's continuing importance, it may surprise readers unfamiliar with the anthropology of Indonesia that virtually no anthropologists consider "Indonesia" to be their field site. It is possible to argue that this book is the first ethnography of Indonesians (rather than an ethnography of Javanese, Dayak, Minangkabau, etc.).[4] The Indonesian absence in anthropological research is shaped by ethnolocality (see chapter 2; Boellstorff 2002). I coin the term "ethnolocality" to name a spatial scale where "ethnicity" and "locality" presume each other to such a degree that they become, in essence, a single concept. This mode of representation originated in the colonial encounter as a means of impeding the possibility of translocal spatial scales other than colonialism (in particular, nationalism and Islamic movements). As reified in the work of the Leiden school, "custom" (*adat*) was understood to belong not to the Indies as a whole but to groups framed in terms of the equation of ethnicity and place. This assumes culture is the property of "the Balinese," "the Makassarese," "the Javanese," and so on. Although a large body of scholarship has denaturalized ethnolocality, it remains influential: national culture is often treated as a force impacting local culture rather than the possible location of culture in its own right. Indonesianist anthropology has produced an archipelago of literatures keyed to an archipelago of unitary cultures, discrete units *secondarily* shaped by an "Indonesia" conflated with the political, the urban, the modern, and ultimately with the inauthentic.

If a goal of John Pemberton's work (Pemberton 1994) is to demonstrate that the subject of Java is really a subject of "Java" (that is, that the notion of "Java" is a discursive formation, not a priori), my analysis works in reverse, seeking to erase the implicit scare quotes and show that the subject of "Indonesia" is a *subject of Indonesia*—amenable to an ethnographic analysis with strengths and weaknesses not fundamentally different from those found in ethnography conducted with reference to any other spatial scale. Ethnolocality marks this boundary between ruler and ruled and also between knower and known. In anthropological inquiry it became the "investigative modality" (Cohn 1996:5) demarcating the conceptual threshold between the ethnographic and the comparative. To the degree that ethnicity is understood in terms of kinship and reproduction, *heteronormativity also demarcates this threshold.* Can there be subject positions with spatial scales that are foundationally national, even if persons inhabiting such subject positions might consider themselves in terms of ethnolocality with respect to other aspects of their lives? Could one think of oneself, for instance, as "Madurese" with relation to conceptions of religion, but "Indonesian" with relation to sexuality?

The most radical theoretical and methodological intervention of this book is that I take Indonesia as an ethnographic unit of analysis. A queer reading of the category "Indonesian," it is an *ethnography of Indonesians*, not of the Batak, Buginese, Madurese, or any other ethnolocalized group. Indeed, it often seems that political scientists and anthropologists study two different objects: "Indonesia" versus "local culture." There is a theoretically sophisticated body of literature on Indonesian, the national language, as a language of the public and the translocal (e.g., J. Errington 1998, 2000; Keane 1997, 2003; Siegel 1986, 1997). Yet rarely in the corpus of Indonesianist anthropology is one reminded that Indonesian is the "mother tongue" of a growing percentage of Indonesians, learned alongside rather than subsequent to ethnolocalized tongues like Javanese or Balinese. Never to my knowledge is one reminded that millions of Indonesians (including some of my interlocutors) are functionally *monolingual* in Indonesian (Sneddon 2003:202, 205). It is not solely due to his upperclass status that Sakti, the *gay* protagonist of the hit 2004 film *Arisan!* (Nia diNata, director), speaks only Indonesian (and not also Batak, his family's ethnolocal language).

Monolingual Indonesian-speakers are absent from the ethnographic record because they are inconceivable from the perspective of ethnolocality. They seem to belong to the archipelago but not to any of its component islands. The national motto of Indonesia is "unity in diversity," but monolingual Indonesian-speakers, like *gay* and *lesbi* Indonesians, do not seem to have any "diversity," only unity. They appear improper. Yet while I carry out fieldwork on multiple islands, I ultimately construe them as elements of a single "site." Just as someone studying a city might work in several neighborhoods but consider her or his conclusions to be reflective of that city, so my fieldwork takes "Indonesia" as its subject. In one sense my research is an example of multisited fieldwork (Marcus 1995). Yet since I take the nation-state of Indonesia as the ethnographic unit of analysis, in a fundamental sense my research is neither multisited nor comparative; it is a "multi-sited ethnography in one place."[5]

This book is based on twenty-two months of activism and fieldwork over a twelve-year time span, centered on a period from July 1997 to May 1998, with three periods of earlier work (1992, 1993, and 1995), as well as additional work in 2000, 2001, 2002, and 2004. My knowledge of *gay* and *lesbi* Indonesians is based on participant observation and other qualitative methods. Qualitative methods are not more micrological or localizing than quantitative ones; they illuminate different aspects of social life. When explaining this to students I tell the story of a quantitative researcher and a qualitative researcher who go to Japan to study the Japanese language. The quantitative researcher prepares a survey that can be distributed to a large, random sample, providing valuable data concerning, say, varieties of Japanese dialects. The qualitative researcher studies a far smaller sample; he or she could not learn every vocabulary item of Japanese, for instance, or every dialect. Yet through immersion in daily life this person could learn to *speak* Japanese: from a handful of individuals one can learn how to communicate with millions. Qualitative research can be effective in drawing out cultural logics that, like languages, are shared: it is an approach suited to the study of similitude. There is no necessary relationship between methods and spatial scale: it is not true that qualitative methods like ethnography are "more local" and quantitative methods "more global." As globalization becomes seen as the new default state of affairs in the world, there is a real need for qualitative studies of the global.

The complexities of *gay* and *lesbi* life present further challenges to traditional ethnographic methodologies. Despite the fact that (since at least Leach's *Political Systems of Highland Burma*) anthropologists question that cultures are integrated, there remains a strong sense that ethnography should portray a total way of life (Leach 1964). But there is no *gay* and *lesbi* village I could study: *gay* and *lesbi* worlds are fragmented, taking form in stolen moments in places like apartments and parks. It is not a community with the kinds of recognized leaders that anthropologists often rely upon for authoritative accounts. One reason I find the ethnographic vignette so useful in this book is that *gay* and *lesbi* lives are lived in vignettes.

Because *gay* and *lesbi* lives are so self-consciously not a product of locality, I decided to conduct research in three sites: Surabaya in East Java, Makassar (formerly Ujung Pandang) in South Sulawesi, and Bali. I chose these sites because they are relatively close to one another yet contrast in ethnic and religious makeup, degree of contact with non-Indonesians, and position in the Indonesian nation-state. I have also spent periods from a few days to a month in Jakarta, Kediri (East Java), Bandung (West Java), Yogyakarta, Samarinda (East Kalimantan), Balikpapan (East Kalimantan), and several rural sites in East Java and South Sulawesi.

With a population of over three million, my first site, Surabaya, is the capital of the province of East Java. Located on Java's north coast across a narrow strait from the island of Madura, it is a major port as well as a financial and commercial center. Predominantly Javanese and Muslim with a large Madurese community, there are also significant numbers of Javanese Christians, Christians from other ethnolocalized groups, and smaller numbers of Hindus, Buddhists, and Confucians. Makassar, my second site, is the sixth-largest city in Indonesia, provincial capital of South Sulawesi and "gateway" to eastern Indonesia. Like Surabaya, it lies on the coast and has an active port. It has a reputation for conservative Islam. The Bugis and Makassarese are the dominant ethnolocalized groups. My third site is predominantly Hindu Bali: Denpasar (the capital, with a population of approximately 375,000), the Kuta/Legian/Seminyak tourist corridor in south Bali, and the Lovina/Singaraja tourist corridor on the north coast. Kuta, Legian, and Seminyak, on the western coast approximately seven miles south of Denpasar, were sleepy fishing villages until the 1970s, when tourism became dominant. It has remained so (Picard 1996), even after the 2002 bombing in Kuta.

Before beginning fieldwork, I expected to find fundamental differences in *gay* and *lesbi* subjectivity between these three sites. Surely Muslim, Christian, and Hindu *gay* and *lesbi* Indonesians would differ, as would those in the tourist zones of Bali versus urban Makassar or Surabaya. However, I was continually confronted by similarity among my sites and across demographic variables. Such similarity challenges the theoretical apparatus of anthropology, attuned as it is to discovering difference.

Since being *gay* or *lesbi* is rarely linked to one's working life, my participant observation took place mostly in the evenings. With *gay* men this meant innumerable nights hanging out in parks, discos, or apartments; with *lesbi* women my socializing, like theirs, was largely in the more domestic environments of homes and apartments, but sometimes shopping malls and other semipublic spaces as well. My participant observation also gave me ample opportunity to explore the *normal* world; that is, the dominant, heteronormative ground of national popular culture and ethnolocalized "tradition" against which the *gay* and *lesbi* worlds are figured.

I was openly gay throughout my fieldwork; this certainly aided the process of becoming familiar with those I was studying, but it gave me no privileged access (a heterosexual ethnographer could have conducted this research, though of course not in the same way). I built up relationships (often friendships) with my interlocutors over a period of years, but since *gay* or *lesbi* persons often suddenly leave the *gay* or *lesbi* world because of marriage or migration within Indonesia, I lost contact with many interlocutors over time. During the day I would conduct interviews and type up fieldnotes from the previous evening's experiences. I also engaged in extensive HIV prevention as well as *gay* and *lesbi* rights work with nongovernmental organizations. In addition to participant observation and interviews, I conducted focus groups with *gay* men in Surabaya and Makassar. I have also done extensive textual and archival research, involving everything from items of popular culture (newspaper articles, books, magazines, television and film) to materials produced by *gay* and *lesbi* Indonesians themselves (Boellstorff 2004c).

One long-standing concern in ethnographic work concerns conscious explanation: "the Ethnographer has in the field . . . the duty before him of drawing up all the rules and regularities. . . . But these things, though crystallized and set, are nowhere explicitly *formulated*" (Malinowski 1922:11). This has also long been recognized as "the fundamental task the anthropologist concerned with gender and sexual orientation must take on: dealing with diversity while challenging the transparency of individual experience" (Lewin 1991:791). Only occasionally are the cultural logics explored in this book the topic of explicit commentary: *gay* men and *lesbi* women do not speak of "dubbing culture," and rarely do they talk about a *gay* archipelago. I see my task as an interpretive one that draws out largely implicit assumptions. I find that moving beyond conscious explanation gives me greater humility regarding my conclusions: an approach that constructs ethnographic authority by claiming "they say so-and-so is the case" can lead to a false sense of certainty.

A possible misconstrual of this study is in terms of scope: have I misidentified the viewpoint of a few politicized, intellectual, or wealthy *gay* and *lesbi* Indonesians for Indonesians as a whole? My goal is to describe the most dominant conceptions of *gay* and *lesbi* subjectivity without implying that the possible ways of living a *gay* or *lesbi* life are thereby exhausted. After all, anthropologists write all the time of "the Javanese" or even "the Javanese of the southern neighborhoods of Kediri" with the understanding that they are not ascribing unanimity to those they study. To misinterpret my claims as more overarching would constitute a "confusion of closure with scale"; ethnolocalized explanations of social phenomena can be as totalizing as translocal ones (Gupta 1998:12). Maintaining that *gay* and *lesbi* persons are found throughout Indonesia is not the same thing as saying that they are found everywhere in Indonesia. Even in urban centers many Indonesians with same-gender desires remain unaware of the concepts *gay* and *lesbi*. The metaphor of the archipelago is useful here: there can be "islands" of *gay* and *lesbi* Indonesians nationwide, yet also places "nearby" where *gay* and *lesbi* are not taken up as subjectivities.

I am often asked if those on the oppressed periphery see *gay* and *lesbi* in national terms. There are indeed persons in Aceh, Papua, and elsewhere who see themselves as *gay* or *lesbi* Indonesians, as well as many ethnic Chinese. This does not mean that there are not separatists who reject the idea that they are "Indonesian"; it means that there exist Acehnese and Papuan persons who, like some Javanese, Makassarese, Chinese, or otherwise ethnolocalized persons, also see themselves as *gay* or *lesbi* Indonesians. While neither I nor my interlocutors know of ethnolocalized *gay* or *lesbi* subjectivities (like "*gay* Javanese" or "*lesbi* Bugis"), my argument is descriptive, not prescriptive. Ethnolocalized *gay* or *lesbi* subject positions could form in the future, which would raise fascinating new questions. However, it seemed that my methodology should not render local what *gay* and *lesbi* Indonesians have experienced as national.

Another possible misconstrual of this analysis concerns exceptionality: one could argue that *gay* and *lesbi* may be irreducible to ethnolocality, but that they are the exception that proves how most "Indonesians" are first and foremost ethnic. Yet it is clear that many persons in the archipelago who are not *gay* or *lesbi* see themselves in Indonesian as well as ethnolocalized terms. *Gay* and *lesbi* Indonesians exemplify, not exceptionalize, emergent patterns of national culture.

I hope to leave the reader with some sense of the great camaraderie, joy, and creativity of the *gay* and *lesbi* worlds, but these are also worlds of heartbreak and pain, and what the future holds for *gay* and *lesbi* Indonesians remains uncertain. Therefore, I have gone to great lengths to protect the confidentiality of my interlocutors. All names except for that of Dédé Oetomo are pseudonyms, and details of persons, places, and situations have been altered.

SECOND PRELUDE: NATIONAL IDENTITY CARDS

Setting: Surabaya, capital of the province of East Java. *Place*: near the Joyoboyo bus terminal, not far from the city zoo. *Time*: Saturday, October 18, 1997, ten o' clock at night or so.

I have come here via minibus with some *gay* friends after watching a performance by male transvestites at the Taman Remaja amusement park. Paying our fare of 450 rupiah, we exit the terminal—an open space filled with over a hundred minibuses—and walk down a narrow street that runs alongside the Brantas River, a still sweep of inky water winding through Surabaya to the sea on the north edge of town. Under blue tarps, sellers in stalls lit with harsh fluorescent light watch over shoes, shirts, and music cassettes. Past the stalls the street gets quiet; almost no traffic here. To the right minibuses are lined up like locomotive cars, drivers sleeping in front seats or ambling to the river with plastic buckets, gathering brown water to rinse away a day's dirt and dust. A railing runs along the left side of the street, four feet high and made of horizontal metal bars with vertical supports. Two working streetlights filter dimly through the branches of large trees lining the road. Beyond the trees, the river slides along silently, streaked with white and gold from the lights of the shantytown on the other bank, wooden houses perched on stilts right over the river. A child laughs in the distance.

The bus station now at a safe remove, we see the expected groups of men extending down the street for a hundred yards or so, sitting or leaning on the barrier, half-hidden in shadow from the trees above. *This* left side of the street, past *this* bus station, along *this* railing, at *this* time of night, is *Texas*. Under this name, which plays off the term "*terminal*," Texas has been one of the best-known places for *gay* men to meet in Surabaya since the 1980s. Its popularity has ebbed and peaked over the years (men desirous of other men have met in this area since at least the 1920s), but in the late 1990s Texas was quite popular. Like most of these places in Surabaya, Texas is named for a locale outside Indonesia. When you come here you are also, in a sense, elsewhere.

The first groups of men we encounter at Texas stare with hungry interest; only one or two smile in recognition. This part of Texas nearest the bus station is usually dominated by closed (*tertutup*) men; they generally come here once a week at most. Toward the middle of Texas the groups of men get larger and denser. While men in this area are sometimes looking for a sex partner, most seek conversation; indeed, many come here with friends or lovers. As a *gay* man put it one night, "I like to go to Texas because even if we have a partner we can still feel alone, feel how narrow this world is!"

Entering the central part of Texas I see a man I'll call Anwar, someone I saw year after year; he's been coming to this spot since the early 1980s. Anwar is the kind of person you could talk to about problems in your life—about a boyfriend who is having sex with another man, about pressure from your family to marry a woman (or your own desire to marry), about missing a partner who's moved elsewhere in search of work. You could also depend on Anwar to entertain you with his effeminate clowning around. Swishing from side to side, exaggerating his hip motion in a hilarious way, he will wag his finger at someone, berating them good-naturedly and then suddenly breaking out in an a cappella song before returning to a monologue. One thing that seems to make him so hilarious is that he can poke fun while bringing up larger issues. On this night I find Anwar in the midst of a group of about twenty *gay* men, engaging everyone in uproarious conversation, when suddenly his head snaps to the right and he turns his attention to a space about ten yards down the road where a large tree provides shelter from the feeble street lamp—a darker periphery of Texas. Anwar has noticed a young man sitting on a motorcycle, someone no one knows. The young man sits in shy silence, watching the scene with apparent fascination and discomfort.

Never one to let an opportunity for drama slip by, Anwar takes the young man's shyness as a challenge. Dropping whatever line of commentary had been occupying him to that point, Anwar walks right up to the young man, who now appears positively embarrassed as all the eyes of Texas turn to see what Anwar will do. Anwar begins with a few short, teasing sentences, each of which contains a term in *gay* language: "my, isn't he young (*brondong*)!" "You are so handsome (*cucok*)!" The young man responds with a fetching but silent smile. Anwar concludes that the young man doesn't know *gay* language, is too shy to speak, or both. Clearly, more effort will be required to obtain the desired entertainment effect.

Anwar suddenly stands up straight and formal as a government official, turns one fist into an impromptu microphone, raises his voice to just below a shout so all Texas can hear, and taking on the measured and mellifluous tones of a television reporter, says "Are you new here?"

The young man answers haltingly into Anwar's "microphone": "Yes, this is my first time at this place."

Anwar's voice shifts to that of a cheery game show host: "well, you just keep coming back here, okay? Come back here tomorrow and it will be even more busy. This place will make you happy. Just bring your National Identity Card and we'll get you a second, *gay* National Identity Card. Bring some forms and two photographs and fifteen thousand rupiah and we'll get it for you." The audience bursts out in laughter: one shouts "What will he get with his new *gay* National Identity Card?" and Anwar answers: "A man!"

GLOBALIZATION, SIMILITUDE, AND DIFFERENCE

Similitude is the ultimate challenge both homosexuality and globalization pose to social theory; in both cases we appear to be confronted with a "desire for the same." As a result, a central theoretical project of this book is to develop an archipelagic framework for understanding similitude and difference. It is not enough to ask if globalization is "making the world more the same" or "making the world more different," because how we decide when two things are "the same" or "different" is itself part of what is being globalized. Our rubrics for determining similitude and difference are not exterior to the object of study—globalization itself. It is in recognizing this fact that the anthropological study of globalization has the potential to move beyond, on one hand, the diffusionism that remains a legacy of the Boasian tradition (and indeed goes back to Herder), and, on the other hand, the scientist evolutionism that comes down to us from Tylor and Spencer, among others.

Anthropologists have tended to see sameness as a threat and difference as a solution, the self-prescribed medicine for what ails both anthropology (with its poorly thought-out evolutionisms) and Western culture (with its racisms and sexisms). In this sense anthropology has been (and remains) largely heteronormative, in the etymological sense of *hetero* as "different." It seems that we have reached a point of theoretical and political exhaustion with this trope of difference. The idea that we should value difference is nowadays either taken up as self-evident by all parties (even the Religious Right, for instance, talks about the value of difference) or imagined to be an inadequate formulation for the post–9/11 world. The multiculturalist trope that asks for the recognition of difference meets its limit when it encounters forms of incommensurability that refuse the sameness upon which that difference depends (Povinelli 2002). Our failure to realize that the sameness/difference binarism is also our "folk" model contributes to this conceptual logjam. An unfortunate consequence of the focus on difference within anthropology and cultural studies has been the ceding of similitude to sociobiology and evolutionary psychology, permitting these reductive and deeply compromised modes of inquiry to lay claim to categories of encompassment—the human, the universal, the panhistoric. And if languages of difference were central to the colonial encounter (Stoler 1995), experiences of postcoloniality are marked by rubrics in which difference reacquaints itself with similitude, regarding it with the skeptical familiarity of a long-lost love.

The task is not to reclaim sameness or the universal, but rather to scrutinize the very sameness/difference binarism and imagine alternative rubrics for knowledge that sidestep this binarism altogether. How can we use the methodologies and theoretical insights of cultural anthropology to do more than call for context? During "gay marriage" debates of the early 2000s, for instance, anthropologists intervened largely by showing that heterosexual monogamous marriage is not the only form of marriage worldwide. How could anthropology have contributed in ways other than this demonstration of difference? What may push anthropology toward new relevance and insights may be not just the call for valuing difference, but a challenge to the implicit logics of sameness and difference that structure both the knowledge claims of anthropology and the systems of inequality that operate through the management of difference. Systems of oppressive power do not always obliterate difference; they also work through producing difference. I am thus interested in the theoretical and political possibilities of an anthropological deployment of the Other not predicated on difference. Contemporary dynamics of globalization demand an anthropology of similitude that does not reinscribe dominant subject positions (be they white, male, Western, heterosexual, or elite).

My analysis reexamines four binarisms shaping the literature on globalization and nonnormative sexualities and genders outside the West. The first binarism concerns genres of this literature. One focuses on political mobilizations that recall Western gay and lesbian movements. This genre tends to produce stories of convergence, assuming that terms like *gay* or *lesbi* are spread through international activism. The second genre focuses on "traditional" nonnormative sexualities. At its most romanticizing, such work takes the form of ethnocartography, "looking for evidence of same-gender sexuality and gendered ambiguity in 'other' societies . . . [this] 'salvage anthropology' of indigenous homosexualities remains largely insulated from important new theoretical work on postcolonial relations" (Weston 1993:341, 344). A second binarism consists of two recurrent reductionisms. The first—the reductionism of similitude—sees these persons as "just like" gay and lesbian persons in a homogenized West. They represent the transcendental gay man or lesbian woman, characterized by a supposed essential similitude that has been there all along, hidden under a veneer of exotic cultural difference. The second reductionism—the reductionism of difference—assumes these persons suffer from false consciousness and are traitors to their "traditional" sexualities, victims of (and, ultimately, collaborators with) a global gay imperialism. They represent the Westernized, inauthentic gay or lesbian. From this perspective these persons have an essential difference that is masked by terms like *gay* and *lesbi*. The third binarism concerns spatial scale: nonnormative sexualities and genders outside the West are seen as foundationally local phenomena (altered or not by globalization), or as foundationally global phenomena (altered or not by local contexts). The fourth binarism concerns celebratory or pessimistic attitudes toward globalization.

The four binarisms tend to line up as follows: gay and lesbian movements, structured by similitude, are assumed to be globalizing and positively affected by globalization, while traditional and indigenous cultures, structured by difference, are assumed to be localizing and negatively affected by globalization. This produces the two dominant tropes of global-

TABLE 1–1.
Two tropes of globalization and sexuality.

	Gay Planet	McGay
Genre	gay and lesbian movements	traditional and indigenous cultures
Reductionism	similitude	difference
Spatial scale	global	local
Attitude toward globalization	positive	negative

ization and sexuality, which I term "Gay Planet" and "McGay" (as in "McDonald's-ization") (table 1–1). I set these up intentionally as straw men; while there is much work on nonnormative sexualities and genders outside the West that demonstrates a much more subtle understanding of globalization (including most of the works cited in this book), these tropes remain prevalent in academic and everyday discussions of sexuality and globalization. Both tropes oversimplify. The limitations of the Gay Planet trope are evident in its teleological assumption that nonnormative sexualities and genders worldwide will converge on Western models of identity and politics. Less discussed are the limits of the McGay trope's doggedly pessimistic interpretation of globalizing processes.

The possibility of a nonthreatening and nonantagonistic relationship to processes of cultural globalization is almost completely absent in the literature on globalization and nonnormative sexualities and genders outside the West.[6] This reflects a common misconception associated with the reductionism of difference: namely, that gay men and lesbian women are products of the executive, jet-setting classes. Here the cultural effects of globalization are thought to correlate with class in a linear fashion: the richer you are, the more you are affected by globalization, and thus the less authentic you are. The proletarian becomes the new indigene. As any Nike factory worker in Indonesia could tell you, however, class is poorly correlated with the degree to which someone is impacted by globalizing forces. Often it is precisely the rich who have the time to acquire "tradition" (for instance, by learning "traditional" dances and music).

Understanding *gay* and *lesbi* lives will require reconfiguring the binarisms that structure the tropes of Gay Planet and McGay. A central goal of this book is to develop a third way of conceptualizing the apparent globalization of "gay" and "lesbian" that avoids these tropes. A first step is to reconsider what "globalization" means. A useful preliminary definition is "a social process in which the constraints of geography on social and cultural arrangements recede and in which people become increasingly aware that they are receding" (Waters 1995:3); in other words, who you are is less determined by where you're at. Globalization, however, is more than a definition; it is a narrative—a story with settings, a cast of characters, and a plot that moves through time. Gibson-Graham (1996) notes its similarity to rape narratives: both present a masculinized entity (the rapist, global capitalism) as always already in a position of dominance and a feminized entity (the rape victim, the local) in a position of weakness. This is more than a metaphorical parallel: as narratives about relationality and transfer, stories of sexuality are stories of globalization and vice versa. Gibson-Graham hopes that "a queer perspective can help to unsettle the consonances and coherences of the narrative of global commodification" (144). This narrative of globalization as rape underlies the McGay trope.

My analysis deconstructs the reductionisms of similitude and difference by insisting that the issue is not the world's becoming more the same or more different under globalization (neither homogenization nor heterogenization per se), but the transformation of the very yardsticks by which one decides whether something is the same or different in the first place; that is, reconfigurations of the grid of similitude and difference. In *The Order of Things*, Foucault (1970) characterized shifts in Western European thought in terms of conceptualizations of similitude and difference. What analytic purchase might be gained by positing, under some circumstances at least, a postcolonial order of things in which relationships between same and other were characterized not as boundaries transgressed but as boundaries blurred, not as borders crossed but as borderlands inhabited, not as spheres adjoined but as archipelagoes intertwined?

In other words, what is needed is an approach that recognizes how conceptions of similitude and difference do not stand outside the globalizing processes they seek to describe.[7] The very notion of "cross-cultural research" must be rethought when the cultures in question have been "crossing" in advance of the ethnographic encounter. This challenges dominant theories of knowledge, since difference typically constitutes the "Aha!" moment justifying knowledge production in the Western academy. *Gay* and *lesbi* subjectivities break the equation of "the local" with similitude and "the global" with difference. This is not a cosmopolitanism by which national subjects (usually urban elites) imagine themselves as part of a community transcending the nation. Nor is it a diaspora in which gay or lesbian selves disperse from an originary homeland, or a hybridity in which two prior unities turn difference into similitude via an "implicit politics of heterosexuality" (Young 1995:25). Careful attention to *gay* and *lesbi* lives will show conceptions of selfhood, desire, and belonging that transcend the tropes of McGay and Gay Planet. This shows the limits of approaches that frame the emergence of postcolonial gay and lesbian subjectivities in terms of dualisms of rupture versus continuity, indicating instead how "what is happening in Bangkok, Rio, and Nairobi is the creating of new forms of understanding and regulating the sexual self, but it is unlikely that they will merely repeat those forms which were developed in the Atlantic world" (Altman 2001:100; see also Jackson 2004). In this regard my analysis shares a theoretical agenda with anthropological work on Indonesia that is concerned to "avoid the pitfalls of both . . . an essentialized native identity celebrated for its heroic resistance to the incursions of externalized powers—or of the complete loss of self in which cultural alterity would be thoroughly subsumed, dominated, and erased" (Spyer 1996:27). Like Spyer and others, "What I hope to show instead is a third possibility, one in which the inescapable insertion within a wider world is infused and, at times, unsettled by the sense of coming from a 'different' place" (Spyer 1996:27).

THIRD PRELUDE: AT THE RESTAURANT

Setting: the north coast of Bali, where lush southern vistas give way to dry slopes of the great Agung volcano. *Place*: a tourist zone outside the city of Singaraja. *Time*: Monday evening, slow and quiet, a sky of brilliant stars save a black wall to the south where Agung lies as if in wait.

Ita's family runs a restaurant at the end of a lane snaking toward the ocean, lined with shops hawking the familiar paraphernalia of any tourist area in Bali—souvenirs, film processing, guided tours. Like many tourist restaurants, the main dining area is an open pavilion, with the kitchen and owner's home in back. Tonight Ita has Tracy Chapman, one of her favorite lesbian Western singers, on the stereo. Save for a Western couple eating dinner, the restaurant is empty of patrons. This is one of the main places that *lesbi* women along this stretch of the coast come to socialize. Tonight there are ten *lesbi* women sitting around an empty table at one end of the restaurant, including Ita and her lover, Tuti. Ita, thirty years old, has been with Tuti for ten years. "When we met Tuti was still in high school and I had just graduated. I moved here from my village a couple miles away when my parents built this restaurant. Tuti works at her parents' souvenir shop just a few buildings down; that's how I met her. For almost ten years I didn't go back to my village, even though it's so close you can walk there. Because whenever I'd go back, people would always pester me about getting married: 'Where's your boyfriend?' And they would tell me that I was ruining the family name, and stuff like that. Now I go back, because they don't pressure me to marry anymore."

Tuti sits with Ita, noticeably affectionate in the safety of the restaurant: one hand holding Ita's hand, the other on Ita's knee. Tuti says: "I'm twenty-seven years old and was raised in this village. My parents are still here too; I work at their art shop down the street. From the moment I saw Ita I wanted to be with her. I was afraid she'd be mad at me and reject me, so I approached her slowly, got to know her, and soon it was clear that the feelings were mutual. Now we sleep together every night, either here at her house or mine. My parents still pressure me to get married, but they know about us and are okay with our relationship. I think they're just used to it because we've been together so long. The only one who doesn't accept it is one of my older siblings. He still gets really mad. So if he comes to the art shop, Ita runs back to this restaurant. I'd like to coordinate the *lesbi* women here, but it's hard. But what does happen is that we get together in the evenings, like we're doing right now, to give each other advice. And I've found work for a couple *lesbi* women at my parents' souvenir shop. Most of our *lesbi* friends here are very closed. When we meet as a group, it's always at my souvenir shop, or here at the restaurant, because the others are too afraid to have us over as a group. *Lesbi* women have a hard time getting a job around here, especially if they look masculine. It's hard for us to meet each other, find out about each other, because women can't go out alone at night."

Irma and her girlfriend have been sitting next to Ita and Tuti this whole time. They've come to the restaurant tonight to ask for advice: Irma's parents have threatened to throw her out of the family unless she ends the relationship. Irma says, "I said I had stopped seeing her, that now I come to the coast just to work. Now I'm due to go back to my village and they'll expect me to bring back presents as proof that I'm working. But of course I'm not working and I don't have any money. So what should I do?" Ita talks to Irma about what she calls the "right to love": "You should tell her parents, 'If you say I can't be with her, why don't you just kill me at the same time and be done with it.' Maybe that will make them realize how you feel." This night, as so many other nights, *lesbi* women talk about belonging. It might sound at first like a language of tradition: parents, villages, and shame. Yet these women call themselves *lesbi*, talk about the "right to love," socialize not only with each other but with *gay* men, and find it perfectly reasonable that a gay Western anthropologist, not unlike the occasional gay or lesbian Western tourists they meet, should want to join them at the restaurant for a night's conversation.

POSTCOLONIALITY AND POSTMODERNITY

Part 1 of this book, "The Indonesian Subject," lays the groundwork for my cumulative argument. Following this introduction, chapter 2 addresses the history of "homosexuality" in Indonesia up to the 1980s. Chapter 3 brings together the fact that most *gay* and *lesbi* Indonesians come to their sexualities through mass media, and a recent debate in which the dubbing of foreign television shows into the Indonesian language was banned on the grounds Indonesians would no longer be able to tell where their culture ends and the West begins, to analyze how the *gay* and *lesbi* subject positions shape the lives of those Indonesians who take them up as lived categories of experience.

Part 2, "Opening to *Gay* and *Lesbi* Worlds," turns in greater detail to the everyday lives of contemporary *gay* and *lesbi* Indonesians. Chapter 4 explores desire, sexual practices, and romantic relationships, as well as the fact that most *gay* and *lesbi* Indonesians marry "heterosexually" and may not see this as inconsistent with being *gay* or *lesbi*. I continue my theorization of an anthropology of similitude through these ethnographic materials and discuss how the shift from arranged to "love" marriages in modern Indonesia, and the link between this shift and ideals of the good citizen, has powerfully linked heterosexuality and choice with national belonging. Chapter 5 explores the differing geographies of the *gay* and *lesbi* worlds, their intersections, and how they are influenced by Indonesian national culture. Chapter 6 examines the "style" of being *gay* or *lesbi*, from gender performativity to language use. It links this to the idea of "national style" and explores the relationship between practice and subjectivity. I also address the place of religion in *gay* and *lesbi* lives.

Part 3, "Sexuality and Nation," builds on the ethnographic, historical, and theoretical work of parts 1 and 2 to examine the imbrication of *gay* and *lesbi* subjectivities with national discourse. Chapter 7 examines how the "archipelago concept" and "family principle," two key ideologies of the postcolonial nation-state, have shaped the *gay* and *lesbi* subject positions. *Gay* and *lesbi* Indonesians stand as the greatest success story of the postcolonial Indonesian state—the truest example of national subjectivities, irreducible to ethnicity, locality, or tradition. Yet as success stories the state never intended to facilitate into being, they are also doomed to failure since they cannot be ethnolocalized. They are of the "archipelago" but ultimately belong to no "island" and thus do not "belong." This shows how discourses of race and ethnicity are pertinent not just to the United States, but to that subset of the "new queer studies" that examines sexuality outside the West (Manalansan 2003:6). Chapter 8 summarizes the theoretical and ethnographic arguments of the book, addressing its broader implications for sexuality, national belonging, and globalization.

While the term "postcolonial" can be problematic (Shohat 1992), I find it crucial for understanding the *gay* and *lesbi* subject positions: "its theoretical value . . . lies precisely in its refusal of this 'here' and 'there,' 'then' and 'now,' 'home' and 'abroad' perspective" (Hall 1996:247). My theorization of Indonesian postcoloniality begins from a dilemma: not only Indonesia's boundaries but much of its bureaucracy, economic structure, and even "cultural" elements were produced through the colonial encounter. The dilemma is one of authenticity: is "Indonesia" nothing more than a new label for the Dutch East Indies; is it merely a derivative discourse (Chatterjee 1986)?

Postcolonial rhetoric unites state and nation: the country is no longer occupied by a foreign power; rulers and ruled are one. Postcolonial states share with their former overlords a use of "the family" not only as metaphor but as "a cheap and efficient surrogate for the state" itself (Mosse 1985:20). As Mosse notes in his study of nationalism and sexuality in Europe, the family is particularly useful for inculcating and monitoring notions of sexual propriety in a context where respectability is seen as crucial. In the Indonesian context, concerns over respectability often take the form of debates over authenticity and belonging.

Beyond a foundation in heteronormativity, perhaps the only common element all postcolonial contexts share is an understanding of modernity as the goal toward which the nation-state should strive while preserving its unique "traditions." *Gay* and *lesbi* Indonesians themselves speak of being "*modern*," a highly visible concept in Indonesian public culture. Increasingly, anthropologists and other social researchers have taken up modernity as a topic of investigation under the rubric of "alternative modernities." In doing so they seek to transcend an earlier modernization paradigm that framed the modern as the realization of a historical teleology based in the West, in favor of exploring how modernity is reconfigured in non-Western contexts. The body of scholarship is so large as to constitute "modernity" as a new ethnographic present—increasingly, it stands in for "culture" itself (Rutherford 2003a:93). I thus locate this book within a larger field of interest in modernity within Asian studies. Asians are consuming modernity (Breckenridge 1995), inhabiting modernity (Chakrabarty 2002), making modernity (Das 2000), swallowing modernity (Mintz 1998), performing modernity (Schein 1999), overcome by modernity (Harootunian 2002), entangling with modernity (Spyer 2000), messianically modern (Rutherford 2003b:137–171), suitably modern (Liechty 2003), or simply "being modern" (Vickers 1996). Modernity in Asia is at large (Appadurai 1996), alternative (S. Brenner 1996), translated (Liu 1995), with its mediums (Morris 2000), imagined (Rodgers 1991), linked to matriliny (Stivens 1996), or simply "other" (Rofel 1999).[8]

There has been little critical attention to this interest in modernity; for instance, Steedly's review on the state of culture theory in Southeast Asia makes no mention of it, despite its importance to her own work (Steedly 1999, 2000). The growth of interest in "alternative modernities" demands an exploration of how this very notion of a fractured and reconfigurable modernity is postmodern and can thus destabilize the normative Western white heterosexual male subject (Massey 1994:215). Postmodernity is a specific, if debated, historical phenomenon linked to the loss of faith in human perfectibility and progress in the wake of world wars, decolonization, and a shifting global economic order (Harvey 1989; Jameson 1991; Lyotard 1984). One aspect of the collapse of metanarratives is the possibility of multiple modernities, "alternative" to each other and with no overarching expectation of synthesis. There has been a striking retreat from the anthropology of postmodernity, perhaps induced by the lamentable vulgarization of "postmodern" from a specific theory of political economy, representation, and culture to an epithet hurled at methodologies or writing strategies one finds difficult to apprehend.[9] Yet what is the anthropology of alternative modernities if not an anthropology of postmodernity? I wish to banalize *gay* and *lesbi* Indonesians and indicate their embeddedness in the general trajectories of Indonesian public culture. For these Indonesians *difference* is no longer isomorphic with *distance*. *Gay* and *lesbi* subjectivities are imagined not in terms of concentric spheres of decreasing familiarity, but archipelagically; someone thousands of miles away might be "closer" than someone next door who is not *gay* or *lesbi*. An ethnographic investigation of *gay* and *lesbi* experience holds the promise of illuminating how a "modern" way of being persists at the intersection of postcoloniality and globalization. A stance of respect toward the Indonesian subject is the precondition for any such investigation.

CHAPTER TWO

Historical Temptations

Who Needs History?

Subject positions, the topic of this book, do not always have names, but like any aspect of culture they always have a history. They come into being at a certain period of time, which shapes them, and they also change through time as long as they persist. Subject positions also always contain spatial scales within them (N. Brenner 1998; Harvey 2000). To be a "Yale student" has a different spatial scale than to be a "New Yorker" or "Japanese." The various subject positions through which one lives at any point in time may not have isomorphic spatial scales: one's sense of self as a youth could be global, as a man local, and as a laborer national, all at the same time. Or to be a youth could be both local and global at the same time, intersecting. Thus, three crucial issues in the ethnographic investigation of subject positions are (1) their historicity (that is, the way they are shaped by their embedded notions of their own history and what counts as history); (2) their spatial scales; and (3) how they intersect with other subject positions and the histories and spatial scales of those other subject positions. This chapter focuses on the first of these issues.

Only since the 1970s or so have people in Indonesia called themselves *gay* or *lesbi*, yet many Westerners seek a clear temporal trajectory connecting *gay* and *lesbi* with "indigenous" homosexualities. This deep-seated desire for unbroken history has many precedents in the Western tradition, most notably the Old Testament chains of "begats" that establish legitimacy through a patriline. While on rare occasions I have encountered *gay* and *lesbi* Indonesians who share this concern with a clear temporal trajectory, what demands explanation is that most do not. It is not a *meaningful* connection; for *gay* and *lesbi* Indonesians, belonging, recognition, and authenticity are legitimated not through history but by the performance of good deeds (*prestasi*) in the present. Since this chapter concerns the historicity of the *gay* and *lesbi* subject positions, it is built around an empty center, a McGuffin—Hitchcock's term for a plot element that is of intense interest (to Westerners, in this case) but has no content. The point is not to unearth the hidden past of *gay* and *lesbi* subjectivities, but to explore contingent contexts of homosexual desire in the archipelago— and why such "history" matters to the Western reader, where notions of the "archive" as scene of legitimation remain powerful, and archives are often mined for their content without attention to the affective assumptions embedded in their form (Derrida 1996; Stoler 2002a).

"Indonesia," after all, is a self-consciously novel concept. The postcolonial nation came into being with the *proklamasi* (proclamation) of Sukarno on August 17, 1945; nationalism dates back only another forty years or so. The term "Indonesia" was coined by George W. Earl in 1850 and first used by his colleague James R. Logan that same year, but it was not used as a political term by "natives" of the archipelago until April 1917 (Avé 1989:220; R. Jones 1973:100–103; Nagazumi 1978:28). It is quite certain that no one in the archipelago called themselves *gay* or *lesbi* in the year 900, 1400, 1900, or probably even 1960. Yet by the early 1980s *gay* and *lesbi* existed in the archipelago as nationally distributed subject positions. These subject positions challenge narrativizing; their "history" seems to be all change and no continuity. This threatens the dualism of change (modernity) and continuity (tradition) that has been a motif of Indonesianist historiography (Benda 1972).

This problem—"can there be a history of sexuality?"—is not unique to Indonesia; it has been the topic of debate in scholarship on Western sexualities. But it takes on new urgency when globalization and postcoloniality are brought into the discussion. The most careful scholarship on Western homosexualities takes continuity into consideration while foregrounding "the irreducible cultural and historical specificities of the present" (Halperin 2002:17). In a postcolonial context, it can appear that without an unbroken historical timeline one must view gay and lesbian non-Westerners as derivative, converging on a single global conception of homosexuality.

One response to the problem of radical change accepts the premise that an unbroken historical timeline is needed to establish authenticity. Since the nation-state form is deeply bound up with conceptions of modernity, the idea of tradition is a central paradox of national thinking: nation-states are young, but they imagine themselves as of great antiquity (Anderson 1983:5). Tradition is the shadow modernity casts back in time to see itself whole. Often it is postcolonial nation-states that display a particular concern with an unbroken historical timeline because this appears to bracket the colonial encounter. Although one does not assume that a Western man born in 1980 is first shaped by conceptions of homosexuality dominant in the 1920s before calling himself "gay" in 2001, this response suggests that gay and lesbian non-Westerners are first and foremost products of indigenous locality—as if the history of a person repeats, in miniature, the ostensible history of a society. This developmentalist perspective assumes that non-Western "homosexualities" like *gay* and *lesbi* originate in homosexualities and transgenderisms of the past. It makes it difficult to understand how a *lesbi* woman in northern Bali could say "I don't know of any cases in the past where there were actually women having sex with each other" and not find this a cause for concern.

A more theoretically informed response to the problem of radical change questions the need for "the narrative continuity of history and identity" (Clifford 1988:341). Can there be a subject position without a direct historical predecessor? Is such a subject position necessarily less authentic? How can one think historically about the *gay* and *lesbi* subject positions without assuming that what came before is the foundation of what comes after? Concerns for "discovering gay and lesbian history" sometimes participate in the widespread assumption that such history always already exists; that its real or apparent absence is inevitably problematic; that its existence by definition has validating effects; and that these effects are necessary to the sexualities in question. This tempting chain of reasoning creates the desire for narrative continuity and delegitimates sexualities for whom such continuity really does not exist (and is not only waiting to be uncovered).

I am not saying that historical research on nonnormative sexualities and genders is misguided, but that tradition is not the same thing as history and that proper historiography requires being open to a variety of causal relationships between the past and present, including no relationship at all. There may be no "perfect path" between past and present, just as there may be no *genealogical* lineage between "gay" and "lesbian" sexualities in the West and non-West (Boellstorff 1999). A less reproductive and heteronormative metaphor is needed in place of the genealogical grid. One such metaphor I develop in this book is that of the archipelago.

Forging histories of nonnormative sexualities and genders outside the West presents methodological as well as theoretical challenges. While the barriers to historical research on homosexuality in the United States may only "appear, at first glance, to be unusually daunting" (Chauncey 1994:365), outside the West much more than appearances are involved. The available documentation is often so minimal that one is forced to make do with limited sources and craft the best narrative possible (Jackson 1999a:369). Written documents by persons from the archipelago now called "Indonesia" are primarily limited to courtly texts. These sometimes address homosexuality and transgenderism, but not in a sustained manner; it is unclear to what extent they reflect everyday life outside royal circles. One can often read between the lines of colonial documents to find data concerning homosexuality and transgenderism (e.g., Proschan 2002). In Indonesia, the remarkable lack of colonial documentation on male (and female) homosexuality underscores how Dutch civil law paid little attention to sodomy until the end of the three-century presence of the Dutch in the archipelago. Stoler (1995:96) notes that her own "silence on this issue and the prominent place I give to heterosexuality reflects my long-term and failed efforts to identify any sources that do more than assume or obliquely allude to this 'evil,' thereby making the other 'lesser' evils of concubinage and prostitution acceptable."[1]

This chapter examines past nonnormative sexualities and genders in what is now called Indonesia without assuming that this past contains the present in embryonic form. *Gay* and *lesbi* subjectivities can represent an innovation, even a radical break, with understandings of sexuality in Indonesia and still be authentic if they are conceptualized in terms of conjunctural, "dubbed" histories of homosexual desire.

RITUAL AND DRAMA

Scholars of sexuality in what is now called Indonesia have tended to focus on what might be called "indigenous" homosexualities and transgenderisms. The best known is probably the *bissu* subject position, associated with Bugis culture in southern Sulawesi. Bissus are linked to pre-Islamic traditions and first entered the Western written record with the visit of Antonio de Paiva to Sulawesi in 1545. They appear in sources from the 1600s, as well as the travelogue of the "white raja" James Brooke in 1840 (Andaya 2000:41; Bleys 1995:117; Pelras 1996:56).

At present it is typically assumed that bissus are male transvestites (Hamzah 1978:6; Pelras 1996:165–167), but female bissus appear in Bugis mythology (Pelras 1996:83), and historically the majority of bissus were apparently women (in the *I La Galigo* myth cycle, for instance, thirty-two of the forty original bissus were women, including We Tenriabeng, twin sister of the cycle's hero Sawerigading).[2] To the present day there are women bissus (known by the terms *bissu makkunrai* or *corecore*) whose presence is required for certain rituals (Lathief 2004:48–49). Although refraining from sex has long been a way for bissus to protect and increase their power, and despite the fact that bissus sometimes married women, since at least the sixteenth century most bissus have been male transvestites who engage in sex with men (Pelras 1996:83).[3] Following what is usually at least three years of training (Lathief 2004:43), bissus historically engaged in a lifelong profession of guarding royal regalia and conducting rituals for nobles, particularly for life events like childbirth and weddings, as well as rituals for the fertility of the rice fields. In performing these activities, bissus would dress in an androgynous fashion, combining men's and women's clothing. One of the best-known bissu rituals involves trance proven through *maggiri*, where bissus attempt to stab themselves with ceremonial knives (*krises*); if the bissus' bodies are truly possessed by gods (*dewatas*), the knives will not be able to enter

(Graham 2003). At present, however, this ritual is not performed by all bissu groups (for instance, it is not performed in the Bone region; Lathief 2004:75).

For several hundred years, bissu rituals coexisted with the Islamic faith now followed by virtually all Bugis. This changed radically with the rise of the Islamic fundamentalist movement of Kahar Muzakar in South Sulawesi in the mid-1960s. One element of this movement, "Operasi Tobat" (Operation Repent), took aim at practices considered un-Islamic, particularly bissu practices. It was also claimed that bissus were in league with the Communist Party of Indonesia, which was in the process of being eliminated by Soeharto's New Order government. Sacred regalia were burned or thrown in the sea, rituals forbidden, and bissus offered the choice of death or leaving the bissu profession, dressing and working like "normal" men (Lathief 2004:79–80). As a warning, the head bissu of the Bone region, Sanro Makgangke, was decapitated and his head publicly displayed; many other bissus were killed as well.

Since the late 1990s there have been attempts to revitalize bissu practices. In part this reflects the refetishization of *adat* (traditional custom) across the archipelago in the wake of Soeharto's fall in 1998, supported by new government policies of regional autonomy. This has included the production of at least two documentary films by Westerners on bissus. However, it appears that these attempts to revitalize bissu practices are failing. Bissu rituals have been radically simplified (for instance, the *Mappalili* agrarian ritual in the Segeri region that once took forty days is now conducted in a single night), many rituals are now performed only for tourists, and the rice fields that were once given to the bissu community for income have been taken away and sold (Lathief 2004:69, 87–89, 83–85). Few persons seem interested in becoming bissus any more (Lathief 2004:92); for instance, in one region of South Sulawesi the arrival of a young apprentice to the head bissu was greeted with hope, but the apprentice soon had a falling out with the bissu and left.

In general, the distinction between "bissu" as a ritual professional subject position and "waria" as a male transvestite subject position seems to be breaking down in contemporary South Sulawesi (Lathief 2004:47); virtually all persons now sometimes called "bissu" in reality make their living through bridal makeup (a national occupation for warias) and as traditional healers, not through rituals. What ritual function remains for bissus has largely shifted from serving nobility to conducting a wide range of rituals for commoners—from insuring a safe pilgrimage to Mecca to a successful harvest (Graham 2003). It appears that contemporary bissus are being caught up in the same state rhetorics of belonging that are central to waria, *gay*, and *lesbi* subjectivities. Good deeds on behalf of "the people" are what *gay* men, *lesbi* women, and warias term *prestasi* and see as the means by which they can become accepted members of Indonesian society. The bissu subject position, repackaged as adat (in other words, as Bugis "custom" or "tradition," rather than the property of a privileged class of courtly elites), can act as one of the "islands" of local uniqueness that national culture incorporates into its archipelago of diversity. The irony is that once freed from the hallows of the courts (the number of which was limited) and transferred to the populist realm of adat and its virtually unlimited clientele, the possibility exists for there to be more bissus than ever before (traditionally the number of bissus in any region was limited to forty).

Bissus have often been interpreted as a third gender (e.g., Andaya 2000:34–38) because bissu rituals often involve the combining of male- and female-gendered characteristics. Some Bugis believe that "while bissu[s] are human, on their descent to earth they did not divide into man or woman, but remained a perfect combination of both. This combination ensures bissu[s] retain their connection with the spirit world" (Graham 2003:186). However, the "third gender" concept is theoretically inadequate for conceptualizing most transgenderisms, including bissu. For instance, it does not explain why most contemporary bissus are male or why being bissu does not involve continual transvestism. A better parallel is the fact that "nurse" is assumed to be a female occupation in the West. One must usually specify "male nurse" (like one specifies "female bissu"), but this does not mean that "nurse" or "bissu" is a gender. "Bissu" is a profession, not a sexuality, for which a particular reading of Bugis cosmology implies transvestism if the person involved is seen as male-bodied. Unlike being male or female, you have to have a special calling and engage in training (memorizing phrases and rituals, for instance) to become bissu. That one occasionally encounters the phrase "men, women, and bissus" does not imply that "bissu" is a gender on par with "man" and "woman," any more than the English phrase "men, women, and children" implies that "children" is a third gender.

A different situation occurs in the *warok-gemblak* relationship, which is found in the Ponorogo region of eastern Java. Contemporary persons occupying the *warok* subject position are male actors in a Javanese drama genre known as *reog*. According to legend, the reog drama was created in the thirteenth century by Kelono Sewandono, a prince of the Bantarangin kingdom (near Ponorogo). He proposed to a princess from the Doho kingdom (near Kediri in Central Java), Dewi Songgolangit, who said she would marry him if he created a performance different from any that existed before (Wachirianto 1991:3). Thus the defining practice of waroks is intended to enable heterosexuality. Wearing a tiger mask (the *singabarong*) weighing over one hundred pounds, waroks are identified with bravery, pride, aggressive masculinity, and mystical knowledge (S. Murray 1992:166; Wilson 1999). However, in the past waroks could be women as well as men. In one story, a man went to a coffee shop on the side of a quiet road near Ponorogo and flirted improperly with the woman running the shop, who just smiled in return. After asking the woman for a light for his cigarette, the woman went to the back of the shop and then reemerged holding a hot coal in her bare hand. The story "shows how waroks in Ponorogo were not only men" (Hardjomartono 1961:16–17).

Like bissu, the warok subject position still exists and is now identified with men. At present, as seems to have been the case in the past, the mystical power waroks possess depends on avoiding sex with women. While most waroks marry later in life (and thereby lose true warok status), while active as waroks they take on younger men between about eight and sixteen years of age (known as *gemblaks*) as understudies and domestic partners. Historically this was welcomed by the families of gemblaks, as the warok provided gifts (e.g., a cow every year the boy was a gemblak), and the gemblak welcomed the gifts of clothes and schooling given to him the warok, not to mention the chance to participate in reog drama.

Since sexual asceticism is key to warok power, waroks usually insist that they do not have sex with gemblaks; one contemporary warok claimed "with gemblaks the most that can happen is a bit of harmless kissing and cuddling" (Wilson 1999:7; Hardjomartono 1961:17, 24). However, it is well known that other sexual activities can take place between waroks and gemblaks, before the gemblak comes of age, marries heterosexually, and stops being a gemblak, or the warok retires from the stage to marry heterosexually. It appears that during some historical periods "the people of Ponorogo allowed these same-gender relations without any reaction," but gemblaks may have become social outcasts upon reaching adulthood (Hardjomartono 1961:24). Waroks have come under attack from the Dutch colonial period (when reog performances were outlawed), to the beginning of Soeharto's New Order in the 1960s (when, like bissus, waroks were labeled communist sympathizers and mystics), to the contemporary period, in which a desire for sanitized "tradition" has led to gemblaks being largely replaced in reog dances by young women.[4]

Beyond the Indigenous: Ethnolocality and ETPs

Bissus and waroks are the kinds of ethnographic objects Westerners like to discover.[5] Seeming to fit well-established assumptions about culture, tradition, and locality, they appear *indigenous*, which is assumed to mean "different from the West." *Gay* and *lesbi* Indonesians seem tainted by comparison. This underlies three common Western responses to my research on *gay* and *lesbi* Indonesians: (1) "Aren't homosexuals more tolerated in traditional Indonesian culture?" (2) "Here in the West we think in binarisms; they can teach us about fluidity," and (3) "Aren't *gay* and *lesbi* Indonesians mostly Westernized, rich cosmopolitans, not really part of any Indonesian culture?" These responses partake of deeply embedded tropes concerning difference, authenticity, and sexuality that took form through the colonial encounter. For instance, the idea that "Western culture" is trapped in the dualism of two genders while "elsewhere" there are three or five genders says more about Western fantasies of multiculturalism than it does about non-Western gender regimes. Such tropes act as implicit theories of indigenity in gender and sexuality studies: "the researcher's theoretical perspectives remain embedded in apparently straightforward reports from the field. In effect, the absence of theory becomes the submersion of theory" (Weston 1993:344).

In what appears to be an already globalized world, it is crucial to ask why the category of the "indigenous" is so attractive in the study of non-Western sexualities. While it is obvious that bissus and waroks deserve respect and support, justifying the recognition of sexual and gendered diversity because it is "indigenous" carries two risks. The first is that if one justifies tolerance of bissus or waroks because they are "indigenous" to "Bugis culture" or "Javanese culture," then what is to be done when there are "indigenous cultures" that do not contain such diversity, or are hostile to it? In southern Sulawesi the Makassarese are an ethnic group so closely intertwined with the Bugis that many persons in the region call themselves "Bugis-Makassar" (e.g., Abdullah 1985). Yet in "Makassarese culture" it is said that should a waria pass under the threshold of one's home, forty days and forty nights of bad luck will follow. If one valorizes bissus (most of whom are warias) in "Bugis culture" based on a discourse of indigenity, there remains no Archimedean point for challenging the denigration of warias in "Makassarese culture" except for a universalizing notion of "human rights," which is precisely the kind of concept "the indigenous" relativizes into nonexistence. The second danger is that the concept of "the indigenous" leaves us with no way to conceptualize self-evidently modern subject positions: they appear as impositions. If indigenity is the lens used to examine non-Western sexualities, *gay* and *lesbi* remain outside the scope of analysis.

Two theoretical steps are needed to transcend conceptions of indigenity as they apply to sexual subjectivities. The first, which is applicable to social inquiry more generally, is a critique of what I term "ethnolocality." The second step is to use the concept of ethnolocality to reconceptualize so-called indigenous or traditional homosexualities. Both for analytical precision and to ironize the empiricism prevalent in many discourses of indigenity, I will refer to these as "ethnolocalized homosexual and trans-vestite professional subject positions," or ETPs for short.

"Ethnolocality" is a concept that links people to place, but in doing so it links them to time as well: the concept plays a central role in the fetishiz-ing of "tradition" that makes it seem necessary for the *gay* and *lesbi* sub-ject positions to display historicity. Ethnolocality, which I discuss in more depth elsewhere (Boellstorff 2002), appears to have originated in the colo-nial encounter, where it was shaped by fears that people living in the archipelago might identify with broader spatial scales like Islam or nation-alism. It occupied a middle ground between the "racial dualism" of colo-nizer versus colonized (Van Doorn 1983) and the myriad localities of the village (Breman 1982). People living in the archipelago would, in theory, be permitted no other forms of spatial imagination. This colonial project of localization is the "sovereign exception" that "traces a threshold" be-tween inside and outside (Agamben 1998:19).

Following Indonesian independence, the spatial scale of ethnolocality lived on through legal, political, and cultural structures that were retained by the postcolonial nation-state. This is exemplified above all in the "ar-chipelago concept," illustrated by Jakarta's Beautiful Indonesia in Minia-ture Park—with its pavilions representing local culture arrayed around an artificial lake with a miniature set of islands representing the Indonesian archipelago—that has captured the imagination of many scholars (e.g., Pemberton 1994; Rutherford 1996; Spyer 1996). Ethnicity and locality are drawn together so as to presuppose each other, and this conjunction becomes the linchpin of state rule (and thus the presumptive ground for "ethnic" or "regional" resistance to state rule). It has become a "doxa"—an apparent isomorphism between a discourse and the world that dis-course claims to describe (Bourdieu 1977:164). Anthropological inquiry in Indonesia and elsewhere draws upon this spatial scale: ethnolocality dovetails with dominant conceptions of "the field" that produce anthro-pology's subject of study (Gupta and Ferguson 1997). For instance, the Leiden school of anthropology historically delimited Indonesia as a "field of ethnological study" in a purely comparative vein: this field was not the "field" in which one did fieldwork (Josselin de Jong 1977).

Following the collapse of Soeharto's New Order, some scholars have critiqued "Indonesian studies" for reifying Indonesia as a unit of analysis (Philpott 2000). As far as anthropology is concerned, it seems that the danger is not going far enough—not taking Indonesia seriously as a unit of ethnographic analysis, no more or less problematic than any other spa-tial scale. It is certainly insufficient to assume that persons within the nation-state of Indonesia see themselves as "Indonesian" in all circum-stances. However, it is equally problematic to fall back on ethnolocality as the default mode of representation for culture, naturalizing a spatial scale that was not just a result of colonialism, but "the very form of colonial rule" (Mamdani 1996:185).

This possibility is of particular import in the current historical moment, when the future of Indonesia is under debate. This is because ethnographic arguments against the cultural reality of the nation-state bear a disconcerting resemblance to colonial ethnology's refusal to grant people living in the archipelago the possibility of identifying in terms of spatial scales beyond that of ethnolocality itself. Anthropologists of the region can therefore find themselves complicit with social movements predicated on ethnic absolutism (Gilroy 1993a). While the state is often an oppressive and violent force, at issue is that persons within the nation-state of Indonesia identify in terms of spatial scales beyond ethnolocality, and understanding their "culture" requires taking all of these spatial scales into account, without assuming that any one spatial scale has ontological priority. For instance, chronological priority does not necessarily mean ontological priority: a subjectivity shaped by "global" forces (like Islam) may be experienced as more foundational than one shaped by "local" forces (see Gibson 2000:53). Additionally, showing the necessity of the foreign object or discourse to social life should call ethnolocality itself into question.

It goes without saying that there will be differences between different islands and ethnic groups, just as there is always difference between households or neighborhoods. At issue is the critical analytical moment when the ethnographer determines the boundaries of "the field," deciding at what point the threshold from similitude to difference has been crossed. This is a culturally located act, and in the context of this act, this heuristic compromise, it seems methodologically sound to take into account our interlocutors' senses of inhabiting subject positions with translocal spatial scales. James Siegel names this compromise when he says, "I want to stress how various Java is. Whatever claims I make about it should be understood to refer to [the city of] Solo alone, relieving me of the tiresome duty to qualify my statements in every instance" (1986:11). Although Siegel is certainly correct in pointing out Java's diversity, the problem of spatial scale is one of not only overreaching but underreaching. It appears unlikely that Indonesians in Solo, even if ethnically Javanese—living in a city where one main cruising area for *gay* men is known as Manhattan— "refer to Solo alone" in their own cultural worlds. What Siegel points out is the ethnographer's tiresome duty of looking not only for solid data but also for a methodological and theoretical construction of the field site pitched as closely as possible to the cultural geographies of those whose lives the ethnographer seeks to interpret.

For Indonesian studies, "writing culture" has tended to mean "writing ethnolocality": in the implicit "I was there" move establishing ethnographic authority, "there" has indexed an ethnolocalized spatial scale (Rabinow 1986:244). Ethnolocality makes an ethnographic approach to Indonesia appear to overgeneralize by definition—how could we speak ethnographically of "Indonesians"? What about Aceh, troubled by insurgency and natural disaster, or the highland peoples of Sulawesi, or any group "distant" from the physical site where the ethnographer conducts research? This way of thinking elides how all ethnographic work is based upon discerning broadly held cultural logics from intensive work with a limited number of interlocutors and then qualifying one's claims accordingly. No ethnographers ever speak to all persons within the spatial scale that they use to conceptualize their work, be that "Torajan," "Acehnese," or a subregion. To critique ethnolocality is not to deliver an apologia for the nation, nor is it to deny the importance of the conceptual work ethnolocality performs in contemporary Indonesian life. It is, instead, to write against the foreclosure of debate, to open a space from which to imagine new geographies of identification, to equip oneself to respond better to an already globalized world.

The concept of ethnolocality permits a more precise definition of subject positions like bissu and warok. I have called these "indigenous" homosexualities and transgenderisms, but a more accurate (and appropriately playful) term is "ethnolocalized homosexual and transvestite professional" subject positions (ETPs). Bissu and warok illustrate features of ETPs throughout Indonesia: they are found only among some ethnic groups; are linked to ritual or performance; and are usually for men, for part of the life span, and do not absolve the persons who take them up from "heterosexual" marriage. It is a misnomer to speak of ETPs as "sexualities" since they are above all professions (usually involving sexual asceticism), not categories of selfhood organized around sexual desire.

When beginning my fieldwork I supposed many *gay* and *lesbi* Indonesians would have originally identified themselves in terms of an ETP, since they are so prominent in the Indonesianist literature on homosexuality. This led to the corollary hypothesis that as a result of such identifications, I would find differing *gay* and *lesbi* subject positions based upon the ETPs prevalent in any one area. I was mistaken. In only two cases have I known someone who saw themselves both in terms of an ETP and as *gay* or waria; most of my interlocutors were not aware of ETPs even if they existed among their ethnic group. Often it is only through the scholarship of Western academics that *gay* and *lesbi* Indonesians know of ETPs at all (Petkovic 1999). I have occasionally heard *gay* men or warias talk about how society should accept them because bissus or waroks have existed "for hundreds of years." This is not surprising given that "the narrative continuity of history and identity" remains a crucial way to claim authenticity. What stands out is how rarely such claims are made: after all, these Indonesians see themselves not as bissus or waroks but as *gay* or *lesbi*. This lack of a link to conceptions of indigenity demands theorization—more than just "globalization" is at work. One reason there has been so little scholarship on *gay* and *lesbi* Indonesians is that if we view the archipelago through an ethnolocalized lens, they (and many other aspects of contemporary Indonesian cultures) are rendered invisible.

COURTS AND TRAVELERS

Outside of ETPs, what little documentation of homosexuality exists appears primarily in Javanese courtly texts. Some examples come from the *Serat Centhini*, an epic poem of which the oldest known manuscript dates to 1616 and the longest version was completed in the early nineteenth century. Providing "detailed descriptions of sodomy, fellatio, mutual masturbation, multiple-partner intercourse, and transvestism," this text shows "that male homosexuality at least was an unproblematic, everyday part of a highly varied traditional Javanese sexual culture" (Anderson 1990:278), at least among elites. Anderson's analysis of a scene in which a nobleman anally penetrates two male heroes and is then himself penetrated by one of them shows how within the text's logic a man can be "a skilled professional in every aspect of sexual intercourse between males, without ever losing his control or manhood" (282). Some texts written during the reign of Pakubuwana II in the early eighteenth century decry male homosexuality. Often framed in terms of Islamic prohibition, these texts address homosexuality at court, for instance, the same-gender affairs of Urawan, brother-in-law of Pakubuwana II, which drew the Dutch East India company's attention (Ricklefs 1998:69, 110, 183–185). Male sodomy was condemned and even punished in these contexts when it interfered with the reproduction of royal families (Ricklefs 1998:222). Sexual relationships between women appear less frequently in these courtly texts, but there are discussions of sex between royal concubines in the Javanese courts during the nineteenth and preindependence twentieth centuries (Blackwood and Wieringa 1999:41–42, 44; Gayatri 1996:90; S. Wieringa 2000:451).

Courtly texts rarely concerned themselves with the world outside the royal residence. What is known of homosexuality among commoners prior to independence comes mostly from merchants, missionaries, ethnologists, and colonial officials. These travelers wrote more frequently on transgenderism, probably because it was more visible to outsiders. Most colonial references to "pederasty," "sodomy," and "homosexuality" (after that term was coined in the 1860s) are actually to ETPs or the archipelago-wide male transvestite subjectivity banci (waria), not homo-sexuality per se. One finds primarily fleeting and dismissive reference to "native" homosexualities. The *Encyclopaedie van Nederlandsch-Indie*, for example,

> stated matter-of-factly in 1919 that in the Indonesian archipelago "*paederastie* is widespread. The Balinese, under the name *menjelit*, indulge in this perversion in a major fashion. . . . in Atjeh, the *sedatis*, children between the ages of nine and twelve, who probably hail from the island of Nias, make a business out of participating in this vice publicly [like the *gandroengs* in Bali]. . . . On Madoera, pederasty occurs in public, without shame, and it is also practiced as a profession on Java." (Gouda 1995:181)

Colonial ethnologists like George Alexander Wilken and Christiaan Snouck Hurgronje wrote in similar terms of "immorality of the worst kind," though "discussion assumed a calmer tone by the end of the colonial period" (Anderson 1990:277–278). One such calmer scholar was Hendrik Chabot, who also provides a rare glimpse of female-to-male transgenderism. In his research village near Makassar in the late 1930s and early 1940s, Chabot found "a woman . . . who did not feel at ease with those of her own sex. She wore her hair like a woman, but her sarong like a man. . . . She carried burdens on a yoke on her shoulders the way a man does, and she would go alone to markets and on roads. Her kin accepted these transgressions of the sex-role prohibitions without further ado" (1996:190–191). There are also brief accounts of women dressing as men whether or not they engaged in sex with other women (S. Wieringa 1999a:216); in Java these women were reportedly called *wandu*, a word now synonymous with waria and used outside Java. The following narrative provides rare documentation of late colonial female non-normative gender and sexuality:

> Last Saturday [February 11, 1939] two women went to the village headman of Alahan Panjang [a highland village about fifteen miles east of Padang in West Sumatra] and asked to be married to each other. Of course this request got a very, very strong rejection. Two women asking to be married to each other! Soon thereafter a mass of people had surrounded the office of the village headman. It's understandable that those people wanted to know as well what the decision would be, and how things had ended up like this.
>
> One of the women, Rakit, lived near Alahan Panjang. She had been a widow for eight years and had never married again, and her actions had never been any cause for suspicion. But she was a close friend of a young woman named Tinur, the child of an Islamic scholar in the village. They had been friends for eight years. The young Tinur didn't want to be married to a man; in fact she didn't like men. With no warning she had asked to be married to the widow

Rakit. Her parents did not want to grant this request, because Tinur was a woman. Since she was small she'd always been a woman. She'd gone to school as a woman. Up to the present people knew that Tinur's way of speaking was that of a woman. Apparently she didn't want to accept the decision of her parents, and had gone directly to the village headman and asked to be married to Rakit. When she arrived she'd cut her hair short, like that of a man.

What was the style of the connection of these two?

They explained they'd already been together as husband and wife as long as they'd been friends. When they were together, the masculine character of the young Tinur was like that of a male duck.

Of course the village headman couldn't just accept this explanation. Right away he telephoned the doctor of Solok [a small town a few miles west of Alahan Panjang] to ask for some clarification about this abnormality. The doctor himself thought all this strange. For that reason, the two women where sent by the village headman to the doctor to be inspected further.[6]

Tinur seems similar to tombois, currently found not only (like Tinur) in contemporary West Sumatra but throughout Indonesia. That both Tinur and her lover Rakit were "sent to be inspected" implies that Rakit was seen as a woman with incorrect desires; this appears to be the first documentation of cewek (effeminate *lesbi*) subjectivity outside courtly texts. Intriguingly, the story centers on an attempt to gain official recognition for a same-gender relationship through marriage. Issues of marriage, particularly "love" versus "arranged" marriages, will prove central to the dynamics of belonging for contemporary *gay* and *lesbi* Indonesians.

THE EARLY TWENTIETH CENTURY

In the mid-1970s, Ulrich Kratz discovered in the National Library of Jakarta the three-hundred-page memoir of "Sucipto," a Javanese man who lived during the final decades of Dutch colonialism.[7] This is the only autobiographical narrative to my knowledge by a person from the archipelago with a homosexual or transgendered subjectivity before 1980, when the first mass media article by a *gay* man appeared. The text was radically edited and published in 1992 by the historian Amin Budiman under the title *Jalan Hidupku* (Path of My Life); it was originally titled *Jalan Sempurna* (The "Perfect" or "Completed" Path).[8] Few inhabitants of the Dutch East Indies produced autobiographies, even among the small educated class (Budiman 1992:x), making the existence of Sucipto's text all the more remarkable. *The Perfect Path* reflects a genre of late colonial literature that framed modern society and modern personhood in parallel terms (Rodgers 1995:7; C. Watson 2000). It is unfortunate that no other memoirs or secondary sources from the 1910s and 1920s currently exist to corroborate and clarify *The Perfect Path*. *The Perfect Path* does not provide a direct prehistory to *gay* and *lesbi* subject positions: certainly no *gay* or *lesbi* Indonesians knew of this text before its publication in 1992. Yet there are clear resonances between Sucipto's world and the contemporary *gay* world.

Sucipto was born in 1910 and lived in eastern Java. In his writings he never used *gay* or any other term, even when discussing the existence of a community of like-hearted men in some of the cities where he lived. The memoir covers the years 1919 to 1927, but its pivotal event takes place less than ten pages into the narrative, in 1919, when Sucipto is attending primary school in Sitobondo on the north coast of East Java. Walking past the town square on the way to school, Sucipto meets a boy about fifteen years old. After a series of long stares and forced smiles—including a moment when, "because it had already been willed by God," Sucipto drops his handkerchief and the gallant older boy retrieves it for him—they speak briefly. The boy asks Sucipto if they could be friends, and Sucipto struggles with unaccustomed feelings of desire for another man.

Wondering about the boy he has just met, Sucipto cannot focus on school that day. The teacher explains there will be a celebration at the town square to observe the twenty-fifth anniversary of the Dutch coronation and encourages the students to attend. During the festivities that night a storm comes up and Sucipto hides from the downpour with other onlookers on a verandah where a stage play had been performed. The lights go out and it is pitch black as Sucipto gropes through the crowd. Suddenly there is a hand upon his shoulder: "Watching the show?" It is the boy Sucipto had met earlier that day. Sucipto implores him not to get too close because he is soaking wet, and the friend suggests they return to his house so Sucipto can borrow dry clothes. Sucipto agrees and they make their way to the boy's house, which is empty because his parents are on vacation. They lie down together on a bed in a darkened room, illuminated only by moonlight streaming through an open window. Their mutual lust becomes increasingly apparent until Sucipto asks the boy if he has ever slept with a woman. "Not even once," the boy replies:

> "Listen. I want to tell you a story. Now you have become my friend. Before, when I lived in Kediri[9] and was only as big as you are now, there was a Javanese man who fell in love with me. He worked as a doctor. At that point, just like you, I didn't understand. I was of the opinion that only a woman could fulfill a man's desire. After I became acquainted with this doctor, he spoke to me of many things. Finally he told me that desire could be fulfilled by a man with a man. We fell in love with each other; then after a time he moved away. After he left, I did as he had. . . . It's the same way with my friends; many of them do this same thing . . ."

"How is it done?" I asked, smiling.

He didn't answer with a single word, but kissed my cheek while his hand caressed my body. At that point I couldn't hold in my desire any longer; I forgot myself and returned his kiss. "This is what I've been waiting for," I said in my heart. He grasped my thigh and then slowly took hold of my sarong, until his hand found my ——— [ellipsis in original]."

"Apparently you like me, yeah?," he said while smiling.

At that point I couldn't explain any longer how strong was my desire . . .

"You are now my sweetheart" he said; his body trembled as he climbed on top of me. In that way, he satisfied his desire on top of my chest . . . Then he fulfilled my desire by using his hand. "Is this what the feeling is like?," I said in my heart . . . Then he held my hand and said: . . . "let us make a promise to each other. You will not forget me. And I will not forget you. The moon that shines upon us is our witness." (Budiman 1992:12–19)

This scene offers clues concerning male homosexual subjectivities in the late colonial period. First, the older boy who becomes Sucipto's lover was initiated into the practice of same-gender love in the early 1910s by a "Javanese doctor" who apparently claimed to be sexually interested only in men. There is clearly a history to this unlexicalized subject position, at least in Java. Second, the earlier lover of Sucipto's boyfriend was a physician, a powerful symbol of modernity in Indonesian literature. This hints at the possibility that educated people who lived in the archipelago encountered notions of homosexual subjectivity from the Western sexological and psychiatric literatures that were beginning to circulate through the colonial world. Third, the physician and the boyfriend belong to a community of men with similar interests—"it's the same way with my friends"—and they assume they will find such men elsewhere in Java. Fourth, while sexual desire is clearly a powerful factor in Sucipto's life, love (not desire in isolation) drives the narrative: the boyfriend and his earlier Javanese doctor had fallen in love, and the romance between Sucipto and his boyfriend begins with an oath of remembrance—witnessed like oaths of marriage, but here by the moon. Fifth, Sucipto holds the colonial presence at arm's length. It provides a background for the narrative—sometimes explicitly, as in the celebration of the queen's coronation anniversary—but Sucipto never identifies with (or against) nationalism and never mentions the nationalist movement. Additionally, Sucipto does not feel any sense of sin or remorse; indeed, references to God's role in Sucipto's homosexuality appear throughout his narrative:

Life is following habits. If someone is used to eating, without food he'll become hungry . . . If someone's used to using a woman, he'll feel less happy or a lack of desire if he uses a man . . . I feel happy with men . . . For that reason I've got to habituate myself to it, because that's the best thing for me . . . In this way God is indeed a generous being towards His creatures. For all bad things on this earth He has provided weapons to turn them into something good (Budiman 1992:26).

After several months Sucipto's lover leaves Sitobondo, and soon Sucipto runs away from home because of family conflicts unrelated to his sexuality. Making his way to Surabaya, Sucipto lives as a homeless youth; many of the parks and other places where he spends his time are the same as those used by *gay* men eighty years later. He has a sexual relationship with a Dutchman; when that ends he becomes a prostitute and decides to spend time only with certain groups of people:

> I carried out my promise to myself. I didn't socialize at all with boys who liked women. I continued my habit of strolling about at night [looking for sex work] without end, adding more and more friends with the same intentions as I. But not all of my friends who liked to "search around" were really like me. There were some who did it just for the money. If they succeeded in getting some, they used it to get a woman. I didn't really spend much time with them . . . Besides that, there were lots of boys who were really and truly interested in men, but their behavior was exactly like that of a woman. I also didn't like hanging out with them, because their disposition was too visible to other people (Budiman 1992:140).

Sucipto divides his homosocial world into (1) men who like women, (2) men who like men (and sometimes have sex with men for money), (3) men who have sex with other men for money but really like women, and (4) men who like men (and sometimes have sex with men for money) but act like women. One might anachronistically term the first and third categories as heterosexual or *normal*, the second as *gay*, and the fourth as waria. However, Sucipto's concept of male homosexuality does not appear to imply a female counterpart. This is only one of several apparent differences between Sucipto's subject position and that of contemporary *gay* men. There appear to be no linguistic, sartorial, or gestural practices associated with men "of the same intentions" as Sucipto. He writes of a broadly shared assumption that such men will *not* marry women. This diverges from the understandings of most contemporary *gay* men, suggesting that the marriage imperative is not simply "traditional." Above all, he betrays no sense of an archipelago-wide or global community. Not only is there no mention of men "of the same intentions" elsewhere in the Indies, but Sucipto first reacts with bewilderment when a Dutchman, "of a different race" than he, evinces sexual interest in men. If, as a thought experiment, Western gay sexuality were held constant, the change from Sucipto's sexuality to contemporary *gay* sexuality could be interpreted as one of divergence, not convergence, with the West.

The Dutch Last Gasp

In his introduction to *The Perfect Path*, Budiman claimed that in the 1930s "for the first time in several Indonesian cities a large number of *gay* people started to make themselves visible" (1992:x). I do not know the evidence upon which Budiman based this claim; Sucipto's narrative ends in 1927. While the persons Budiman describes as "making themselves visible" certainly did not identify as *gay* (if Sucipto's memoir is any guide, they did not have lexicalized sexual subject positions at all), it may be that by the second and third decades of the twentieth century men who desired sex and romance with other men began creating informal groups in the metropolises of the colony. A new relationship to the West was in the making as well. By this time the Indies had experienced significant advances in transportation technology—in particular the emergence of steam shipping following the opening of the Suez Canal in 1869—as well as the final consolidation of Dutch rule. These changes facilitated a growing population of Western men and women unaffiliated with the colonial government. While some of these Western women probably had sex with each other or women from the archipelago, our primary documentation at present concerns Western men who settled in the Indies in the 1920s and 1930s, particularly in Bali, had sex with each other or men from the archipelago, and sometimes saw themselves as homosexual. To my knowledge there are no recognized links between these male homosexual Westerners and the emergence of the *gay* and *lesbi* subject positions in the 1970s and 1980s. I have never heard *gay* or *lesbi* Indonesians indicate any knowledge of this prewar expatriate community. It is of interest not necessarily as a progenitor but because it shows how sexuality and state power articulate in the formation of nonnormative sexual subject positions.

Our knowledge of this community comes primarily from a sinister turn of events. In 1938, toward the end of Dutch rule, the colonial government at the instigation of the final viceroy of the Netherlands initiated an archipelago-wide crackdown on colonial "pederasts." The crackdown is reputed to have begun in Bandung, when an Indonesian student claimed to have been raped by his European teacher (Bijkerk 1988:70). One of the first victims of the crackdown appears to have been Fievez de Malines. This colonial official from West Java was fired from his post but then arrested later in Makassar as he was departing the Indies, charged with sex with someone under the age of consent, and sentenced to a year and a half in prison (Bijkerk 1988:70–71). Also arrested at this time was Assistant Resident Coolhaas, a member of the colony's new parliament, the Volksraad (Budiman 1992:x). While some officials disagreed with the crackdown (for instance, H. J. van Mook, who subsequently became the last lieutenant governor-general of the Netherlands East Indies), it received broad government support and seems to have been most intense on Bali (Gouda 1995:181–182; Rhodius and Darling 1980:43–45). In Batavia (Jakarta), police apparently rounded up street youths and paraded them before lineups of European men; if the youths pointed to any of the men, indicating a claim that the men had had sexual relations with them, the men were arrested (Bijkerk 1988:71). The "native" men involved were usually assumed not to be homosexual (Simons 1939:5579). The crackdown continued into the following year, involving many well-known expatriates such as Roelof Goris and Herman Noosten. Budiman claims that "in Surabaya the police got pretty good results. This need not surprise us since from the 1920s there were lots of gay Dutchmen in this city" (1992:xi).[10]

The most famous target was the German painter Walter Spies (1895–1942), who began living permanently on Bali in 1927 and became a major force in the artistic life of the island. Margaret Mead termed the affair a "veritable witch hunt" and spoke at Spies's trial in support of Spies's "continuing light involvement with Balinese male youth": "she argued that Spies was seeking a 'repudiation of the kind of dominance and submission, authority and dependence, which he associated with European culture.' [Mead claimed that] on Bali homosexuality was not a matter for moral condemnation, simply a pastime for young unmarried men" (Vickers 1989:106).[11] At this point K'Tut Tantri (alias Manx, alias Surabaya Sue)—the British woman whose exploits during the independence struggle made her a controversial figure (Lindsey 1997)—owned a hotel of questionable repute in southern Bali and was a friend of Spies. During the crackdown "Manx" tried to protect Spies and her other homosexual friends, even as the tourist industry suffered. In fact "[i]t was probably only because Manx was not homosexual, and had the support of a number of aristocratic guests, that she herself was not jailed or banished from Bali, given establishment claims that 'Manx's Place' was a brothel" (Lindsey 1997:92). The script for K'Tut Tantri's never-produced autobiographical film contains an unintentionally humorous adaptation of these events:

> SPIES: K'Tut, the Dutch are looking for me! . . .
> K'TUT: But what on earth have you done?
> SPIES: They're rounding up homosexuals. No one is exempt. . . .
> K'TUT: Where will you go?
> SPIES: To the Western part of the Island. . . . I may be safe there till this all dies down.
> K'TUT: I'll drive you.
> SPIES: No. K'Tut. You must not be seen with me. It's too dangerous.

K'TUT: Then Wayan will drive you. You are too good a friend of Bali to be allowed to suffer at the hands of the Dutch.

In spite of Mead's and Tantri's efforts, Spies was convicted and "imprisoned from 31 December 1938 to 1 September 1939 on charges of having had homosexual relations with minors" (Lindsay 1997:64). It is said that Spies's Balinese lover sang to the accompaniment of a *gamelan* orchestra outside the walls of Spies's prison. What little additional information exists concerning "native" reactions to the crackdown comes from the testimony of Europeans:

> Rudolf Bonnet [mentioned in a letter] that the Dutch police had also treated the Balinese in an unduly harsh manner, who "do not understand any of this. They look like frail, frightened birds: after all, a homosexual relationship is nothing special to them!" As the American anthropologist Jane Belo reported in February, 1939, sexuality between men did not constitute a violation of Balinese *adat*: to be *salah mekoerenan* (wrongly married) entailed men's relations with animals, with young girls who had not yet reached maturity, or with higher-caste women. As a result, Belo wrote, the Balinese thought that "the whole 'white caste' had gone stark raving mad." (Gouda 1995:181–182)

The state of homosexual subjectivity in the Indies during this period is an area in which further research is needed, not least because at this point homophile movements existed in many Western metropoles. It seems Spies and his European compatriots understood themselves as "homosexual" as that concept was typically used in Western sexology, and they may have communicated this concept in some fashion to the men from the archipelago they befriended and loved. In 1940 Spies was rearrested, this time as an ethnic German when Germany invaded the Netherlands at the beginning of World War II. He died in 1942 when his prison ship was sunk near Sri Lanka; on the same boat was Hans Overbeck, the never-married German literary scholar of Malay who lived in Surabaya and whose servant, and possibly lover, was none other than Sucipto.[12] The very existence of the Dutch crackdown suggests that homosexuality was visible enough to catch the eye of the colonial apparatus at a time when the colony's future was increasingly in doubt. Even though reproduction and thus miscegenation was not a possibility, sex between men seems to have become seen as threatening the racial hierarchy upon which colonial authority rested. Before giving way to the postcolonial polity it shapes to this day, the colonial "administrative state" (Benda 1966, Anderson 1990:94–96) framed sex between men as the product of global connection and a threat to social order.

HOMOSEXUALITY IN THE YOUNG INDONESIA, 1945–1980

Documents relating to sex between men or between women from the late 1940s to the 1970s are scarce, and little archival work has been undertaken to explore how the early postcolonial state regarded homosexuality. While the European presence in Indonesia during the early postcolonial period was minimal and decreased further with the conflict over the absorption of Irian Jaya into Indonesia in the 1950s, some European men spent time in venues like parks, where they formed sexual and affective relationships with Indonesians. A waria from Makassar born in the 1930s recalled that by 1959 "there were already lots of homo men; I already knew lots of homo men from the Japanese [World War II] and Dutch times, and lots of *lesbi* women too, both those who were hunter [tomboi] and lines [cewek]." Andre, a lower-class Javanese man, recalls this time fondly:

> A: I first came to Surabaya in 1948. Actually the difference was not that great, except that we weren't as visible as nowadays. There weren't any people brave enough to have long hair or an earring or wear effeminate clothing. There wasn't anyone at all like that. . . . At that point I hung out with my friends at Taman Imbong Macang [a park in Surabaya]. There were Dutch men there too . . . some of them from Ambon [in the Moluccas] or Manado [in North Sulawesi]. . . . So I would go there with my [Javanese] lover. This was around 1950. . . . Every night I'd go out. . . . Every night and I never got bored for fifteen years. Until 1965.

Andre's reference to 1965 marks the period when Sukarno, Indonesia's first president, was toppled from power. Hundreds of thousands of Indonesians died in the ensuing unrest; since Surabaya and its environs were a major scene of this violence, it is not surprising that Andre and his friends stopped going to the parks. As noted earlier, many persons with ETPs, like bissus and waroks, were substantially impacted by this violence. It is also in connection with the events of 1965 that women's homosexuality entered public discourse in a frightening manner, with the massacre of Indonesian women involved in the women's Communist Party organization Gerwani. Accusations that Gerwani members had sex with each other played a role in the government campaign to justify discrediting and even murdering these women (S. Wieringa 1999b, 2002). Male homosexuality does not appear to have been targeted, but the turbulence of the transition to Soeharto's New Order meant that men involved in homosexual activities strongly curtailed their public presence.

After a few years a renewed park life began to emerge: Andre notes that "beginning around 1970 there were already very many [of us]. More and more people like me. I felt the worries of my life were reduced a little because I had those friends like me to hang around with." Other interlocutors corroborate Andre's narrative of park socializing with Indonesians and Westerners in the 1950s, severely curtailed in 1965. From the point when park socializing picked up again in the 1970s until the present, there has been a reduced presence of Westerners in parks and other public places of *gay* life: most contemporary Westerners either go to tourist sites or socialize largely with expatriates. There appears to have been a further shift around 1980, when some people began identifying as waria on an ongoing basis in public (as opposed to more circumscribed contexts like theatrical performances) and some men began using the term *gay*. The first edition of the *All Lavender International Gay Guide* in 1971 has a single entry for "Jakarta, Indonesia"—the "Cosy Corner" on 9 Nusantara Street. However, while the terms *gay* and *lesbi* were certainly in existence by the early 1970s, at least in the capital, they do not appear to have been in widespread use before the 1980s, and there is little evidence for a sense of nationwide or worldwide homosexual affiliation before that point.

Through a critique of ethnolocality and the concept of ETPs, it is possible to navigate the historical temptations associated with the study of non-normative genders and sexualities outside the West. The history of the *gay* and *lesbi* subject positions does not conform to Western prejudices concerning narrative continuity. Prior to *gay* and *lesbi* there is little evidence for archipelago-wide sexual subject positions; their appearance is intertwined with Indonesian nationhood. The assumption that the past stands in a causal relationship to the present does not capture the conjunctural manner in which these subject positions have come into being.

Warias, National Transvestites

So far I have made occasional reference to male transvestites (warias). Since the *gay* and *lesbi* subject positions "globalized" to Indonesia in a context where the waria subject position was already well known, the existence of warias has profoundly shaped the *gay* and *lesbi* subject positions and indeed accounts for some of the most significant differences between *gay* men and *lesbi* women, as discussed at several points later in this book. A brief summary of waria subjectivity will thus help illuminate the *gay* and *lesbi* subject positions (see Boellstorff 2004b for a more detailed discussion of warias).

The waria subject position is far better known in contemporary Indonesia than any ETP, or indeed the *gay* and *lesbi* subject positions themselves.

Virtually everyone in Indonesia knows what "banci" or "béncong" (derogatory terms for waria) mean. It appears that the waria subject position took form during the mid-nineteenth century in metropolitan areas (the now-common term "banci" does not appear in early nineteenth-century versions of the Javanese chronicle *Serat Centhini* [Anderson 2001:xiv]). From the beginning it was assumed that warias could be found anywhere in the archipelago, and from the beginning warias were associated not with ritual but with lowbrow entertainment, petty commodity trading, and sex work.

Since the waria subject position is so well known, most warias begin identifying as such while children. You cannot become waria if you are seen to have been born with a vagina: waria subjectivity is an attribute of male bodies. Waria almost never describe themselves as a "third gender" but see themselves as men with women's souls who therefore dress like women and are attracted to men. They usually have sex only with "real" men and are the only major class of persons beyond the disabled who are not typically pressured to marry heterosexually. Many warias enjoy being anally penetrated by their male partners, but it is clear from interview data as well as HIV/AIDS-related sexual behavior surveys that warias often penetrate their male partners anally (Oetomo 2000). In comparison to the *activo/pasivo* sexual regime attributed to much of Latin America, where penetrating is conflated with masculinity and being penetrated with femininity (see Kulick 1998: chap. 3), it appears that in Indonesia, bodily presentation is more important than sexual act in determining gender, a state of affairs that may exist across much of Southeast Asia (cf. Manalansan 2003:26).

Before the late 1970s warias dressed as women primarily at night or when on stage, but at present most warias dress as women all day long, and many ingest female hormones (in the form of birth control pills) or inject silicone to give their bodies a more feminine look. They rarely have sex-change operations, due not only to the cost but to the fact that they ultimately see themselves as men. By the early 2000s warias had become increasingly visible in public life, from their common role as beauticians to appearances in television shows. This visibility has not translated directly into acceptance, but it does underscore how these national transvestites contribute to the complex sexual landscape upon which the *gay* archipelago has taken form.

CHAPTER THREE

Dubbing Culture

MOMENTS OF ORIGIN

It should be clear from the last two chapters that ethnolocalized homosexual and transvestite professional subject positions like "bissu" are distinct from the waria subject position, and that both are distinct from the *gay* and *lesbi* subject positions. This chapter focuses on *moments of origin* for the *gay* and *lesbi* subject positions: (1) on the social level—the historical context in which they first appeared; and (2) on the personal level—how particular Indonesians come to see themselves as *gay* or *lesbi*. I foreground the crucial role of mass media and ask how these moments of origin illuminate the mutually constituting conjunction of sexuality and nation in contemporary Indonesia. In doing so I also develop a framework for rethinking ethnography in an already globalized world. I call this framework *dubbing culture,* where *to dub* means, as the Oxford English Dictionary phrases it, "to provide an alternative sound track to (a film or television broadcast), especially a translation from a foreign language."[1]

With regard to *gay* and *lesbi* Indonesians, my goal is to develop a theory that can account for a contingent, fractured, intermittent, yet powerfully influential relationship between globalization and subjectivities. Two additional requirements for such a theory are as follows. First, it must not mistake contingency for the absence of power; it must account for relations of domination. Second, such a theory must not render domination as determination; it must account for how *gay* and *lesbi* Indonesians transform this contingent relationship in unexpected ways.

The framework of dubbing culture is crucially concerned with agency: it questions both deterministic theories that assume the hailing of persons through ideology and voluntaristic theories that assume persons "negotiate" their subjectivities vis-à-vis structures of power. As a result, it aims to provide a more processual understanding of subjectivity: it gives us a new way to think through the metaphorical construal of hegemonic cultural logics as "discourses." To "dub" a discourse is neither to parrot it verbatim nor to compose an entirely new script. It is to hold together cultural logics without resolving them into a unitary whole.

I see this analysis as linking queer theory and mass-media theory, partaking in a "new queer studies" that highlights "the political stakes in positing a particular understanding or vision of the global" (Manalansan

2003:6). In much the same way that print capitalism presents a general precondition for national imagined communities, but in a manner open to reinterpretation (Anderson 1983), so contemporary mass media present a general precondition for dubbing culture, but not in a deterministic sense. I thus examine ways in which mass-mediated messages that might appear totalizing (because of their association with powerful political-economic actors) are, in fact, susceptible to contingent transformation. Just as the dubbed television show in which "Sharon Stone speaks Indonesian" does not originate in the United States, so the *gay* and *lesbi* subject positions I examine are Indonesian—not, strictly speaking, imported.[2] Yet just as the range of possibilities for a dubbed soundtrack is shaped by images originating elsewhere, so the persons who occupy subject positions that are dubbed in some fashion cannot choose their subjectivities just as they please. I move from a literal, technical meaning of dubbing to a more speculative, analogical usage as a way to explore the relationship between social actors and the modes of subjectivation (Foucault 1985) by which such persons come to occupy subject positions.

The theory of dubbing culture developed in this chapter is central to my analysis of the paradoxes of sexuality and nation in postcolonial Indonesia. The ultimate goal of this chapter, however, is to speak at a broad level to the state of culture theory. Might it be that dubbing culture occurs in the context of globalizing processes not directly related to mass media, sexuality, or Southeast Asia? How, for instance, is the relationship between English "gay" and Indonesian "*gay*" like the relationship between English "beauty" and the concept of *biyuti* employed by Filipino gay men (Manalansan 2003:15)? Indeed, at the end of this chapter I ask if the dubbing of culture Indonesians perform when they constitutively occupy the *gay* or *lesbi* subject position is all that different from the ethnographic project in an already globalized world. This chapter, then, has a reflexive (indeed, postreflexive) dimension. It asks if the ways in which much contemporary ethnography holds together, in tension, multiple cultural logics (like "the local" and "modernity")—in such a way that they are coconstitutive, not just juxtaposed—might not be productively interpreted in terms of dubbing culture.

THE EMERGENCE OF THE *GAY* AND *LESBI* SUBJECT POSITIONS

> In what measure are sexual perversions analogues of incorrect speech? . . . Might there be elements of homosexuality in the modern theory of language . . . in the concept of communication as an arbitrary mirroring?
> —George Steiner, *After Babel:*
> *Aspects of Language and Translation*

As noted in chapter 2, subject positions, like any other aspect of culture, have a history. One reason the *gay* and *lesbi* subject positions present such a quandary for social analysis is that, like homosexual subject positions in the West, they are quite recent. The Dutch crackdown in the 1930s, and the strong influence of Freudian psychology in Indonesian social science (Gayatri 1996:90, A. Murray 1999:142), make it possible that some Indonesians could have started calling themselves *gay* or *lesbi* (or some other term like *homo* or *homoseks*) before 1960.[3] Whereas about one-third of Sucipto's *The Perfect Path* from the 1920s is devoted to a commentary on Javanese mystical texts, Indonesian texts on homosexuality or trans-genderism from the 1970s onward often invoke outdated Western psychological theories. However, I know of no evidence of Indonesians terming themselves *gay* or *lesbi* before the 1970s. Since I am interested in the emergence of the *gay* and *lesbi* subject positions (not in, say, how a handful of Indonesians that might have learned of Western gay and lesbian subject positions in the 1950s or 1960s through travel to the West or an intimate relationship with an expatriate Westerner), this means that *gay* probably took form as a widely (if imperfectly) known subject position between the early 1970s and early 1980s, a decade or two later than in some other Southeast Asian nations such as Thailand (Jackson 1999a). The *lesbi* subject position appears to have a similar time frame, and *lesbi* communities existed at least in large cities by the early 1980s (S. Wieringa 1999a:215). The appearance of the *gay* and *lesbi* subject positions in Indonesia in the 1970s to 1980s is corroborated by a range of archival and oral historical data. One of my interlocutors, an older *gay* man living in Surabaya, noted that "there was a big change around 1978–79. Globalization [*globalisasi*] came in, the mass media came in . . . there were some Western gay magazines that were imported; they had small parts of them summarized and translated into Indonesian so they would sell here. These publications pushed people to be more open; they would read them and realize that 'I'm not alone.' "

That this man is highly literate probably explains why he is the only one of my interlocutors in any of my field sites to describe Western gay magazines being imported. Such imported magazines could not have circulated frequently or broadly enough to have contributed significantly to the formation of the *gay* and *lesbi* subject positions; it is clear that general mass media played the central role. The earliest study of contemporary Indonesian homosexuality to my knowledge, Amen Budiman's 1979 book *Lelaki Perindu Lelaki* (Men Who Yearn for Men), notes that

in this decade [the 1970s] homosexuality has increasingly become an interesting issue for many segments of Indonesian society. Newspapers, both those published in the capital and in other areas, often present articles and news about homosexuality. In fact, *Berita Buana Minggu* in Jakarta has a special column, "Consultation with a Psychiatrist," which often answers the complaints of those who are homosexual and want to change their sexual orientation. It's the same way with pop magazines, which increasingly produce articles about homosexuality, sometimes filled with personal stories from homosexual people, complete with their photographs. (Budiman 1979:89–90)

Budiman added, "It is very interesting to note that homosexuals who originate in the lower classes often try to change their behavior by seeking advice from psychiatric or health columnists in our newspapers and magazines" (116). A similar timeline appears in the *lesbi* autobiography *Menguak Duniaku* (Revealing My World), published in 1988. Here the author reprints an "interesting piece of writing" by a doctor that "relates to my world," one linking mass media, sexuality, and national "style":

About ten years ago [1976 more or less], Indonesian newspapers and magazines discovered a new issue that sold well with readers. This was the problem of adult men who wanted to become women, and though the total was less, women who wanted to change themselves into men.

Nevertheless, before and after that issue circulated as a social issue, what was set forth was the problem of homosexuality [*homoseksualitas*] and lesbianism [*lesbianisme*]. Stories and reports were offered about the social condition of these things in industrial nations, together with commentary from sleazy Indonesian mass media. From time to time it was implied between the lines that even in Indonesia things like this had emerged.

After home electronics entered the consumer market in Indonesia, not all films with sex scenes were censored, because the form of sale was through video cassettes. So Indonesian films became colored by erotic and sexual scenes. The reaction of the Indonesian public varied. Some linked the showing of these films, including those that offered homosexual [*homoseksual*] or lesbian [*lesbian*] scenes, with the "invasion" of foreign values. . . . But those who talked about this didn't really know what was being discussed. . . . A nation that must be made smart becomes a gullible nation. Such a gullible nation is a nation that has a *label*, but does not possess an identity [*identitas*]. . . . So it has happened with homosexuality and lesbianism, or with the problem of "changing ones genitals," and other problems that are connected with a style of life [*cara hidup*] that is "strange but stimulating" [*"aneh tetapi merangsang"*]. (Prawirakusumah and Ramadhan 1988:481–482)

In July 1980 an anonymous author, "X," published a story in the magazine *Anda* (You) entitled "I Found My Identity as a *Homosex* Person." This to my knowledge is the first time *gay* subjectivity appeared in mainstream mass media. The author wished to "provide a picture of what the life of homosex people is like" and "for those who are homosex/*lesbi*, to encourage them to go to experts so maybe they can change. And if they cannot change, to accept themselves." He described a sexual awakening marked by encounters with mass media. When he was eleven years old (in 1964) and beginning to experiment sexually, "I read in a magazine about the meaning of the word *homosex*. I began to compare that explanation of *homosexualitas* with my own situation, but wasn't yet sure." At this point the author claimed the term *gay* was not yet in use. As a young adult in college in 1977, "by coincidence I saw a book entitled *Homosexual Behavior among Males*, which explained that homosexualitas was proper and normal. I slowly developed a positive attitude concerning homosexualitas."[4] This author is Dédé Oetomo, one of a handful of Indonesians willing to identify themselves publicly as *gay* or *lesbi*:

> One of my friends from kindergarten was a psychology student at the University of Indonesia. He had connections at this popular psychology magazine called *Anda* and suggested I write my story. That must have been the spring of 1980. I thought I'd use my real name, but my aunt said "why don't you use a pseudonym for the time being." So we settled on the name "X." It was published in July 1980 and the editors forwarded about fifteen letters from people who wanted to contact me. That was around October 1980. Most people were supportive, saying things like "I'm glad you are so honest; I hope you can be happy now."

Among my *gay and lesbi* interlocutors whose memory extends back to the early 1980s, there is wide agreement that the entry of *gay* and *lesbi* into mass media, and in a sense the beginning of the *gay* and *lesbi* worlds, originates not in the *Anda* article (of which most are unaware), but in the unofficial "marriage" in Jakarta of two *lesbi* women, Jossie and Bonnie (respectively, twenty-five and twenty-two years old at the time). The event took place on the night of April 19, 1981, and was covered soon thereafter by two weekly magazines with a national readership, the May 31 edition of *Tempo* and the June 6 edition of *Liberty*. The Liberty article was that week's cover story (fig. 3–1) and began as follows:

FIRST IN INDONESIA: A LESBIAN MARRIAGE, ATTENDED BY 120 GUESTS

> In a luxurious building in the Blok M Kebayoran Baru district, a large crowd met in the Swimming Pub Bar. . . . The guests coming to this place turned their gaze to the young "groom and bride," both of whom smiled unceasingly. . . . The groom, Jossie, wore a white jacket and a blue tie with red blowers, while the bride, Bonnie, wore a long red gown. . . . The wedding cake was cut by Bonnie's soft hands; over a hundred witnesses, including both sets of parents, watched as they fed each other a mouthful. This celebration of marriage went smoothly. Among the guests who came that night were several friends from the Police. . . .[5]

Figure 3–1. "First in Indonesia: Lesbian Wedding, Attended by 120 Guests," with picture of Jossie and Bonnie. *Liberty* magazine, cover illustration for June 6, 1981, issue.

The *Liberty* reporter covering the event was fascinated by how Jossie appeared masculine and Bonnie feminine. The reporter claimed Jossie had been examined by doctors and found to have 75 percent male hormones and only 25 percent female hormones, while Bonnie was *normal* and "once had a boyfriend." When asked how she and Bonnie had sex, Jossie turned aside the question by referring to mass media, saying "It's precisely like you have seen in imported books."

Even at this early point in the history of the *gay* and *lesbi* subject positions, there was great interest in belonging, productivity, and love, themes tightly interwoven with national rhetorics of the good citizen. The reporter underscored Jossie's unemployed status at the time of the wedding—a disgraceful position for a new head of household—and asked Bonnie if her relationship with Jossie was based on emotion, sex, or love. Bonnie replied, "We want to have an eternal love."

It was the public consecration of Jossie and Bonnie's relationship—their "official" wedding "with invitations, guests, fine clothes, and members of both families present"—that engendered the most anxiety for the media. The *Tempo* article contained a sidebox entitled "There They Have Laws for Them," which spoke about social recognition of homosexual relationships in the West, describing, for instance, how the United States had antidiscrimination laws and gay pride marches. This is the first occasion to my knowledge that Indonesian mass media directly compared *gay* and *lesbi* Indonesians with gay and lesbian Westerners. The *Liberty* reporter openly pondered the social consequences of recognition:

> This event is indeed unique, not least because it is the first time something like this has occurred in Jakarta, maybe in Indonesia, or even the whole world—that the marriage of two people of the same sex is formalized openly, without anything to cover it. . . . If the relationship by Jossie and Bonnie were tied together . . . with an ordinary reception in the presence of their peers, anyone could have done it. It would have been no different than a birthday party. What is unique . . . is a *lesbi* wedding formalized with a joyous ceremony, and thus constitutes a new "dilemma" in Indonesia. Viewing the life of these two young *lesbi* women, it is apparent that they have a different way of thinking about how to solve the problem of lesbianism in our Republic. In our estimation, both of them want to become pioneers for their people who are not small in number. And with them both standing in front, their hopes openly revealed, who knows what will happen.

Why did the *Liberty* reporter see the wedding of Jossie and Bonnie as a new dilemma? Crucially, it was not just the presence of the parents, the lovely cake, and the 120 guests that formalized the marriage, but the coverage of the event in the mass media. These mass media provided the incitement to discourse that inscribed the ceremony in a public sphere, marking it as a problem of the Republic but also part of a globalizing media environment rendering the Republic's boundaries uncertain. Many *gay* and *lesbi* Indonesians recall the mass media coverage of Jossie and Bonnie's reception as life-changing (not the reception itself, which few attended). In making the existence of a specifically Indonesian *lesbi* subjectivity public, the coverage of the reception holds a place in Indonesian popular culture roughly analogous to the coverage of Darrell Berrigan's 1965 murder in Bangkok (Jackson 1999a). When *Lambda Indonesia*, the first *gay* activist organization, sent out its press release in March 1, 1982, one Western gay magazine noted that its "founding resulted in part from increasing coverage of lesbian and gay issues by the straight press, particularly the public marriage of two Jakarta lesbians in May 1981."[6] In the novel *Menguak Duniaku*, the tomboi Hen recounts how while at a friend's house he "picked up a copy of *Tempo* from a pile of magazines in the corner. I flipped through the pages and my eyes froze when I saw an article 'The Story of Jossie and Bonni[e],' like what I had read a few months earlier." Hen then provides what appears to be a full transcript of the article, which identifies Jossie and Bonnie as "the first female couple, properly called lesbians, in Indonesia to publicize themselves through a reception" (Prawirakusumah and Ramadhan 1988:303). The author of a report on *lesbi* women written in the early 1990s stated that "Ten years after their marriage, the echo from the wedding of this female homosexual couple still reverberates. Their marriage is the only lesbian marriage to ever go proudly public in Indonesia" (see also Ary 1987:17).[7] The wedding of Jossie and Bonnie is also mentioned in more recent works on *lesbi* life (e.g., Herlinatiens 2003:12).

In the years immediately following this event, in at least two other instances *lesbi* couples received media attention. In the first, two young women, Suratmi and Isnaini, killed themselves in a rural area of Central Java (near Solo) by running in front of a train rather than be separated by their families. According to the news report (once again from *Liberty*), Suratmi, "Isnaini's best friend and workmate," was asked to dress as a man and stand in for Isnaini's new husband from Solo who had failed to return to the village for an official reception. It is unclear if the two women had been in a sexual relationship before the ceremony took place, but following the ceremony it became well known: "they went everywhere together, including the movies." This visibility "became a problem" for the villagers and the women were ordered to end their relationship, which resulted in the suicides. As in the case of Bonnie and Jossie, social opprobrium revolved around the politics of recognition, not the sexual acts of the women.

The second *lesbi* relationship to gain public attention in the wake of Jossie and Bonnie involved Aty, a twenty-one-year-old pop singer in Jakarta who was arrested for her love affair with the fifteen-year-old Nona. *Tempo* reported the incident on May 23, 1981, noting that it was "The first case of a *lesbi* woman being tried 'for doing it with someone of the same sex.'" In this case, the two women escaped from Jakarta to Malang in East Java, where Nona sent a letter to her parents saying that she would "choose Aty as my friend" until death. Reflecting yet again an emphasis on recognition, Nona emphasized in her letter that she had made a vow on a Bible with Aty.

Articles concerning *gay* men and *lesbi* women continued to appear intermittently throughout the 1980s; determining the exact level of coverage is not yet possible because there has been no systematic attempt to catalogue this coverage. In 1984 a group of Australians translated and published (under the title *Gays in Indonesia*) a set of articles that appeared between 1981 and 1983, collected by Dédé Oetomo (Gays in Indonesia Collective 1984). Given his diligence, the total of forty articles over two years probably represents a substantial percentage of the total number of articles published in major mass media during that time, highlighting that attention to *gay* and *lesbi* Indonesians was ongoing but rather minimal. Topics covered in these articles include the murder of a karate teacher in Bogor by a young man whom the teacher had forced into homosexual sex; "I Didn't Know My Husband Was a Homosexual," the story of a tricked wife who explained that unlike warias, *gay* men cannot be identified by a feminine appearance; and a story of homosexual behavior between men in a village Islamic school (*pesantren*), known as *mairil*. There also appeared a number of articles speculating on the causes of homosexual behavior based on Western sexology, and on notions of sin (usually drawing from Christian or Islamic sources).

It appears that throughout this period there was more media coverage of *lesbi* women than *gay* men. This is probably due to the greater policing of female sexuality in national discourse. The reports emphasized self-identified, lower-class *lesbi* women in couples as a foil to the modern middle-class woman. While *gay* and *lesbi* voices appeared in the early 1980s in Oetomo's *Anda* article and the coverage of Jossie and Bonnie's wedding, most articles were written from an outsider's perspective. Very little of this 1980s' mainstream mass media coverage addressed homosexuality outside Indonesia, raising again the issue of how *gay* and *lesbi* "globalized" to Indonesia at all.

Coming to *Gay* or *Lesbi* Subjectivity

> Any model of communication is at the same time a model of trans-lation, of a vertical or horizontal transfer of significance. No two historical epochs, no two social classes, no two localities use words and syntax to signify exactly the same things, to send identical signals of valuation and inference. Neither do two human beings.
> —George Steiner, *After Babel: Aspects of Language and Translation*

My *gay* and *lesbi* interlocutors of the 1990s and 2000s did not typically know of this history from the 1980s or the Dutch crackdown of the 1930s; they had little interest in, or knowledge of, ETPs. How did these Indonesians come to see themselves as *gay* or *lesbi*? Across what lines of similitude and difference are their selfhoods woven? How did Indonesians appropriate Western notions of homosexuality from the 1980s to the early 2000s, the period when *gay* and *lesbi* subjectivities first spread across the nation?

It is late morning in the city of Makassar, and I am recording an interview with Hasan, a thirty-two-year-old *gay* man I have known for many years. We are speaking about Hasan's youth, and he recalls his first sexual relationship as a young teenager, which took place with an older friend at school. At that point Hasan had never heard the word *gay*:

HASAN: I didn't yet know. I was confused. Why, why were there people like that? What I mean is why were there men who wanted to kiss men? This got me thinking when I was at home. I thought: why did my friend do that to me? What was going on? Was it just a sign, a sign of, what do you call it, just of friendship, I thought like that. I was still blind as to the existence of the *gay* world.

TB: And to learn the term *gay* or about the *gay* world, how did that happen?

HASAN: I knew later, when I was watching television. I saw on the "world news," there it showed a gay demonstration. And according to the information there . . . the people who were demonstrating, um, wanted the government to accept the marriage of men with men. And that made me confused. Why was it like that? That's when I was in high school [about two years after his first sexual experience with a man].

TB: And when you saw that, about that gay demonstration, what was your reaction, your feelings?

HASAN: I felt that an event like that could only happen outside; that in Indonesia there wasn't anything like that. I thought that maybe because we had a different state [*negara*], a culture [*kebudayaan*] that wasn't the same as their culture, so, maybe outside maybe it could be, and in Indonesia maybe it couldn't be, but, at that time I didn't think that there were people like that in Indonesia.

Hasan here recounts a moment of recognition, one that later leads him to look for other *gay* men and eventually call himself *gay*. Through an encounter with mass media, he comes to knowledge of what he takes to be the concept *"gay"* and retrospectively interprets his same-gender relationships before acquiring this knowledge in terms of "blindness." Readers familiar with debates in queer studies over the internationalization of gay and lesbian subjectivities (e.g., Adam, Duyvendak, and Krouwel 1999; Altman 2001) might seize on the fact that Hasan saw a gay demonstration as evidence of activism driving this "globalization," but, in fact, this is the most unusual aspect of Hasan's narrative. Three other elements prove more typical: sexuality is tied to mass-mediated language; an outside way of being becomes intimate; and the border dividing *gay* culture from other cultures is national, not ethnolocal.

Throughout my fieldwork, I have taken great pains to investigate how it is that Indonesians come to *gay* or *lesbi* subjectivity. Unlike ethnicity, religion, or gender, the *gay* and *lesbi* subject positions are not passed down through the family. They are experienced as novel. Unlike ETPs or the waria subject position, they are not something one learns from one's community or traditions: becoming *gay* or *lesbi* has required the reception and transformation of ideas from outside the home. This process appears, on first consideration, to be an ethnographic mystery. Unless they are quite upper class or have traveled to the West, most Indonesians remain surprisingly unaware of the terms *gay* and *lesbi* or think the terms (and *homo*) are English names for warias. Even *gay* men and *lesbi* women who went to elementary school in the late 1980s or early 1990s recall the use on the schoolyard of terms primarily for warias, such as *banci*, but rarely *gay* or *lesbi*. No ethnolocalized tradition (*adat*) or religion sanctions *gay* or *lesbi* or even names them systematically. How, then, do these subject positions take hold in the hearts of so many contemporary Indonesians?

Despite the testimony of my interlocutor concerning Western gay pornographic magazines imported into Indonesia in the late 1970s, during my fieldwork *gay* men and particularly *lesbi* women did not describe such pornography as having given them the idea they could be *gay* or *lesbi*; many have never seen such pornography, and it was certainly never distributed on a national scale or to most rural areas. Early in my fieldwork I learned of the small, informally published magazines or "zines" produced by some *gay* and *lesbi* groups. I initially hypothesized that such zines might play a "conduit" role, indigenizing and disseminating Western concepts of homosexual identity. I was mistaken. Zines are a form of cultural commentary highlighting many aspects of *gay* and *lesbi* subjectivity, including the relationship between love and the nation (see Boellstorff 2004c), but are almost always accessed after first seeing oneself as *gay* or *lesbi*. None of my interlocutors cited zines as how they came to *gay* or *lesbi* subjectivity: they do not represent a significant medium through which *gay* and *lesbi* subjectivities are taken up by Indonesian men and women—or were first taken up historically, since the *gay* and *lesbi* subject positions existed for several years prior to the appearance of the first *gay* zine in 1982.

The majority of *gay* men and *lesbi* women first hear about the terms *gay* and *lesbi* from print media. Others hear of the terms from peers or teachers; in these cases the term is also mass mediated since those who employ it have usually encountered it directly or indirectly through mass media. One *gay* man recalled that "I first heard about *gay* from my biology teacher. She didn't use the term *gay* or *homo*, just the concept. She said it was a genetic mutation and that such a person is a man but his face is pretty like a woman's. Through that I knew that I was that kind of person." Another recalled that "My school friends never called me homo or banci. But I heard other people get called such names. At school some of the boys would tease one of my friends. If he grabbed another boy by the hand, another boy would call him 'homo.' I heard the word and thought 'that's me,' I knew that what was said by that was me [*yang disebutkan itu adalah saya*]."

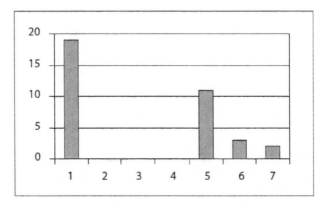

Figure 3–2. Ways in which one sample of 35 gay Indonesians first learned of the term. Categories listed on the horizontal axis: (1) from Indonesian mass media [19]; (2) from imported Western gay/lesbian media [0]; (3) from the Indonesian *gay* media [0]; (4) from religious sources [0]; (5) from friends [11]; (6) by wandering into a cruising area [3]; (7) from a sexual partner [2].

A few *gay* men first knew they could be *gay* after wandering into a public area frequented by *gay* men, and a few *gay* men and *lesbi* women became aware of the subject positions after being seduced. However, these are not the dominant pathways to learning of the *gay* or *lesbi* subject positions.

Figure 3–2 summarizes the responses of one sample of thirty-five *gay* men with whom I conducted extensive interviews. It shows that the element of Hasan's narrative with the greatest resonance is his description of a kind of "Aha!" moment when, during an encounter with mainstream print or electronic mass media, they come to think of themselves as *gay*. But unlike the "Aha!" moments that dominate knowledge production in the West, this is the discovery of similitude rather than difference. About 90 percent of my interlocutors encountered these terms through mainstream print media, or from schoolmates or friends who learned of the terms through mainstream print media. This is true whether the individuals in question are from Java, Bali, Sulawesi, or other islands; whether they are Muslim, Christian, Hindu, or Buddhist; whether they are wealthy, middle class, or impoverished; whether they live in cities or rural areas; and whether they were born in the 1950s, 1960s, 1970s, or 1980s. Rarely is a cultural variable distributed so widely across such a diverse population. The critical role of mainstream mass media in the lives of *gay* and *lesbi* Indonesians is all the more notable when comparing the life narratives of *gay* men and *lesbi* women with those of warias. I have never heard warias cite mass media as the means by which they first saw themselves as warias; they learn of the waria subject position from their social environs. Hasan's narrative rehearses a common story of discovery that most *gay* and *lesbi* Indonesians see as pivotal in their lives, a moment they recall without hesitation, as in the case of the following Javanese Christian man in Surabaya:

> In elementary school the only word was *banci* [waria]. For instance, a boy who walked or acted like a girl would get teased with the word *banci*. So I didn't know about the word *gay* until junior high. I heard it from books, magazines, television. And I wanted to know! I looked for information; if I saw that a magazine had an article about homos I'd be sure to read it. . . . I learned all of that stuff from the mass media. . . . So having someone come and tell me "It's like this," that never happened. I learned it all through magazines and newspapers. . . . And when I read those things, I knew that I was *gay*.

For this man "homo" is an impersonalized descriptive category, whereas *"gay"* is a framework for understanding the self's past motivations, immediate desires, and visions of an unfolding future. For many men an important aspect of this moment is realizing the possibility of a nonnormative masculine sexuality other than waria. Basir, a Muslim man who grew up in a small town in Sulawesi, tells his story in the following interview excerpt:

> TB: When you were in your teenage years, did you already know the term *gay*?
> BASIR: In my environment at that time, most people didn't yet know. But because I read a lot, read a lot of news, I already knew. I already knew that I was *gay*. Through reading I knew about the *gay* world. . . .
> TB: What kinds of magazines?
> BASIR: Gossip magazines, you know, they always talk about such-and-such a star and the rumors that the person is *gay*. So that broadened my concepts [*wawasan*], made me realize "Oh, there are others like me."

A Balinese Hindu man in his late twenties notes that: "In my first year of high school, I started to think. I started to think very hard: why do I like men? Because my other friends liked women. So from that my questions began, but they weren't yet answered. . . . I turned to the print media. So if there was news about *gay* stuff I'd be sure to read it—letters to the editor that asked 'why am I like this?,' reports in women's magazines, and so on."

One afternoon I was speaking with Darta, an unmarried Ambonese man in his early thirties living with his family in Surabaya. We were alone in the living room, but family members bustled about in the back of the house. I realized that since we were speaking Indonesian, they could be listening in on the conversation, yet Darta didn't seem bothered. Sitting on the cool tile floor, I looked up at him and asked, "Does your family already know about you?" Darta answered, "Yeah, they know that I'm effeminate and I have sex with men. It's no problem. They don't say it's a sin or anything. After they read magazines, they knew and understood, and accepted me."

"What magazines did they read?" I asked.

"Women's magazines, like *Kartini*. Those magazines always have gossip columns. So that's how they knew."

"When did you hear about *gay* for the first time?"

"I also read about it from magazines. When I first heard the word *gay*, it was in fifth or sixth grade [c. 1985], on the island of Ambon where I grew up. It was there that I first heard about *lesbi*. Earlier, you know— *gay* wasn't around yet [*gay belum ada*]. But *lesbi* was already in women's magazines . . . and I read lots of those magazines because mom was a regular subscriber. Mom and I loved reading the articles on sexual deviants. I was always effeminate, and one day she even said I was *lesbi*! Because she didn't know the term *gay*; the term wasn't public back then. But eventually I learned the term *gay* as well [*dapat gay juga*]. That was also from a magazine. There was some story about historic English royalty . . . Richard someone. When I saw that, I thought 'there're others like me.'"

Because *gay* and *lesbi* representations mingle in these mass media, most *lesbi* women, like the following Balinese woman, also trace their subjectivities to encounters with mass media: "I didn't use the word *lesbi* because I didn't even know the term [when I was young]. I didn't hear about the word *lesbi* until about 1990, when I read it in a magazine. And right away, when I read about *lesbi* and what that meant, I thought to myself, 'That's me!'" Sukma, a Muslim who terms herself a masculine *lesbi* woman (*hunter yang lesbi*), recalls that although she had sexual relations with other women in her early teenage years, "I didn't know *hunter* yet, but I already knew *lesbian, lesbi*, I knew. I'd already—I'd already read it, don't you know? In magazines, through hanging out with friends who mentioned it, through means like that." Sukma talked about short articles in newspapers that would occasionally mention how women could have sex with women, concluding, "Through that I could know that I was *lesbi*" (*lewat itu saya bisa tahu bahwa saya itu lesbi*).

For these Indonesians, the prerevelatory period of sexual subjectivity is usually experienced locally; the local is the social space of the not-yet (*belum*) gay or not-yet *lesbi*. What they describe when they encounter the concepts *gay* or *lesbi* through mass media is a moment of recognition that involves a shift in sexualized spatial scale; it is not only that same-gender desire can be constituted as a subjectivity, but also that its spatial scale is translocal. The deictic "*That*'s me!" places the self in a dialogic relationship with a *distant but familiar Other.* On one level this spatial scale is national. One reason for this is that the mass media through which Indonesians come to *gay* or *lesbi* subjectivity employ the national language, Indonesian (not ethnolocalized languages like Javanese or Buginese), and incorporate themes of national unity and patriotism. A second reason is that, unlike ETPs, the concepts *gay* and *lesbi* are seen as self-evidently incompatible with ethnolocality: no one learns what *gay* or *lesbi* means through "Makassarese culture" or "Javanese culture." *Gay* and *lesbi* persons think of themselves as *Indonesians* with regard to their sexualities. On a second level, *gay* and *lesbi* Indonesians, unlike warias, see their subjectivities as linked to a transnational imagined community: it is as if they are one island in a global archipelago of gay and lesbian persons. How can mass media have such unexpected effects from the margins?

The role of mass media is striking because there has been little coverage of openly *gay* or *lesbi* Indonesians: while coverage is increasing, what Indonesians still usually encounter through mass media is gossip about Indonesian celebrities and particularly gossip about Western celebrities. In contrast to some other postcolonial states like India, imports now represent a substantial amount of cinematic and televised fare in Indonesia, and most Indonesians, not just *gay* and *lesbi* ones, learn about the West through mass media rather than "the direct experience of living abroad" (Utomo 2002:211). Although there is a long tradition of filmmaking in Indonesia dating back to the early twentieth century and at some points garnering nationwide audiences, in the late 1990s the Indonesian film industry generally produced only fifteen to twenty films per year, mostly low-budget erotic films that went directly to second- or third-run theaters (Ryanto 1998:42).[8] Homosexuality appears so rarely that in 1997 a representative from Virgo Putra Film Corporation noted with regard to the film *Metropolitan Girl* "that film is really great, because there is a lesbian [*lesbian*] scene in it, something that has never existed in an Indonesian film up to this point."[9] Print media frequently run articles on "hetero" sex crimes, with descriptions of police breaking up "sex parties,"[10] arresting sex workers, or seizing pornography. Such musings on sexuality are sometimes linked to globalization, but homosexuality typically receives at best indirect mention, as in the following 1996 editorial:

> The speed of information and the high mobility of people on the face of this earth has resulted in sociocultural interaction [*interaksi sosio budaya*]. Within this sociocultural interaction there occurs a process of influence, imitation, and identification. . . . [We] must guard against this sociocultural interaction. . . . it's possible that we will lose our self-identity as Indonesians. . . . So don't be surprised if premarital relations, sexual relations outside of mar-

Figure 3–3. *Gay* men portrayed as possessed by animal lust. *Bali Post*, March 1, 1998:12.

riage, sexual harassment, rape, living together without being married, sexual deviations, infidelity and similar things are already no longer considered strange.[11]

In the 1990s *lesbi* women continued to receive more attention (i.e., surveillance) than men in mass media, but the focus shifted from lower-class *lesbi* women to entertainment figures, from couples to individual women, from ceremonies to sex acts, and from self-identified *lesbi* women to speculation on concealed homosexuality. An example is *Nusa*'s 1998 interview of the actress Inneke Koesherawati.[12] The article, entitled "I Indeed Embrace Devi Frequently," revolved around accusations that Inneke was the *lesbi* lover of another actress, Devi Permatasari: "To give the public certainty . . . [Devi] married [the male actor] Candra Priatna. 'Society now has proof I'm not a *lesbi* woman,' said Devi. But what about Inneke? For her the news of Devi's marriage is already enough to disprove the gossip. 'What more proof do you want. What's clear is that I'm a *normal* woman.'"

Coverage on *gay* men has tended to follow the same pattern, with a particular interest in *gay* sexuality as a vice of the *kalangan eksekutif* or "executive classes." A 1998 *Bali Post* article "*Homoseksual*" is typical.[13] Opening with an image portraying homosexual men as "after meat" or possessed by animal lust (fig. 3–3), the columnist, an "andrologist-sexologist," reprints two letters. In the first, "DP" describes befriending another man who showered DP with kindnesses and invited DP to spend the night in a hotel, where he seduced DP. In the second, "WA" describes feeling aroused by seeing men in tight pants or underwear. Both ask the columnist, "Am I homoseksual?" The columnist replies "No" to both, because the first was "receiving intensive sexual stimulation" and the second because "just because he likes a handsome man does not indicate that WA is homoseksual." Emphasizing the importance of conditioning, the columnist warns DP never to repeat his experience with another man and WA to avoid seeing men in their underwear, lest either become habituated to *homosexualitas*.[14]

When Indonesians encounter Western homosexuality in the mass media, what they usually see is not a one-hour special on "Homosexuality in the West"; rarely is it even the kind of demonstration described by Hasan. *Gay* and *lesbi* Indonesians typically speak of brief, intermittent coverage: a single fifteen-second item on Rock Hudson's AIDS diagnosis; an editorial about Al Pacino's role in the movie *Cruising*; reports on the 1991 death from AIDS of Freddie Mercury, lead singer of the British rock band Queen; a gossip column about Elton John or Melissa Etheridge; or gossip in the wake of the hit movie *Titanic* that Leonardo DiCaprio might be gay. The contrast to *Liberty's* coverage of Jossie and Bonnie's marriage in 1981 is evident: the emphasis has changed from Indonesia to the outside, from couples to individuals, from the acknowledged to the imputed, and from impoverished criminality to elitism. Alongside this attention to Western entertainers has come greater coverage of homosexuality outside Indonesia.[15]

Throughout the 1980s and 1990s a growing number of imported programs presented gay and lesbian characters.[16] Particularly when homosexuality is a relatively minor element of the plot—as in movies like *Cruising* or *The Wedding Banquet*, and television shows like *Melrose Place*—such programs are difficult to censor on the basis of their homosexual elements.[17] Although some *gay* men and *lesbi* women actually see such films, because the films either make it onto Indonesian screens or, increasingly, are available on video or VCD, what *gay* and *lesbi* Indonesians found most significant through the 1990s and early 2000s are national print media, particularly newspapers and women's magazines like *Kartini* and *Femina*. In most cases the references to homosexuality are negative—psychologists presenting homosexuality as a pathology, crime exposés, or disapproving gossip columns. The mystery of how Indonesians come to *gay* and *lesbi* subjectivity deepens in the face of this paradox: it is mainstream mass media that play the crucial role, yet "homosexuality"—Western or Indonesian—appears quite infrequently and inconsistently in these mass media. Denunciations of sexually decadent programming from the

West usually cite premarital sex, adultery, and unmarried cohabitation between men and women rather than homosexuality.

Beginning in the mid-1990s there has been an increasing, if still small, presence of *gay* and *lesbi* voices in general mass media, with a substantial increase after 2002. This remains a radical act because it collapses the boundaries between the *gay* and *lesbi* worlds and the *normal* world; it could thus have serious repercussions, including bringing shame upon the family or being expelled from the household or workplace. The scholar and activist Dédé Oetomo has remained the most salient *gay* or *lesbi* voice in mass media; few articles on homosexuality fail to interview him, and on several occasions he has appeared in full-color photo essays, complete with partner, house, and car—elements that mark him (and most images of *gay* and *lesbi* subjectivity in mass media in the 1990s) as middle class.[18] On June 9, 1997, Oetomo appeared on the talk show *Buah Bibir* (Topic of Conversation). Emceed by Debra Yatim, a woman known for her connections to women's rights circles, the show was well known for its sensational topics such as adultery and domestic violence. The topic for discussion on June 9 was *lesbi* women, but Oetomo, willing to be publicly identified as *homoseks*, was the guest star (several *lesbi* women appeared with their faces blackened out). This marked the first time that *gay* or *lesbi* subjectivities had appeared so openly on national television. When Minister of Information Hartono criticized RCTI (the station producing *Buah Bibir*) as well as station SCTV, which produced a similar program, *Portret*, Yatim defended the show by appealing to ETPs and style: "gemblak in [the area of] Ponorogo [in East Java] have been around for a long time, in [the West Java city of] Indramayu there are *tayuban* dances in a homo style [*gaya homo*], and even at the Borobudur temple there are reliefs about homosexuality."[19] When Minister of Religion Tarmizi Taher added that the "promotion of *gay* and *lesbianisme*" must not be "provided with opportunities" in television, radio, or other public forums, the editors of *Kompas* joked, "But how is it that béncongs [warias] are in almost every telecomedy, sir?"[20]—highlighting how the waria subject position is less threatening than the *gay* and *lesbi* subject positions, so clearly novel and with transnational resonances.[21]

Lesbi women appear much more rarely in mass media of their own accord. One Balinese *lesbi* woman appeared in the tourist magazine *Bali Eko* in the mid 1990s: "It was in English . . . and in the article I came out, using my real name, and talked about how hard it was being a *lesbi* here. . . . My parents and family were mad at first—'how can you do this?, they said'—but I think it's been good. It forced us to talk about things more, but they still pressure me to marry."

Since 2002 several private television stations have run segments of ten to thirty minutes on *gay* and *lesbi* life in Indonesia, including face-to-face interviews. *Gay* and *lesbi* topics have appeared on talk shows with greater regularity, with celebrities like Ivan Gunawan openly identifying as *gay*. The film *Arisan!* included a major plotline concerning the struggle of Sakti, a *gay* man, to accept himself and find love with another man. Though Sakti's upper-class life bears little resemblance to the lives of most *gay* men, the film, with its two on-screen kisses between Sakti and his lover, was widely viewed in theaters or on video. Additionally, a growing number of books on *gay* life have appeared that focus on rich Jakartans, detailing an elite world of sex parties and wealth alien to the lives of most *gay* and *lesbi* Indonesians (e.g., Priaga 2003). This greater coverage of *gay* and *lesbi* lives in the mass media, however biased, will surely have unintended ramifications for how *gay* and *lesbi* Indonesians in ensuing years understand their subjectivities.

Occasionally *gay* or *lesbi* Indonesians respond to unfavorable coverage, as in an exchange of letters from the Surabaya newspaper *Surya* in 1998. On January 8 the newspaper published a letter by someone using the initials "M.Y.R." that claimed, "In this era of globalization, everything demands openness. . . . Up to now I have always regarded the life of *gay* people as something normal, with the note that everything has always been limited to friendship and communication. But after more than a week of research in Surabaya, I've become nervous. Apparently the life of *gay* people there is just a business mask, to get money easily." A week later the newspaper published the response of "A.T." After stating how he had known the *gay* world since 1984 and had even appeared on the cover of *Intisari* magazine in May 1993 for an article about *gay* issues, A.T. emphasized that "For all that time I have never known that there are *gay* men who sell themselves for money. What I know is that there are *hetero* people (there are some who already have families) who prostitute themselves for money. . . . Don't just base your research on a week's work and then draw conclusions."

Such back-talk can appear in other formats. One day in March 1998 I was hanging out in the salon of a *gay* man in southern Bali when two members of a local *gay* group suddenly entered the door. Tossing their motorcycle helmets on the sofa and pushing aside a stack of glossy fashion magazines, they sat down and started speaking animatedly: "We got invited to participate in this radio show about being *gay* three days ago, and earlier this morning we went on-air [anonymously] with a parent and a psychologist." The other man chimed in: "But that psychologist was so stupid! He didn't know his material. He kept saying that it was a disease, that if a client got married and had kids that meant he was cured. We argued with him for the whole show."

Rarely, mainstream mass media address the organizational activities of *gay* and *lesbi* Indonesians. One of the most extensive examples was the five-part series run by the newspaper *Nusa* from November 23 to 28, 1997, covering the Third National Congress of *Gay* and *Lesbi* Indonesians in Denpasar, Bali. Most of the reportage was sensationalistic, focusing on sexual practices and the supposed shame and secrecy of the attendees. However, the final installment—entitled "The 'Medicine' That Makes the People Who Like the Same Kind [*Kaum Sejenis*] Happy: To Be Recognized by Society"—explored, albeit briefly, the politics of acceptance articulated by many of the conference attendees. Focusing on the fact that no *gay* or *lesbi* organization has ever been recognized by the government, in a context where many waria organizations are so recognized, the article noted that "it is difficult for [*gay* and *lesbi* organizations] to be legalized by the government for the reason that *gay* identity [*identitas gay*] does not exist in the [system of] government administration."[22] As in the case of Bonnie and Jossie's wedding almost two decades before, the issue was not sex acts but belonging and recognition.[23]

The *gay* and *lesbi* subject positions thus lead us to a specific sociological problem. As a new, consumerist middle class emerged following the oil crisis of the 1970s, Indonesians began to learn of the possibility of thinking of oneself as *gay* or *lesbi* through the intermittent reception of messages from mass media. These messages do not intend to convey the possibility of a kind of selfhood. They are often denigrating and dismissive, but above all they are *fragmentary*. Because I have bundled together a series of examples, I may have given the false impression that such coverage is an everyday occurrence. But normally these discussions of "homosexuality" are but isolated moments in the buzz and confusion of other reportage, even in the early 2000s. It is not an incitement to discourse or a coherent "hailing." But the sum of these partial asides, sporadic human-interest stories, and irregular interviews has been a slowly increasing hum of discourse tenuously linkable to *gay* and *lesbi* subjectivities, reaching the farthest corners of Indonesia. It has implied that one could understand one's selfhood in terms of same-gender desire, and thus that *gay* and *lesbi* subjectivities are somehow akin—suggesting that *gay* is conceptually closer to *lesbi* than to waria. These media disseminate the idea that *gay* and *lesbi* subjectivities exist, while being vague, incomplete, and contradictory as to what they might entail in terms of everyday practice. They also imply that these subjectivities are Indonesia-wide phenomena, non-ethnolocalized and bearing some kind of "family resemblance" to gay and lesbian subjectivities outside Indonesia. From their beginnings to the present, these media have "exposed" not a fully articulated discourse of homosexuality, but a series of incomplete and contradictory references, in translation, sometimes openly denigrating and hostile. It is not a transmission of self-understanding so much as a fractured set of cultural logics reconfigured within Indonesia. Yet from "translations" of this intermittent reportage come subjectivities by which myriad Indonesians live out their lives. In the 1980s an Indonesian might encounter such reportage a few times a year at most, if an avid reader; in the 1990s and 2000s it became more frequent but still minimal given the universe of topics appearing in the mass media. The question, then, is how modes of subjectivation become established when the social field in which they arise establishes them neither as discourses nor as reverse discourses. Indonesian mass media certainly do not intend to set forth the possibility of *gay* and *lesbi* subject positions, nor do the imported programs they frequently rebroadcast; in fact, they rarely take a negative stance on *gay* and *lesbi* subject positions. Yet it is these mass media that, in a very real sense, make *gay* and *lesbi* subjectivities possible, just as the national imagined communities that are so socially efficacious worldwide could not have existed before Gutenberg struck type to page.

The "Problem" of Dubbing

> Eros and language mesh at every point. Intercourse and discourse, copula and copulation, are subclasses of the dominant fact of communication. . . . Sex is a profoundly semantic act . . . human sexuality and speech [together] generate . . . the process . . . whereby we have hammered out the notion of self and otherness.
> —George Steiner, *After Babel: Aspects of Language and Translation*

Mass media were important in the archipelago long before *gay* and *lesbi* subjectivities. From the late nineteenth century to the middle of the twentieth, print media played a central role in the formation of nationalism among the diverse and far-flung peoples of the Netherlands East Indies. Print media were also important in the establishment of Indonesian (a dialect of Malay formerly used as a lingua franca of trade) as the language of this new imagined community, a language that could permit communication among a populace speaking about 550 languages, or approximately "one-tenth of all the languages in the world" (Sneddon 2003:5).[24] Electronic media have become increasingly significant: by the late 1990s each of Indonesia's then-five private television stations was importing approximately seven thousand shows per year, many of which originated in the United States (Republika 1996), and beginning in the 1990s dubbing became an increasingly popular way of presenting these broadcasts to Indonesian audiences (Lindsay 2005).[25]

It was in this context that, in a joint news conference on April 4, 1996, one year after one of Indonesia's private television stations went national for the first time, Minister of Information Harmoko and Minister of Education and Culture Wardiman Djojonegoro announced that "foreign films on television should no longer be broadcast in their original language version with Indonesian summaries or subtitles but were to be dubbed into Indonesian" (Lindsay 2005). This regulation on dubbing (*dubbing, sulih suara* [to substitute sound]) was to take effect by August 16, in accordance with a soon-to-be-passed broadcasting law, which included the first set of broadcasting regulations to be issued in eighteen years.[26] This bill, which had been debated in Parliament for several months at that point, was to become one of the most contentious legal documents of the New Order's twilight years. The requirement that all programs be dubbed into Indonesian was greeted with little fanfare: as the public relations manager of TPI noted, many of the programs imported each year by private television stations were already dubbed in response to viewer demand. Acquiescing to the state's long-standing goal of building nationalism through language planning, the public relations manager of RCTI added that the requirement was "a good policy that will help build Indonesian skills in society" (Republika 1996).

Within a month of the announcement, however, Aisyah Aminy, a spokesperson from the House of Representatives, suggested "this problem of dubbing is going to be discussed in more depth" (Suara Pembaruan Daily 1996). Revealing dissent within the state apparatus, Aminy expressed concern that "at present, foreign films on television are not dubbed selectively and show many things that do not fit well with the culture of our people" (Suara Pembaruan Daily 1996). The influential armed forces faction also weighed in against the measure, but the House forged ahead, incorporating the dubbing requirement in its draft broadcast law of December 6, 1996.

What made the broadcasting bill such a topic of discussion was the way in which it was debated and revised, extraordinary even for the arcane machinations of the New Order bureaucracy. A first draft of the bill was completed by a legislative committee early in 1996 and sent to Parliament for approval. As usual in the New Order, the bill had been essentially crafted by the president and even bore his initials (McBeth 1997:24). In December 1996 Parliament duly rubber-stamped the bill, returning it to Soeharto for his signature. After seven months, however, on July 11, 1997, Soeharto dropped a bombshell: in an official letter he refused to sign the draft broadcast law and returned it to Parliament for revision, claiming that "several articles will be too difficult to implement from a technical standpoint" (Kompas 1997; Soeharto 1997). This unconstitutional act was the first time in national history a president refused to sign a draft law already passed by the House, a refusal made all the more perplexing by his approval of the original bill (Kompas 1997). House debate on the president's proposed revisions began on September 18, 1997, and was marked by unusual (for the Soeharto era) interruptions from Parliament members and heated argument over executive–legislative relations.

In the wake of the president's refusal, government sources gave conflicting accounts of the issues at stake. One issue, however, stood out above the others for its cultural, rather than directly economic, emphasis: the edict on dubbing. What was notable was the total reversal that occurred during parliamentary revisions: when the dust cleared in December 1997, Article 25 of the draft law, concerning dubbing, "had been completely reversed. All non-English language foreign films henceforth had to be dubbed into English, and all foreign films shown with Indonesian subtitles" (Lindsay 2005). Why this sea change? As one apologist later explained:

> Dubbing can create gaps in family communication. It can ruin the self-image of family members as a result of adopting foreign values that are "Indonesianized" [*diindonesiakan*]. . . . This can cause feelings of becoming "another person" to arise in family members, who are in actuality not foreigners . . . whenever Indonesians view television, films, or other broadcasts where the original language has been changed into our national language, *those Indonesians will think that the performances in those media constitute a part of themselves. As if the culture behind those performances is also the culture of our people.* (N. Ali 1997:341–342, emphasis added)

In the end, the final version of the bill indeed forbids dubbing most foreign programs into the Indonesian language. What is of interest for our purposes here, however, is the debate itself. Why, at this prescient moment in 1997—as if foreshadowing the New Order's collapse the following year—did translation become a focal point of political and cultural anxiety? What made the ability of Sharon Stone or Tom Cruise to "speak Indonesian" no longer a welcome opportunity to foster linguistic competency but rather a sinister force threatening the good citizen's ability to differentiate self from Other? Why, even with widespread discontent in many parts of the archipelago, was the state's fear suddenly recentered, not on religious, regional, or ethnic affiliation overwhelming national loyalty, but on transnational affiliation superseding nationalism and rendering it secondary? And what might be the hidden linkages between this dubbing controversy and the crucial role mass media play in *gay* and *lesbi* subjectivities?

DUBBING CULTURE

> An error, a misreading initiates the modern history of our sub-
> ject. Romance languages derive their terms for "translation"
> from *traducere* because Leonardo Bruni misinterpreted a sen-
> tence in the *Noctes* of Aulus Gellius in which the Latin actu-
> ally signifies "to introduce, to lead into." The point is trivial
> but symbolic. Often, in the records of translation, a fortunate
> misreading is the source of new life.
> —George Steiner, *After Babel:*
> *Aspects of Language in Translation*

We now have two problems centering on mass media. First: how do Indonesians come to see themselves as *gay* or *lesbi* through the fragmentary
reception of mass mediated messages? Second: why would the question
of dubbing foreign television shows into the Indonesian language provoke
one of the greatest constitutional crises in Indonesia's history? I suggest
that the first problem can be addressed through the second. In effect, these
two sets of social facts can be "dubbed," throwing up striking conver-
gences and unexpected resonances. Both of these problems raise issues of
translation and authenticity in an already globalized world. This conjuncture of translation and authenticity is powerfully gendered and sexualized
in the Western tradition, which "suggests that in the original abides what
is natural, truthful, and lawful, in the copy, what is artificial, false, and
treasonous . . . like women, the adage goes, translations should be either
beautiful or faithful" (Chamberlain 2000:315). The "authentic" originary is masculinized, the "inauthentic" translation is feminized, and the
process of translation heterosexualized. From this dominant perspective
both dubbing and homosexual sex appear sterile, failed, unfaithful. The
gay and *lesbi* subject positions demand a queer take on translation: How
long before a word is no longer a "loanword"?

It was long after becoming aware of the link between mass media and
gay and *lesbi* subjectivities that I learned of the dubbing controversy. I
had been struggling with the question of *gay* and *lesbi* subjectivities for
some time without a clear conclusion, particularly concerning questions
of agency. Were *gay* and *lesbi* Indonesians simply mimicking the West?
Were they severed from their traditions once they occupied the subject
positions *gay* or *lesbi*? Alternatively, were these Indonesians queering
global capitalism, subverting its heteronormativity and building a movement dedicated to human rights? Were they deploying the terms *gay* and
lesbi tactically, as a veneer over a deeper indigenousness?

A notion of "dubbing culture" allowed me to move beyond this impasse of "puppets of globalization" versus "veneer over tradition." Through individual encounters with mass media—like reading one's mother's magazines or an advice column in the local newspaper, or viewing television coverage of a gay pride march in Australia—Indonesians construct subjectivities and communities. *Construct* is the wrong word; it connotes a self who plans and consciously shapes something.[27] Better to say that these Indonesians "come to" *gay* and *lesbi* subjectivity through these entanglements with mass media; their constructive agency, and the *gay* and *lesbi* subject positions themselves, are constructed through the encounter. This is not a solely individual process; although the originary encounters with magazines or newspapers are typically solitary, as soon as the person begins to interact with other *gay-* or *lesbi*-identified Indonesians, he or she reworks these mass-mediated understandings of sexuality. Romance, for instance, is a crucial element of *gay* and *lesbi* subjectivities but rarely appears in media treatments of homosexuality.

A set of fragmented cultural elements from mass media is transformed in unexpected ways in the Indonesian context, transforming that context itself in the process. In other words, *gay* and *lesbi* Indonesians "dub" ostensibly Western sexual subjectivities. Like a dub, the fusion remains a juxtaposition; the seams show. "Speech" and "gesture" never perfectly match; being *gay* or *lesbi* and being Indonesian never perfectly match. For *gay* and *lesbi* Indonesians, as in dubbing culture more generally, this tension is irresolvable; there is no "real" version underneath, where everything fits. You can close your eyes and hear perfect speech or mute the sound and see perfect gesture, but no original unites the two in the dubbed production. This may not present the self with an unlivable contradiction, however, since in dubbing one is invested not in the originary, but rather in the awkward fusion. Disjuncture is at the heart of the dub; there is no prior state of pure synchrony, and no simple conversion to another way of being. Where traditional translation is haunted by its inevitable failure, dubbing rejoices in the good-enough and the forever incomplete. Dubbing is not definitive but heuristic, interpretative—like many understandings of the ethnographic project.

It is this dimension of dubbing that transcends the apparent dilemma of "puppets of globalization" versus "veneer over tradition." The idea of dubbing culture indicates that the root of the problem is the notion of authenticity itself, the colonialist paradigm that valorizes the "civilized" colonizer over the "traditional" colonized. In line with the observation that postcolonial nationalisms usually invert, rather than disavow, colonial categories of thought (inter alia, Gupta 1998:169), the Indonesian state simply flips the colonial binary, placing tradition over modernity as the ultimate justification for the nation. To the obvious problem of justifying a recently formed nation in terms of tradition, the Indonesian state (like all national states) has worked ever since to inculcate a sense of national culture *(kebudayaan nasional)*. This is built on the pillar of the Indonesian language and propagated via mass media. Through mass media, citizens are to come to recognize themselves as authentic Indonesians, carriers of an oxymoronic "national tradition" that will guide the body politic through the travails of modernity. By speaking in one "Indonesian" voice, a hierarchy of tradition over modernity can be sustained and reconciled with statehood.

Dubbing, an inevitably and openly unfaithful translation since words and lips never match, threatens this hierarchy: it is lateral, rhizomatic (Deleuze and Guattari 1987). The authoritative voice is at odds with the visual presentation. Dubbing culture sets two elements side by side, blurred yet distinct. It is a performative act that, in linking persons to subject positions, creates subjectivities (Butler 1990); but this dubbing link is *profoundly not one of suture,* a term originating in film studies regarding "the procedures by means of which cinematic texts confer subjectivity upon their viewers" (Silverman 1983:195). In dubbing culture, subjectivity is constituted not through suture but through collage. Yet this productively partial incorporation of the self into discourse is not a failed performance: in its iteration, its holding together of two ostensibly incompatible cultural logics without conflating them, a space for subjectivity—a subject position—appears.

I have described dubbing in terms of a disjuncture between image and voice, and many Indonesians see it that way, but another way to conceptualize dubbing is as the substitution of one voice for another, as indicated by the phrase *sulih suara,* a common term alongside dubbing. Early twentieth-century Russian linguists like Bakhtin (1981) and Vološinov (1973) became interested in "reported speech," a topic that has also gained the attention of current scholars of language and culture (e.g., Gal 1998; Rumsey 1990; Silverstein 1993). Reported speech, which in Indonesian as in English can take the form of direct or indirect discourse ("She said, 'I'm exhausted'" versus "She said that she was exhausted"), typically operates as what Bakhtin termed authoritative discourse, which works "to determine the very bases of our ideological interactions with the world" (Bakhtin 1981:342). For Bakhtin, "authoritative discourse . . . remains sharply demarcated, compact and inert . . . it enters our verbal consciousness as a compact and indivisible mass; one must either totally affirm it, or totally reject it" (343).

Dubbing destabilizes the very notion of reported speech. It is highly indirect discourse—not just paraphrasing speech but rendering it into a different language—yet it is hemmed in by a double authority: the original dialogue it reworks, and the image of moving lips with which it must attempt to unify. Yet the attempt is intended (not doomed) to fail; a dub rejects the binarism of "totally affirming" or "totally rejecting" the discourse it transforms, just like *gay* and *lesbi* Indonesians are neither imitating Western homosexualities nor utterly distinct from them. Dubbing demands a new grid of similitude and difference, one appropriate to an already globalized world.

The original television show or movie may preexist its Indonesian dub temporally, but to the interpreting audience neither voice nor image is prior. They happen together; neither dominates. Agamben, citing Benjamin's concern with the relationship between quotation and the new "transmissibility of culture" made possible by mass media, notes that quotation "alienat[es] by force a fragment of the past . . . mak[ing] it lose its authentic power" (1999:104). But dubbing culture (in a literal sense as well as the metaphorical sense I develop here) is more than just quotation; it adds a step, first alienating something but then reworking it in a new context. The power of the dub comes not by erasing authenticity but by inaugurating new authenticities not dependent on tradition or translation. It is a form of reported speech that disrupts the apparent seamlessness of the predubbed original, showing that it too is a dub, that its "traditions" are the product of social contexts with their own assumptions and inequalities. Thus it is not the case that *gay* and *lesbi* subjectivities in Indonesia are disjunctive and heuristic while Western sexual subjectivities (queer or otherwise) are seamless. What we can learn from the Indonesian case is that the apparent coherence of all subjectivities is a cultural effect, and the inevitable "failure" of coherence does not mean that subjectivity is flawed or inauthentic.

The Indonesian authorities were keenly aware of these disruptive implications during the dubbing controversy. For decades, Indonesian had been the vehicle allowing Indonesians to speak with one voice. But now the possibility that Sharon Stone could "speak Indonesian" meant that this vehicle was spinning beyond state control—into the control of globalizing forces, but also into an interzone between languages and cultures, a zone with no controlling authority: "the Indonesian dubbing was so successful in making the language familiar that viewers lost any idea that it was strange for foreigners to speak Indonesian. . . . The language was too familiar, too much like real speech, too colloquial, and therefore the speech was too dangerous" (Lindsay 2005:11).

The sudden shift during the dubbing controversy—from an insistence that *all* foreign television programs be dubbed into the Indonesian language to an insistence that *none* of them could be so dubbed—reveals a tectonic shift in the position of mass media in Indonesian society. For the first time, fear of this juxtaposition, of Westerners "speaking" the national tongue, tipped the scales against a historically privileged concern with propagating Indonesian as national unifier. Now the ability of dubbing (and the Indonesian language itself) to explode the national imagined community—to show that one can be Indonesian *and* translate ideas from outside—presented a danger greater than the potential benefit of drawing more sharply the nation's archipelagic edges.

Dubbing itself is clearly not how Indonesians come to *gay* and *lesbi* subjectivity; I have never heard them specifically mention dubbing, and dubbing did not become ubiquitous until the 1990s. This is why the dubbing controversy took place in 1997, not 1981, 1961, or 1861. However, the controversy was about more than the technique of dubbing or even mass media generally: it concretized a sense that the relationship among scale, selfhood, and belonging had been cast into what for some was a disturbing state of flux. The trajectory of this process stretches back over one hundred years, for "the path by which recognition became centered in the Indonesian nation . . . is indissociable from the history of 'communication' . . . the history of the nation is made not from autochthonous sources and not from foreign borrowings but from the effects of these connections." Not similitude, nor difference, but the dubbing of these two, so that the originary moment of Indonesian national culture lies in "the history of hearing and overhearing that went on between groups of the Indies and between the Indies and the world" (Siegel 1997:7, 6).

What does it mean when what you overhear is a dub?

Dubbing culture is about a new kind of cultural formation in an already globalized world, one for which the idiom of translation is no longer sufficient. It questions *the relationship between translation and belonging,* asserting that the binarisms of import–export and authentic–inauthentic are insufficient to explain how globalizing mass media play a role in *gay* and *lesbi* subject positions but do not determine them outright. For queer studies, one lesson is that binarisms of rupture versus indigenity do not capture the possibility of subject positions with more nuanced and conjunctural relationships to the West, ones that may stand outside usual definitions of identity politics. In a metaphorical sense, one could say that *gay* and *lesbi* Indonesians dub Western sexual subject positions: they overwrite the deterministic "voice of the West," yet they cannot compose any script they please; their bricolage remains shaped by a discourse originating in the West and filtered through a nationalistic lens. This process of dubbing allows *gay* and *lesbi* individuals to see themselves as part of a global community, but also as authentically Indonesian. Unlike warias, they never ask, "Are there people like me outside Indonesia?" because it is already obvious—"built into" the dubbed subjectivities—that there are such people. These Indonesians imagine themselves as one national element in a global patchwork of gay and lesbian national subjectivities, not as "traditional," because *gay* and *lesbi* have a national spatial scale.

More broadly, dubbing culture as a metaphor speaks to the nonteleo-logical, transformative dimensions of globalizing processes. It is useful for questioning the ability of globalizing mass media to project uniform ideologies. Contemporary mass media have enormous power, but this power is not absolute; it can lead to unexpected results—like *gay* and *lesbi* subject positions themselves. The metaphorical use of dubbing cul-ture fleshes out theories linking ideological apparatuses with Althusser's thesis that "ideology interpellates individuals as subjects" (1971:160–162). By this, Althusser meant that ideology forms the subject positions by which individuals come to represent their conditions of existence to themselves and to others. Althusser terms this function of ideology inter-pellation or hailing and illustrates it in terms of a person on the street responding to the hail, "Hey, you there!" When the person turns around to respond to the hail, "he becomes a *subject*. Why? Because he has recog-nized that the hail was 'really' addressed to him" (Althusser 1971:163). Many social theorists, particularly those interested in mass media, have found this a useful analytical starting point. The question most commonly posed to this framework by these theorists concerns the issue of structure versus agency: "How and why does the subject turn? . . . What kind of relation already binds these two such that the subject knows to turn, knows that something is to be gained from such a turn" (Butler 1997:107)?

Part and parcel of this dilemma of agency is the question: how to ex-plain the circumstance when people "recognize" something an ideology does not intend? Indonesian mass media never meant to create the condi-tions of possibility for national *gay* and *lesbi* subject positions. One way to address this problem might be through the dubbing culture concept, where what is recognized in the hail is itself a product of transformation. This does not entail compliance with state ideology. Yet neither does it imply a freewheeling, presocial, self-assembling of an identity from ele-ments presented by mass media, independent of social context.

Gay and *lesbi* Indonesians often playfully employ the notion of authen-ticity (*asli*)—I have often heard gay men describe themselves as *asli gay.* In doing so, they implicitly challenge the state's monopoly on designating what will count as tradition in Indonesia. Authenticity is crucial for mass media studies as well. For Benjamin, the very concept of authenticity is put under erasure by mass media. Because mass media depend on mechan-ical reproduction (no mass media circulate as a series of handcrafted origi-nals), and for Benjamin "the presence of the original is the prerequisite to the concept of authenticity," it follows that "the whole sphere of authen-ticity is outside technical . . . reproducibility." Benjamin sees the most significant aspect of this reproducibility to be that of movement: "above all, [technical reproduction] enables the original to meet the beholder halfway. . . . [The] cathedral leaves its locale to be received in the studio of a lover of art; the choral production, performed in an auditorium or in the open air, resounds in the drawing room" (1955:220–221).

Gay and *lesbi* subjectivities are not moved from one place to another, as Benjamin saw mechanical reproduction, but are the dubbing of cultural logics in new ways. Dubbing culture is thus articulation in both senses of the term, an interaction of elements that remain distinct—like the image of speech and the dubbed voice—and also the "speaking" of a (dubbed) subjectivity.[28] This lets us "queery" globalization without posing either an oppositionally authentic "native" or globalization as simple movement.

Dubbing culture also speaks to conceptions of translation in the age of mechanical production. As Benjamin notes with reference to magazines, "For the first time, captions have become obligatory. And it is clear that they have an altogether different character than the title of a painting" (1955:226). This is because captions are a guide to interpretation, juxtaposed to the work of art yet at a slight remove. They serve as "signposts" that "demand a specific kind of approach; free-floating contemplation is not appropriate to them" (Benjamin 1955:226). They are a mediation internal to mass media, a translation within.

Dubbing, far more than a subtitle, is a caption fused to the thing being described. It comes from the mouth of imagic characters yet is never quite in synch. The moving lips never match the speech; the moment of fusion is always deferred, as dubbed voice, translation-never-quite-complete, bridges two sets of representations.[29] *Gay* and *lesbi* Indonesians dub culture as they live a subjectivity linked to people and places far away. They are completely Indonesian, but to be "completely Indonesian" requires thinking of one's position in a transnational world. In speaking of translation, Benjamin wrote that "unlike a work of literature, translation does not find itself in the center of the language forest but on the outside facing the wooded ridge; it calls into it without entering, aiming at that single spot where the echo is able to give, in its own language, the reverberation of the work in the alien one" (1955:76). *Gay* and *lesbi* Indonesians have made of that echo subject positions that bespeak subjectivity and community even under conditions of oppression. They live in the echo, in the mass-mediated margin of incomplete translation, and find there authenticity, meaning, sex, friendship, and love.

The concept of dubbing culture has a reflexive dimension for ethnography in an already globalized world. To the extent that translation is a structuralist enterprise framing movement between languages and cultures in terms of grammar and meaning, many contemporary ethnographers engage in dubbing culture when they employ poststructuralist frameworks that question received understandings of the relationship among signifiers, and between signifiers and signifieds. One reason dubbing culture profoundly challenges established frameworks for anthropo-logical analysis is that in it the act of interpretation precedes the anthropo-logical encounter, so the analytical moment is not external to the ethnographic moment.

Contemporary ethnography, then, can be said to be engaging in dub-bing culture when it brings together parts and wholes, data and theory. *Gay* and *lesbi* Indonesians engage in dubbing culture as they come to sexual subjectivity; they show not that "authentic Indonesian tradition" is a lie but that this authenticity is processual, constructed through active engagement with an unequal world. And if tradition and belonging are not given but constructed, they can be contested and transformed. The playing field is certainly not even—*gay* and *lesbi* Indonesians are not about to become fully accepted members of Indonesian society—but it is a playing field nonetheless, and there is space for change. Similarly, even in an already globalized world, non-Western cultures are not doomed to the status of reruns, even when confronted by Western hegemony.

PART TWO

Opening to *Gay* and *Lesbi* Worlds

CHAPTER FOUR

Islands of Desire

Toward an Anthropology of Similitude

> We do not know whether two things are to be regarded as
> the same or not unless we are told the context in which the
> question arises. However much we may be tempted to think
> otherwise, there is no absolute unchanging sense to the words
> "the same."
> —Peter Winch, *The Idea of a Social Science*

If becoming *gay* or *lesbi* typically begins with mass media, how is a whole
gay or *lesbi* life forged from this first moment of dubbing culture?

Many *gay* and *lesbi* Indonesians express the idea of a *gay* or *lesbi* life by
speaking of a *gay* world and *lesbi* world (*dunia gay, dunia lesbi*), partially
overlapping worlds they distinguish from the *normal* world (*dunia normal*). As Howard notes in his study of *gay* men in Jakarta, "the use of
the term 'normal' is telling, as normal life (*kehidupan normal*) is also
recognized in national political rhetoric as a recognition of social stability
and order" (1996:177). *Gay* and *lesbi* sexuality have no place in the *normal* world, and during the time of my fieldwork *gay* and *lesbi* Indonesians
overwhelmingly had no interest in a Western-style politics seeking a place
in that world. Less contiguous spaces than distributed archipelagos, the
gay and *lesbi* worlds were the primary "sites" of my fieldwork. Part 2 of
this book delves into these worlds to gain a better understanding of how
gay and *lesbi* subjectivities are lived. This chapter explores sex, desire,
love, and relationships, including "heterosexual" marriage. It may seem
strange to discuss "heterosexual" marriage in a chapter on homosexual
erotics, but the importance of marriage to *gay* men and *lesbi* women offers
important clues about the relationship between sexuality and nation for
all those living in the postcolonial nation-state of Indonesia.

Most "homosexualities" in Indonesia and elsewhere in Southeast Asia
share with dominant Western "homosexualities" an assumption that sexuality and gender overlap. While "race" is sexualized in the United States,
I do not know of any case where, for instance, sex between one African
American and another, regardless of their gender, is labeled "homosex-

ual" while sex between an African American and an Asian American, regardless of their gender, is labeled "heterosexual." Nor do I know of a case where an older person having sex with a younger person is seen as "heterosexual" while sex between two younger people or two older people (regardless of the genders involved) is seen as "homosexual." "Homo" and "hetero," as terms of sexuality, are assumed to index gender; thus, what is referred to as gender is more accurately glossed "heteronormative gender." The partial fusion of sexuality and gender appears universal, an apparent similitude that invites biologizing or the search for counterexamples. Another possibility is to reconceptualize the grid of similitude and difference itself, asking how conceptions of gender and sexuality are forged and sustained in specific contexts.

Gay and *lesbi* desires are unique in Indonesia in that they are erotics within, not between, sexual subject positions. Both *gay* men and *lesbi* women speak of their sexualities as a "desire for the same." This contrasts with the desire for difference characterizing the desire of *normal* women for *normal* men, *normal* men for *normal* women, warias for *normal* men, and *normal* men for warias. Even when *gay* or *lesbi* erotics are articulated across a heterogendered divide—between effeminate and masculine *gay* men, or between tombois and ceweks—this is seen to take place within a field of homosexual desire.

Similitude is the style (*gaya, cara*) of *gay* and *lesbi* desire, revealed in phrases like *sama jenis* (same type) or *sejenis* (one type) in distinction to *normal* desire, which is for *lain jenis* (different type). *Sama* is a common word for "same"; in *gay* language it can be transformed into *sémong* "gay man." *Sama* can also mean "together, with." *Suka* means "joy, pleasure, desire," and the phrase *suka sama suka*, roughly "desire with desire," is a colloquialism meaning "by mutual agreement, especially with regard to sex and marriage" (Echols and Shadily 1997:530).[1] *Gay* and *lesbi* Indonesians often use *suka sama suka* to describe their desires. Their *gay* or *lesbi* sexual relationships are never arranged by their families; they are always chosen, like the "love marriages" that have become the ideal in contemporary Indonesia. Later I discuss how marriage based on love and choice has long been linked to modernity and national belonging, and how this rhetoric of similitude intersects with *gay* and *lesbi* views of having a difference or deviance (*kelainan*, from the root word *lain*, "other") in regard to Indonesian society. Here I wish to linger over *gay* and *lesbi* desire—a desire for the same (*suka sama*) realized through choice (*suka sama suka*)—and the complexities hinted at in *sama*'s polysemy.

This polysemy recalls how *gay* and *lesbi* Indonesians often say they are the "same" across Indonesia. It also recalls the common view that they are the "same" as gay and lesbian Westerners, as indexed by the terms *gay* and *lesbi* themselves, even if their understanding of these Westerners' lives is unclear. The *gay* and *lesbi* subject positions confront us with questions of similitude in reference to both scale and desire.

Westerners have advanced theoretical tools—feminist, psychoanalytic, deconstructionist—for analyzing difference, but only a handful of clichés for theorizing similitude. The focus on difference is not misguided or unproductive; it is incomplete without an equally thoroughgoing theorization of the similitude it implicitly evokes. In anthropology, difference is seen to be our contribution to social theory. It is expected: unproblematic, obvious, and authentic. It asks nothing more than to be recorded, typologized, interpreted, and rhetorically deployed. Similitude, however, awakens disturbing contradictions. On the one hand, similitude is uninteresting: if you study the Other and they are the same, what is there to say? Are they a proper Other at all? At the same time, there is discomfort: similitude cries out for explanation and modeling. It must have a reason: is it diffusion or convergent evolution? There is a sense that contamination has occurred and authenticity compromised. The tendency for ethnographic work to structure itself around difference renders *gay*, *lesbi*, and other nonethnolocalized aspects of Indonesian culture invisible to Western observers.

The lifeworlds of *gay* and *lesbi* Indonesians demand an anthropology of similitude—of *sama*. Not only do they employ a problematic of similitude in understanding their desires, but much of their daily lives seems familiar. *Gay* men hang out in parks and shopping malls, perform in drag shows at discos, and engage in sexual practices that recall those of many gay Westerners. *Lesbi* women meet in each other's homes, listen to American lesbian folksingers, and appear to identify in terms recalling "butch" and "femme." Difference has often stood as the default paradigm for understanding sexuality, gender, and globalization. A "homo" approach may prove productive: "Can similarities encode difference, and differences similarities?" (Weston 1995:92). In an already globalized world, an anthropology of similitude can illuminate how what appear to be Western ways of being are transformed through dubbing culture.

DESIRE

How do *gay* men conceptualize their desire for men? One clue is offered by the term *orang sakit* (sick person), which can be used with reference to any man who desires men. There is certainly an element of self-hate in the phrase "sick person," and some politically minded *gay* men have called for its abolition. But when I have heard *gay* men use the phrase, the connotation has been more specific and neutral: *gayness* is like a chronic illness, something for which accommodations must be made on an ongoing basis. It is something important but not necessarily central to one's sense of self, and it can be "transmitted to susceptible individuals" (Howard 1996:8).

From the evidence of my interlocutors, other researchers, and narratives published in zines and mass media, it appears most *gay* men start thinking of themselves as *gay* in their late teens to early twenties. Some *gay* men recall feeling same-gender attractions while boys—toward another young boy or an adult man in the neighborhood, or toward someone on television (Indonesian or not; one *gay* men was attracted to the actor Lee Majors on the 1970s' show *The Six Million Dollar Man*). However, a frequent pattern is for *gay* men to emphasize the agency of others. A common view is that to be *gay* is willed by God. Same-gender desire may be viewed as innate, "carried from birth"; as one man put it, "my instinct calls me to men, not women." This can also take the form of a belief one is biologically *gay*, a notion reinforced by reportage some *gay* men have encountered concerning "gay gene" research in the West. These are all essentialist understandings of becoming *gay*, recalling the penchant of Westerners for understanding sexuality in terms of immutability (Halley 1994).

However, environmental, constructionist explanations are the most popular etiology for *gay* subjectivity, phrased in terms of addiction (*keta-gihan*) or habit (*kebiasaan*), recalling Sucipto's 1920s claim that "life is following habits."[2] Such an addition can permanently alter the self as surely as one cannot forget one's mother-tongue. Sammy, a man from Sumatra, mused on how his life could have been different: "I think that if I'd never left my village, it's possible that I wouldn't have become *gay*. Because every time I go back to the village, my feelings are different than my feelings here: I can have feelings for women. I hang out with my father and brothers, I talk about girl problems and stuff like that. And it's *normal* life, it's no problem! So from that I think there's a big possibility that if I'd never left my village, I'd have a house by now, children, a family. Maybe I'd just have a little bit of feelings for men."

Environmental explanations rarely cite effeminacy: few *gay* men cross-dressed regularly as children or thought they might be warias. When I asked one Balinese man if he ever thought he might be waria, he said that "No, I didn't think of myself as waria. I just knew that if I looked at a man I wanted [*suka*] him." Another kind of environmental explanation is the claim that someone became *gay* because his heart was broken by a woman. Above all the language of addiction and habit usually refers to being seduced by another male while a child or adolescent.[3] Often the seducer does not see himself as *gay*, indeed does not know of the term, so it is more accurate to say such seduction makes *gay* subjectivity more possible. The seducer is often an older male neighbor, uncle, or cousin, but seduction can also take place away from home:

I used to live in the pesantren, from the last year of junior high school until the end of high school. About four years . . . it was at that time that I started to understand same-gender relations [*hubungan sejenis*] because I was seduced by my Koranic recitation teacher. . . . I was 18 or 19 years old at the time and he was 25 years old. The first time we were together I didn't have any emotions [*belum rasa*]. . . . When we were sleeping together he liked to hold me and he'd ejaculate. . . . [At] the beginning I felt very uncomfortable. I didn't like feeling the sperm in his *sarung* . . . but he started asking me to hold his penis . . . eventually I started to like it. . . . He had his own room, so we could do it easily. He was always very helpful to me in my studies; perhaps at the beginning he was only sympathetic and eventually there arose desire [*suka*]. I don't know about him for sure, but there arose love in me for him as well. Eventually his own studies at the pesantren were finished and so he had to return to his home province. And I was sad half to death, because he got married at that point; he was pushed to get married by his parents. I was so sad that I fled here to the city.

This environmental understanding of same-gender desire can be a source of confusion because many *gay* men prefer sex and even romantic relationships with *normal* men. *Gay* men often call such persons authentic (*asli, tulen*) men: on one occasion a *gay* man asked me, "Have you ever had sex with a *normal* man, with an asli *normal* man [*lelaki normal asli*]?" *Normal* men are desired for a variety of reasons: they are (it is assumed) never effeminate, and they are also better at keeping relationships secret because they do not like to hang out and gossip like *gay* men do. Most *gay* men believe that all men are capable of same-gender arousal and love given the opportunity, but they insist that these *normal* men could not become *gay* themselves: as one *gay* man put it, "That's not possible. If a *hetero* becomes *gay* temporarily [*jadi gay sementara*], he'll go back to being *hetero*." Another *gay* man described how *gay* men seduced *normal* men by saying "we insert our selves [*pribadi*] into the other person." In this view a *normal* man can be seduced into desiring a *gay* man, but these temporarily acquired desires do not persist: one persona is "inserted" into another. Relationships with *normal* men can make the distinguishing character of being *gay* unclear:

> We can't be hypocrites: if a man likes a man that means he's *gay*, right? That's the opinion of all people, right? But in my own view, what I've experienced, it's not always that way—there are certain men who like *gay* men from a certain structure, a certain form. He wants to be with me, but it's not for certain that he wants to be with another *gay* person. . . . But what's strange is that there's a feeling of jealousy and anger on his part if I'm with someone else. Now, from that we can know from a psychological perspective he's already started to enter, to feel the *gay* life [*merasakan kehidupan gay*].

Family enjoying leisure time.

Figure 4–1. The fatherly modern male. Office of State Minister for Population (1999):25.

Most *gay* men prefer men who are masculine—using terms like *macho*, *maskulin*, and, most frequently, "fatherly" (*kebapakan*). Effeminate *gay* men attracted to masculine men thus have somewhat heterogendered desires. Desirable masculine men (*normal* or *gay*) ideally have an absence of effeminacy and a quiet, assertive demeanor; height and a mustache are pluses, as is employment as a policeman or military man. This is a narrow notion of acceptable masculinity. Historians and anthropologists have noted how across the archipelago the range of masculinities has been much broader; for instance, " 'Pure' Javanese tradition . . . regards a very wide range of behavior, from he-man to rather . . . 'effeminate,' as properly masculine" (Peacock 1968:204). The more restricted conception of masculinity prevalent in contemporary Indonesia, the conception *gay* men draw upon in their views of the ideal lover, is linked to idealized images of the modern middle-class male (fig. 4–1). This notion of the fatherly modern male took form during Soeharto's New Order and was promulgated by state discourse, particularly the state's powerful family planning program. Soeharto, after all, called himself "father" (*Bapak Soeharto*) in opposition to his predecessor's moniker "brother" (*Bung Karno*). *Gay* desire is colored by national discourse.

For *lesbi* desire a heterogendered form predominates: it is considered unusual for a tomboi to desire another tomboi, or for a cewek to desire another cewek. *Lesbi* women who do not experience their desires through a heterogendered lens tend to reject the tomboi/cewek binarism altogether. While this could be seen as evidence of influence from Western notions of butch and femme, it seems to originate in the fact that no female-to-male analogue to the waria subject position existed as "gay" and "lesbian" translocated to Indonesia, so that both female homosexuality and female-to-male transgenderism have been taken up within the scope of *lesbi*. Waria preexisted *gay*, but they now form a binarism making thinkable a noneffeminate male homosexuality (cf. Jackson 1999a). The tomboi subject position, however, appears not to have had a separate existence before the *lesbi* subject position; it tends to form a subtype within *lesbi*, troubling the distinction between homosexuality and transgenderism under the sign of "female."

Many tombois speak of themselves as the pursuer of women—as indicated by the term *hunter*, used by tombois in southern Sulawesi and supposedly in parts of Java as well. To be a hunter is to hunt women, be they cewek or *normal*. Hen, the protagonist of the tomboi autobiography *Menguak Duniaku*, explains how he seduces women in terms tombois across Indonesia would find familiar (cf. Blackwood 1999; Graham 2001):

> I begin by trying to fathom her feelings. I treat her like a beloved by protecting and helping her, taking her wherever she wants to go without being asked to do so. I go to her house every few days. If in the end she can sense that my attitude towards her is more than that of a friend, slowly I'll tell her who I really am. And if she can accept [*menerima*] my love, I'll give her all I own and I'll do anything for her happiness . . . just like how any *normal* man would act towards their beloved. (Prawirakusumah and Ramadhan 1988:206)

Clearly Hen assumes his beloved cannot be another tomboi. This understanding of *lesbi* desire occasionally crosses over into popular culture, as in figure 4–2, from a 1996 article entitled "Lesbians and Lifestyle." This cartoon from the newspaper *Kompas* depicts a tomboi and cewek couple, figures dimly familiar to the Indonesian public since the wedding of Jossie and Bonnie. A tomboi fails to connect with a man (possibly because he is effeminate); Cupid's arrow strikes the tomboi instead and the tomboi's desire is misdirected toward a woman, who does not reciprocate that desire but is only a object to be pursued. It is not clear from the image whether the pursued woman is supposed to be a *normal* woman or a cewek: the distinction is irrelevant from the cartoon's perspective, which assumes desire is always of masculine for feminine.

Figure 4–2. Image accompanying article on "Lesbians and Lifestyle." *Kompas*, January 13, 1996.

This understanding of *lesbi* desire as one of masculinity for femininity fits the widespread pattern of devaluing women's sexuality (Blackwood and Wieringa 1999:55). But it does not tell the whole story, for ceweks do sometimes "hunt" tombois: in the words of one tomboi, ceweks are "far the most aggressive partners, they are always the first to ask for sex" (Graham 2001:fn9).[4] Some tombois even say they became tomboi because a cewek seduced them (Graham 2001:21). While some lovers of tombois do identify as *normal*, others see themselves as a kind of *lesbi* woman.[5]

In *Menguak Duniaku*, Hen views desire between a tomboi and cewek as a kind of homosexuality: "I'm not *normal* because I love someone of the same kind as me [*sejenisku*]"; later he adds, "I have the soul of a man not because of my strength, bravery, or firmness, but because the objects of my love are women" (Prawirakusumah and Ramadhan 1988:12, 280). Many tombois would agree with Hen that what they see as homosexual desire is more foundational than their masculine gendering: the tombois "wanted to love women, and they had noticed that persons with male bodies had much less trouble in finding women partners than they had" (S. Wieringa 1999a:218). In other cases it appears that a desire for women follows from a prior sense of being masculine and having a man's soul that begins in childhood (Blackwood 1999). Two dominant viewpoints concerning etiology exist among warias: someone is waria because they (1) have a woman's soul or (2) dress like women. It appears that having a man's soul or dressing like a man can make one tomboi, but so can sexual desire for women—a multiplicity of possible understandings of "desire for the same" reflecting the *lesbi* subject position's complexity.

For both *gay* and *lesbi* Indonesians, another common element of their sexual subjectivities is a lack of desire for difference. Many *gay* men talk about not feeling a desire for women—and *lesbi* women of not feeling a desire for men—as important to their sense of self. In the West as well, a lack of desire often plays a central role in gay and lesbian subjectivities, distinguishing them from bisexual subjectivities. While most *gay* and *lesbi* Indonesians marry "heterosexually," they tend not to see themselves as bisexual, not only because *biseks* is still a rather academic term in Indonesian but because they see marriage as, so to speak, another island of desire.

Sex, Identity, and Behavior

I did not conduct a survey of sexual practices during my research, since subject positions are my primary interest. Sexual practices are neither necessary nor sufficient conditions for *gay* subjectivity; there are both *gay* virgins and men sexually active with other men who do not think of themselves as *gay*. However, through my ethnographic and HIV prevention work I gained familiarity with the range of sexual practices in which *gay* men engage. As a male researcher it was more difficult to talk with *lesbi* women about sex practices, but particularly through HIV prevention work I was able to broach this topic.

The greatest difficulty in discussing the place of sex in *gay* and *lesbi* subjectivities is not a lack of data but the identity-behavior binarism that still dominates discussions of sexuality. This binarism is of limited value because it entails a behaviorist approach that assumes behavior precedes and determines identity (and often valorizes a vague notion of "fluidity"). The concept of "men who have sex with men" or MSM illustrates this process. This term (which by the early 2000s had been dubbed in Indonesia as LSL (*lelaki suka lelaki*)) was invented in HIV prevention circles to refer to men who had sex with other men but did not identify as gay (as the saying goes, it's not who you are, it's what you do). "MSM" is to "gay man" as "behavior" is to "identity." This assumption that one could label behavior without identity failed to take into account how what we do (our "behaviors") always shapes how we think about ourselves (our "identities"). Through many channels, including the program planning requirements of organizations that fund HIV prevention and treatment, the distinction between "identity" and "behavior" that the MSM category was to stabilize has broken down. Despite the fact that HIV prevention discourse intended "MSM" to label behavior without identity, there soon emerged talk of the "MSM community," "self-identified MSM," and "MSM peers." The most remarkable term in this regard—one I have heard used in international HIV/AIDS conferences—must be "male partners of MSM." A moment's reflection should convince that, by definition, the male partner of an MSM is himself an MSM. Yet this term exists and can make sense because "identity" versus "behavior" is a false dichotomy (Elliston 1995): "identity" is not simply a cognitive map but also a set of embodied practices, and "behavior" is always culturally mediated through self-narrative.[6]

While many cultures of the Indonesian archipelago have had well-developed erotic vocabularies, in contemporary Indonesia sex is also shaped by the "family principle." The common word for "sex," *seks*, is itself a loanword, and a widespread circumlocution is *hubungan suami-istri* or "husband-wife relations." One result of this is that many *gay* men gloss the practices they engage in with other men as *main-main* (playing around) rather than "sex," which is often understood to be something that occurs between men and women, involving penile-vaginal penetration and the possibility of pregnancy. This is reinforced by religious norms that define sex in terms of adultery or premarital relations between women and men. For some *gay* men, one thing that distinguishes them from *normal* men is that they recognize what they do with other men as "sex" at all. This is often linked to the complaint that *normal* men are passive (*pasif*); they just want to ejaculate and "lie there" as the *gay* man fellates them or sits on their penis, while a *gay* lover will engage in kissing and foreplay. One *gay* man asserted that "It's much nicer having sex with a *gay* man. There's more give and take. With a regular man it's just an act of devotion. I'm active, he's just quiet. After he ejaculates he doesn't pay attention to me!" *Gay* men often claim that Western men are more romantic and active than *normal* or *gay* Indonesian men, based on mass media images, Western gay pornography they have seen, or a sexual experience they or a friend has had with a Westerner. With the rise of video technology and growing Internet access, Western gay pornography has become more common, though still somewhat difficult to obtain and even more difficult to find a place to watch it without the knowledge of family members.

Since most *gay* men come to *gay* subjectivity via mass media, sex with other *gay* men usually begins in the late teens or early twenties. *Gay* men who have had sex with men earlier in life usually see those experiences as distinct. They fall into two main categories: sex with childhood peers and sex with older men. *Gay* men sometimes talk of the latter in terms of their being a victim (*korban*) and see it as sexual abuse. For example, "It was first by my uncle, when I was in the fourth or fifth grade of elementary school. He put his penis between my thighs. I rejected being anally penetrated, but my uncle wanted to try it. It was very painful and was a kind of trauma that made me not want to be given it like that."

Adult *gay* men engage in a range of sexual practices roughly familiar to most gay Westerners. Kissing and hugging are considered erotic and things *normal* men are less likely to agree to do. Oral sex is very common and there are many slang terms for it: *karaoke, oral, ngésong,* even *gaya 69* "69 style" for mutual oral sex (the symbolism of "69" for this practice is suggested by the way the digits 6 and 9 wrap around each other). All of these terms can take active or passive grammatical forms in Indonesian (for instance, *(me)ngesong* or *diesong*); for oral sex the active form always refers to the man using his mouth. Some *gay* men enjoy swallowing semen when they have oral sex. Rimming (oral-anal contact) is probably less common but by no means unknown; a widespread *gay* term for it is "cleaning the toilet" (*cuci WC*). Interfemoral sex (placing one man's penis between the thighs of another) is a much more familiar sexual practice than in the West and is known in *gay* language as *jépong* from *jepit* (pinching, in this case pinching the thighs together). Mutual masturbation is also widely practiced; anal penetration with fingers is well known, with dildos less so. Anal sex itself, while perhaps not having the symbolic centrality it often possesses in the West for understandings of male homosexuality, is significant for many *gay* men. *Gay* men who penetrate (and *normal* men who go to male, female, or waria sex workers) often say that they prefer anal sex over vaginal sex because the anus is drier and thus "tighter." This reflects a preference for "dry sex" in much of Indonesia; women, for instance, sometimes take traditional medicines (*jamu*) or insert alum wands into their vaginas to dry them out. Terms for anal sex can also have passive or active grammatical markers. For instance, one of the most widespread *gay* language terms for anal sex, *tempong,* can be rendered *(me)nempong* (to penetrate another man anally with one's penis) or *ditempong* (to be penetrated anally by other man's penis). This division is so clear that the prefixes can be used in isolation; *gay* men sometimes ask if a person prefers "*me-*" or "*di-*" or can say they don't like anal sex "*baik di- atau me-*" ("whether penetrated or penetrator").

Beyond kissing and hugging, the most popular sexual practices in which *lesbi* women engage, in order, appear to be oral-vaginal contact, rubbing vaginas together (referred to in Makassar as *pompa kosong* or "empty [gas] pump"), vaginal penetration with fingers, and more rarely, vaginal penetration with dildos. I have not heard of oral-anal contact or anal penetration as recognized forms of *lesbi* sexuality but assume they take place. In *Menguak Duniaku*, one of Hen's lovers loses her virginity to Hen's finger and they find blood on the sheets afterwards; when the lover asks how Hen learned to be so good in bed, Hen replies that she learned from books about sex between men and women (Prawirakusumah and Ramadhan 1988:489). Across Indonesia there seems to be an understanding that when desire is structured across a tomboi/cewek divide, it is the tomboi who penetrates the cewek, not the other way around.

LOVE AND MARRIAGE: CHOOSING TO BELONG

To the extent *normal* Indonesians know of *gay* and *lesbi* Indonesians, they assume them to be interested only in sex. But while sex is certainly important to *gay* and *lesbi* Indonesians, they consistently valorize same-gender love as more consequential; through it, sex gains meaning and social significance. *Gay* and *lesbi* Indonesians across the archipelago emphasize that they fall in love with persons of the same gender: nowhere in Indonesia is there a predominant belief that *gay* and *lesbi* desire is limited to sex alone. Love (*cinta*, less often *kasih sayang* or *kasih*) is extremely important to *gay* and *lesbi* Indonesians, and it is a key way in which their sexualities are linked to national discourse. What is distinctive about being *gay* or *lesbi* is not same-gender sex (it is usually taken for granted that both men and women will engage in it, given the chance) but love. Like most tombois, Sukma insisted that "sex has to be based on love. I must date a woman first and start to care about her and love her before I want to have sex with her." Love is the epitome of being *gay* or *lesbi*. *Gay* and *lesbi* Indonesians even speak of their love as greater than the love between *normal* men and women. The distinction between authentic (*asli*) and inauthentic or false (*palsu*) is crucial: *gay* and *lesbi* Indonesians speak of love as asli or caution against palsu love.

There are no models for *gay* and *lesbi* love; like all aspects of *gay* and *lesbi* life, one cannot learn about this from family, tradition, religion, or state. *Gay* and *lesbi* Indonesians instead dub dominant heterosexual models of love that in the contemporary period are shaped by the state's family principle. The meanings of *gay* and *lesbi* love track assumptions about marriage in the *normal* world; this is one reason why most *gay* and *lesbi* Indonesians marry "heterosexually." The resonances between same-gender love and "heterosexual" marriage in *gay* and *lesbi* life speak to how these subject positions are formed at the conjuncture of globalization and postcoloniality.

The expectation in Indonesia that adults will marry (barring some special circumstance, like being a Catholic priest or waria) is well documented (G. Jones 1994:61); across Indonesia, "individuals, whether male or female, are not considered adult until they have married heterosexually" (Blackwood 1999:191) and "notions of celibacy or single life styles are virtually unknown" (Hoskins 1998:17).[7] But if sexual desire is (arguably) a human universal, there is nothing natural about why it should take particular forms of marriage. The apparent universality of the marriage imperative compels a critical response that appreciates the varied meanings "marriage" takes in different historical and cultural contexts, particularly how marriage has come to link coupledom, national belonging, and the consumerist self of capitalism (Abelove 1992; Collier 1988; Collier, Rosaldo, and Yanagisako 1997; Engels 1972; Freeman 2002; Rubin 1975; Zaretsky 1976).

As is the case elsewhere, marriage in Indonesia is in the midst of enormous change (Ahearn 2001; Castells 1997:221–235). In comments regarding Spain that are appropriate for Indonesia as well, Jane Collier notes a shift in the latter part of the twentieth century toward a notion of marriage based on love, a shift often understood as being from "following social conventions" to "thinking for oneself," but in fact shaped by larger cultural forces including the rise of wage labor (so that the inheritance of property from one's parents was no longer central to one's class status) (1997:45 and passim). Collier concludes that "television and opportunities for urban employment did not simply offer villagers exposure to different ways of behaving. . . . people taking advantage of new opportunities changed the wider socioeconomic context for everyone, transforming the consequences of individual action" (47). In Indonesia as well, social transformations have led to new dubbed understandings of marriage, desire, and selfhood that are not simply the direct product of globalization.

With a growing degree of socialization between the sexes (even among adolescents) has come a steady increase in the age of marriage in Indonesia. Between 1971 and 1990, overall age at marriage rose from 19.3 to 21.6 years for women; between 1970 and 1990 it rose from 23.8 to 25.4 years for men (G. Jones 1994:80, 104). During the social upheavals of the late colonial period, World War II, and the independence struggle, there were no detectable changes in age of marriage in Indonesia (G. Jones 1994:68–69); these marriage trends are associated with persons born since the early 1960s, just like *gay* and *lesbi* subjectivities. One apparent constant is that "the proxy data (percentage of women single at ages 45–49) . . . give no evidence that [not marrying] is becoming any more than an aberration in a resolutely family-centered Malay world" (G. Jones 1994:63). A triply compulsory heterosexuality makes marriage in contemporary Indonesia appear as the overdetermined imperative of tradition, religion, and nation. Mainline doctrines in Islam, Christianity, and Balinese Hinduism view marriage as essential. The great ethnolocalized variation in adat or "local tradition" across Indonesia seems to evaporate in the face of marriage. The postcolonial state takes great interest in redeploying such "tradition." Historically marriage has been a key institution shaping statecraft within the archipelago (Pemberton 1994:71, 142, 215) and elsewhere, but attention to marriage was largely limited to royal circles and the ritual event of the wedding itself, with little provision for officialized marriage among commoners. With the rise of modern forms of governmentality that view societies in terms of national "populations" (Foucault 1991), interest has shifted to the proper and successful marriage of each citizen: "no modern nation-state can ignore marriage forms, because of their direct impact on reproducing and composing the population" (Cott 2000:5).

This national vision of marriage is shaped by and promulgated through family planning discourse (Dwyer 2000; Robinson 1989; Warren 1993) and based upon the state's family principle, which stipulates that the nation is made up not of citizens but of families. The marriage envisioned by the state involves a single husband and wife where the husband is head of household, but increasingly the wife is to have a career in addition to her domestic duties. It assumes a middle-class conception of the self organized around responsibility, consumerism, and career, even if one is not middle class oneself. For instance, when one *gay* man said that "in Indonesia if you're not married you're not seen as mature in your thinking. Because you don't shoulder any responsibility . . . you can just go wherever you want," it is this national rhetoric of marriage "in Indonesia" that he referenced.

One day in Makassar when I was discussing marriage with Umar and Hasan, *gay* men who had been friends for years, Umar tried to sum up what he saw as the prevailing attitude by saying, "Here in Indonesia you have to marry to prove you can make a small, harmonious family." Almost every term in Umar's statement—"Indonesia" (rather than "Makassar" or "among the Bugis"), "small, harmonious family"—comes from the state's family principle. I then asked: Why is it that I've never seen a case anywhere in Indonesia of a *gay* man and *lesbi* woman marrying each other? Wouldn't that solve all the problems? Hasan eyed me resignedly and shook his head: clearly I didn't understand. "The most important reason why that doesn't happen is that it wouldn't be a real marriage. Marriage isn't just for show, it isn't to hide who we are. It's something that you must take seriously." The model of love *gay* and *lesbi* Indonesians internalize from childhood pivots around this ideal of *authentic* heterosexual marriage actualized through love and choice.

The meanings of marriage that circulate in Indonesian popular culture are strongly shaped by the state and mass media. Many scholars have commented on the decline of arranged marriages in Indonesia.[8] While a range of marriage practices still exists, and there are claims that polygamy is on the rise due to Islamic revivalism, the dominant model of marriage is based on monogamous love and choice. The importance of this to *gay* and *lesbi* subjectivities cannot be overstated. In Indonesian and many ethnolocalized languages, the verb "to marry" can take active or passive forms: one can "be married off" or "marry someone." For decades the latter has been eclipsing the former, a process linked to conceptions of nationalism and modernity that also draws from Western models of romantic love transmitted through mass media (Robinson 1989). It strongly emphasizes notions of authenticity and choice; love should be true and freely chosen by individuals, not families (E. Wieringa 2003).

Late colonial literature brought together nation, people, and language through the power of love, particularly around the conflict over "arranged" marriages, associated with tradition, versus "love" marriages, associated with modernity and nationalism. Such conflicts figure centrally in nationalist literature, condensing debates over tradition, modernity, and collective identity.[9] Love and choice imply democracy, equality, and a horizon beyond the family and locality. This literature frames love as selfless when directed toward either the nation or the hoped-for spouse: "nationalism and love are linked because through it, peoples are mixed and a new authority is created" (Siegel 1998:16). This is a love that "demands recognition" and is "inseparable from the struggle for progress" (Siegel 1997:140); by definition it breaks from ethnolocalized custom (adat). Properly chosen love makes you a proper citizen. It is for this reason that the failure of national-love is not barrenness, but sickness (sakit), an unnational love that can kill:

> What would the cure for love sickness be if not proper recognition, that is, recognizing cinta [love] for what it is: *the power to compel recognition*. More precisely, it is the power to compel recognition of desire transformed into idealism. That idealism is directed towards the advancement of the Indonesian people. At that time [in the 1920s and 1930s], this meant not independence and not equality. It meant rather *the possibility of having a certain identity*. One which marked one as progressive. A progressive person was in touch with the modern world outside the Indies. (Siegel 1997:146, emphasis mine)

Thanks to a love performed through choice rather than arrangement, Indonesian national literature enacts a "twin approach to constructing a modern self and imagining a modern society," whereby "in gaining a modern self, [Indonesians] gain a modern vision of the world, and vice versa. Selfhood becomes permeated with political meaning" (Rodgers 1995:44).[10] Thus, in the decades before independence, love, choice, modernity, and national belonging became interlinked. While there are still arranged marriages, and many that fall between arrangement and choice,

Figure 4–3. Love should make *gay* and *lesbi* Indonesians equal to normal ones. *GAYa Nusantara* 59 (February 1999):36.

the ideal of chosen marriage now dominates images of the proper Indonesian citizen; purely arranged marriages are viewed as unsophisticated, and women and men are increasingly assumed to play an active role in choosing their future spouses (Hatley 1997; Hull 2002). This is a love that does not just happen to you through arrangement but is performed through choice. (One possible reason for the popularity of the film *Titanic* in Indonesia was its dramatization of a triumph, beyond the grave, of choice over arrangement.) It is based on a paradox of modernity that crops up in contexts beyond Indonesia: love enables choice but is not chosen. Thus, one cannot choose not to choose love. As Ahearn notes in the case of Nepal, "while love empowers lovers in non-romantic realms, people do not have any control over love itself" (2001:150); and as Collier notes in the case of Spain, "'modern' courtship customs were as culturally constructed, and socially enforced, as 'traditional' ones" (1997:101). Another paradox is that love overcomes difference and creates sameness—as the editors of the zine *GAYa Nusantara* once wrote, "with love we can learn to overcome differences between all people." [11] Ideally, *gay* and *lesbi* love should make *gay* and *lesbi* Indonesians equal to *normal* ones (fig. 4–3), but their "desire for the same" is not recognized as having this ability to overcome difference.

Performatives depend on cultural context: only an umpire can declare "strike!" and only a judge or jury can pronounce someone "innocent" in a court of law. The ability of love to compel national recognition depends on a modern conception of heterosexual desire (termed, after all, with transformed English terms [*normal* or *hetero*] just like *gay* and *lesbi*). *Gay* or *lesbi* love does not get you national belonging: heteronormativity lies at the heart of national love.[12] Indonesians who term themselves *gay* or *lesbi* mark themselves as in touch with the modern world outside the archipelago, but in terms of a love that receives no recognition. It does not belong.

The pivotal cultural logic is that when marriage is arranged, sexual orientation is secondary, but sexual orientation comes to the fore-ground—to some extent, comes into being—through a language of choice. The failure to "be married off" is a failure of the family to see one of their members properly married. However, when marriage hinges on choice—on a relational, choosing self animated by love—that self and that love fail if not heterosexual. It is a failure of the self and a failure of citizenship. As one married *gay* man put it when advising un-married *gay* men, "marriage is up to us." The shift from arranged to chosen has not implied a parallel shift from public to private; this "choice" remains a highly public act. To be national and modern, this choice must be heterosexual choice. It is through heterosexuality that self and nation articulate.

A heteronormative worldview can dismiss same-gender sex as devoid of deeper implication, but same-gender love leans dangerously close to kinship. Since many *gay* and *lesbi* Indonesians see their capacity for loving people of the same gender as their distinguishing characteristic, more than same-gender attraction (which is seen as ubiquitous), this hegemony can bring incredible pain and desperation. Many *gay* and *lesbi* Indonesians love their partners passionately: wed them in unrecognized ceremonies in the dead of night at the homes of sympathetic preachers, sleep cuddled in their arms, trade rings, go to the photographer's shop for portraits that are carried in wallets until faded and scarred by creases. It is this love, far more than the actual sexual acts themselves, which is prohibited by dominant discourses of national belonging.

GAY AND *LESBI* RELATIONSHIPS

Within the *gay* and *lesbi* worlds, love thus ideally leads to an ongoing same-gender relationship. The common Indonesian term for a boyfriend or girlfriend is *pacar* and the relationship *pacaran*, and these terms are sometimes used by *gay* and *lesbi* Indonesians to refer to their same-gender relationships. Other terms used are *jodoh*—"marriage partner, future spouse" (Idrus 2003)—and even husband (*suami*) or wife (*isteri*). How-ever, many *gay* and *lesbi* Indonesians avoid using these terms in the *gay* or *lesbi* world; as a *gay* man from Central Java put it, "if we say 'suami' or 'isteri' it means marriage." Most *gay* men have girlfriends in addition to any love relationships in the *gay* world, and the question "Do you have a pacar?" is typically interpreted to mean "Do you have a girlfriend?" One term less linked to the *normal* world is *join*: "Do you have a join?"

Regardless of the term used, *gay* and *lesbi* Indonesians see themselves as "joined" to their lovers within the *gay* or *lesbi* world. These relationships can persist for decades and involve great fidelity, devotion, and passion. Most *gay* and *lesbi* Indonesians see no benefit in having their same-gender relationships known to the *normal* world. When I once told one *gay* man that some gay Westerners adopted children, he replied that the idea horrified him because if with two men "people can assume they're just friends," but a child would make the relationship visible to the *normal* world. The "marriage" of Jossie and Bonnie in 1981 was influential because it was atypical (see chapter 3).

Most sexual relationships in the *gay* and *lesbi* worlds are with other Indonesians, not Westerners, since there are relatively few Westerners in Indonesia and they travel mostly in expatriate circles. However, in all three of my major field sites I met *gay* men in relationships with Western men. Early in my fieldwork I hypothesized that these relationships might represent a significant modality by which Western conceptions of homosexuality translocate to Indonesia. This now appears unlikely. Such relationships are fairly rare, and language barriers often impede communication. Additionally, since a Western lover offers prestige, money, and sometimes travel to the West, *gay* men who find a Western lover often try to keep that Westerner from meeting other *gay* men, curtailing the couple's involvement in the *gay* world. As a result, gay or lesbian Westerners with Indonesian partners do not affect the *gay* and *lesbi* worlds as often as might be expected. I have knowledge of only a handful of *lesbi* relationships with Western women; two reasons for this beyond my own status as a man are the smaller number of Western women expatriates and the greater difficulty *lesbi* women face in meeting Westerners, given restrictions on women's movement.

A constant threat to *gay* relationships is for one member to have sex outside the relationship, a practice most often termed *selingkuh*, which normally means "dishonest, corrupt" (Echols and Shadily 1989:494). Selingkuh refers to sexual dalliances within the *gay* world; many *gay* men have girlfriends or wives, but I have never heard them term sex with women selingkuh. Selingkuh is a concern in the *lesbi* world as well; many tombois say one reason they do not spend more time socializing with each other is the fear that another tomboi will "hunt" their own girlfriend. While *lesbi* sexuality has a strong erotic component that should not be underestimated, *lesbi* women, like *gay* men, consistently rank romance and the goal of a long-term relationship as important priorities.

MARRIAGE AND SELFHOOD

The Mystery of Marriage

One night in a park I met Andy and four of his friends. Andy identified as *gay*, explaining that his boyfriend of ten years was married with two children. When I asked if the boyfriend should get divorced he stared in shock: "Of course not. He needs descendants and a wife. I want to get married in five years—I already have a girlfriend. You mean you won't marry as long as you live?" When I nodded, the other men confronted me in astonishment: "How could you not want to get married? You'll be lonely when you get old! Everyone must have descendants. According to Islam, if you don't yet have children, you haven't yet entered the society of the Prophet Muhammad."

In this story *gay* men implicate me in their world while discussing marriage in terms of the triple compulsion of religion, tradition, and nation. The story is from Surabaya and involves primarily Muslim men, but Hindu and Christian men speak in similar terms. When I told a Hindu *gay* man in Bali that *gay* men in Surabaya tended to speak of marriage as their number-one problem, he replied, "Here it's the same. Most of my friends who are the same age as me, around thirty, have already started to think: am I going to get married or not?" In Makassar, Michael talked about how his lover Arief already had a fiancée and would probably marry next year; Arief's younger sibling had married, increasing the pressure on Arief. Michael also expected to marry someday, in response to his own desires and pressure from his aunt and grandmother, yet he hoped to sustain his relationship with Arief. A Bugis Muslim from Makassar, who unlike most *gay* men had told his family he was *gay* and moved away from the parental home, nevertheless said that "I'm one hundred percent sure I'm going to get married. I'm sure that my family will demand it. . . . The problem is, in Indonesia—maybe outside it's different—everyone has to get married. Lots of *gay* people get married. Even if [your family] knows that you're *gay* they want you to marry." In Howard's study of *gay* men in Jakarta, marriage was viewed as "an essential step in becoming a whole person" regardless of religion, ethnicity, or class (1996:246).

While the stereotypical response of Western parents to a son's coming out is "I'll never have grandchildren," Indonesian parents who learn a son is *gay* sometimes say they can accept this so long as he marries a woman. This parental sentiment may sound contradictory to Western ears, but it reflects a cultural logic shared with most *gay* men and most *lesbi* women, as revealed in their "heterosexual" marriages and their assumption that that gay and lesbian Westerners marry "heterosexually." During my 1997–1998 fieldwork I always placed on my desk a picture of my partner that shows him standing with a female colleague. *Gay* men and *lesbi* women who saw this picture would invariably point it out and say, "Your partner is already married," or "His wife is taller than he is!" My explanation that she was a friend and that neither my partner nor I wanted to marry a woman was be met with disbelief and pity. In their eyes we were deviants, transgressing what they understood *gay* subjectivity to entail.

During my Surabaya fieldwork I conducted three focus groups bringing together approximately ten *gay* men for an evening in a neutral environment. Toward the end of one focus group a debate broke out between the members of the group and Faisal, a *gay* man who assisted me in moderating the groups. We were discussing marriage when the focus group members asked if Faisal or I would ever marry. My negative reply brought surprised looks, but it was Faisal's firm contention that *he* would never marry ("because I am *gay* after all") that brought an air of distress to the room. No one was more upset than Ikbal, a friend of Andy who was married to a woman. "Maybe you are more modern and liberal, Faisal. I am absolutely in disagreement and unhappy with your decision. I'm sure you could do it with a woman if you tried."

"Ikbal, I think you are *biseks*," Faisal said, using a term unfamiliar to most *gay* men that reflected his work in HIV prevention.

"But I only became able to have sex with a woman after I got married. You've already condemned yourself to be *gay*," Ikbal replied.

Murmurs broke out around the room. One person said, "I think that Faisal is really waria, not *gay*, because he never plans to marry."

Ikbal leapt on the statement: "Faisal, the problem with you is that you don't want to take any steps toward being *normal*. You're being shallow." Then, in exasperation, Ikbal turned to me: "I just can't imagine you not getting married, Tom. I'm trying to understand it, but my mind just can't believe it. I've always assumed that all men get married, even warias, even *gay* men."

For the Western observer, the starkest difference between *gay* and *lesbi* Indonesians and gay and lesbian Westerners is probably that the former usually *choose* to marry "heterosexually," have children, and see this as part of a complete *gay* or *lesbi* life (Boellstorff 1999).[13] Across the archipelago unmarried *gay* men and *lesbi* women cite marriage as the most important issue in their lives. Most *gay* men past their early thirties have married, and most *lesbi* women, particularly ceweks, marry before turning thirty. Cases of *gay* men or *lesbi* women forced into marriage certainly exist. For some, marriage is a traumatic event: people have committed suicide rather than be compelled to marry, or at the news that their long-term lover has decided to marry. However, such cases are easy to explain in terms of oppression.

What poses the greater theoretical challenge is that unmarried *gay* men and *lesbi* women can look forward to their wedding day with all the anticipation of any *normal* Indonesian. This is a compromise between homosexual desire and social norms concerning marriage, but it is not just an external imposition: for many *gay* and *lesbi* Indonesians, it is a source of meaning and pleasure allowing them to enjoy homosexual relationships while pleasing their parents, carrying on the family name, minimizing sin, raising dearly loved children who can care for them in old age, and becoming full members of national society. For both *gay* men and *lesbi* women, the causality of marriage is complex, and my analysis is predicated on taking seriously the meaningfulness of their marriages. Because marriage brings together in such stark relief sexuality and belonging, it is crucial to how *gay* and *lesbi* Indonesians see their place in national culture.

The Marriage Imperative

During the time period of my fieldwork (1992–2004) it was considered acceptable for a man to stay unmarried until about twenty-five or so. But while Western models of homosexual identity presume that the pivotal emotional crisis takes place during adolescence (see chapter 7 and Howard 1996:125), for *gay* men the key predicament typically takes place in one's twenties as the pressure for marriage increases. To not marry by thirty represents a crisis, requiring excuses of not having a good enough job to support a new household or not having found the right woman, and age thirty-five is what one interlocutor called the "peak" (*puncak*) where the pressure to marry is nearly overwhelming. While age of marriage for women is rising, it has been difficult for a young woman to remain single past twenty-five, even when engaging in forms of white-collar work identified as a "career." For *gay* men and *lesbi* women, the marriage of a younger sibling frequently increases the pressure to wed; across Indonesia there is often an assumption that members of a sibling set should marry in order. These dynamics were remarkably uniform across all of my field sites (as well as in Howard's study of *gay* men in Jakarta) and did not appear to vary systematically by ethnicity or religion. Like *gay* and *lesbi* Indonesians' relationship to mass media and other aspects of their worlds, what begs explanation is not ethnolocalized difference but national similarity.

Across Indonesia *gay* and *lesbi* Indonesians identify marriage as something of a mystery. For instance, married *gay* men sometimes talk about marriage to a woman as one of the greatest joys of life, something they could not imagine living without. They almost always want their lovers to marry women as well, because the lover will be happy and successful and also less likely to have sex with other men. Yet they also complain about the strictures marriage brings. If a husband finds it difficult to go out at night once married, it can drastically curtail involvement in the *gay* world:

> We were lovers for seventeen years, until 1996 when he married, and now I am so sad. I cry every night. He lives with his wife now. Sometimes at night I go walking past his house and see him and his wife inside. I don't even say hello; I just look on him from afar. It just causes me too much stress to go in. . . . Even his parents knew about us. They didn't have any problem with it; they thought of me as one of their own children. . . . Then one day his parents came to me: "Our child wants to marry. And we beg permission of you, please let him marry." Oh, it was so hard! I didn't want that at all. I said, "Go right ahead," but I felt as if I'd died. He was pushed into marriage by his parents. So I just told him, "From now on, just think of me as a father to you." Even his new wife calls me "father." She doesn't know a thing!

Some *gay* men complain about the difficulties of the marital bedroom: one *gay* man advised that those who couldn't get an erection with their wife should note how their penis had spontaneous erections several times during the day and that they should call their wives and have sex with them right away. Others insist they enjoy sex with their wives because they find them attractive or that the sex demonstrates their love and care for their wife. Unmarried *gay* men sometimes say they wish they did not have to marry, or they plot how to delay it (a common phrase is they will marry "in five years"). *Lesbi* women speak of marriage as a necessity for full social womanhood yet fear the male domination and severe limits on participation in the *lesbi* world that almost always follow marriage. The role of social pressure channeled through family dictate is crucial for both *gay* and *lesbi* Indonesians: parents, siblings, even cousins hound them about their single status as they age. Such pressure is strongest for ceweks and *gay* men (as opposed to tombois and warias) because their same-gender desire is not unambiguously embodied; they appear *normal*. Nira, a Javanese cewek, said, "I will probably get married, but I'll keep having my relationship with Ati and it will be the most important thing to me. My parents will push me to marry because I'm the oldest child." Ati added, "Ceweks always get married." When I asked Karim what led him to decide he should marry, he employed reported speech in his reply, citing the authoritative voice of social expectation: "I couldn't stand all that pressure, especially the pressure from home, from my mother. I worried she would start saying that if I didn't get married people would say, quote, 'maybe you're impotent' or 'maybe you're a béncong' [waria]." For Karim "the outside pressure [*tekanan luar*] became an inside pressure [*tekanan batin*]," but many married *gay* men state emphatically that they were *not* pressured into marrying by family, religious leaders, traditional authorities, or anyone other than themselves. *Gay* men across Indonesia appear not to "recognize a distinction between being a man and being a husband, for they believe that the only way to become recognized adult members of society is by getting married and eventually having children" (Howard 1996:156).

Lesbi Women and Marriage

Across Indonesia there are no socially sanctioned life narratives for Indonesian women that do not result in marriage (Blackwood 1999). As for men, this is shaped by the triple compulsion of religion, ethnolocalized tradition, and state discourse. State ideologies of womanhood, which under Soeharto took the form of a "State Ibuism" (State Momism), "define women as appendages and companions to their husbands, as procreators of the nation, as mothers and educators of children, as housekeepers, and as members of Indonesian society—in that order" (Suryakusuma 1996:101). As in many postcolonial nations, women's sexuality becomes the site of "tradition" and authenticity, and controlling women's sexuality the symbolic equivalent of resisting colonial oppression (Chatterjee 1993). This offers little conceptual space for the "career woman," even as women are increasingly exhorted to work outside the home in addition to their domestic duties (Anderson 1996). While the notion of the affluent career woman has become a favored image of Indonesian femininity (Sen 1998), she is still presumed to marry a man and bear children. This new woman has a dual role (*peran ganda*)—career and parent; the career is additive rather than supplanting. The choices *lesbi* women make to marry or delay marrying, to divorce or to stick with a husband, take place within the horizon of these discourses of femininity and belonging. Many *lesbi* women thus struggle with the limits imposed by conceptions of normative heterosexuality: as repeated obsessively by Paria, the *lesbi* protagonist of *Garis Tepi Seorang Lesbian*, "I am a normal woman who can do what's normal" (*aku perempuan biasa yang terbiasa bisa*) (Herlinatiens 2003).

Marriage to a man does not necessarily end same-gender relations or *lesbi* subjectivity (A. Murray 1999:141). However, while marriage does not usually place insurmountable barriers to a man's involvement in the *gay* world, it makes it much harder for *lesbi* women to participate in the *lesbi* world. Marriage presents Indonesian women with a set of time-consuming activities that make privacy nearly impossible: not only caring for the husband and any children, but also economic responsibility for maintaining the household. Nonetheless, many married *lesbi* women find a way to participate in the *lesbi* world in some fashion.

One way in which some tombois say they are like warias is that they do not wish to marry. Unlike warias, however, tombois are not typically released from the marriage imperative, even if their appearance is highly masculine, because tomboi subjectivity is so poorly recognized. As a result it appears that many tombois marry, divorce, and do not remarry. The divorce can take place within weeks of the wedding or even sooner, as in the case of one tomboi in Makassar who was married for a single day.[14] In another case from Makassar, a tomboi reportedly married a man, but the tomboi's cewek girlfriend slept between the bride and groom on their wedding night, and the two women ran away the following day. Another common pattern is for tombois to marry (and often bear children) but then separate from their husbands, remaining formally married but independent in daily life, with their children under the care of other family members. Because tombois are typically visible as gender nonconforming, they, like warias, say that the idea of living in two worlds (as most *gay* men and feminine *lesbi* women do) is impossible and undesirable.

It appears that the husbands of *lesbi* women rarely know of their wives' former (and ongoing) sexual relationships with women. Before moving to Surabaya, Rita, a tomboi, was involved for five years with Anti, a woman in her early forties who was married with three children. Rita was known by Anti's family as Anti's "close friend" and was on good terms with Anti's husband and three children, who Rita claims never knew of the sexual relationship he shared with Anti. Interlocutors with married *lesbi* friends often said that since married *lesbi* women find it difficult to leave the home unaccompanied, especially if they have children, these *lesbi* women often have their partners come to their home while the husband is away, either in the evening or especially during the day while he is at work. Even if other family members are around, the women can often steal a few moments together. The ability for *lesbi* women to continue same-gender relations after marriage is aided by a variety of factors, including that female-female sex is even more unfamiliar to Indonesian public culture than male-male sex, the greater emphasis on male homosexuality in Islam and Christianity, and the lack of a well-known female analogue to warias.

The Wives of Gay Men

For a woman to marry a *gay* man, knowingly or not, presents issues not completely foreign to those faced by other Indonesian women in their marriages. Many wives know of their husband's *gay* subjectivity to some extent and sometimes even befriend their husband's male lover. In one of my field sites a *gay* man lived with his wife and three children in a two-story house that also contained his salon. The man's wife lived on the top floor with a male lover, while the husband lived on the bottom floor with his male lover, and a peaceable arrangement was reached. In another of many examples, one young *gay* man's wife invited his male lover to live at home with them, preferring this arrangement to having her husband absent on evenings and weekends. While I find the gender politics of this disturbing, it is important to recognize the situated rationality at play in the production of these new inequalities, and why it is the case that although some wives divorce *gay* husbands, many "choose" to remain married even if they know their husband pursues sexual relationships with other men.

Across Indonesia a double standard of masculinity is common. On one hand, men are seen as possessing more rationality (*akal*) than women, who are driven by desire (*nafsu*) (Siegel 1969). At the same time, women are seen as more rational than men, particularly in matters of household finances, while men are naughty and mischievous like children, apt to be carried away by sexual desire, which is tricky to control (cf. Peletz 1996). As a result of this second view, "many women tolerate, and even expect, a certain amount of sexual infidelity from their husbands, although they certainly do not encourage it" (Brenner 1998:151).[15] As Brenner notes, the crucial issue is not the existence of such affairs, but the potential for such affairs to (1) siphon financial resources away from the home in the forms of gifts or cash support to the illicit partner; (2) lead to a pregnancy out of wedlock, which would entail financial drain and social shame; (3) lead to a second wife being taken by the husband (if he is Muslim), which many Indonesians find improper and which could affect inheritance and property rights; and (4) bring shame to the family through public knowledge of the affair. The acceptance of many Indonesian women for the same-gender affairs of their husbands must be placed in this context: (1) a male lover is more likely to have his own income, (2) pregnancy is impossible, (3) a male lover cannot become a second wife, and (4) it is far easier to hide a sexual relationship between two men than between a man and a woman. Male friends routinely move about alone at night, sleep over in each other's houses—even bathe together—without arousing suspicion, since it is unclear to many Indonesians if activities between men (and even more, between two women) count as sex or are just "playing around." One married *gay* man summed up this state of affairs, animating the voices of wives through reported speech:

> Because I provide for the family, because I strive to become, what's the word for it, the head of the family, then as I see it how could [my wife] know I was *gay*? Even if she knew, I'm sure she'd just say "Oh, that's probably just seeking variety." It's like the waria Cindy's boyfriend. He has a wife and the wife knows her husband is Cindy's partner. The wife says "it's no big deal if it's a waria,

it's not competition. Cindy won't become a second wife, right? There won't be polygamy." And the wife sees lots of benefits. Because the husband gets money from Cindy. It's always like that, right? So rather than have him having sex with women, spending lots of money, whatever, it's better this way. He can get sexual satisfaction and money.

Marriage and Hegemony

I examine the overall linkages between the *gay* and *lesbi* subject positions and national discourse in chapter 7; at this point I wish to explore how these linkages shape the archipelago-wide pattern of "heterosexual" marriage. In particular, I am interested in how this discourse shapes not a single stance on marriage, but a complex and contradictory range of desires—a desire to marry and a desire not to marry, an understanding of selfhood as unitary and an understanding of selfhood as multiple. The great power of hegemonies lies in this ability to define a "horizon of the taken for granted" (Hall 1988a:44) that informs a spectrum of viewpoints, desires, and practices. The mystery of "heterosexual" marriage speaks to the existence of oppressive heterosexist norms, but it also indicates how ostensibly Western sexual subject positions have been dubbed: this "homosexual" self can desire marriage. *Gay* and *lesbi* persons are self-reflexive but not self-congruent. Amin, a Muslim *gay* man from Surabaya, expressed this when he noted that "one of the benefits of being *gay* is that you can enjoy two worlds." The benefit lies not in an integrated self, out of its closet and always the same, but in the ability to maintain distinct worlds keyed to distinct subjectivities. Could *gay* and *lesbi* Indonesians become poster children for the ultimate postmodern subject? The mystery is more complex.

Ikbal was a friend of Andy, who earlier reacted in shock when I told him I did not plan on marrying a woman. Like Andy's boyfriend, Ikbal was already married; his wife lived in a nearby village with their child while he cohabited in Surabaya with Dodi, his male lover for over ten years. Hand in hand with Dodi at the parks almost every night, Ikbal frequently lectured other *gay* men on the obligation to marry and the joys it brought. It was a point of pride that his wife and parents "knew about him" and that he and Dodi had married cousins so they would never be separated. One day Ikbal insisted that I come to the village to meet his wife. Once there, however, we would stay in a nearby town with his parents until Sunday; he would end up spending only two hours with his wife before we had to return to Surabaya. En route to the meeting, Ikbal told me about the months of sexual frustration he and his wife had experienced: they had been able to consummate their marriage only by admitting Dodi to their bed, where he lay alongside Ikbal and, as Ikbal's wife sobbed, stimulated him so that penetration could take place. On this Sunday, when he could delay his visit with his wife no longer, Ikbal warned me to be extra macho: "Now is the time to begin 'playacting.'" Apparently his family's knowledge of him was more fractured than I had suspected. Later that day he would comment, "This life is theater." As our little minibus, adrift in a green flowing sea of rice paddies, approached the village and a tense afternoon of silent squabbles and awkward smiles, Ikbal looked out the dusty window and almost whispered: "These parts of my life cannot be unified."

Theoretical physicists may believe in God's creation; social constructionists may believe that they were born gay or lesbian. The mystery of "heterosexual" marriage is that most *gay* men and *lesbi* women evince—simultaneously, within a single subjectivity—a multiple self for which marriage is not only compatible but pleasurable *and* a self for which it stymies a desire to "unify" one's spheres of life into a single narrative trajectory. This is a mystery not only to the "external," non-Indonesian observer, but also to the *gay* men themselves; many of them, like Ikbal, experience it as a contradiction. Ceweks also appear to experience this contradiction, as do those tombois who wish to marry. The source of this mystery lies in the origins of the imperative to marry itself. While marriage is a powerful norm throughout Indonesia, the particular form of this imperative certainly does not stem from a primordial localism: it is an imperative to *choose* marriage that is deeply bound up with nationalist conceptions of marriage as symbol and exemplar of proper citizenship.

In modern societies, forms of kinship and forms of governmentality shape each other. A key element of Indonesian state ideology is the "family principle," which holds that the family is the fundamental unit of the nation. Crucially, this is not the extended family but the nuclear family, whose ubiquitous smiles illuminate television ads and government posters: husband, wife, and two children, with a car, a home with smooth white tile floors, a television set, and other paraphernalia of the new middle class. It is this "public domesticity" that the state equates with citizen subjectivity and summons into being through a range of development practices (cf. Morris 1997). For the most part the influence of nationalist rhetoric is implicit: when *gay* men and *lesbi* women speak about the imperative to marry, they emphasize parental pressure. Parents' hopes that their children marry reflect not just nationalist discourse but ethnolocalized beliefs about kinship. My interlocutors were mostly twenty to thirty years old, and their parents are thus of the generation born around the time of independence. Their expectations about marriage incorporate understandings of marriage as social duty; visions of the romantic couple tended to play a subordinate role. In this regard there is a generational divide in beliefs about marriage. Yet it is crucial not to portray the imperative to marry as more traditional than *gay* and *lesbi* subjectivities. Both *gay* men and *lesbi* women can have their marriages "arranged" to some degree by their families, but the norm for them, as for most contemporary Indonesians, is a marriage actualized through choice and love. However, their love, sick in its desire for the same, forever estranges them from truly choosing marriage and thus disqualifies them from truly belonging as proper citizens of the postcolonial nation-state.

Since both postcolonial thought and capitalism orient themselves toward modernity, it is understandable that rhetorics of economic globalization converge with ideals of the modern Indonesian (Weber 1994). While a considerable body of work has pointed out the gender inequalities of the new international division of labor, less attention has been paid to its foundation in the naturalization of the couple formed though heterosexual love and choice as the basic unit of the postcolonial nation. More effectively than Henry Ford's fabled management of his workers' lives ever could, the heterosexualization of the labor force constitutes the domains of public and private, locates the family as the unit of consumption, and naturalizes gender inequalities. Heterosexuality made real through love and choice (associated with independence, democracy, and modernity), not arrangement (associated with dependency, colonialism, and tradition), provides a critical bridge between capitalist ideologies of production and nationalist ideologies of reproduction. Voting and marriage: proper choice is to underlie both sex and citizenship, and the nuclear, middle-class family is to stand as metonym for the nation. As constituted by this moral economy, the unmarried self is an incomplete economic and national subject. It has not "chosen" to marry; its love is inauthentic, a miscast vote for national belonging. It is this context, not ethnolocalized tradition, that explains most *gay* and *lesbi* Indonesians' assumption not just that they will "marry," but that *they will choose marriage through heterosexual love and form a nuclear family.*

State rhetoric claims that the prosperous family produced by chosen heterosexual marriage will be middle class. This notion of the family is strongly influenced by shifting economic rationalities. In 1982, following the oil boom, Soeharto's technocratic ministers gained ground and enacted economic and fiscal reforms that resulted in massive inflows of capital, which accelerated a shift away from agriculture and toward the service and industrial sectors (Hill 1996; Winters 1996). This shift led to the rise of a substantial middle class for the first time in Indonesian history (Robison 1996:79). Daniel Lev dates its consumerist and self-reflexive consciousness to a special edition of the magazine *Prisma* on the "new middle class" in 1984, during the same period in which *gay* and *lesbi* subjectivities first became national phenomena (1990:26).

These economic changes did not affect *gay* and *lesbi* subjectivities in a determinist manner; *gay* and *lesbi* Indonesians were not suddenly wealthy, able to travel to the West, or obtain Western gay and lesbian publications. Like other Indonesians, many of them are members of the "populist lower middle classes," "a much-neglected and underresearched category of the middle class [in Indonesia]" (Robison 1996:88). Anthropological studies of new middle classes, however, have emphasized how "the middle class's position is determined less directly by its relations to the 'means of production' . . . than by its relations to the market, that is, by its ability to consume" (Liechty 2003:16; see also Pinches 1999:8). In Indonesia as well, it has long been realized that middle-class consciousness thus cannot be "read off" raw income (H. Geertz 1963:37). Many observers identify the Indonesian middle class in terms of aspiration and "mode of consumption": "among the *rakyat* [lower classes], consumer durables are shared: it is anti-social to restrict the access of one's neighbors. Middle class households, by contrast, confine the enjoyment of such goods to members of the household. . . . In other words, there is 'privatization of the means of consumption'" (Dick 1990:64). Another important theme of the Indonesian middle class is equality (Dick 1985, 1990:66)—a kind of desire for the same, but one that unlike homosexuality engenders national belonging through "assumptions of kinship in the place of the assumptions of difference . . . giving [the middle class] the recognition that they too [are] part of the Indonesian family no matter what their regional origins" (Siegel 2002:209).

Like middle-class subjectivities, *gay* and *lesbi* subjectivities are not passed down through "tradition." With this consumerist ethic comes a modernist, narrative self defined in terms of autobiography. While far from universal, the notion of the self as something constructed is hardly new. What is at issue in the Indonesian context is the conjunction of a fashioned self with middle-class consumerism. It is not a fantasy of the sultan or the super-rich cosmopolitan who selects at will from the world's bounty. It is a circumscribed personhood-as-career in which, given limited resources, one budgets one's life trajectory within a marketplace logic that guides the crafting of choices. The self becomes the self's profession: this middle-class subjectivity is a story that the self tells to itself about itself, rather than a story passed down primarily through religious or ethnolocalized background, as the stories of lower and upper classes historically were in Indonesia and elsewhere (Appadurai 1996:53). Like middle-class subjectivities, *gay* and *lesbi* subjectivities are not passed down through "tradition"; they become their own stories, and the telling of those stories becomes a problem. A palette of possible lives spreads out before the subject, whose only prohibition is not to choose heterosexual love. One self-consumes, struggling to forge one's self-story. Like M. C. Escher's

Figure 4–4. "A poor *hetero* family that does not follow Family Planning. In the end they create not heaven but a 'hell' on earth. How far can this husband and wife guarantee that their children will become successful children later on?" Maengkom (1997:44).

image of two disembodied hands gripping pens, conjuring each other into existence on a drawing pad, the self and the self's story form a loop of personhood. As Escher's loop breaks down without the pens with which to draw, so heterosexual love and the commodity represent the conduits by which the middle-class self writes its story. In this sense, the *gay* person is self-contingent. Is this the same old liberal, bourgeois subject that has received such scholarly attention (Collier, Maurer, and Suárez-Nava 1995; Macpherson 1962)? The mystery is more complex.

The Desire Not to Marry

Given the overdetermined character of the marriage imperative, it is remarkable that any *gay* and *lesbi* Indonesian would ever reject marriage. Yet such Indonesians exist (including about 10 percent of my interlocutors). In "choosing" not to marry, however, these Indonesians have not stepped outside Indonesian culture into a realm of purely globalized homosexuality.

On rare occasions *gay* men critique the conjunction of class, nation, and the imperative to marry, as the following examples from a manifesto published in Jakarta in 1997 show. Figure 4–4 shows "a poor *hetero* family that does not follow Family Planning." Utensils and toys are strewn about a dirt floor; a mother, weighed down by an infant, screams over a gas stove, while the father is incapacitated in bed by the fighting of the other four children. One child is urinating on the floor; curtains hang precariously from unhinged shutters. The line-drawing format of the pic-

Figure 4–5. "A *lesbi* couple who are professionals. They can live together comfortably, with greater plenty, greater prosperity, and . . . fewer problems on average than *hetero* families." Maengkom (1997:45a).

ture recalls those that have appeared in Family Planning brochures since the 1970s.

By contrast, figures 4–5 and 4–6 show "a *lesbi* couple who are professionals" and "can live together comfortably" and "a young *gay* couple who, besides being happy, also can enjoy life optimally": the author notes that the *lesbi* couple can live "with . . . fewer problems on average than *hetero* families" and asks, if the *gay* couple "were each married in the *hetero* manner, could it be guaranteed that they would live as comfortably as shown above? Only if they were descended from wealth."

What is shown in figures 4–5 and 4–6 are beautifully coiffed hair, upholstered furniture, clean clothes, smooth white tile floors, television sets, automobiles, two servants (men for the *gay* couple, women for the *lesbi* couple), gardens being watered, and the calm aura of leisure. The message is clear: *gay* and *lesbi* couples can "outfamily" the family. But what constitutes the ideal family is not challenged: it remains the modern middle-class, professional household. When the author compares marriage unfavorably with *gay* and *lesbi* couples, it is a particular vision of marriage and heterosexuality in mind, one oriented around the nuclear family made modern through family planning, consumer goods, a notion of the home as private leisure space, and ethnolocality confined to the television set. The author argues that *gay* and *lesbi* Indonesians achieve this national ideal better than *hetero* couples can, but without questioning the vision of national couplehood: their actions "bring benefit to others, without regard to race, religion, line of work, education, or status" (Maengkom 1997:9).

While direct denunciations of marriage like these cartoons are uncommon, traces of their sentiment emerge in the words of other *gay* and *lesbi*

Figure 4–6. "A young *gay* couple who, besides being happy, also can enjoy life optimally. If they each married in the *hetero* manner, could it be guaranteed that they would live as comfortably as shown above? Only if they descended from wealth." Maengkom (1997:45b).

Indonesians who reject marriage. Some *gay* men base a desire not to marry on a sense that *gay* men marry to "hide who they are," solely due to social pressure, and also that marriage is unjust: "In Indonesia many men hide themselves by having a girlfriend. I think they're hypocrites! They don't want to accept themselves as *gay*. I feel sorry for the woman. She gets toyed with. I have a friend who has a girlfriend. He's an authentic gay [*gay asli*]. Eventually they got married. But they were married only for one week and then they got divorced because he couldn't have sex with her. He was only looking for status by marrying."

Another *gay* man said, "I'm afraid that I'd break the heart of the woman. . . . All the women that I've ever been with want me to stop being *gay*, and I don't think I could do that." A third said, "So many gay men do that; they just marry a woman to close themselves [*menutupi diri sendiri*], and then as soon as they're married they run off and have sex with men. . . . It's unfair to the woman." Sometimes an unmarried relative provides a precedent. Michael, a *gay* man in Makassar, had an older uncle who never married; the uncle knew about Michael, but since he and his uncle were the same (*sama*) they could "close each other" (*saling menu-*

tupi). In north Bali, the *lesbi* woman Ita noted that "Another reason my parents accept me is because I have an aunt in the village who never married and has always lived by herself. So I can point to her and say 'I'm like that,' even though that aunt doesn't have sex with women. There are actually a couple other women in my family who didn't marry. But there's no one like that in Tuti's family, and that makes things harder for her."

Choosing not to marry usually has enormous social and economic repercussions, even in urban areas; like other Indonesians, *gay* men and *lesbi* women usually say they have "not yet" married (*belum nikah*) rather than say they are not married at all (*tidak nikah*), regardless of age. While a few of my older *gay* interlocutors in their forties and fifties had never married, most of my interlocutors were in their twenties and thirties; absent a future longitudinal study, it is not possible to predict how many of them will "choose" marriage as they age. Despite the pressures to marry, those who say they will not marry can find cultural rationales for coping with this choice. To not marry for life certainly presents challenges, but some *gay* and *lesbi* Indonesians find ways to live with them, particularly if they are upper class (cf. Howard 1996:247). In response to the need for children, *gay* men and *lesbi* women say that they will adopt the children of siblings, cousins, or other relatives (or have already done so), or will pay for their schooling to build bonds of reciprocity. Most reconcile their religious beliefs with not marrying (see chapter 6).

Paradoxically, another way to avoid marriage is to marry and divorce, a solution that seems to be especially popular amongst tombois. Across Indonesia seeing one's child married is often seen as the ultimate duty of parenthood. The transition from arranged to chosen marriage has not obviated this; parents should ensure that their children "choose" marriage, and the parents should provide a wedding appropriate to the family's status. However, whether or not a divorcee remarries tends to be seen as a more individual decision.

The question is why so few *gay* and *lesbi* Indonesians "choose" not to marry and why this "choice" does not appear to be gaining popularity. That Islam or tradition demands marriage does not explain the particular form the marriage imperative takes, or its similitude across religion and ethnolocalized difference. The answer seems to lie in intersections between the *gay* and *lesbi* subject positions and national discourse. My goal is not to adjudicate between apparently contradictory notions of personhood, the multiple (where "heterosexual" marriage is not problematic) or the congruent (where "heterosexual" marriage is problematic). I wish to hold them in tension, as a mystery I attempt to solve in chapter 7, because it is precisely in such a multiply mediated contact zone that *gay* and *lesbi* subjectivities exist.

Marriage, Similitude, and the Nation

Some coverage of Jossie and Bonnie's 1981 wedding mentioned Western homosexual rights legislation, and since the mid-1990s rumors of gay and lesbian marriage in the West have fascinated *gay* and *lesbi* Indonesians. The topic is interesting because *gay* and *lesbi* Indonesians usually assume that gay and lesbian Westerners marry "heterosexually" as they do and are confused as to whether such same-sex marriages are acknowledged in the *normal* world or are limited to the *gay* world. One tomboi concluded after speaking with me about the West that he was more like Western gay men than Indonesian *gay* men because he did not plan on marrying. In a few cases *gay* men told me that were *gay* marriage legal in Indonesia, they would not marry women, but most find this inconceivable and imagine an ideal life in which there would be a *normal* marriage for the *normal* world and a formalized *gay* relationship for the *gay* world. Marriage links *gay* and *lesbi* subjectivities to the *normal* world; *gay* men, for instance, often believe that through marriage they can become "real men" (*laki-laki asli*; cf. Howard 1996).

The following episode from *The Perfect Path* (introduced in chapter 2) suggests how these spatial scales of homosexual desire in Indonesia are not the direct product of globalization. The year is 1926, and Sucipto, young and homeless in Surabaya, has been walking along the river at night. He pauses to rest on a bridge near the Gubeng train station, near one site where *gay* men hang out in the contemporary period. Lost in thought, he hears a voice call out to him. It is a Dutchman, who invites Sucipto to his house and pays Sucipto to have sex with him. After leaving the house, Sucipto returns to the bridge, "thinking about what had just happened. . . . It was completely impossible that a Dutch person could desire things like that. . . . He was of a different race than myself. Apparently my assumptions had been turned upside down. . . . How did he know that I like this kind of thing? This was what astonished me" (Budiman 1992:111–114).

The Westerner of Sucipto's imagination did not have same-gender desires prior to this encounter. Even after learning that a colonial Westerner could have these desires, Sucipto does not identify with him; he sees the Westerner as interested only in commodified sex, incapable of the love that Sucipto shares with other Javanese men. Sucipto sees his homosexuality in the 1920s as a local, Javanese phenomenon; he also sees it as incompatible with marriage and discourages his Javanese friends from marrying. Living at the high point of Dutch colonialism, he does not imagine himself as part of a national or transnational community, but in some ways his subjectivity is closer to Western gay subjectivity than to contemporary Indonesian *gay* subjectivity, since normative *gay* Indonesians marry and normative gay Westerners do not. Clearly, a theory of globalization that holds that things become more similar as time marches on is insufficient. Contemporary *gay* and *lesbi* subjectivities are not just the evolutionary end points of Sucipto's subjectivity. They represent a dubbing culture, a reterritorialization of Western discourses of homosexuality.

While *gay* and *lesbi* Indonesians' homosexual "desire for the same" and their desire to marry "heterosexually" may seem worlds apart—one the core of identity and the other imposed by society—these desires are part of *gay, lesbi,* and *normal* worlds all shaped by Indonesian national culture. Sexual desire is the source of great pleasure and meaning for most *gay* Indonesians (even if sometimes lived only in fantasy and also the source of sorrow and heartbreak), but it is not always central to selfhood. In Western thought sexuality has become seen as a psychic Prime Mover that radiates outward into every aspect of one's life. Foucault (1978) identified this as the rise of "confessional" discourse and noted that modern gay and lesbian sexualities retain this view of sexuality, as revealed in the concept of "coming out."

Gay and *lesbi* Indonesians have dubbed national discourse with concepts of homosexuality originating outside Indonesia. This is why the *gay* and *lesbi* subject positions are not ethnolocalized, why belonging to society is so important, and why issues of love and marriage take the particular forms they do. *Gay* and *lesbi* desire typically appears as an island of desire among others, keyed to a *gay* or *lesbi* world rather than seeking to "come out" to the whole world. Recalling again the polysemy of *sama,* *gay* and *lesbi* love is a "desire for the same" and a desire to be "together with" others in the *gay* or *lesbi* world. In marrying heterosexually, *gay* and *lesbi* Indonesians desire to be the "same" as *normal* Indonesians, "together with" them in the national culture they epitomize.

CHAPTER FIVE

Geographies of Belonging

PLACE AND SUBJECTIVITY

Warias are usually identified as such by playmates or neighbors long before they take up waria subjectivity. There is no need for learning of the concept "waria" through mass media and little notion of a "waria world"; warias are part of the recognized social mosaic. In contrast, *gay* and *lesbi* Indonesians' "desire for the same" has no place in the *normal* world. They must contend with a society that is largely unaware of their existence, living their sexual subjectivities within the *gay* and *lesbi* worlds.[1] There is more to a *gay* or *lesbi* life than being *gay* or *lesbi*, but other discourses shaping their lives—the family, ethnicity, religion, nation—are sustained through institutions like bureaucracies, households, and mosques. In Southeast Asia such institutions are publicly recognized through architecture, ritual, and everyday social interaction: "it is the ubiquity of publicly displayed cultural forms that gives the region its distinctive aura" (Bowen 1995:1048). The *gay* and *lesbi* worlds lack such recognition; *gay* and *lesbi* Indonesians must thus live out their sexual subjectivities on the margins of the *normal* world.

For *gay* and *lesbi* Indonesians there is usually a distinction between "becoming" (*menjadi*) *gay* or *lesbi*, which refers to self-awareness, and opening oneself (*membuka diri*), which refers to participating in the *gay* or *lesbi* world. To my knowledge *gay* and *lesbi* Indonesians never speak of "opening oneself to oneself" in the way that Western gay men and lesbian often speak of "coming out to oneself" as the first stage in an incremental process of coming out to the world.

No census of the *gay* and *lesbi* worlds exists, but for thousands (and possibly tens or hundreds of thousands) of Indonesians these worlds are spaces of sociality—camaraderie, desire, and love—a source of great pleasure and meaning. The places of the *gay* and *lesbi* worlds are sites of belonging and recognition, places to find people who are the "same" (*sama*) as oneself because they too "desire the same." One *gay* man who regularly went to a park at night observed that "people think that the only reason people go to this park is to find a [sex] partner. That guess is correct for those who are newcomers. But 'old stock' like me go to this park only for refreshing [*refreshing*]." Another came to the park to "get rid of feelings of boredom and frustration, so I don't feel alone in the middle of my neighborhood."

This chapter focuses on the geography of the *gay* and *lesbi* worlds—a geography of belonging—and "the role of spatialization in social reproduction" (Shields 1997:192).[2] I am interested in how being *gay* and *lesbi* is shaped by spatial dimensions of domination, by the relationship between space and desire: desire operates across space, and space "unleashes desire" (Lefebvre 1991:97). The fragmented character of the *gay* and *lesbi* worlds influences a sense that these subjectivities are fragmented as well: like the *gay* men in Jakarta studied by Howard, *gay* men and *lesbi* women in all of my field sites overwhelmingly saw Indonesia "as being divided into distinct social worlds, and they recognized the fact that in some sense they had to become different people in different locations in social space" (Howard 1996:263). This fragmentation shapes a powerful sense of separation from what one desires—separation from other *gay* and *lesbi* Indonesians, from *normal* society, from the nation itself. How is a marginalized "desire for the same" articulated through geographical imaginaries?

GEOGRAPHIES OF THE *GAY* WORLD

Tempat Ngebers

Across Indonesia nighttime in the city marks not the end of the day but a beginning. The sun's searing heat is replaced by electric streetlights, whose orange glow mixes with dust and smoke to form a gentle haze pressing downward. The streets take on new life: exhausted factory workers nodding asleep on minibuses, teenagers on motorcycles en route to the cinema, husbands and wives strolling down the street. And among these varied groups of people, *gay* men meet at "hanging-out places," known in many parts of Indonesia as *tempat ngeber* (*tempat* means "place"; *ngeber* is a *gay* language term for "hang out") and sometimes by other terms like *tempat ngumpul* ("gathering place"). One tempat ngeber, Texas (in Surabaya), appeared in chapter 1. The largest tempat ngeber in Bali during my fieldwork was probably *PPT*, a contraction for Puputan, the town square of Denpasar, Bali's capital. This is a broad expanse of grass alternating with groves of trees and bushes: a statue of the warrior Udayana stands at one end of the square as the inhabitants of Denpasar cross en route to the nearby government office, hospital, or temple. On the south side of the square sits a bench, where in the late evenings one can often find five or ten *gay* men talking and laughing with each other, more on a Saturday night. The bench is on the perimeter of the park and faces the street; occasionally a man will circle once or twice on a motorcycle, then pull up to greet his friends. Many Indonesians who have moved to Bali from other islands prefer the tourist zones to PPT: the promise of a Westerner, cash payment, or both compares favorably to the relatively nonsexual atmosphere here. Some Balinese men do not like to come here either; they fear being seen by family or neighbors. "The Balinese here are very closed," said Bagus, a *gay* man from Bali, sitting on the curb with Nyoman, his lover, also from Bali; in the *gay* world they use the same last name as a token of their relationship. "Surabaya is more opened," Nyoman added. They live together at the house of Bagus's parents, who think they are just friends.

The *gay* world is a constellation of conceptually linked sites ranging from bedrooms to shopping malls. It is the more public of these sites that are termed tempat ngebers, and most *gay* men see these as prototypical elements of the *gay* world. *Gay* men across Indonesia describe their city or village—and other cities or parts of Indonesia they have visited or heard about—as being relatively "opened" or "closed." This indexes not the visibility of the *gay* world but its extensiveness: a city can be seen as "opened" even though *normal* Indonesians are unaware of the *gay* geography in their midst. One thing that makes a place "opened" is the presence of tempat ngebers, and tempat ngebers are considered the most "opened" parts of the *gay* world because they occupy civic space. An "opened" city has lots of busy tempat ngebers. If you call yourself a "member of the *gay* world" (*anggota dunia gay*), you probably spend a lot of time in tempat ngebers. Even *gay* men who do not go to tempat ngebers usually know they exist and see them as important sites of the *gay* world. Along with the other elements of the *gay* world discussed below, they are places of *gay* geography forged within spaces of modern Indonesia, places to find friendship, sex, and love.[3] As an ethnographer, tempat ngebers allowed me to enter the *gay* world in a new city and connect with *gay* men over months and years.

The general concept of tempat ngebers is familiar to *gay* men across Indonesia. Tempat ngebers tend to occupy civic spaces like parks, town squares, bridges, waterfronts, or bus stations. This is often the case even in towns with only a few thousand inhabitants. Late on a Thursday or Saturday night at a major tempat ngeber like PPT in Denpasar, *kampus* (campus), located at Karebosi, Makassar's town square, or Pattaya in Surabaya, I have seen a hundred persons gathered together. More usually there are five to twenty men at a tempat ngeber at any point in time. Tempat ngebers are rarely coextensive with an entire civic space; only a portion, usually at the periphery, becomes the tempat ngeber. This permits a degree of invisibility within the most public places. Texas corresponds to no feature of everyday geography: it is one side of a street, along a river, behind the Joyoboyo bus station. Kampus is not identical to Karebosi (even when "Karebosi" is used as a shorthand for it); it is part of the square's edge, as is the case for other tempat ngebers found in town squares, like PPT in Denpasar and *LA* (Los Angeles) in Yogyakarta.

The civic location of tempat ngebers can be explained in utilitarian terms. Since physical violence and police harassment against *gay* men have been rare, a central location is preferable because it is easy to invent an excuse for being seen there; this also makes them accessible to *normal* men who may be looking for sex. Such locations are also easy to access by public transport even at night, which is crucial since many *gay* men cannot afford a motorcycle. But a utilitarian characterization misses the specific conjunction of place, practice, and power at hand—what de Certeau addressed through his distinction between strategies and tactics. For de Certeau a strategy is formed through the hegemonic power to set the geographic terms of discussion; it "postulates a *place* that can be delimited as its *own* and serve as the base [for managing] relations with an *exteriority*" (1984:356). Tactics lack this power and thus both institutionalization and control over place. They cannot construct "a borderline distinguishing the other as a visible totality. The place of a tactic belongs to the other. A tactic insinuates itself into the other's place, fragmentarily, without taking it over in its entirety" (xix). Like all nodes of the *gay* and *lesbi* worlds, tempat ngebers are tactics, "situational" territories of the self (Goffman 1971:29) that insinuate themselves into civic space, national space—the "other" that will not acknowledge one's existence.

De Certeau also emphasized that "a tactic depends on time—it is always on the watch for opportunities that must be seized 'on the wing.' Whatever it wins, it does not keep" (xix). This seizing of place "on the wing" is not unlike the dynamic of dubbing. Few tempat ngebers are such twenty-four hours a day. It would make no sense to tell someone "Let's meet at Texas at eleven in the morning"; Makassar's kampus is nothing more than Karebosi square during the day. As one man said when we drove past Texas one afternoon, "It's closed right now," using the same term (*tertutup*) used in reference to "closed" persons. Most tempat ngebers are associated with particular days of the week. Saturday night is generally a big evening for leisure and thus a good night for tempat ngebers. Many businesses are closed in the afternoons on Friday in observance of weekly prayers for Muslims, and as a result Thursday nights are also busy. Though some *gay* men go to tempat ngebers nearly every day of the week, many go only on these busier days. A few tempat ngebers, such as Pattaya in Surabaya, have daytime visitors, including men who have office jobs and make a brief visit on their lunch break to socialize.

Hasan spoke in chapter 3 about first seeing himself as *gay* after an encounter with mass media. Several years following this shift in subjectivity:

I was walking by Karebosi. I thought there were only warias there and didn't know *gay* men gathered there. And by coincidence when I walked by someone called out to me. I thought "this is a nice person" and didn't think about it, it was just small talk, relaxed, and then one of them started speaking openly [*terbuka*] to me, admitting that he was attracted to me. And I was surprised. "How can someone be so open?" When I was a man and he was a man. And that was when I started to think that "oh, apparently in Indonesia we can already find people like this, not only outside [*di luar*]."

For Hasan it was at tempat ngebers that *gay* started to index a geography located neither "outside" nor "in Makassar" but "in Indonesia." Even though mass media are usually how *gay* subjectivity is first entered, and quite a few *gay* men have their first sex with men who do not term themselves *gay*, tempat ngebers are often the sites where they learn a *gay* world exists, as illustrated by Karim:

There was a nighttime event at Karebosi, and I was walking by and met some *gay* men [*hémong*]. . . . And I really didn't know anything, even though I lived and grew up in Makassar, I only knew that it was a place for warias, only that, I didn't know it was a *gay* place [*tempat gay*]. After I was taken into it, oh, I started to know "oh, the northern part of Karebosi, that's the place where *gay* men gather," and I started to learn. . . . In the end I made a lot of friends. And someone that I met at Karebosi became my partner for a year or two.

The story leads from learning about a tempat ngeber to friendship and finally love; when speaking of what he discovered, Karim introduces a term of *gay* language (*hémong*), language that indexes the *gay* world. Tarik learned the term *gay* "from watching television, from health consultations in magazines." When he encountered the term "it was like a harpoon struck me. . . . I was reading the magazine, and it was like 'this is the same [*sama*] with what I've experienced.' " Only after graduating from high school did he "start to get together with *gay* men [*sémong-sémong*]"; to find them he "met them on the street . . . from one to one information was passed." Like Karim, Tarik introduces a term of *gay* language (*sémong*) when describing the moment of meeting other *gay* men. This relationship to tempat ngebers takes roughly the same form across Indonesia. In Bali, Made was attracted to men from a young age and learned about the term *gay* from "letters to the editors of newspapers asking 'why am I like this?,' reports in women's magazines, and so on." But then:

It turned out that a brother-in-law got sick, so I had to spend a lot of time at the hospital at Denpasar, helping take care of him. So I would go walking around at night. And one night just by chance I happened to walk by Puputan. That's how I found it, just by chance! I was so surprised. I walked by there and was hanging around, and someone said, "So you realize this is a place for *gay* men?" I was shocked! Because Puputan, then as now, was mixed: the *gay* men just hung out on one side of the park. Once I knew, I started going there again. My questions started to get answered, and I didn't feel lonely anymore. I knew there were other people like me, and I would go there a lot to make friends. I'd already known the term "*gay*" before then, but I'd never actually known any *gay* people other than myself.

Puputan was also important to Agus, like Made a Hindu *gay* man:

> In my first year of high school I heard you could find warias at the town square at night. My classes were in the morning, so one afternoon I walked by there. But it was around five o'clock and there wasn't anyone there of course! I thought to myself, "How strange, there's no one here but little kids and their parents!" About two weeks later I went again around 7 in the evening, but there still weren't many people there. After that, a week later I went for the third time, even later, around 8 P.M. And it was a Saturday night. And so I sat down there, right there at the bench where we still sit today. And a guy came up to me. It was around 9 P.M. by then. He asked me "What time is it?" but I didn't have a watch on. After that, he started asking me where I lived, with whom I lived, where I went to school, stuff like that. He asked me what I was doing there, what I was looking for, and I said, "I'm not looking for anything; I'm just hanging around." After that, I went the following day again, around 10 P.M., and I met another guy.

Tempat ngebers are sites of belonging, not sex in isolation: *gay* men (and some *normal* men) use them to find a sex partner, but more often they are places to talk about the joys and sorrows of life, to discover romance, or simply to sit quietly in the presence of men like yourself. As a *gay* man in Makassar put it, you can "get together, joke around, things like that, get to know each other." A *gay* man in Surabaya recalled how "I met friends who . . . were of the same fate [*senasib*] as me. So I had a lot of friends and I wasn't sad." *Gay* men usually go to tempat ngebers as the last event of their day before returning home, spending an hour or two beginning around 10 P.M. There is great variation—visits from five minutes to all night long; beginning as late as 2:00 or 3:00 in the morning and as early as 8 P.M., though rarely before sunset. However, this variation does not correlate with cities or ethnic groups; the broad patterns of inhabiting tempat ngebers appear to be roughly consistent across the archipelago.

Gay men often use pseudonyms when in the *gay* world and do not reveal if they are married to a woman: two *gay* men may get to know each other quite well without knowing much about their life in the *normal* world. The topics of discussion at tempat ngebers are usually internal to the *gay* world—joking, gossip about relationships and sex, occasionally talk about personal problems like a lover who has ended a relationship or family pressure to marry a woman. As a *gay* man from Surabaya put it: "I only became brave enough to enter the *gay* world two years ago. And new people want to know about things, right? It makes us happy. I want to know about things, know and know and know. Want to hang out at places like *Kalifor* [a tempat ngeber located on a bridge near a major shopping mall in central Surabaya, near a river (*kali*) and named after California]. Just to talk with my friends, and then go home."

Distinctions usually develop between tempat ngebers within a city, primarily between those visible to passers-by and those more hidden. Across Indonesia, tempat ngebers in the former category are termed "opened" (*terbuka*) and in the latter "closed" (*tertutup*)—the same framework used with reference to entire cities and even nations, and also with reference to persons. Opened tempat ngebers tend to attract opened *gay* men, while closed tempat ngebers tend to attract closed *gay* men as well as men looking for sex who may not term themselves *gay*. Pattaya was created around 1997 and quickly become the most popular tempat ngeber in Surabaya because of its location: *gay* men described it as closed and quiet (*sepi*), allowing closed persons to socialize more easily than at Texas and Kalifor, which many saw as too public (*umum*). Socializing is so central to *gay* men's use of tempat ngebers that many choose different places for sexual encounters:

> I like *gay* men for friendship, but not for sex. So I go to Texas to meet friends and hang out, but I go to the Bungarasih bus terminal to find men for sex. There are lots of men from out of town who arrive on an evening bus and spend the night there sleeping on the curb. So I say "hey, I live near here and you can just spend the night with me." When we get to my room, I tell them that I want to have sex with them. Sometimes they refuse at the beginning, but I show them gay porn videos and seduce them, and so far I've never had a man who didn't eventually have sex with me.

Most tempat ngebers also have an internal structure calibrated along the opened-closed continuum. While it might seem that the outer fringes of a tempat ngeber would be considered opened and the center closed, the reverse tends to be the case. For instance, the more central part of Texas, away from the *normal* world, is where opened men gather, while its ends, cloaked in shadow and closer to large streets, are frequented by closed men. The more opened men of the center may come to Texas five nights a week, while the closed men who frequent its periphery may show up only once or twice a month.

This metonymic linking of opened men to opened parts of tempat ngebers and opened cities, and closed men to closed parts of tempat ngebers and closed cities, shows how the opened-closed continuum references the *gay* world. You are an opened *gay* man not because your parents or co-workers know about you, nor because you go to rallies or write letters to the newspaper, but because you spend time in the *gay* world and particularly in parts of that world considered opened. Sometimes a *gay* man who comes frequently to a tempat ngeber will be regarded as a kind of leader to whom others turn for advice, the "queen of Texas" or "the person who shuts down Pattaya every night." The movements of *gay* men through different parts of tempat ngebers constitute them as more opened or closed; it is the kind of social practice by which subject positions become instantiated as subjectivities. The relationship is, in Piercian terms, indexical rather than iconic: to shift one Saturday night from one's typical perch on a railing at the perimeter of a tempat ngeber to its center does not just mark one as opened, but is part of the process of opening oneself (see Butler 1990; Mahmood 2001).

Malls

Tempat ngebers have begun appearing within shopping malls, making them important elements of the *gay* world (cf. Leong 1995). Malls in Indonesia range from the basic to the truly spectacular, signifying modernity and economic transformation. The shift from open-air markets (*pasar*), with their connotations of earthy trading and the selling of foodstuffs, to enclosed malls (*mal*), where prices are fixed and the most common items are consumer goods like clothes and electronics, represents an emerging ideal of conspicuous, collective consumerism as a social activity that, separate from the items actually purchased, marks middle-class status and modernity. Surabaya's Tunjungan Plaza, one of the largest malls in Southeast Asia, comprises four linked atria ranging from four to eight stories high, boasting hundreds of shops (including McDonald's, Kentucky Fried Chicken, and Dunkin Donuts); Tunjungan 1 features a multiplex movie theater, and for several years Tunjungan 3 featured an ice-skating rink.[4] On most afternoons the mall is filled with Indonesians—the wealthy to make their purchases and others to socialize, enjoy the free air conditioning, and watch the spectacle of shopping and ice skating. Without an ice skating rink or movie theater, Tunjungan 2 is quiet. On its third floor, near the Gunung Agung bookstore, are a few wooden benches. Sitting on them or leaning over the rail in front of the store are often a few *gay* men, alone or in small groups. There is a public bathroom nearby, and men sometimes stare a little too long at the man next to them, signaling interest through eye contact. If the interest is reciprocated, the men may leave the mall together or sneak into one of the fire escape stairwells in the mall for oral sex.

Some *gay* men go to both malls and tempat ngebers, but most go predominantly to one or the other. *Gay* men often go to malls in small groups to spend time with *gay* friends; after opening in 2000, the Ratu Indah Mall in Makassar became popular among *gay* men. Others, like Suprati, use malls primarily to find sex partners. A regular at Tunjungan Plaza, Suprati rarely goes to outdoor tempat ngebers like Texas because he is *takut dihafal* (literally, "afraid of being memorized"). For this reason his knowledge of many practices of the *gay* world is minimal; for instance, *gay* language: "I don't know all those *gay* terms." He likes *normal* men as sexual partners; one current partner is a doctor, another in the military. He prefers such men to *gay* men because he and they "close each other" (*saling menutupi*); that is, keep their relationship hidden.

While malls have become quasi-civic spaces in contemporary Indonesia, their private ownership and orientation toward moneyed classes makes them less public than a park or town square. Malls are not open late at night, so *gay* men must visit them at the same time others do. This makes it is easier to find *normal* men for sex and to be inconspicuous, but one must be careful lest gossip make its way back to friends, family, or workplace colleagues. Effeminacy is rare in malls, as are groups of more than a handful of men. Nevertheless, provided one dresses in a manner reflecting the modernity associated with malls (e.g., not in "traditional" dress or as a waria), accessing malls is not difficult even if one's income is low.

If looking to find a sex partner, *gay* men usually come alone and communicate through "playing eyes" (*main mata*). One *gay* man who liked to go Tunjungan Plaza said, "I would know who is *gay* there. They'd usually be hanging out around the glass walls in Tunjungan 1, just looking around. Or at Gunung Agung. And lots of people also hanging out in Tunjungan 3, looking down on the ice skating rink. . . . You'd see someone standing there alone, watching the ice skating for a long time. With someone like that there'd be a possibility that they were 'sick.'" While in the West parks are stereotyped as cruising grounds saturated with sex, for *gay* men malls are often more sexualized than parks, attracting men interested solely in finding sexual partners. Seemingly so public, malls are good places to be closed.

Discos

Normal Indonesians usually walk past a group of men in a park or mall without realizing they have passed through a node of the *gay* world. One element of *gay* geography has a slightly more stable presence—discos that have a *gay* night, usually informally recognized but occasionally openly declared. *Gay* nights have taken place in discos in several Indonesian cities since at least the mid-1980s. In major cities like Jakarta and Surabaya, or in the Kuta tourist zone of Bali, disco patrons on some nights can be almost entirely *gay* men with a few warias and *lesbi* women. Elsewhere *gay* nights are usually mixed (*campur*), with *normal* Indonesians present. In these cases *gay* men hang out more discreetly. Because discos have owners, *gay* nights are less stable than tempat ngebers or malls; they end when the owner sells the establishment or decides the *gay* night is unprofitable. Particularly in the capital of Jakarta, *normal* Indonesians who know of the *gay* world sometimes conflate it with discos. Since 2002, several private television stations have run segments about *gay* Indonesian life; such segments almost always begin with footage from a disco "exemplifying" what *gay* life is like.

Sensation was one disco where I conducted fieldwork during the late 1990s: located on the second floor of an otherwise nondescript building in a southeastern district of Surabaya, its *gay* night was on Thursdays. One Thursday I took a minibus from Texas to Sensation with Robert, a *gay* friend. On the night in question Robert forgot to wear shoes: "they won't let me in with these sandals," he said dejectedly. In the ground floor entryway the walls quaked from the music above as we entered (Robert made it in, self-consciously looking away from his feet). About forty feet deep with a narrow second-floor balcony on three sides, the small disco was packed with over two hundred men and about twenty warias. Underneath the balcony and behind the dance floor, sofas and chairs were lit by the intermittent constellations of innumerable cigarettes; a bar to the right of the stairs served drinks to thirsty patrons. Hip-hop music filled the room, making it difficult to converse as men filled the dance floor. Elsewhere, pairs of men sat together or even stole a kiss under the darkness of the balcony.

After half an hour the music stopped, leaving behind a sudden cacophony of conversation and laughter. Everyone backed away from the dance floor to form a tightly packed circle as the deejay's voice filled the room: "Welcome to Sensation! It's time for the evening's show." Sensation's show was a weekly event; the music was mostly Western pop, with only a few Indonesian songs thrown in. The performers were both warias and *gay* men but there was no live band; they sang what in Indonesian is termed *playback*, lip-synching to the recorded voices of others (see Boellstorff 2004b). The show began with a man playbacking a Western pop ballad, followed by a waria playbacking the theme from the movie *Titanic*. As each performed, beautifully dressed and face full of emotion, audience members walked onto the dance floor and stuffed thousand-rupiah bills (about 15 cents each) into bosoms, pants, or shorts.

The third performer was another waria, with short hair and a tight-fitting knee-length white dress. She began playbacking to an Indonesian pop song of love gone awry, *Aku benci* ("I hate"). Each verse of the song lists a grievance suffered by a woman from an uncaring lover, followed by the phrase *aku benci*. By the second or third repetition a few mischievous *gay* men were singing along, substituting *aku banci* ("I am a waria"). Soon the entire audience had picked up on the joke and at the end of each verse the room echoed with *aku banci!*, *gay* men pointing at themselves in mock pity or rolling on the floor in laughter. Above the fray, the waria kept her composure with a wry smile.

This joking play on the *gay*/waria boundary (see chapter 6) was possible because of the greater degree of privacy offered by discos. While upper-class *gay* men prefer discos and rarely enter tempat ngebers, many middle- and lower-class *gay* men go to both discos and tempat ngebers; some even socialize exclusively in discos. There is always the matter of the fee (five thousand rupiah [about seventy-five cents] in 1998 at Sensation, fifteen thousand rupiah [about two dollars] in 2002 at the disco that replaced it), but *gay* men will save all month to afford the ticket. Anzar lived in Bali during my fieldwork but was from Surabaya: "When I'm in Surabaya, I don't go to Texas much, because I'm afraid of being seen by my family. *Gay* people at that place are too overboard, they're too open [*terlalu terbuka*], they even kiss each other out there. But at Sensation it's no problem, because it's enclosed; it's not outside. And the people who go there are all like us, so it's not possible they'd tell." In Makassar, Abdul pointed out how he felt uncomfortable (*risih*) hanging out in parks because of "people's stares. You can't embrace, you can't do anything together in public." For Abdul and some other *gay* men, discos are where they first entered the *gay* world. Though married to a woman and the father of a child by the latter stages of my fieldwork, when I first knew him Abdul was a bachelor and heavily involved in the *gay* world. Attracted to men since elementary school, as a child he didn't know the word *gay*, only banci. By his early teens he knew the term *gay* "from reading magazines all the time . . . women's magazines like *Femina* and *Populer*." However, he only began socializing with other *gay* men in high school after stumbling upon a particular disco: "what I knew was that it was a crowded disco; I didn't know that it was special for *gay* men and warias."

Domestic Sites: Salons, Homes, and Koses

While the home is generally a place where *gay*ness must be hidden, *gay* men forge sites of *gay* subjectivity in ostensibly domestic places, the best-known of which are salons, homes, and *koses* (rented rooms). *Gay* men can be opened in them only if the salon provides a welcoming atmosphere; usually this means the salon in question is owned and/or operated by a *gay* man or waria. Such salons can become so well known in the *gay* world that they are listed as tempat ngebers in *gay* zines. Salon work is a common line of employment for *gay* men and warias, and most Indonesians know that warias (and *gay* men, to the extent they distinguish the two subject positions) can be found in salons. *Gay* men drop into such salons at all hours of the day as clients or visitors, gossiping about everything from sexual escapades to romantic squabbles. Salons are an important venue by which knowledge of the *gay* world (including *gay* language) crosses, however fitfully, into Indonesian popular culture.

Since simple salons are often physically connected to homes, the dividing line between salon and home can be indistinct. Like most Indonesians, *gay* men rarely live alone. Many *gay* men spend time at the homes of *gay* friends and lovers despite the presence of parents, siblings, or a wife. For *gay* men who even fear being seen in discos, homes are the only places they can live out their sexual subjectivities. This is particularly true for upper-class men, who often look down upon the predominantly lower-class users of tempat ngebers (one upper-class *gay* man confessed that he sometimes drove by a tempat ngeber—with his car windows rolled up). Thus the widespread segregation along lines of class and status in Indonesia persists in the *gay* world (cf. Howard 1996:265). The larger homes of the wealthy make it easier to find space with some *gay* friends away from other members of the household. The difficulty is that it is educated, wealthier families who are more likely to know what *gay* means. In more lower-class households, *gay* visitors can socialize with little fear of discovery. I have seen drag show rehearsals and HIV prevention rap groups with twenty *gay* participants take place in a *gay* man's home without the host's parents understanding what was happening. Sometimes a *gay* couple can live together in the home of one of their families without raising suspicion, as in the case of Nyoman and Bagus above, or a married *gay* men can have a male partner live in the home without his wife understanding that he and the partner are lovers (see chapter 4). One *gay* man recalled how he and his former lover shared a life: "Most of the time we were at his house, because his mother was nice and would say 'just stay here tonight and be a friend to my son.' So that whole time we were together we never had our own place. We had to be careful; even if we were fighting because of a broken promise or something, we had to keep our voices down so no one would hear."

If his wealth is great enough, a *gay* man can occasionally live alone in a home without family members, avoiding marriage or living separated from his wife. Such homes may become well-known sites in the *gay* world, though their use is limited by who is on friendly terms with the owner. On one occasion during my Surabaya fieldwork, over forty *gay* men crowded inside the home of a wealthy *gay* man to celebrate his birthday. In the living room we chatted and watched Western porn videos (a rare treat for most *gay* Indonesians) with the sound turned off while others held Muslim evening prayers in a bedroom. No one seemed to find this juxtaposition of sex and religion worthy of commentary. Sitting on the floor eating dessert in the living room, one man turned to me and said: "Let's not bother going to Texas tonight! This is much more fun!"

The term *kos* is sometimes translated as "apartment," but this is a misnomer since most koses are single unfurnished rooms no more than ten feet on a side, with shared bathing and cooking facilities. A *rumah kos* or "kos house" can be a dormitory-like building composed of koses, or a series of koses added to a house where the landlord's family lives. Even if there are no other known *gay* boarders, the relative lack of social ties between boarders can make a *gay* man's kos a safe haven that other *gay* men regularly visit. Such koses are some of the most ubiquitous nodes of the *gay* world. Occasionally *gay* men live in koses located near each other, as in the case of Ridwan, who lived with his parents in a large house with eleven small koses on the second floor. Ridwan's parents owned a second residence out of town, spending only one or two nights a week at the house. Ridwan was left to act as landlord:

> This house has had lots of *gay* men and one *lesbi* woman living here for the last three months; eight out of the eleven boarders now! What happened was that the other people would move out because they married or found work elsewhere, so there were lots of empty rooms. And it spread by word of mouth, "You should board at Ridwan's place." . . . I said, "Okay, we can gather here together, we can take care of each other." . . . If they have a problem with their boyfriends or whatever, they come to me. It's like one of those sitcoms on television.

Rural/Urban Dynamics

A major factor in the rural *gay* world's existence is that rural Indonesians have become avid media consumers; it is by no means unusual to find rural homes with dirt floors and no running water, but enough electricity for a handful of light bulbs and a television set. Given the key role mass media play in *gay* subjectivities, it should not be surprising that *gay* men can be found even in small villages. While many rural *gay* men move to cities, others remain in their villages of origin because they are caring for a relative, have married a woman and do not wish to be separated from their family, or do not like urban life. Others engage in cyclical migration, living in a kos in the city and returning to the village on a regular basis.

In rural areas, malls and town squares either do not exist or are too small for hanging out beyond the earshot of passersby. As a result, salons are important sites of the rural *gay* world; there exist salons run and frequented by *gay* men surrounded by nothing but rice fields. However, in both Java and Sulawesi (and, I suspect, elsewhere in Indonesia), certain villages have become known as places where men have sex with each other; *gay* men sometimes come from such villages and these villages are also sometimes visited by *gay* men from nearby cities. One *gay* man from outside Surabaya noted that "in my village sometimes there are men who live with each other and have sex with each other. One is a man and one is a banci; everyone knows about it and it isn't seen as a problem or a sin. Eventually the man marries, but often the banci does not." When visiting one such village I was impressed by the way men joked openly about sexual practices with other men. However, even in such circumstances it is assumed all men will eventually marry.

Events

Beyond sites like tempat ngebers, malls, and salons are events (*acara, pertemuan, show*). These are time-delimited but important elements of the *gay* world. Events with up to a thousand attendees occasionally take place in large cities, and smaller events with a handful of performers and fewer than thirty *gay* men in the audience occur even in rural environments. Set apart from the rhythm of daily life and requiring a level of planning not found in the more regularized patronage of tempat ngebers and discos, events invite explicit commentary on topics like authenticity and belonging. There have been skits performed at discos in Surabaya, for instance, where the story revolves around love and separation, and the lead characters are named *gaya* (style) or *nusa* (island).

One well-known *gay* event is September Ceria (Joyous September), held near Solo; when I attended in 1997 the event had taken place every year since 1989, drawing spectators from across Java and occasionally beyond. For several weeks before September Ceria in 1997, *gay* men hanging out at Texas and elsewhere talked excitedly about the event, and as the time drew near, small groups of them made their way toward Solo on buses or trains. The event took place in a resort village outside the city, on the slopes of a volcano extending up to ten thousand feet. On the day before the event, the village was full of *gay* men strolling around between the small hotels where they were staying four or more to a room. Friends from distant cities greeted each other with hugs, and the dress all around was sharp: tight white T-shirts, jeans, smooth silk button-down shirts. But not everyone was outside, because at 4:30 P.M. local time the casket of Princess Diana began its procession toward Westminster. In every hotel room men watched the television intently, gossiping about the attractiveness of Elton John's lover, a tantalizing glimpse of the Western gay world. By 6:45 P.M. the coverage ended and we left the hotel room in darkness, walking up to the large, high-ceilinged concrete-and-glass hall where September Ceria would take place. Over six hundred *gay* men together with a few *lesbi* women and warias waited outside: excitement was in the air, and it was clear that most had never been in the company of so many *gay* men at once. I purchased my ticket for 15,000 rupiah right before the doors opened at 7 P.M. The *gay* men from Solo who organized the event informed the guests that (as in years past) photography was forbidden. One attendee from Surabaya whispered under his breath: "Why are they so worried about being exposed? They are so closed."

The hall was filled with chairs, the stage at one end decorated with white steps topped with five Greek columns and bouquets of plastic flowers. Attendees took their seats as the program began with an introduction from the emcees—Ardi, a *gay* man from Surabaya, and Maria, a *gay* man from Jakarta famous for his dressing up as a woman. Maria's glossy painted nails flashed under the lights as he exchanged mile-a-minute jokes with Ardi and then performed playback to a pop song. Afterward, Ardi stuffed money in Maria's bosom in appreciation of his performance, joking that he had considered doing the same in "back" (slapping Maria's rear end for emphasis) but was afraid because "who knows what's authentic (*asli*) and what isn't!"

Suddenly the sounds of Richard Strauss's *Also Sprach Zarathustra* filled the air. All eyes turned to the back of the hall as Toni, the head of the organizing committee from Solo, moved toward the stage, looking down imperiously from a golden throne resting upon the shoulders of four beefy, bare-chested men in golden loincloths. Upon reaching the stage, Toni stepped off the throne and read a short speech, expressing hope that the audience, who he referred to as *senasib* (of one fate) and *sehati* (of one heart), would enjoy the evening's events. Following over two hours of performances by *gay* men from across Java and Bali, Ardi appeared on stage to make a few comments. Noting that both performers and attendees had come from all over Indonesia, he repeated the nationalist saying, "From Sabang to Merauke we become one."[5]

Organizations

Events are the most common type of organizational work in which *gay* men engage: very few participate in activism as that term is usually used in the West. This near absence of political work is one reason why *gay* Indonesians remain quite invisible to Westerners and *normal* Indonesians. The organizational and activist work that does exist, however, certainly affects the *gay* world. *Gay* men have been organizing since quite soon after the *gay* subject position was probably first formed in the archipelago. Most of the largest and longest-lasting *gay* organizations are on Java, but substantial organizations have arisen in many other parts of Indonesia. While not representative of the lives or interests of most *gay* men, *gay* organizations have engaged in a range of activities from telephone counseling hotlines to a wide variety of HIV prevention programs; they have played a crucial role in creating entertainment events and fostering *gay* zines, volleyball clubs, and other activities that build a sense of local and national sociality.

The first *gay* organization to publicly proclaim itself was Lambda Indonesia, which in 1982 began publishing a zine and holding events in Surabaya, and which quickly gained members from other areas (Ary 1987:52). The successor organization to Lambda Indonesia, GAYa Nusantara, remains the best-known *gay* organization and plays an important role in articulating a sense of national belonging for organizations across the archipelago. The phrase *GAYa Nusantara* indexes (1) an organization based in Surabaya, (2) a nationally distributed zine produced by (1), and (3) a national network for which (1) is the clearinghouse. Each term in the phrase *GAYa Nusantara* has two meanings. *Gaya* is Indonesian for "style," but the unusual capitalization highlights its similarity to "*gay.*" *Nusantara* means both "archipelago" and is an everyday term for "Indonesia." The phrase can thus be parsed in four ways (since in Indonesian adjectives follow nouns, while in English they precede them): "archipelago style," "archipelago *gay*," "Indonesia style," and "Indonesia *gay.*"

This multilevel aspect of the term is illustrated in figure 5-1, the August 1994 cover of the magazine *GAYa Nusantara*. The image shows two *gay* men wearing Muslim *topi* hats. The man on the left carries the Indonesian flag (red on top, white on the bottom) while the man on the right carries the rainbow flag that has become an international symbol for gay men and lesbians (which has two small vertical red and white strips at its base, recalling the Indonesian flag). While the term *GAYa Nusantara* is by no means used or even known to all Indonesians who identify as *gay*, it manifests a common conception of *gay* subjectivity as national in scope. Many *gay* groups name themselves "*GAYa X*": GAYa Semarang in the city of Semarang in Java, GAYa Betawi in Jakarta (Betawi is an old name for Jakarta and its ethnolocalized inhabitants), GAYa PRIAngan in Bandung (*Priangan* is a local term; the first four letters are capitalized to evoke *pria*, Indonesian for "male"), GAYa Celebes in Makassar (Celebes is the French term for the island of Sulawesi), the former GAYa Intim in Ambon, GAYa Siak in the city of Pekanbaru in Sumatra (the Siak is a major river in the province), GAYa Dewata in Bali (*dewata* is Indonesian for "gods," and in contemporary Indonesia Bali is termed the "island of the gods" or Pulau Dewata), GAYa Khatulistiwa in the city of Pontianak, near the equator in Kalimantan (Khatulistiwa is Indonesian for "equator"), GAYa Tepian Samarinda in the city of Samarinda in Kalimantan, and others. A *gay* group on the island of Batam near Singapore, Bagasy, changed its name

Figure 5–1. Sexuality and nation intersecting. *GAYa Nusantara* 32 (August 1994), cover illustration.

to GAYa Batam in the late 1990s, marking more clearly its place in the national *gay* archipelago. Several *lesbi* organizations have also used *GAYa* or other terms to link themselves to this network. Since adjectives follow nouns in Indonesian, this pattern ontologizes the national; the "local" term appears as modifier of *GAYa*, incorporating the state's "attempt to construct local identity in such a way that it can be encompassed by national culture" (Keane 1997:38).

The activities of *gay* organizations differ in several respects from dominant Western models. *Gay* organizations rarely engage in work whose goal is social rights or visibility; most focus on entertainment and social activities. *Gay* men who participate in organizations rarely see their goal as changing social norms or find the notion of visibility compelling. Many members of *gay* organizations, even their leaders, are married to women or plan to get married in the future. *Gay* men who contribute time and energy to *gay* organizations (they are rarely paid) sometimes say they are *aktif* or refer to themselves as an *aktivis* but more commonly identify as a member (*anggota*) or participant (*peserta*) in an organization. Organizations tend to be small, with three to eight core members, and many cease to exist after a few years. Those that are able to survive for longer periods have usually obtained international funding, generally linked to HIV/AIDS prevention and treatment. *Gay* organizations engage in such work out of a real concern about HIV/AIDS and a sense that doing good deeds proves that they are worthy of inclusion in national society. While linkages to transnational HIV/AIDS discourse undoubtedly shape *gay* subjectivity (for instance, the rise in the early 2000s of the concept *lelaki suka lelaki* or LSL, based upon "men who have sex with men" or MSM), such discourse is not how *gay* men come to *gay* subjectivity and does not play a major role in shaping the *gay* world. Among other things, this reflects the reality that funding for HIV/AIDS prevention and treatment in Indonesia remains relatively minor and the profile of HIV/AIDS organizations quite low.

The struggles *gay* organizations face reflect the "tactical" geography of the *gay* world; except for a handful of organizations with HIV/AIDS-related funding who can rent an office, meetings typically must take place in homes or koses, and problems arise if no such places are available or if conflicts develop between the lucky person with a place to meet and others. It testifies to the crucial role of place in *gay* subjectivity that organizations often arise from tempat ngebers rather than the other way around. In 1993 an organization came into being in one of my field sites when a group of men who knew each other from a tempat ngeber began meeting in my rented room. In a different city an organization began with a group of *gay* men who rented koses in the boarding house described earlier: "We had a group of people at this place, so we thought 'why not become an organization?'" Some organizations even incorporate tempat ngebers into their names.

The Working World

Warias hold a limited range of occupations (salon work, bridal makeup, sex work), and at work they remain visibly waria. In contrast, the working world is almost never part of a *gay* man's *gay* world unless he works in a salon. When in the *gay* world, *gay* men often avoid speaking about how they earn a living, since they wish to keep the *normal* and *gay* worlds distinct. *Gay* men who have high-paying jobs in corporate management exist, and mass media usually conflate *gay* men with the *kalangan ekseutif* or "executive classes." However, because they come to their sexual subjectivities through mass media rather than travel to the West or reading English-language magazines, *gay* men can be from any class and most are rather poor even in Indonesian terms. Although detailed survey work on the class backgrounds of *gay* men has not yet been conducted, about 90 percent of *gay* men I interviewed during one fieldwork period (1997–1998) made under 500,000 rupiah a month (about 100 dollars at the time), many much less. Very few *gay* men I encountered during my fieldwork owned a car, and most did not even own a motorcycle. If living separate from their families, most *gay* men live in koses; few own their own homes. The jobs of *gay* men have the same range as other Indonesian men, from street sweeper to elementary school teacher, pharmacist, salesman in a motorcycle dealership, hotel worker, and store cashier. As is the case for other Indonesians, there is a fair amount of unemployment and underemployment among *gay* men.

GEOGRAPHIES OF THE *LESBI* WORLD

As noted earlier, the *gay* and *lesbi* subject positions took form around the same time, as gendered analogues of a "desire for the same." However, while both *gay* men and *lesbi* women sometimes speak of a single "*gay* and *lesbi* world" and cogendered sociality certainly exists (see below), the *lesbi* world is generally distinct from the *gay* world. This reflects the widespread gender segregation in Indonesia: socialization between men and women connotes sexual impropriety unless carefully managed.

A theme in *lesbi* narratives is the difficulty they face in meeting others "like themselves." *Gay* men also speak of isolation and invisibility, but not so consistently and emphatically. The most fundamental issue is that *lesbi* women have difficulty accessing public or civic space, even in the "tactical" way that *gay* men do, because generally they cannot leave the home (particularly at night) unless in the company of a male guardian. This is not an absolute prohibition. Women in much of Southeast Asia have historically had significant freedom of movement, often due to market activities or agricultural work (Reid 1988). While the aristocratic nationalist figure Kartini complained of confinement during the late colonial era, nonelite women have often been expected to move about outside their homes. However, this is extended primarily to married and older women, and nowhere in Indonesia is it considered acceptable for an unaccompanied woman to spend a couple hours at night hanging out in a park. Were a woman to do so, she would risk bringing shame to her family by being seen as a prostitute or *perek* (an abbreviation for *perempuan eksperimen* or "experimenting woman").

Across Indonesia, tombois have somewhat more freedom of movement than ceweks: "[tombois] go out alone, especially at night, which is men's prerogative" (Blackwood 1999:188). This is particularly the case if their appearance is so masculine that they are mistaken for men on the street. Even so, parents or husbands may limit their time away from home. Tombois speak of rivalries over their cewek partners as a major barrier to sociality between tombois. There are few social activities to bring tombois together along the lines of the shows and contests of waria and *gay* life. Ceweks find it easier to move about in the company of a tomboi; in *Menguak Duniaku*, the tomboi Hen talks about how he can move about with a cewek after dark because people "see how my presentation reflects the character and attitude [*sifat dan sikap*] of a man" (Prawirakusumah and Ramadhan 1988:280). While a few upper-class tombois own cars, most tombois drive motorcycles or take public transport.

Given the restrictions on women's movement in civic space, it is not surprising that tempat ngebers, such important sites of *gay* subjectivity, do not exist for *lesbi* women. The primary sites of *lesbi* subjectivity are homes or semiprivate civic spaces like shopping malls, cinemas, coffee shops, salons, or restaurants, as in the story from northern Bali in chapter 1. *Menguak Duniaku* shows the *lesbi* world in the western Javanese city of Bandung to be composed primarily of semiprivate civic spaces, a pattern similar to *lesbi* geographies elsewhere: "A few months ago I was always spending my Saturday nights with Dewi. Whether it was going to the movies, sitting together in a restaurant, or going to a friend's party" (Prawirakusumah and Ramadhan 1988:239). On another occasion the tomboi protagonist reminisces about places he would go with a former lover: "We'd go study [at each others' homes], go to the bookstore looking for schoolbooks, to the mosque every Friday morning, to movies, to friend's parties" (1988:66). The upper-class characters in more recent *lesbi* fiction move in similar spaces (Herlinatiens 2003; Kartini 2003; Ratri 2000). Since the early 1990s the relatively enclosed, private spaces of discos have become sites of *lesbi* subjectivity in some Indonesian cities.

Like the *gay* world, the *lesbi* world is constructed by forging rooms of one's own in the space of another. Indeed, the *lesbi* world is more tactical than the *gay* world; its sites are less distinguished from those of the *normal* world. Keeping the *lesbi* world safely separated from the *normal* world presents challenges. *Lesbi* women are aided by patterns of gender segregation in Indonesia: men tend to socialize with men and women with women. This does not solve the problem of prying female family members, and at home men are often present as well. For instance, Tina and Tri were a *lesbi* couple who lived together in Tina's house, tucked down a side alley on the outskirts of Denpasar where houses become interspersed with rice fields. They had to be on guard since Tina's brother lived in the house but was unaware that his sister and Tri were *lesbi*, much less that they were lovers; *gay* and *lesbi* friends were led to a back room out of earshot.

While *gay* men or warias may encounter violence, it plays a special role in the *lesbi* world. Many *lesbi* women have direct or indirect experience of violence at the hands of fathers, husbands, brothers, or other male family members. That the *lesbi* world is comparatively oriented around the home makes this threat of violence difficult to escape. One of my upper-class *lesbi* interlocutors was hit in the jaw by her older brother so strongly that she had to be hospitalized; the family also tried to have her committed to a psychiatric hospital. The tomboi protagonist of *Menguak Duniaku* is locked up for several months in such a hospital.

While images of "criminal" lower-class *lesbi* women were quite common in popular Indonesian mass media during the 1980s, by the 1990s the dominant stereotype among both Indonesians and Westerners was that *lesbi* women were upper class. The image is that of the career woman or entertainment figure, living in Jakarta, for whom sex with women is another sign of foreign contamination and excessive modernity. While rich *lesbi* women certainly exist, they seem to represent the segment of *lesbi* women most visible to outsiders rather than a numerically or discursively dominant group. As is the case for *gay* men, *lesbi* geographies are class specific, and the worlds of poor *lesbi* women and wealthy *lesbi* women have little in common (A. Murray 1999).

State discourse presents Indonesia as neither becoming a nation of millionaires nor forever mired in poverty, but a nation of "prosperous" middle-class households centered on the heterosexual conjugal pair. The new middle class is highly gendered: "gender relations are central to the making of middle classes and modernity in [Southeast Asia]. . . . in particular, the development of elaborate new femininities based on the consumer/wife/mother and the consumer/beautiful young woman in the region can be seen as central to the very development of these burgeoning economies" (Stivens 1998:1, 5). As for *gay* men, *lesbi* middle-class subjectivity must be understood in terms of "mode of consumption": "the economic forces which have produced the new 'middle classes' of affluent Asia have had transformative effects for people not directly benefiting from being members of an urban rich or self-consciously modern stratum. . . . One does not have to have a high disposable income to desire consumption of new commodities, or to aspire to associated lifestyles" (Robinson 1998:63).

Since most Indonesians cannot distinguish *lesbi* women from *normal* women, they work anywhere other women do, from club deejay to restaurant waitress to office manager. There are feminine *lesbi* women who engage in sex work (with male clients). Survival in the working world usually means not telling anyone one is *lesbi*. This is also true for *lesbi* women who are married to men and work as housewives; these probably form the largest category of *lesbi* labor. Due to their visibly nonnormative gender practices, tombois face a more limited range of career options than ceweks and sometimes work in traditionally male domains like driving a taxi. Many tombois are unemployed, but even poor tombois do not usually engage in sex work, since they do not fit dominant conceptions of female beauty. Like warias, however, some tombois work in salons, even though they do not wear makeup or have feminine hairstyles. Tombois say they obtain salon work because salons have a reputation for employing persons who do not conform to gender norms, and also because it permits interacting with women clients with whom they can potentially have sexual relationships.

A handful of *lesbi* organizations have existed, based mostly in Jakarta (with one predominantly lower-class *lesbi* HIV/AIDS organization in Makassar), but their activities have been limited due to their relative exclusion from HIV/AIDS-related funding and difficulties in finding a place to meet. Whereas some *gay* men are able to access transnational gay networks through HIV/AIDS prevention and treatment programs, *lesbi* women's linkages to the transnational (beyond mass media) are largely limited to women's rights networks; in some cases such women first enter these networks while in college abroad rather than in Indonesia itself.

INTERSECTIONS OF THE *GAY* AND *LESBI* WORLDS

Across Indonesia, men and women tend to socialize in single-gender groups and remain segregated in daily life. It is relatively rare (but becoming more common) for men and women not related through kinship or marriage to spend time with each other outside carefully delimited contexts of school or work. In such environments it is to be expected that *lesbi* women spend time mostly with other *lesbi* women, and *gay* men with other *gay* men.

However, instances of cogendered sociality across Indonesia beg explanation. A *gay* man who owns a salon in Bandung rents out a front room to a *lesbi* couple, which they use as a photography studio. In Surabaya, Rita, a tomboi, emphasizes that *gay* language is "for our group alone, so we can talk without other people understanding." One night Rita and I were in a taxi en route to the Sensation disco with Rano, a *gay* man. They fell to talking and Rano said: "I feel so sorry for *lesbi* women. We have to pity them, because they're so closed." Rita nodded her assent. I added, "Yeah, it's so hard for *lesbi* women to meet," and Rita replied, "Yes, we meet mostly at each other's homes." I mentioned that at the home of a certain waria "It's nice that *gay* men, *lesbi* women, and warias are together. Why doesn't that happen everywhere?" Rita answered "It used to be like that: *lesbi* women and *gay* men were together." Rano added: "Around 1990 it ended, because some authentic men [*laki-laki asli*] pretended to be *gay*. They used it as a ruse to get at the *lesbi* women. So we became separated." I asked, "Was this just in Surabaya?" and Rita replied, "I think it happened all over East Java." Just as memories of "traditional" Java were constructed through the encounter with colonial modernity (Pemberton 1994), this example shows how *gay* men and *lesbi* women can imagine a past in which they were a single community, rather than seeing *gay* and *lesbi* as having distinct ontologies.

In Surabaya and Makassar, *gay* zines have published *lesbi* zines as inserts, allowing them to benefit from the *gay* zine's larger distribution network. In Makassar, a *gay* organization grew to include not only warias but *lesbi* women as staff and clients. In northern Bali, Ita's family's restaurant was a gathering place not only for *lesbi* women but for *gay* men and warias, and *lesbi* women would visit *gay* men and warias at their own homes and salons. One afternoon Tuti invited a respected *gay* man and several warias to a meeting in her family's souvenir shop. Everyone moved racks of batik clothing and carved wooden fruit to the sides of the shop, clearing a space in the middle to sit. Tuti began by thanking everyone for attending, saying, "It's good that we're all meeting here together, *lesbi* women, *gay* men, and warias, because we're all of the same fate [*senasib*], of the same soul [*sejiwa*]." It was decided that a new organization would be created for northern Bali that would network with *gay* men and *lesbi* women in southern Bali, and that the organization would have three chairs—one *lesbi* woman, one *gay* man, and one waria.

Without multiplying examples further, it is clear that the geographies of the *gay* and *lesbi* worlds can intersect. This is not a function of wealth or urbanity; there appears to be more cogendered sociality in rural areas, where networks are smaller and thus less likely to become distinct. When *gay* men and *lesbi* women do socialize it is on the more restricted terms of the *lesbi* world: not in parks at night but in salons (where *gay* men and *lesbi* women often work together) or at homes. *Lesbi* women have been involved with male-dominated *gay* groups in many different contexts. This was first documented in the article "Welcome Sisters!" by Dédé Oetomo, which appeared in *Gaya Hidup Ceria* in July 1983. The article recounts that the organization Lambda Indonesia was founded by Oetomo and five other men on March 1, 1981, and that in May of that year the women's magazine *Sarinah* interviewed the group. Lambda Indonesia received a large number of letters from women, including *lesbi*-identified women, in the wake of the *Sarinah* reportage.[6] In *lesbi* zines *lesbi* women can speak of a "*gay* and *lesbi* movement" (e.g., *MitraS*, Nov. 1997:8) or judge *lesbi* women to be politically infantile compared to "our *gay* male compatriots, our older siblings" (*Gaya LEStari* 3:9; in *GAYa Nusantara*, July 1994).

To my knowledge no *lesbi* women are unaware of the existence of *gay* men, or vice versa. Mass media as well as *gay* and *lesbi* Indonesians themselves speak frequently of *homoseks* and *homosexualitas* in terms that unite *gay* men and *lesbi* women. In southern Bali, Kari once explained that "*lesbi* means the same as *gay*, it's only the type [*jenis*] that differs." In a meeting between *gay* men and *lesbi* women in Makassar, Karim spoke of *gay* men and *lesbi* women as of "the same fate"—the same term, *senasib*, used by the *lesbi* woman Tuti in Bali and the *gay* man Ardi at September Ceria—and also as having a single emotional state (*seperasaan*) and vision (*kesamaan visi*).

The language of unity that permeates these understandings of cogendered sociality recalls nationalist tropes of unity across difference, as canonized in the nationalist Youth Pledge of 1928: one nation, one people, one language. For *gay* and *lesbi* Indonesians, sociality across a gendered divide can be sustained in terms of a shared "desire for the same." The resonances between a sense of cogendered sociality and national discourse indicate that this assumption of sharedness is not simply due to notions of gender complementarity that can be found in many "traditional" cultures of the archipelago. It also has to do with the dubbing culture by which the *gay* and *lesbi* subject positions took form, and the continuing importance of mass media in *gay* and *lesbi* subjectivities. Concepts of gayness and lesbianness have for the most part translocated to Indonesia together: the *gay* and *lesbi* subject positions originated around the same time through the same process. In Indonesia, homosexuality has implied heterosociality.

GAY AND LESBI ARCHIPELAGOES

The dominant belief in contemporary Indonesia is that sexual and gendered subjectivities are to be clearly embodied. *Gay* and *lesbi* subjectivities, however, pivot around a homosexual desire that is not immediately visible. They do not just have different geographies from *normal* and waria Indonesians; their geographies have different meanings. On many occasions in all my field sites, a *gay* man would invite me and some *gay* friends to his family's home but warn us not to be effeminate because his mother, wife, brother, or neighbors did not know he was *gay*. Warias do not request such discretion because others typically know they are waria. Yet it is possible for twenty *gay* men to gather in the living room of a *gay* friend who lives with his parents and siblings and discuss how difficult it is to tell one's parents one is *gay* while the mother and sisters offer drinks to the guests. "They just think we are all friends," one guest said.

For no *gay* and *lesbi* Indonesian is the *gay* or *lesbi* world their whole world. Despite the many years that homosexuality has appeared in Indonesian mass media, most Indonesians do not have a clear understanding of male or female "desire for the same"; they know primarily of warias. These worlds are not the spatially and culturally contiguous units that constitute the settings for traditional ethnographic work, nor the transnational circuits assumed to constitute "globalization." The notion of a gay or lesbian "community," which suffers from definitional confusion in the West, makes even less sense in Indonesia. There is no Indonesian term for "community"; the closest glosses are probably *masyarakat* (society), *himpunan* (association, as in a "community of scholars"), *kampung* ("village" or "quarter"), and the as-yet rarely used loanword *komunitas*. *Gay* men never use himpunan or kampung to refer to themselves, and they consistently use masyarakat to refer to society in general, as in the phrase "we are not yet accepted by society" (*kita belum diterima oleh masyarakat*). When referring to themselves collectively, *gay* men are most likely to speak of a *gay* "people" using the terms *kaum* or *bangsa*, which usually refer to dispersed social groups like Muslims (*kaum Muslim*) or nationals (*bangsa Indonesia*).

The splintered and marginalized worlds of *gay* and *lesbi* Indonesians do not correspond to "community" in Redfield's (1995) classic sense of the term as a localized, distinctive, homogeneous group, or as used in Western gender and sexuality studies, where it refers to interpersonal relationships, shared values, commercial venues like bookstores and bars, and social service or activist organizations. This lack of institutional support or social recognition means that the *gay* and *lesbi* worlds are seen as incomplete and on some level incapable of sustaining a full life. This is why Howard's *gay* interlocutors in Jakarta could describe the *gay* world as fulfilling but also "a dangerous and disorderly place, where those who stayed too long could be destroyed emotionally, financially, and sometimes spiritually" (1996:178).

Through their everyday interactions, *gay* and *lesbi* Indonesians create the *gay* and *lesbi* worlds over and over again at the center of the *normal* world, not its periphery—in centers of consumer life like malls, centers of domestic life like homes, and, for *gay* men, centers of civic life like parks. When *gay* and *lesbi* Indonesians hang out in a corner of a park or a friend's home, a piece of the globe becomes part of the *gay* and *lesbi* worlds. Subjectivity shapes place. And place shapes subjectivity, as exemplified in how *gay* men (and *lesbi* women) often employ deictics, referring to themselves as "people like this" (*orang begini*), "members of here" (*anggota di sini*), "people like that" (*orang begitu*), or "people like here" (*orang kayak sini*). These are exophoric categorizations; unlike anaphoric pronouns whose reference is to an item in the linguistic chain (as in "Sally gave Joe a shirt. *He* liked *it*"), for these terms the reference point is outside language (as in "*That* table is blue"). Some *gay* men feel they become *gay* only in certain places: when I asked one frequent visitor to Texas, "Would you call yourself *gay* or *homo*?" he answered, "Yeah, words like that are used here often, but in other places [*tempat lain*] it's different."

Such geographical transformations make it possible for a *gay* man in Bali to say that "[*gay* men] might become friends in particular places [*tempat tertentu*] like the tempat ngeber at the town square, but then if we meet in a public place [*tempat umum*] like a movie theater or a supermarket, we pretend like we don't know each other." A town square—usually a prime example of a public place—is here reframed as part of the *gay* world: through the agency of *gay* men, a "tempat umum" becomes a "tempat tertentu."

The relationship between *gay* and *lesbi* Indonesians and place recalls not only how historically "privacy could only be had in public" for gay men in New York (Chauncey 1994), but the more general Western dynamic by which "*public* vs. *private* does not refer to properties inherent in any locale, so much as it specifies two different interpretations . . . of the visibility or accessibility of a particular locale" (Leap 1999:9). The places of the *gay* and *lesbi* worlds are literal "subject positions" shaping the selfhoods of those inhabiting them. In the West the phrase "the gay world" has existed historically and at present, but there is no evidence that this translocated to Indonesia. The mass mediated messages have been too fragmentary; after all, *dunia* is an Arabic "loanword" that in standard Indonesian refers to nonlocalized social phenomena: the world of Islam, the world of fashion. The channels of globalization once again turn out to be dubbed, linked to popular culture and national discourse rather than international gay and lesbian human rights activism or gay and lesbian tourism.

The *gay* and *lesbi* worlds are not ethnolocalized: they seem to be conceptualized as localities connected in a national network that is in turn part of a global network. This queerscape or homoscape (Ingram 1997; Parker 1999) is a complex grid of similitude and difference that references not "tradition" but the nation: while *gay* and *lesbi* persons identify in ethnic terms in many respects, with reference to their *gay*ness or *lesbi*ness they are *Indonesians*. In addition, the *gay* and *lesbi* worlds invoke the transnational despite the near absence of Westerners in them. Such indirect and fragmented linkages to globality recall nothing so much as the dubbing culture relationship between mass media and *gay* and *lesbi* subjectivities. This can be seen in the terms "*gay*" and "*lesbi*" themselves, and in tempat ngeber names like Texas, *Kalifor, Paris, Brasil*, and Pattaya in Surabaya, *Manhattan* in Solo, LA and *Paris* in Yogyakarta, or Texas in Mataram on the island of Lombok (which probably indexes both the West's and Surabaya's Texas). Global imaginings are not unique to tempat ngebers named after non-Indonesian sites, but they provide clear examples of them. When *gay* men in Texas speak of being a "person of here" or "from Texas" (*dari* Texas), they reference a "here" that is simultaneously a "there," a "here" caught up in imagined communities both national and global. A commonality between *gay* and *lesbi* Indonesians is that in general, what fascination the gay and lesbian West holds for them stems from a perception that it is *familiar*, not exotic. Feminist geographers have long noted a widespread "association between the feminine and the local" (Massey 1994:9); inhabitants of the *lesbi* world challenge this association as they think of themselves in national and transnational terms. *Gay* men may imagine that the Texas in the United States is more opened than Texas in Surabaya, or *lesbi* women may imagine that discos with lesbian patrons are ubiquitous in Europe, but these are seen as distinctions of degree, not kind.

There is a very specific grid of similitude and difference at work: it is as if the *gay* and *lesbi* worlds are islands in a national *gay* and *lesbi* archipelago, and on another level that archipelago is one island in a global archipelago of homosexuality. This archipelago metaphor does not originate in "tradition": as discussed in chapter 7, since 1957 state ideology has explicitly proclaimed Indonesia a nation organized by the archipelago concept (*wawasan nusantara*). *Gay* and *lesbi* Indonesians dub the archipelago concept in conceptualizing their worlds as isolated places linked into constellations or networks of affiliation. This is an implicit blurring of domains: I have never heard a *gay* man or *lesbi* woman refer to a tempat ngeber or café as an island, yet it appears that the various elements of their *gay* worlds are construed implicitly as islands in a *gay* and *lesbi* archipelago.

How can such a largely unspoken leakage from one cultural domain (nation) to another (sexuality) take place in Indonesia, the "East Indies"? To answer this question it is productive to turn to work on the "West Indies," the Caribbean, where the concept of cultural transformation is a familiar theme. Mintz and Price's (1976) classic study of African American culture responds to an intellectual milieu in which two unsatisfactory interpretations of African American culture predominated: (1) due to the tremendous dislocations and oppressions of the slave trade, African American culture had originated solely in the New World and there was nothing particularly "African" about it, and (2) scholarship could uncover "retentions and survivals" from Africa, which made African American culture "African." These two interpretations participate in the same Western conceptualization of similitude and difference that, as noted in chapter 1, inform the reductionisms of "Gay Planet" versus "McGay." Mintz and Price, drawing from Herskovits, developed the idea of a "cultural grammar" that could be shared even if surface manifestations differed, just as related but mutually unintelligible languages can share grammatical features: "though 'witchcraft' may figure importantly in the social life of one group and be absent from that of its neighbor, both peoples may still subscribe to the widely held African principle that social conflict can produce illness or misfortune" (10).

The influence of the archipelago concept on the *gay* and *lesbi* worlds is mostly covert. These worlds are not "mapped" as archipelagoes because the idea of culture as cognitive map is an artifact of the researcher's position as outsider: "it is the analogy which occurs to an outsider who has to find his way around in a foreign landscape and who compensates for his lack of practical mastery . . . by the use of a model of all possible routes" (Bourdieu 1977:2). The tactical way in which the *gay* and *lesbi* worlds are built up through practice—innumerable daily acts of hanging out, visiting a salon, going to a disco, watching television at a friend's kos—means they are experienced processually. The impact of the state's archipelago concept can be seen in the conceptualization of the *gay* and *lesbi* worlds as distributed networks of places: homes, shopping malls, salons, and tempat ngebers like Texas or Kalifor (fig. 5-2) are like islands in an archipelago.

The state's archipelago concept has as its central goal the creation of unity from ethnolocalized diversity. State rhetoric often lexicalizes this ideal through terms based on "one" (*satu*), as in the phrase "unity and integrity" (*persatuan dan kesatuan*) or the verbal form *(me)nyatu* (unify). This shapes how the *gay* and *lesbi* worlds have *never* to date been ethnolocalized—there has never been a specifically Javanese or Sundanese or Makassarese tempat ngeber or salon (or slang or zine). There is no evidence for the idea that, say, two tempat ngebers in Surabaya—Texas and Kalifor—might be for Javanese and Balinese persons, respectively. One finds instead commentary like that of the *gay* man from Surabaya who explained his love of tempat ngebers as follows: "It's always a sense of being close, caring, it's like that, because although there are some different characteristics . . . personal matters, we'll meet in a town square and feel 'oh, we're already close.' So we quickly unify [*menyatu*]—although we're Bugis, we're Javanese, still we quickly unify." *Lesbi* women articulate subjectivities that presume being tomboi or cewek is to participate in a network of affiliation that is not ethnolocalized but both national and transnational. Indeed, given that terms like "tomboy" are used worldwide while *waria* is understood as a specifically Indonesian concept, *lesbi* women may be *more* imbricated with global discourses of gender and sexuality than *gay* men.

Figure 5–2. "Kalifornia," a bridge in downtown Surabaya. *GAYa Nusantara* 29 (May 1994:28).

My hypothesis is that *gay* and *lesbi* Indonesians draw cultural logics from both the archipelagic spatial metaphor of the state and its "family principle." This conjunction of nation and sexuality shapes the desire to marry "heterosexually," the sense that *gay* and *lesbi* are nationwide subjectivities (that is, found throughout the archipelago, though not necessarily everywhere in the archipelago), and the sense that these subjectivities nonetheless do not really belong. The archipelago concept represents a powerfully institutionalized, nonethnolocalized rubric for conceptualizing "desire for the same" in terms of unity.

The *gay* and *lesbi* worlds are isomorphic with Indonesia. They stretch "from Sabang to Merauke," as Ardi put it during September Ceria—though they do not cover every point in between, as a continental rather than archipelago imaginary would imply. One *gay* man in Makassar tried to describe what being "opened" meant by saying "openness is between our groups" (*keterbukaan di antara kalangan kita*). In speaking of openness as between (*di antara*) rather than within (*di dalam*) "our groups," he evoked a geography in which the *gay* and *lesbi* worlds exist as a distributed network of realms; that is, as an archipelago.

The *gay* and *lesbi* worlds cannot be explained as products of a top-down globalization where a "Gay International" imposes homosexual identities on the non-Western Other. They are linked but distinct geographies of "desire for the same." State hegemony shapes *gay* and *lesbi* sub-

Figure 5–3. Intersecting global, national, and local discourses; the *GAYa Dewata* symbol (original in red).

jectivities, yet *gay* and *lesbi* Indonesians rework that hegemony in unexpected ways. This is simultaneously a local archipelago of tactically created places in which *gay* men and *lesbi* women live their sexual subjectivities, a national archipelago of cities and rural sites where the *gay* and *lesbi* worlds are known to exist, and a global archipelago where *gay* and *lesbi* Indonesia is like an island alongside Holland, Australia, Thailand, and the United States. To be *"gay"* in *"Texas"* is not just local.

Just like a person fluent in English may be unable to explain the English grammar they use every time they speak, persons cannot always comment directly on the assumptions that shape their consciousness and social relations. Yet sometimes the influence of national discourse is explicit, as in the *"gay* identity card" story from chapter 1, or in statements like "When I was still with my former lover I never went to Texas or any other places. . . . It was only afterward that I entered the 'Republic' [*Republik*]." An explicit linkage also appears in the name GAYa Nusantara, which means both "archipelago style" and *"gay* archipelago," and the fact that groups of *gay* men and *lesbi* women across the archipelago name their groups with terms incorporating *GAYa*. The symbol for the group GAYa Dewata in Bali, which engages in some HIV prevention work (fig. 5-3), is an AIDS ribbon inverted and turned around so that it looks like a ceremonial Balinese male headdress. This image intertwines discourses of local, national, and international provenance with AIDS discourse and the archipelago concept's requirement that every ethnolocalized region have a distinct character.

To analyze how state discourse shapes something as ostensibly intimate as sexuality, it is necessary to read between the lines of participant observation and divine cultural logics that may not be on the lips of one's interlocutors. Yet situations arise in which these logics—the idea of the *gay* world, for instance—shine forth, if only in an offhand remark that otherwise passes unnoticed. Doel, a *gay* man from Surabaya, had flown to Makassar in July 2002 to meet with a *gay* organization. One afternoon we accompanied a group of about thirty *gay* men to volleyball practice in a big field near the Azhar mosque. Ten yards away another group of men were playing volleyball. Doel was sitting next to me watching our *gay* friends play when he suddenly sat up and exclaimed: "Those guys over there are speaking Javanese!" Karim, sitting nearby, said, "Yes, they're Javanese men who work in the market." Then he added jokingly, "Doel, you should go hang out with them. You're Javanese, after all!"

I think most *gay* and *lesbi* Indonesians would understand why Doel just turned to us and smiled: "Here is my world [*di sini dunia saya*]."

CHAPTER SIX

Practices of Self, Tests of Faith

NATIONAL STYLE

As noted in the last chapter, the *gay* or *lesbi* worlds are "tactical" and cannot lay claim to the physical spaces of *normal* society. As a result, embodied practices shoulder the burden of constituting the "islands" of *gay* and *lesbi* lives. Through practice there is more to being *gay* or *lesbi* than same-gender sex: it is a *style* of life. To speak of style is tricky because in the West nonheterosexual sexualities are delegitimated as "lifestyles." Interpreted on its own terms, however, the notion of style proves useful for thinking through the dynamics of *gay* and *lesbi* subjectivities. It has been important in the archipelago since colonial times and is salient to *gay* and *lesbi* Indonesians.

The term *gaya* (style, fashion) has already appeared in the name GAYa Nusantara (archipelago style, Indonesia style) and the groups who link themselves to this national network by appending an ethnolocalized term to *GAYa*. *Gaya* also crops up in the everyday speech of *gay* and *lesbi* Indonesians when talking about everything from a modern style (*gaya moderen*) to styles of hanging out (*gaya kumpul*), styles of having a same-gender partner (*gaya pacaran*), and masculine and feminine styles of acting and dressing (*gaya lelaki, gaya perempuan*).

Gaya and its near-synonym *cara* have been popular terms in the archipelago more broadly. A concern with style was central to how Indies "natives" construed themselves as distinct from Dutch colonists (Pemberton 1994:23, 65–66). The idea that style can distinguish self from Other persists in the postcolonial concept of national style, which in distinction to ethnolocalized "tradition" is modern, animated by consumerism, and oriented around the figure of the middle-class family. The concept of style has long worked to establish social boundaries: it is a performative rather than status-based logic of belonging.[1]

Western social theorists have found style a useful concept as well. The mid-twentieth-century "culture and personality" school of anthropological theory developed the notion of culture as a configuration of beliefs and practices that "is [no] more mystic or difficult to understand than, for example, the development of an art style" (Benedict 1932:26, cited in Patterson 2001:79). In literary theory, Hayden White has defined narrative style as "the modality of the movement from a representation of some original state of affairs to some subsequent state" (1978:96). This notion of style as difference-across-time echoes the notion of difference-across-space developed in the work of Birmingham School theorists like Dick Hebdige, for whom style indexes signifying practices that mark difference within cultures—a middle "subcultural" ground between individual difference and difference between cultures as a whole. Building on the work of Hebdige (1979) and Judith Butler (1990), Ferguson has advanced the notion of "cultural style" in terms of "practices that signify differences between social categories" (1999:95).

This chapter examines what it means to be *gay* or *lesbi* "archipelago style," *gaya nusantara*. It is concerned with the nonsexual practices by which Indonesians sustain a sense of being *gay* or *lesbi*. I thus examine style in terms of performativity, a concept long linked to gender and sexuality (Butler 1990, 1993; Goffman 1971; Kessler and McKenna 1985). There is something Ferguson and Hebdige's analyses of style share with those of Benedict, Butler, Pemberton, White, and others: across continents, disciplines, and theoretical traditions, *style is assumed to be productive of difference*. Understanding *gay* and *lesbi* subjectivities—and the character of life in an already globalized world—requires rethinking the grid of similitude and difference that "style" mediates. Can similitude be more than a means to difference? This is the question posed by "archipelago style"—a style that, paradoxically from the standpoint of continental thinking, deploys difference in the service of similitude.

The Performed *Lesbi* Self

The Cewek/Tomboi Boundary

A longstanding and robust conclusion of feminist scholarship has been that "very commonly the same axes that divide and distinguish male from female (and indeed rank male over female) also crosscut the gender categories, producing internal distinctions and gradations within them" (Ortner and Whitehead 1981:9). On some level this is not surprising: the masculine-feminine binarism forms the structuring principle for heterosexualities worldwide, and many female and male homosexualities around the world have been shaped by this dominant framework. Yet the internal genderings of the *gay* and *lesbi* subject positions diverge.

One of the most consequential distinctions between the *gay* and *lesbi* subject positions concerns masculinity and femininity. The distinction is not an organizing principle for *gay* subjectivities; some *gay* men prefer masculine men *(laki-laki yang kebapakan)*, but this is seen to be a matter of personal taste and does not denote a category of person. In contrast, for most *lesbi* women the *lesbi* subject position cannot be occupied in the abstract. A sharp division between feminine and masculine structures selfhood, sexual relationships, and sociality: the norm is that sexual relationships take place between masculine and feminine *lesbi* women, not between two masculine or two feminine *lesbi* women.[2] Some *lesbi* women (primarily but not solely upper class) do not structure their desires around this gendered divide, but it is predominant. This heterogenderal (Faderman 1992) character of *lesbi* subjectivity and desire might seem to be imported, since butch-femme distinctions often play an important role in lesbian communities in the West and elsewhere (Halberstam 1998; Kennedy and Davis 1993; S. Wieringa 1999a), without a clear parallel in gay men's sexual norms. However, when *gay* took form in (not "globalized to") Indonesia, it did so in the context of the well-known waria subject position. The *gay* subject position thus came to structure "desire for the same" within the category of masculinity. *Gay* men and warias are often friends, but it is considered highly abnormal for them to have sex with each other. Crucially, however, no female analogue to waria existed at the time that *lesbi* took shape in Indonesia: masculine women and female-to-male transgenders certainly existed but were not publicly known as a category of person, as warias were. As a result, the *lesbi* subject position includes not only women attracted to women (of masculine or feminine gendering) but also tombois, persons born with women's bodies who feel themselves to have the soul of a man and strive to be considered social men.

The consequences of this are manifold. The sense that tomboi and *lesbi* might be separate subject positions is complicated by the fact that whereas *gay* men and warias rarely have sexual relationships, tombois and ceweks are ideal sexual partners. Additionally, like *gay* and *lesbi* (but unlike *waria*), tomboi is understood to be a "foreign" concept that has been Indonesianized. Tomboi does not appear in a 1976 Indonesian dictionary (*lesbian* does, but *gay* is absent [Poerwadarminta 1976:592]); by 1991, however, it appears with the definition "an active girl, full of adventuring like a boy." That tomboi was Indonesianized by this point is indicated by the fact that the term could already occur with the circumfix *ke-an* to form the abstract noun *ketomboian,* "tomboi matters" (Salim and Salim 1991:1630). These common Indonesian uses of *tomboi,* however, do not mark a minoritized sexual subject position but indicate what is understood to be a temporary and benign characteristic of young girls.[3] The use of the term *tomboi* to label an adult sexual subject position builds from this understanding in a manner that has no parallel for the terms *waria, gay,* or *lesbi.* Tomboi subjectivity thus appears to be dubbed with relation both to the West and to Indonesian popular culture.

The most important consequence of this dual dubbing is that there is active debate among tombois as to whether they are a subcategory of *lesbi* or a separate transgendered subject position analogous to waria. As a Balinese *lesbi* woman phrased it: "not all tombois are *lesbi,* and not all *lesbi* women are tomboi." In chapter 5 I described the formation of an organization in northern Bali with three leaders—one *lesbi*, one *gay*, and one waria. The idea of a fourth, tomboi leader seems not to have occurred, reflecting how tombois are seen as a kind of *lesbi* woman whereas waria is a distinct subject position. While warias would never list themselves in the personals section of a *gay* zine, tombois have listed themselves in *lesbi* zines. For instance, in the April 1998 issue of *MitraS*, "Ray," twenty years old, listed herself as "L" (*lesbi*) but then said "I'm a tomboy, with fair skin and medium build." In the February 1998 issue, "Wiewid Thomboy," twenty-five years old, entered a personal ad looking for a woman who "is intimate and warm." In the first of a series of pivotal encounters with mass media in *Menguak Duniaku*, the tomboi protagonist Hen reads about the first waria sex change operation (performed on a waria named Vivian): "in the silence of the night, I prayed to God that he would give the reverse [*sebaliknya*] of what he gave Vivian to me. . . . I wanted to tell my mother, my father, that I was the same as Vivian" (Prawirakusumah and Ramadhan 1988:51).

The "desire for the same" that characterizes *gay* subjectivity is thus more fractured for *lesbi* women. The border between *lesbi* and tomboi is so fraught that it can be difficult to know if a particular woman thinks of herself as homosexual or transgendered—as *lesbi*, tomboi, or both. As Rita, a tomboi originally from Central Java but now living in Surabaya, put it, "I don't feel like a woman, I don't feel like a man. And most of my *lesbi* friends feel this way." Blackwood (1999) describes how she fell in love with what she thought was a *lesbi* woman in South Sumatra; only after a period of time did she realize that Dayan, her tomboi lover, thought of himself as male. It would be almost impossible for someone to mistake a waria for a *gay* man in such a way; warias tell of being mistaken not for a *gay* man, but for a woman.

Thus, while being tomboi can be framed as a form of female masculinity (as when a tomboi states, "Well, I wouldn't want to be a man. Not that I could with this body" [Graham 2001:1]), it is often linked to transgenderism. This is certainly Hen's understanding in *Menguak Duniaku*; when reading about the 1981 "wedding" of Jossie and Bonnie (see chapter 2), Hen is surprised that Bonnie, a cewek who "was beforehand called *normal* and always paired up with a boy," did not want Jossie, a tomboi who had been called "banci" as a child, to have a sex change operation (Prawirakusumah and Ramadhan 1988:306). Later he tells a cewek lover: "I'm not a lesbian [*lesbian*] because I play the part of a man [*berperan sebagai seorang laki-laki*] when I'm with women. You're the one who's better called a lesbian" (265).

In this understanding a masculine "style" precludes considering oneself as a woman, an attitude I have encountered in my own fieldwork: when I once asked Sukma if any of his hunter friends felt they were men, he replied, "You don't have to speak about my friends, I myself feel that way." While female-to-male sex change operations are rare in Indonesia (I do not know of any cases), some tombois express an interest in having them. Regardless of their views on this issue, however, all tombois to my knowledge see themselves as in some sense possessing a man's soul in a woman's body. This is a parallel between tombois and warias, whose possession of women's souls is often understood to produce both the performance of femininity and the desire for men.

The question of whether tombois' performance of masculinity produces a desire for women, or vice versa, has been a key point of discussion in the literature on *lesbi* women. The former causality seems to better fit the ethnographic data: "the dominance of the normative model of gender and heterosexuality persuades tombois to construct their actions and desire for women on the model of masculinity . . . having already established a masculine gender . . . [tombois lay] claim to a sexual desire for women" (Blackwood 1999:189,190). As for warias, gender nonconformity may come not only chronologically but causally before a desire for women in tomboi lives. Yet paralleling some warias' claim that their desire for men motivates nonnormative gendering, some tombois view their desire for women as key to their subjectivities: "You don't understand what I mean by saying I have the soul of a man [*berjiwa laki-laki*]. Not because of my strength, bravery, or firmness, but because the object of my love [*obyek cintaku*] is a woman" (Prawirakusumah and Ramadhan 1988:280).

Regardless of how they see the origination of their subjectivities, tombois remain linked to national culture. For instance, the ideal life course for most tombois—one they know is impossible to obtain—is to build a middle-class household along the lines figured in national discourse: "I've decided to live as a man, and I long to create a home [*rumah tangga*], have a wife and some children, even if they're children I take from an orphanage. Don't they understand that God didn't just make men and women, but also people like me, like [the waria] Umi Yasumi?" (Prawirakusumah and Ramadhan 1988:201–202).

Ceweks and tombois tend to have distinct life courses that recall differences between the *gay* and waria subject positions: tombois (like warias) tend to exhibit gender nonconformity as children, whereas ceweks (like *gay* men) tend not to see themselves as such until their late teens or early twenties and do not necessarily deviate from gender norms. Nonetheless, movement across the cewek/tomboi boundary does occasionally happen.

Ati, a tomboi in Makassar, referred to this as "cewek can run to hunter [tomboi]" (*lines bisa lari ke hunter*); his tomboi friend Sukma even termed this "going to another area" (*ke luar daerah*). Ati and Sukma, like most *lesbi* women I encountered during my fieldwork, felt that tombois could not become ceweks. It may be that that the embodiment of tomboi subjectivity, as well as the early age at which most tombois begin to occupy that subject position, make leaving that "style" particularly difficult.

Comparative questions are raised by the fact that in much of Southeast Asia (Indonesia, Malaysia, the Philippines, Thailand, etc.) there are women with same-sex desires who name themselves with a term dubbing in some fashion the English term "tomboy" (e.g., Sinnott 2004). This stands in sharp distinction to male-to-female transvestites, the terms for whom are country-specific (*waria* in Indonesia, *mak nyah* and *pondan* in Malaysia, *bakla* and *bantut* in the Philippines, *kathoey* in Thailand, and so on). Even though "tomboys" rarely know there are similar persons in neighboring countries, they share many characteristics. Is *tomboy* a nascent translocal female-to-male transgendered subjectivity, more caught up in globalizing networks of identification than male-to-female transgendered subjectivities like waria and kathoey?

Being Cewek, Being Tomboi

From my own fieldwork and that of other scholars, it is clear that in their dress, mannerisms, and speech, ceweks are virtually indistinguishable from *normal* women: they appear as "authentic women" (*asli wanita*). A typical cewek has "shoulder-length, permed hair, wears makeup and lipstick and has long fingernails" (Blackwood 1999:188). They "could always pass as 'normal' women . . . [they] dressed in an exaggeratedly feminine fashion, in dresses with ribbons and frills. They always wore heavy makeup and high heels. Some of them had jobs as secretaries or were selling cosmetics. Others did sex work" (S. Wieringa 1999a:217). In the words of one tomboi, a cewek is "a woman who feels like a woman, but she does not like men; she likes females who have the style of men" (Graham 2001:fn9). As a result, "there are no definite signs or 'secret handshakes' [to identify ceweks] . . . except for [*gay* language] expressions for lesbian like '*Lisa Bonet/Lisbon*'"(A. Murray 1999:146).

The style of being cewek is not typically performed in terms of dress or bodily comportment, but at the level of desire. Throughout Indonesia and much of Southeast Asia, there is an expectation that gender presentation will reflect sexual desire, in line with the broader pattern that "bodily behaviors—one's posture and demeanor, the tone of one's voice—are constantly attended to and read as signs of inner moral states" (S. Errington 1990:17). As a result, ceweks (and masculine *gay* men) present a *greater* challenge to dominant sex/gender regimes in Indonesia than tombois (and warias): their "desire for the same" transgresses the assumption that sexuality operates across a gendered divide. Ceweks "flaunt femininity and yet rebel against proscriptions usually applied to women" (Graham 2001:fn9). This presents a challenge to theories of gender performativity, since "for much gender theory, ambiguity has become that which permits and even necessitates the formation of gender difference" (Morris 1995:570).

Just as you cannot be waria if you are born with a vagina, you cannot be tomboi if you are born with a penis. Tombois across Indonesia share the experience of movement away from normative femininity, and tombois often acknowledge that in the end their given nature (*kodrat*) is that of a woman: this is one of many ways that the tomboi subject position mirrors the waria subject position. These might appear to be gendered analogues, as the Western language of male-to-female (MTF) versus female-to-male (FTM) transgenderism implies. Warias and tombois occasionally talk about how they share the conditions of (1) having the soul of one gender trapped in the body of another and (2) cross-dressing, and tombois are sometimes called "banci" or "female banci" by *normal* Indonesians. Yet *waria* and *tomboi* are not seen as parallel in the way *gay* and *lesbi* are. This is because the waria subject position is part of public culture to a vastly greater degree than the tomboi subject position: for most Indonesians the word *tomboi* still refers to girls who do things boys are expected to do, like climbing trees.

The performativity of tomboi subjectivity typically begins in childhood and focuses on boyish clothing, haircuts, and play activities (tombois frequently emphasize how they never liked dolls). In these respects, the trajectory of tomboi subjectivity appears the inverse of waria subjectivity, but with the crucial difference that the tomboi subject position is virtually unknown. While gender-nonconforming men can be quickly slotted into the category *waria*, gender-nonconforming women can play off the ambiguity between the standard Indonesian term *tomboi* and the less-known transgendered meaning of *tomboi*.[4] This is why Sukma was rarely bothered on the streets of Makassar, even at night: "They might think I'm a tomboi woman, but they don't know I'm a hunter."

Some tombois say they became tomboi because their parents dressed them like boys. One tomboi interlocutor recalled, "I've been masculine since I was little. All of the children were girls, so my father dressed me in men's clothes when I was small" (see also Graham 2001:21). Others say they became tomboi after being seduced by a cewek (*never* by a tomboi). Most tombois claim that they dressed and acted like males before they started desiring women—often while children. Yet some of my tomboi interlocutors also report desiring women from a young age, as does the character Hen in *Menguak Duniaku*: "When I was in third grade, everyone called me banci. . . . I understood why each and every girl that I approached—that I liked—retreated from me, pointing at me and shouting 'You banci! You banci!'" (Prawirakusumah and Ramadhan 1988:263). The dominant understanding of tomboi subjectivity, however, is that one is created tomboi by God, and being tomboi is therefore one's fate; this is linked to having the soul (*jiwa*) of a man.

As adults, tombois tend to dress as men twenty-four hours a day and engage in stereotypically male activities. Taking care of and protecting a cewek partner is typically seen as important to being tomboi: tombois say they are brave (*berani*) and responsible (*tanggung jawab*) toward their partners. The performance of tomboi "style" typically involves what one tomboi focus group called "identifying themselves with men and a rough lifestyle" (*gaya hidup yang keras*); this includes wearing men's clothing and engaging in male activities like smoking, drinking, and riding a motorcycle alone (Blackwood 1999; Prawirakusumah and Ramadhan 1988:153).Tomboi pastimes include playing dominoes or cards. Unless they speak, some tombois are mistaken for men. Quick to laughter—punctuated with short, sharp gestures and a burst of smoke from his ubiquitous cigarette—one tomboi interlocutor in Surabaya always wore blue jeans and a button-down shirt, keeping his dark hair in a short boyish cut. After he visited me one day, my landlady remarked, "I wonder why that man uses a woman's name."

As noted earlier, most tombois are relatively able to move about unaccompanied at night: this relative access to public space is a common feature of tomboi "style." Particularly in Bali but sometimes in Jakarta and other parts of Indonesia, tombois occasionally visit tempat ngebers, building friendships with other tombois as well as *gay* men and warias. Tombois have even been reputed to go to female and waria sex workers. A waria in southern Bali told the story of a person who "came into the park on a motorbike, sitting like a man and looking just like a man. We kissed for a long time and then I went to open the person's pants and the person said 'no,' and I suddenly realized it was a woman."

The relative mobility of tombois made it possible for me to accompany Rita on a two-day trip to a *kejawen* (Javanese mysticism) pilgrimage shrine located high on the slopes of a volcano several hours south of Surabaya. A young woman with long hair and stylish clothes took a seat directly ahead of us on the bus after our departure from Surabaya; Rita was soon exchanging small talk with her as we careened down the narrow highway. When the young woman disembarked, she gave Rita her phone number. As the bus pulled back onto the highway, Rita was visibly agitated. "Do you think she was 'sick'? She might have been. But I suspect she thought I was a man, not a woman." I asked, "Does it offend you when people mistake you for a man?" Rita replied, "No, I'm not offended if people mistake me for a man, only if they point me out and make fun of me."

Once at the shrine Rita and I stayed in separate rooms with Dadang, a man who rented his home out to pilgrims; our traveling together elicited none of the stares or remarks that I have experienced when walking with female Indonesian friends. The evening after our arrival, Dadang's wife and daughters stayed back in the kitchen preparing dinner as the men of the house—and Rita—smoked, drank whiskey, and traded news of the world. However, when the meal was finished Rita alone stood up to help the women take dirty dishes back to the kitchen. Rita was frequently mistaken for a man. Yet he used a woman's name; when asked about his appearance, Rita replied he was a woman and preferred to dress the way he did.

Despite the advantages of mobility, to the degree tombois become visible they encounter discrimination. Tombois receive far more social disapproval than ceweks, not for their sexual orientation so much as their gender transgression. It is difficult for tombois to obtain employment (S. Wieringa 1999a). The purpose of Rita's pilgrimage was to pray for a steady job: living in Surabaya as an immigrant from another province without relatives nearby, and with the additional burden of looking decidedly unfeminine, he was in dire financial straits, surviving on odd jobs. When I first met Rita he was staying at the home of a *normal* woman he had met while working in a salon washing people's hair. Rita had little privacy at the home, and to make matters worse he feared the host had figured out Rita was a tomboi. Tombois face an additional difficulty in that they are more likely than ceweks to be estranged from their families of origin (as in Rita's case), depriving them of what for most Indonesians is the most important source of financial security. One *lesbi* zine summed up the image of tombois: "a comedic form that sickens and nauseates; that is our people in the eyes of the general public" (*GAYa LEStari* Oct./Dec. 1993:4).

While tombois do not normatively have sex with each other, the performance of tomboi subjectivity often includes a masculinized sociality between tombois—taunting, joking, and discussing their relationships with ceweks (Blackwood 1999:188–189). I once encountered Ati and Sukma in a mixed group of tombois, *gay* men, and warias in Makassar as they were joking with each other as to who had the bigger penis: Ati insisted that his was long and thin, and Sukma countered that his was short and fat. Then an older *gay* man came into the room with drinks and his own joke: "I brought coffee for Ati and Sukma, because I know men prefer coffee."

The Performed *Gay* Self

Ngondhek

Gay men new to the *gay* world often ask: how can you tell who is *gay*? In response to this question *gay* men with more experience speak not about sexual practices but ways of acting, dressing, and talking—the performativity of *gay* subjectivity.

Some *gay* men see themselves as consistently feminine or consistently masculine and may prefer sexual relationships with a man who has the opposite gendering, but it is not considered abnormal for two feminine or two masculine *gay* men to have sex with each other.[5] Becoming *gay* thus does not involve the all-important decision between masculine or feminine that characterizes the life courses of most *lesbi* women. However, to "open oneself" (*membuka diri*) to the *gay* world usually means not only socializing in certain places but also effeminacy, known in Surabaya and some other parts of *gay* Indonesia as *ngondhek*.[6] Opposed to masculinity (*macho, maskulin, kebapakan* [derived from *bapak,* "father"], or *laki-laki asli* [authentic man]), ngondhek is a male body's performing of feminine gender at a slight remove. It is the normative but not essential "style" of *gay* subjectivity.

Ngondhek is manifested above all in practices of bodily comportment seen as feminine in contemporary Indonesia: this includes things like florid hand gestures, a lilting walk, or sitting with one's knees tightly together. As elsewhere in Southeast Asia and beyond, these conceptions of femininity originate in colonial (often Victorian era) norms that postcolonial states take up and propagate as "tradition" (cf. Jackson 2003, Chatterjee 1993:116–157). To my knowledge warias never refer to each other as ngondhek or lacking in ngondhek, nor do others refer to warias as ngondhek. Ngondhek differs from most core practices of waria subjectivity in that it is made up of actions—gesture, language, clothing—that can be quickly set aside; it is not strongly linked to bodily modification. A few *gay* men wear light foundation makeup on their faces, tweeze their eyebrows, paint their fingernails, or wear an earring, but even *gay* men seen as particularly ngondhek may have no ongoing bodily modification of this kind. Clothing is also an unreliable marker of ngondhek. *Gay* men say they dress more neatly (*rapi*) than *normal* men; this can include button-up shirts with collars, or a belt whose end hangs down like an iconic penis. Some also wear men's clothing with feminine accents, like long, flowing sleeves. But not all *gay* men dress in such a manner, and their dress overall is a male "style"—they are not warias who dress "like women."

Ngondhek is also practiced though gender play. Occurring anywhere in the *gay* world, from tempat ngebers to koses, this includes things like men teasing each other about really being waria, *lesbi*, or simply a woman. Some *gay* men joke about being "a man above the belt, but a woman below the belt," or vice versa; one night at Texas a *gay* man humorously explained, "My whole body is man except for here [making a circle with his hands around his crotch]: here I'm locally a woman (*lokal perempuan*)." One man will come up to another and reach for his breasts in jest, exclaiming "it's a waria!" to which the man being accosted will respond in mock seriousness "*asli lho!*" ("authentic, of course!"). In such joking the undercurrent is that masculinity and femininity are contextual. Some *gay* men (and warias) suffer from (or engage in) *latah*, a "culture-bound syndrome" usually associated with women that results in sufferers blurting out obscene words or mimicking those around them when startled. For some *gay* men, latah is a source of amusement and is seen in positive terms (*hal yang positif*).

The ultimate expression of ngondhek is to wear women's clothes and makeup; *gay* men often refer to this as *déndong* (a *gay* language variant of *dandan* ["put on makeup" or "groom oneself"]). Warias also use the term *déndong*, but for most *gay* men déndong holds no potential to blur the line between *gay* and waria. This is because *gay* men déndong in circumscribed contexts of performance internal to the *gay* world like drag shows. They do not déndong in the *normal* world or a more public node of the *gay* world like a tempat ngeber or shopping mall; above all, they do not déndong to attract sexual partners. One *gay* man in Bali explained that "What surprises me is that when I'm dressed up as a woman, I don't want to be bothered by men. For instance, if I'm dressed up and a man approaches me, I don't like it. I feel like I'm being insulted and disrespected." For *gay* men, déndong is not typically associated with sexual desire because they understand themselves as "desiring the same"; the kind of men who would respond to déndong (as opposed to the subtle markers of ngondhek) are men interested in sex with warias, not with other men. Déndong marks the outer limit of ngondhek.

Most *gay* men have conflicted views on male effeminacy. It plays an important role in *gay* desire because it is a key way to signal to *gay* men and especially to *normal* men that one is interested in sex. It is associated with being *gay*, helping to "tactically" constitute sites of the *gay* world. Yet ngondhek is often denigrated. Most *gay* men do not find effeminate men attractive; effeminacy weakens their "desire for the same." *Gay* men will criticize each other for being too ngondhek and usually emphasize they are attracted to men who are "macho." This is another point of similarity with effeminacy in Western gay male cultures, where effeminacy, camp, and drag are both valorized and disavowed in line with a broader devaluing of women.

Most *gay* men believe that they can display or hide their ngondhek practices with a fair degree of control. In tempat ngebers and other sites of the *gay* world, *gay* men often switch between effeminate and masculine mannerisms. During a discussion between a group of *gay* men in Makassar, one man asked what one should do if people made negative comments at the mall because one was effeminate. Other men responded that one should just ignore such slights, but then the man asked further: "What if I'm effeminate on purpose? For instance, if a cute man walks by?"

The way in which ngondhek skirts the boundary between visibility and invisibility has consequences for *gay* sociality. Most *gay* men believe that ngondhek practices are a sign of *gay*ness that allows them to identify many, but not all, *gay* men. One *gay* man in Surabaya talked about how he could tell who was *gay* "from their style [*gaya*], their way of walking, talking, things like that." At Surabaya's Texas, Anto said that "I am masculine, but when I'm here at Texas I become feminine so I won't be such an object of desire, since I know all these people already and don't want to have sex with any of them." Anto also talked about the signs of *gay* men, emphasizing speaking "style" (*gaya ucapan*) and a feminine presentation. But he noted emphatically that "only 50 percent of the men are like that. There are also those who are masculine." Another man, who was active in a *gay* organization and also worked part-time as a clerk, was concerned that:

> At my work I'm very afraid that people will find out I'm *gay*. I'm worried that I'll be gossiped about, or that a ngondhek man will telephone for me at the office . . . so I have to be smart about the way I hold myself, about the way I express myself. Fortunately, I've been able to do that. My life is 50–50. If I'm with a *gay* group, sometimes I have to be ngondhek. And I really like that; I like being able to express myself like that. But in the hetero life I have to guard myself. Sometimes I can get away with being ngondhek a little bit; after all being hetero is not authentic for me. I think that I'm living in two worlds. . . . My shrieking and carrying on is really an expression from my *gay*ness [*ekspresi dari kegayan saya sendiri*]. If I was a real man [*laki asli*] it's not possible that I would shriek like that.

During my fieldwork such joking was extended to myself. I would be described as ngondhek when purposively acting in ways seen as effeminate, but *gay* men also commented that I was sometimes ngondhek due to being "carried along by the environment" (*terbawa lingkungan*), as was often the case for them as well. On the other hand, it is well known in the *gay* world that there are *gay* men (and *normal* men interested in sex with men) who are not effeminate. Such men are often idealized sexual partners, but identifying them can be difficult, particularly outside the *gay* world. One *gay* man in Surabaya recounted how he seduced a former boyfriend:

I met him at the mosque. I was actually interested in his younger brother; he was very cute and I thought "he might be like me," judging from the way he held himself when he prayed and walked around. So I went up to him and talked to him, and eventually got invited to his house. But when I went to his house it was his other brother who opened the door! He introduced himself and we talked for a while and became friends. He was very handsome and masculine, so I thought to myself, "He's a real man, he can't possibly be homo." We started spending lots of time together . . . eventually we went to a drumming competition one night, and it was the first of two days of the competition, so he told me, "Don't go home; just stay with me tonight at my grandmother's house which is near here." So we went there and slept together in one bed. I still didn't have any idea, I just couldn't believe he would be interested in men. We were in bed and he said, "Hey, there's no pillow here, can I use you as a pillow?" I said "yes," and he threw his leg over me. Oh my! My heart started pounding and racing; it felt like it'd jumped into my throat. I just sat there . . . then he said, "Hey there's no blanket here, can I use you as a blanket?" I said "yes," and he came toward me and kissed me. We started kissing and making love. I couldn't believe it! He was interested in me! So from that time on we became lovers.

Gay men draw a distinction between being an authentic man (*laki-laki asli*) and an authentic *gay* man (*gay asli*): *gay* men can become authentic men in the *normal* world through marriage (see chapter 4; Howard 1996) yet perform their *gayness* in the *gay* world through ngondhek. There is a pleasure in this expression of the *gay* self through effeminacy; it is an enjoyable practice often conceptualized in terms of performance. There is also danger in ngondhek: it becomes a habit and thus ever in danger of surfacing inappropriately outside the *gay* world. As I once heard a group of *gay* men in Makassar put it, there is a need to "look at the situation" (*lihat situasi*) when acting ngondhek. Ngondhek is a style: of speaking, of hanging out (*gaya kumpul*), of acting in the world that surfs the border between visible and invisible, authentic and inauthentic, local and global, masculine and feminine. It dubs culture in the sense that it holds feminine practice and male embodiment together over time without conflating them (like dubbed language and filmed mouths that do not match up), unlike the practices of waria subjectivity, which fuse—symbolically and literally—femininity and male bodies.

Like the geography of the *gay* world, the practices of ngondhek seem to invite comparison to Western homosexualities of the early twentieth century: "in the right context, appropriating even a single feminine—or at least unconventional—style or article of clothing might signify a man's identity as a fairy" (Chauncey 1994:51). It is easy to posit a homosexual identity that is forced into marginal places (parks, public toilets) and marginal practices (covert codes of behavior) until socioeconomic conditions permit it to be liberated. In the absence of an anthropology of similitude, such an evolutionist and determinist timeline may seem the only analytic option. With the historical and cultural context of *gay* subjectivity in mind, however, it seems clear that even when structures of power create superficially similar conditions of marginalization, the differing dynamics of those structures of power result in quite different practices and desires. For instance, *gay* effeminacy takes place in an Indonesian postcolonial context with a specific set of linkages between manhood, marriage, and national belonging.

Gay men typically see ngondhek (and déndong) as something *gay* men do across Indonesia, but that distinguishes them from Western gay men, whom they assume to be more masculine. One night at Texas I was speaking with Anwar and another *gay* man about differences between Indonesia and America when suddenly Anwar exclaimed: "Take the Indonesian style [*gaya Indonesia*] back to America!" When I asked, "What do you mean by the 'Indonesian style?'" Anwar replied, "You know, ngondhek, like this [moving his arms in a wavy, effeminate manner]. In America the gay people are all macho, right?" This common view that Western gay men are masculine is somewhat surprising, since portrayals of Western gayness transmitted through Indonesian mass media usually emphasize effeminacy. Some *gay* men say they developed this view from seeing Western gay pornography, commenting on how men in these films are macho even when they play the anal-receptive role in sex. Since zines document that the view of Indonesian *gay* men as more effeminate than Western gay men has existed since at least the early 1980s, it may draw from the legacy of colonial discourses that oppose a feminine Asia to a masculine West.

My initial reaction to Anwar's request to "take the Indonesian style back to America" was to deny I took styles anywhere. Reflecting on his words later that night, I realized he had insightfully summed up the ethnographic project in an already globalized world. It is a dubbing project of forever-imperfect translation in the wake of—not preceding—forms of contemporary globalization that are unequal, but no longer novel.

Opening and Closing

During the period of my fieldwork, the vast majority of *gay* Indonesians did not know the phrase "come out of the closet," and there is no Indonesian-language equivalent. *Gay* Indonesians use a variety of metaphors for becoming *gay*, including *terjun ke dunia gay* "falling into the *gay* world" (Howard 1996), but the most common metaphor is "opening to the *gay* world." Like the Western metaphor of being "in" or "out" of the closet, this spatial metaphor is bi-directional: one can be in a state of being opened or closed (*terbuka, tertutup*) and can open or close oneself (*membuka diri, menutupi diri*); one can also speak of the abstract condition of openness (*keterbukaan*). Like the concept of world (*dunia*), the concept of being open (*buka*) or closed (*tutup*) originates in the *normal* world: one can speak of a neighborhood unreceptive to outsiders as tertutup (S. Brenner 1998:47), or speak of a terbuka Muslim.

This dynamic of opening and closing is a theory of performativity specific to the lifeworlds of *gay* men (and to some extent feminine *lesbi* women), but it draws upon notions of public propriety found in Indonesia's *normal* world and elsewhere in Southeast Asia (Jackson 2003). Warias usually feel their selfhood originates in disjuncture (between male body and female soul, between a desire to wear women's clothes and a male body), a disjuncture that is unambiguously marked on the body in all contexts of their lives. They do not speak of being open or closed because their social interlocutors usually recognize a waria as such day and night, at home or in public. In contrast, being *gay* is not explicitly embodied: *normal* Indonesians often miss the subtle signs of *gay* effeminacy. The disjuncture lies not between body and soul, both of which are male, but between appearing *normal* and "desiring the same." This is a "style" deployed and managed, something that can even slip from control and manifest itself out of place, like at work or at home.

Being *gay* is about practices as much as internal states. Dominant Western traditions typically assume that the body is less important than the soul. The notion of coming out of the closet builds on a confessional discourse that begins from an interior self and works outward to body, family, and society: "In our folk psychology, between inner subjectivity and outer form lies a radical break, a disconnection that can be disguised, but not overcome, by self-conscious and instrumental manipulation" (S. Errington 1989:76; see also Foucault 1978). Not all Westerners subscribe to this discourse—there are Western men who have sexual relations with other men without any expectation of "coming out"—but it holds a dominant place in the structuring of Western sexualities; persons that reject confessional discourse are in some way resisting or rejecting a structure of power. Multiple notions of exterior and interior are certainly present in Indonesia as well, originating in "traditional" beliefs, religious doctrine (like the Islamic distinction between *lahir* and *batin*), and the translocation of Western discourses. However, an apparent point of continuity across Indonesia and much of Southeast Asia is a sense that the boundary between inner and outer self is weak, and each can be affected by the other. Since Western confessional discourse does not appear to have translocated to Indonesia to any great extent as the *gay* subject position was dubbed into its contemporary configuration during the 1980s and 1990s, this sense of a porous boundary between embodied and interior self continues to shape *gay* subjectivities.

In Indonesia (and much of Southeast Asia) importance is placed on a match between social presentation and interior self: "Although in English we may speak of a 'well-balanced personality,' we have no expectation that that fortunate person will have good posture; but in [much of Indonesia] . . . balance or centeredness is taken literally" (S. Errington 1989:76–77; see also Jackson 2003:61; Keeler 1983). This presents special difficulties for the disjuncture between the relatively normative gender presentation of *gay* men and their "desire for the same." It is not that waria subjectivity is "gender" and *gay* subjectivity "sexuality," that being waria is something one "is" while being *gay* is something one "does." The distinction lies rather in visibility-to-society, in recognition. The nonrecognition of the *gay* subject position in the *normal* world results in a reciprocal relationship between practice and place. Practices define places: what makes a place *gay* is not physical features or an official permit; practices—speaking *gay* language, evincing *gay* mannerisms, caressing another man's hand—transform places into nodes or islands of the *gay* world. Places define practices: *gay* men are recognizably *gay* only when they are in the *gay* world; when in the *normal* world, gayness is visible only to those who know how to read its subtle signs. This reciprocal relationship between practice and place means that not only the *gay* world but the *gay* self is, in a certain sense, archipelagic—it is a selfhood exercised intermittently, first at one place and then at another, but not in the space between.

Particularly when "exterior" embodiment is not assumed to be the expression of an "interior" subjectivity, persons embodying the same style need not have the same subjectivities, beliefs, even "culture"; style is not necessarily the "expression" of a preexisting subjectivity: "Not all British punks were alienated, nor are all Zambian localists 'traditional'" (Ferguson 1999:97). This dynamic was neatly summarized for me one day in Surabaya when I showed Ali, a young *gay* man, a copy of the *GAYa Nusantara* zine, which features photographs of *gay* men on the front cover. In our earlier conversations Ali had spoken about how he didn't like being *gay* and wanted to be cured. I was thus surprised when he leafed through the zine with interest, pronouncing, "I'd like a photo of me to be on the front cover someday." When I replied, "I thought you said you didn't want to be *gay* and wanted to be cured," he looked at me blankly, seeing no contradiction between wanting to become *normal* and also wanting to be on the cover of a *gay* zine: "I said that right now I'm *gay*. But in eight years, when I'm twenty-seven, I will get married. So if I do things like appear on the cover of the zine maybe I'll be able to use up my *gayness* [*menghabiskan kegayan saya*]."

Some *gay* men are aware of the concept of "coming out" because they are wealthy, well educated, or have worked in HIV prevention. When I asked one such interlocutor how "coming out" differed from "opening oneself," he answered, "Opening oneself [*membuka diri*] is more toward the group [*kelompok*], but the term has been equated [*disamakan*] with 'coming out' by some AIDS groups, which is rather dangerous.... What's meant by opening oneself is how to access the groups that exist."

This has direct consequences for how *gay* men conceptualize national belonging. Abdul, a *gay* man in Makassar, referenced these intermittent practices when he once said you can tell who is "*gay* from their style" [*gay dari gayanya*]. Practice is key to the gaya of *gay* men, the "archipelago style" by which they imagine their place in a *gay* world distributed throughout a national body politic. In place of the status-based discourse common in Western sexuality and gender rights movements, *gay* men emphasize actions (*perilaku*); a common phrase is that society's potential future acceptance of *gay* men will "come down to our actions" [*kembali ke perilaku kita*]. The three keywords that link *gay* men's discussions of selfhood and belonging are "good deeds" (*prestasi*), "society" (*masyarakat*), and "to be accepted" (*diterima*): through good deeds, society will accept them, but since they are not visible to society as *gay* men, their good deeds are not recognized as such, and without recognition belonging lies beyond reach. The notion of being "opened" to the whole world is nearly unthinkable for most *gay* men and appears primarily when discussing impossibilities: "The majority of *gay* men aren't open as *gay* [*terbuka sebagai gay*] and able to say 'oh, I'm *gay*, I can't get married.'"

The crucial point is that homosexuality (like any other cultural logic) "globalizes" (or "translocates") not as a monolithic discourse but as a multiplicity of beliefs and practices, elements of which can move independently of each other or not move at all. In comparison to the religious, colonial, and mercantile infrastructures that drove "globalization" in the past, and the "print capitalism" that made nationalism possible (Anderson 1983), contemporary mass media and other aspects of late capitalism make possible the kinds of fractured and contingent translocations I term "dubbing culture." In the case of *gay* and *lesbi,* the notion of homosexual selfhood has moved, but other aspects of the dominant Western discourse of homosexuality have not. Foucault's genealogy of homosexuality in the West locates the intersection of power and knowledge at the confession. Identity reveals and renders intelligible an interior, private self but is not authentic until exteriorized to an authority who interprets and acknowledges this confession. Only then is the person "out of the closet," even in the remarkable case of the "intralocutor" operative in "coming out to yourself." Many theorists have shown how this model construes homosexual identity as a constant, iterative process of articulation and reception, an incitement to discourse that contributed to the "reverse discourse" of the gay and lesbian rights movement.[7]

But when the terms *gay* and *lesbian* moved to Indonesia, this conjunction of sexuality and confession neither preceded nor followed it. While psychoanalytic discourse has found its way into Indonesia through academic and pop psychology, the mass mediated translocation of concepts of homosexuality to Indonesia has been too fragmentary for this discourse to have had a formative role in the constitution of the *gay* and *lesbi* subject positions. As a result, the ontological status of *gay* and *lesbi* subjectivities does not hinge on disclosure to spheres of home, workplace, or God. Construed not as coming out but in terms of opening and closing oneself, these subjectivities are additive rather than substitutive; opening them does not necessarily imply closing others. In English the term "closet" is etymologically related to the adjective and verb "close," but what is opposed to the closet is presumed to be the world in general. For *gay* and *lesbi* Indonesians, however, being opened or closed is typically in reference to the *gay* or *lesbi* world; confessing to other worlds in society is irrelevant. When *gay* men speak of someone being terbuka, they index participation in tempat ngeber and not, for instance, telling family or coworkers of homosexual desires. One finds not an epistemology of the closet but an epistemology of life worlds, where healthy subjectivity depends not on integrating diverse domains of life and having a unified, unchanging identity in all situations, but on separating domains of life and maintaining their borders against the threat of gossip and discovery. It is this epistemology, for instance, that makes it thinkable that a *gay* man can be opened in the *gay* world yet married to a woman in the *normal* world.

As with practices of ngondhek, *gay* and *lesbi* notions of being opened or closed to the *gay* or *lesbi* world may call again to mind the work of George Chauncey and other scholars on the history of Western homosexuality (Chauncey 1994). In early twentieth-century New York, for instance, the term *coming out,* derived from the notion of a debutante ball, implied coming out to a select community, not to all spheres of life. Furthermore, many homosexually identified people married and did not see their doing so as incongruous. Nonetheless, I would caution against a teleological reading of Indonesians as followers in these footsteps and against a structuralist reading of contemporary Indonesia and historical New York as presenting a mutual set of necessary and sufficient conditions. Such interpretations beg the question of how similitude and difference are measured in the first place. Contemporary *gay* and *lesbi* subjectivities diverge in important respects from earlier Western homosexual subjectivities, not least because they imagine themselves situated in an transnational archipelago of gay and lesbian persons. Crucially, their "desire for the same" has been formed in a postcolonial context: it sexualizes the "deep, horizontal comradeship" associated with nationalism (Anderson 1983:7).

The Gay/Waria Boundary

For the most part, *gay* men never feel they are warias, though they have typically been familiar with warias since childhood and may have been called *banci* (waria) by children or adults in their midst. This is because most *gay* men feel their *gay*ness is motivated by a "desire for the same," not a desire to wear women's clothes or a sense they have a women's soul. Some *gay* men say that warias are really *gay* men who are forced into that role because of social norms. While this may be true in some cases, given that the waria subject position is much better known than the *gay* subject position, warias themselves state quite consistently that looking like a woman and the experience of having a woman's soul is what makes one waria, not the "desire for the same" that characterizes *gay* subjectivity.

However, there are many linkages between the *gay* and waria subject positions. Both are assumed to co-occur with male bodies, both share practices of effeminacy like déndong, and in many parts of Indonesia they socialize with each other to the extent that phrases like "the *gay* and waria world" (*dunia gay waria*) or that *gay* man and warias "become one" (*menjadi satu*) are common. As a result of these linkages, there are men who see themselves as simultaneously *gay* and waria. In some cases they will identify as *gay* for a period of months or years and then switch to waria for a time, as in the case of one *gay* man from Surabaya who wrote about becoming a waria for six months while living in Kalimantan because his friends there were waria and it was easier to find male sex partners as a waria (Faisal 2003). One night I was watching waria show with several *gay* men and a few warias. Agung, a *gay* man, introduced me to Tina, a waria I had never met before, noting that "last month she was *gay*, now she has become waria" [*sebulan lalu dia hémong, dia sekarang jadi waria*]. I asked Tina why she had changed and she replied, "I was tired of being *gay*. Now below [pointing to her genitalia] it's asli [authentic] and above [pointing to her made-up face] it's *spesial*." Here gender play served to indicate humorously how being waria was a kind of addition to a male self rather than a third gender.

Occasionally men navigate between *gay* and waria on a daily basis. Vera was unusual: she almost always wore men's clothes and used the term *gay* during the day. One day I asked Vera if she had dressed as a woman since last week and she replied, "No, I only become waria one night a week; I like both." She saw little point in trying to rank one over the other: "I adapt."

Tensions over the *gay*/waria boundary can be seen in excerpts from letters written to the *gay* zine *GAYa Nusantara* in response to the question: Is it proper that *gay* men make themselves up (déndong)?[8]

> "*Gay* déndong?" Go right ahead . . . just don't do it forever. [*Gay* men] have to remember that they were created as *gay* and not as waria. So if you want to déndong, just do it in the correct proportion and context. Don't do it to the point it becomes a daily occurrence.

> It's clear that I have objections if *gay* people déndong. Their name is *gay* after all, so they have to have the attributes of men in their daily appearance. Although there are a few *gay* men with feminine characteristics, they still have to look like men so that they can be differentiated from warias. Especially because the wider society equates *gay* with waria, even though we're very different. So if there are *gay* men that like to déndong, automatically they exemplify and justify society's view that *gay* is the same as waria.

> "*Gay* déndong?" Please do, it's not forbidden! Just do it occasionally, for instance when taking the stage for a dance or drama . . . don't do it when looking for men; if it's like that then I don't agree with it. Then it's not necessary to become *gay*, better to join a waria organization.

The *gay*/waria boundary, however, can be a source of pleasure as well as anxiety. For Vera, movement across the boundary was experienced as an enjoyable ability to adapt, providing the benefit of sex with *normal* men who did not "desire the same." The pleasures of the *gay*/waria boundary are also indicated in a semi-autobiographical narrative written for me in October 1997 by Yanto, a *gay* man from Surabaya who was married to a woman and whose first child had been born one month earlier. Entitled "A Doll Behind Glass" [*Boneka Dalam Kaca*], the narrative reveals a complex relationship between gender, sexuality, and desire:

> When I made the *gay* world my own world, what I experienced seemed like the usual thing. In fact, I sometimes felt fed up with matters of sex, those same old things without any challenge. . . . Maybe it was for this reason that I wanted to wander, to become something different, to do things that other people would not want to do. I started thinking about crazy things and my attitude became extremely desperate. I wanted to study a life of the night that was darker and rougher than the one I found when I became *gay*.
>
> I had already prepared my outfit with its déndong attributes and only now needed to wear it to begin my new adventure. When I wore my outfit I became aware that beginning from that day I was no longer *gay* but WARIA. Aah . . . I enjoyed my beauty privately in a mirror and only needed to change my speaking accent to fit my new path. I did a pretty good job and it made me laugh at myself. That night I took off with a friend who had also changed himself into a waria.

On the streets I bowed my head to keep down the feelings of shame that flamed up inside when a person passed by, laughing and teasing me. "This is my challenge," I thought to myself until I reached the place. . . . I'd been sitting on the curbside for more than an hour when suddenly from out of nowhere a man sat down next to me. "You're beautiful, like a doll behind glass," he said while looking me over. I inspected him in turn . . . aah, how handsome, fair-skinned, with a thin moustache and still young. "What's your name, Sir?" I asked shyly. "Call me Jono." With his answer I was even more awestruck at his handsomeness. We exchanged formalities and then Jono asked me to service him. I was confused as to where we could fool around but Jono invited me to follow him into the bushes. Apparently Jono was a spontaneous person, because as soon as we were in the bushes he took off his shirt and pants. "Take off your shirt," he said. I was stupefied to see his clean and broad-chested body. "Oh, no," I said, refusing to take off my shirt. Jono didn't force things and straightaway we started to make out. . . .

That's how easy it is to get a man, as easy as turning over the palm of your hand. This eventually made me comfortable continuing my adventure. Every Saturday night I would change myself and become a waria [*aku merubah diriku jadi waria*] and from these adventures I learned a thousand lessons.

This narrative indicates how the *gay*/waria boundary can be unstable, but in terms of movement between *gay* and waria, not their conflation. A common theme is that when déndong is linked to places like sex work areas or outdoor public areas, rather than entertainment events, the border between *gay* and waria becomes defocused. When the made-up doll leaves her display case, the border between *gay* and waria can, for some, become a line to be transgressed across the frontier of gender.

Since the late 1990s or so, the term *"gay waria"* has appeared with increasing frequency. While still rare, this term for warias appears to ontologize *gay* over *waria*, despite the fact that *waria* is the historically prior term and the one with greater public recognition. Should this term become more common, it would reflect an increasing presence of the concept *gay* in Indonesian public culture, and perhaps also the influence of HIV/AIDS discourse, which with its concept of "male sexual health" tends to regard warias as a type of *gay* man. Interestingly, when on occasion the terms *waria* and *tomboi* are combined with reference to masculine women, the phrase is *waria tomboi* (not *tomboi waria*), reflecting how there remains uncertainty as to whether *tomboi* is a subtype of *lesbi* or a distinct subject position.

Gay Language and the National Voice

Gay men often emphasize that they have a way of speaking in the *gay* world that differs from speech in the *normal* world: *"gay"* language" (*bahasa gay*). *Gay* men not only informed me of the existence of bahasa *gay* but eagerly taught it to me. I also observed such men teaching bahasa *gay* to other Indonesian men who were new to the *gay* world. I explore this "*gay* language" (bahasa *gay*, also sometimes called bahasa béncong) in detail elsewhere (Boellstorff 2004a, 2004e); in this section I review how speaking bahasa *gay* contributes to the performance of *gay* subjectivity and its linkages to national culture.

To date, the fundamental condition of bahasa *gay*'s existence is that although some terms transform words from ethnolocalized languages like Javanese or Balinese, at the overall grammatical level bahasa *gay* is always based on Indonesian (*bahasa Indonesia*), the national vernacular. Bahasa *gay* is a self-consciously nationwide way of speaking. *Gay* men sometimes explicitly comment on the national character of bahasa *gay*, as in the case of Eddy, an ethnically Bugis *gay* man in Makassar who emphasized there was no such thing as a *bahasa gay Bugis* (Bugis *gay* language,) but only a *bahasa gay Indonesia*.

The significance of bahasa *gay*'s founding in Indonesian is a consequence of the unusual position of Indonesian in the nation-building project. Language played a vital role in the state's enormous effort to build a sense of nationalism among the denizens of the Dutch East Indies. At the time of independence in the late 1940s, many of these groups shared little more than the Dutch colonial encounter, which itself exhibited great regional variation in length and intensity. One core element of most nationalisms is the belief that to be modern and authentic, nations need national vernaculars (Anderson 1983). What would become Indonesia's mother tongue? Dutch clearly would not have sufficed, not only because of its association with the colonizing power but also because of Holland's antipathy toward having its subjects speak the colonial language. As noted in chapter 1, at the time of independence, after 350 years of Netherlands rule, less than 2 percent of Indonesians spoke Dutch. Javanese, spoken by almost 40 percent of "natives," seemed a logical choice, but selecting any ethnolocalized language had the disadvantage of privileging one group.

A solution was found in Malay, "the language of certain courts and of villages, though not the language of the largest groups of the archipelago" (Siegel 1997:14), the lingua franca of the Dutch East Indies. Due to prior centuries of trade in which Malay had become distributed not only across the Indies but as far away as the Philippines, Japan, Sri Lanka, and Madagascar (J. Errington 1998:52), Malay was construed as a placeless, peopleless tongue. A lingua franca like Malay produces something "not completely foreign or completely domestic" (Siegel 1997:8–9), something "dubbed":

> The lingua franca was exterior to all speakers in that no one thought it origi-
> nated with them. It existed merely, as it were, between them. Of course, all
> languages mediate. But the lingua franca is always, by definition, a language
> in some way foreign to both the speaker and his interlocutor. It contains the
> possibility, therefore, of changing the "I" of the original language into a second
> "I," an "I" incipient in dual form in the other as well as myself. (Siegel 1997:32)

For Malay to become a language of nationhood, a concerted effort was
needed to transform a language of colonial domination into one of national unity, transforming the plural society (Furnivall 1944) into a nation
by constructing a paradox—an authentic lingua franca. Since under colonialism Malay/Indonesian had been contrasted with languages seen as
native, to this day its "un-nativeness crucially enables and informs its
place in the Indonesian national project" (J. Errington 1998:3). There is
a misunderstanding that Indonesian is an invented language; what has
been invented is its speech community. This language frequently appears
in grammars as "Malay/Indonesian": the slash simultaneously linking
and separating *Malay* from *Indonesian* marks a shift not just in grammar
but in the manner of imagining community—from a lingua franca of trade
and colonialism to the archipelagic key in which the new nation's authenticity would be played.

The spread of Indonesian testifies to the success of the New Order
state's educational initiatives: "[Indonesian was] intimately bound up
with the New Order's fortunes, as is clear from one of Soeharto's very
first unilateral decisions: a 1965 Presidential Instruction which mandated
the government-supervised building and staffing of elementary schools
throughout the country, particularly in rural areas" (J. Errington
1998:59). As a result, "among the New Order's most enduring effects on
the Indonesian landscape [was] its success in propagating Indonesian-ness
with and through the Indonesian language" (J. Errington 1998:2). The
success of Indonesian language planning has been seen as a "greater mira-
cle" than the revitalization of Hebrew: "It has taken on the aura of an
omnipresent verity, viewed and experienced as reaching back into antiquity and forward into eternity as a component of the Indonesian genius"
(Fishman 1978:227, 338).

For my interlocutors, Indonesian is a feature of everyday life (J. Errington
2000:209). All of my interlocutors speak Indonesian, as does almost 90
percent of the Indonesian populace, approximately 15 percent of whom
now speak it as their first language. This percentage is increasing, and the
use of Indonesian as a first language is increasingly linked to middle-class
identity (Hill 1996:208; Oetomo 1996b). For decades many Indonesians
have taught Indonesian, not an ethnolocalized language, to their children
as a mother tongue (e.g., Robinson 1989:32). Indonesian is the language

of national belonging (Keane 2003), and for some it is also the language of family intimacies, romance, and emotion; for most of my interlocutors it is learned from the earliest years of life, and in some cases it is the only language they speak. The enduring power of ethnolocality is indicated by the fact that the existence of monolingual Indonesian-speakers is almost never acknowledged in the anthropological literature.

While *gay* Indonesians sometimes say that bahasa *gay* is a secret language, its actual pragmatics appear to reflect more closely the second consciously articulated ideology about it: bahasa *gay* is a "slang" in the sense of a language of association and sociality (*bahasa gaul*). Several pieces of ethnographic evidence indicate that bahasa *gay* is not a secret language. The first is that not all *gay* men know it; they are not all privy to the "secret." *Gay* men who avoid *gay* places (for instance, interacting only with a small circle of friends) may have little or no knowledge of this form of language. Second, whole clauses of bahasa *gay* are rare. Bahasa *gay* is usually formed by altering only a single foregrounded word in the utterance, as with "hungry" in the example below.

Standard Indonesian:	*Saya sudah lapar dua jam* I already hungry two hours
Bahasa *gay*:	*Saya sudah lapangan dua jam* I already open field two hours

Here *lapar* is replaced with *lapangan*, an Indonesian term for "open field." The result is somewhat like an English speaker saying, "I've been Hungarian for two hours." But this makes bahasa *gay* rather easy for outsiders to decipher: the meaning of *I've been Hungarian for two hours* soon becomes clear to someone overhearing the phrase. The fact that only one or two lexemes per utterance are typically changed into bahasa *gay*—often lexemes that do not reveal sensitive information—makes doubtful the argument that it serves primarily as a secret register.

A third reason why the "secret language" ideology seems insufficient is that bahasa *gay* is usually spoken in the *gay* world, when outsiders are not immediately present—in a deserted corner of a park, in an apartment, on a bench in a shopping mall. It is rarely spoken in mixed company as a social screen; it typically acts not to distinguish but to include. When this happens (I have heard it used on a bus to comment on an attractive man, for instance), it may temporarily mask the content of what is being said, but such utterances attract rather than deflect attention by their oddity. Finally, bahasa *gay* cannot act as a secret language because it is increasingly appropriated by Indonesia's *normal* world. While friends and family often do not know if someone is *gay*, *gay* men can sometimes be openly *gay* in the presence of *normal* Indonesians, especially if they work in a salon. These interactions make it possible for bahasa *gay* terms and even derivational patterns to become part of a national vernacular or *bahasa gaul*. In the *normal* world, the register created by switching a word or two in an utterance to bahasa *gay* appears to invoke an Indonesian public culture of freedom from official stricture. In recent years the dissemination of bahasa *gay* has been extended by the entry of bahasa *gay* terms into mass media.

Bahasa *gay* appears to act most often to invoke a sense of the *gay* world in a context where many *gay* men can socialize extensively in civic spaces like parks but have almost no institutional infrastructure—no places to call their own beyond the corner of a town square, no social recognition beyond the occasional (and often lurid) gossip column. Language here works to stabilize social relations, creating a sense of similarity and shared sociality.

Since the story of the Tower of Babel, difference has been central to understandings of language, as it has long been central to understandings of style. This has been demonstrated by work on language ideology showing the importance of "the ideas with which participants frame their understanding of linguistic *varieties* and the *differences* among them, and map those understandings onto people, events, and activities that are significant to them" (Gal and Irvine 1995:970, emphasis added), and by work showing how register "construes *differences* of speech habit as emblematic of *differences* in identity, employing language to motivate *differences* in social identity" (Agha 1998:168, emphasis added). But how can language constitute not only difference but belonging, beyond the mere fact of shared membership in a linguistic community? This is one key question raised by bahasa *gay*, both in its use in the *gay* world and in its use in popular culture.

Gay Indonesians might seem to epitomize difference: they seem to lie radically outside the norms of Indonesian society. Within the *gay* and *normal* worlds, however, bahasa *gay* appears as a register of belonging, not one of hierarchy or distance. The "social stereotyping" (Hervey 1992:195; Agha 1998:168) that co-occurs with bahasa *gay* consistently points toward inclusion in national culture, not ethnolocalized cultures. Nowhere do *gay* Indonesians think that the concept *gay* comes from Javanese or Balinese "tradition." And nowhere do *gay* Indonesians think that there are persons outside Indonesia who speak bahasa *gay*. While bahasa *gay* is neither necessary nor sufficient for *gay* subjectivity, it concretizes nodes of the daily *gay* world, as well as a sense that these nodes are linked in a national network. When *normal* Indonesians use bahasa *gay*, they are seen to be hip, not queer; it marks them not as *gay* but as in tune with popular culture. One possibility is that the "national" character of bahasa *gay* can be delinked from its original association with homosexuality in this manner because *gay* subjectivity is so strongly linked to national culture in the first place.

The increasing ease with which bahasa *gay* has moved from parks and other sites of *gay* life to Indonesian popular culture suggests it is shifting from a "genre register," linked to context, to a "social register," linked to "stereotypical personality types" (Hervey 1992:198). Its referent is coming to be "user" more than "context of use." Bahasa *gay* can index two domains that appear opposed: the world of *gay* life, still lived largely in secrecy and shadow, and the dominant world of popular culture. What these two worlds share is that they are *national* worlds. The "stereotyped personality types" bahasa *gay* invokes are no longer necessarily homosexual, but they are necessarily national.

The desires of *normal* Indonesians are understood to operate across difference—female for male, and male for female. *Normal*, waria, and tomboi desires are understood in "heterogendered" terms. This is what *gay* (and *lesbi*) Indonesians have to offer Indonesian society: they alone articulate a "desire for the same," one that bears uncanny resemblances to the "imagined community" of the nation. What leaks from bahasa *gay* as it is appropriated into the national vernacular is a sense of similitude, of shared identity across islands of difference. Bahasa *gay* sometimes *indexes* homosexuality, but like the archipelago style of *gay* and *lesbi* Indonesians more generally, it *registers* belonging; this is its "style."

Tests of Faith

For most *gay* and *lesbi* Indonesians religious belief is important, but few can or wish to link that faith to the *gay* or *lesbi* world (I discuss gay Muslims more extensively in Boellstorff 2005). In postcolonial Indonesia religion is ever present; it is never simply a matter of personal belief. It is linked to family, society, and state: the first of the Pancasila, or Five Principles of the state, concerns belief in a single God (*Tuhan yang Maha Esa*). Understanding the place of religion in the *gay* and *lesbi* worlds demands distinguishing orthodoxy from lived religious experience. *Gay* and *lesbi* Indonesians find the domain of religion conflated with the *normal* world. Yet as they move through the *gay* and *lesbi* worlds, these Indonesians do not leave their faith behind. As a result, there is a need to approach *gay* and *lesbi* religious experience in a manner that takes into account how doctrine travels and is reinterpreted in different contexts.

In Islam, the religion of most *gay* and *lesbi* Indonesians, the central concept organizing sexuality is that of marriage (*nikah*) between men and women. If asked directly, most Indonesians say that Islam disapproves of sex between men or between women. In practice, however, historically homosexuality has not represented a major concern in Indonesian Islamic thought. While Islamic thought acknowledges and celebrates the sexuality of women, properly controlled, women are often understood as the receivers of sexuality rather than initiators. Since homosexuality in Islam tends to be defined in terms of penile-anal penetration, it is unclear to what degree various erotic practices between women are classed as "sex" at all. Many *lesbi* Muslims struggle with a sense of sin. Yet *lesbi* women across Indonesia find ways to live with, if not reconcile, faith and desire, from tombois praying on the men's side of a mosque to deciding that their desires are the result of God's plan (Prawirakusumah and Ramadhan 1988:427, 122, 250).

As also appears to be the case for *lesbi* Muslims, *gay* Muslims take two main stances with regard to their sexuality. At one extreme are those who see their sexuality as a serious sin. One *gay* Muslim in Bali, citing the story of Lot, said, "Being gay is a big sin in Islam, one of the sins that cannot be forgiven." However, most of my *gay* Muslim interlocutors either did not see being *gay* as sinful or understood it to be a minor sin easily forgiven by God. The starting point for these men is a belief in the God's omnipotence and omniscience. Given that God is all-knowing, all-wise, and all-merciful, most *gay* Indonesian Muslims conclude they were created *gay* by God, and thus that their subjectivities and sexual practices are not sinful. In this view, *nafsu* or desire is planted in each individual by God and represents an irresistible force that cannot be denied, a common view among Indonesian Muslims (Siegel 1969; S. Brenner 1998:149–157). *Gay and lesbi* Indonesians face these tests of faith as they face the other challenges of their lives, and through practices of self they find ways to live within the *gay* archipelago.

PART THREE

Sexuality and Nation

CHAPTER SEVEN

The Postcolonial State and *Gay* and *Lesbi* Subjectivities

HEGEMONY AND SUBJECTIVITY

> Ruling or dominant conceptions of the world [may] not directly prescribe the mental content of . . . the heads of the dominated classes. But the circle of dominant ideas does accumulate the symbolic power to map or classify the world for others; its classifications do acquire not only the constraining power of dominance over other modes of thought but also the inertial authority of habit and instinct. It becomes the horizon of the taken for granted: what the world is and how it works, for all practical purposes.
> —Stuart Hall, "The Toad in the Garden"

Part 2 of this book explored what it means to be *gay* or *lesbi* in daily life. Building upon these materials and also the discussions of history, mass media, and globalization in part 1, this chapter further theorizes the relationship between sexuality and nation. In the postcolonial Indonesia of the 1970s through the 1990s, when the *gay* and *lesbi* subject positions first took form, the authoritarian New Order (*Orde Baru*) regime of Soeharto had the resources to impose its agenda to a greater degree than the Old Order regime of Sukarno (1945–1969) it replaced, or the colonial regimes of Japan and Holland. Indonesians did—and continue to—resist this state power. What is of interest is that such resistance often takes the form of transformation rather than rejection. The very terms "*gay*" and "*lesbi*" might be taken to indicate that *gay* and *lesbi* Indonesians identify with a global gay and lesbian movement and thus stand outside national discourse. However, it seems quite clear that they lie deeply within that discourse. They also imagine global linkages despite the fact that *gay* and *lesbi* Indonesians rarely travel outside Indonesia or encounter gay or lesbian Westerners.

Stuart Hall notes that "ruling ideas may dominate other conceptions of the social world."[1] Theories of ideology tend to view this influence in binary terms: one either believes the ideology and suffers from false consciousness or sees the ideology as such and rejects it. One is hailed, or one turns away (Althusser 1971). Theories of hegemony, which typically trace their origin to the work of Antonio Gramsci (1891–1937), offer a more nuanced framework for analyzing "stories that find sustenance in pervasive commonsensical, almost unconscious, dominant ways of understanding, experiencing, and acting in the world" (Helmreich 1998:12). In developing his theory of hegemony in the 1930s, Gramsci was concerned with orthodox Marxism's inability to explain the failure of the peoples of Western Europe to revolt against their states in the manner of the Russian Revolution twenty years earlier. Gramsci located this theoretical failure in an orthodox Marxist "economism" that "asks the question: 'who profits directly from the initiative under consideration,' and replies with a line of reasoning which is as simplistic as is it fallacious: the ones who profit directly are a certain fraction of the ruling class" (1971:166).

In response Gramsci refined the notion of hegemony, a term already in use in Marxist analysis at the time. Gramsci did not see most societies as controlled solely through physical coercion; while it could certainly exist (as Gramsci's imprisonment must have made clear to him), Gramsci saw it as a means of last resort. He believed that most contemporary societies were controlled by a hegemony functioning first and foremost through "leadership"—the winning of consent through cultural means. Such consent is not reducible to false consciousness because it requires real concessions; it is partial and historically unstable, vulnerable to transformation particularly when such transformation does not directly threaten the hegemony itself. For Gramsci, "hegemony was, in effect, the basis for the reformulation of the doctrine of historical materialism to allow room for the influence of ideas and the powerful effect of human will" (Kurtz 1996:108; see also Crehan 2002:104). One way in which hegemonies differ from ideologies is that the former tend to be taken for granted (Comaroff and Comaroff 1991:25). Such naturalization is possible because, in contrast to the specific content of ideologies (Althusser 1971:162), hegemonies "hail" persons to a range of debate. This nonspecificity gives hegemonies their flexibility and dynamism—you can argue as a Republican or Democrat over a variety of issues, but more important is the range of debate such "extremes" define. Hegemony permits, even requires, diversity. If ideology clothes the self from a specific wardrobe, then hegemony is a style—a loose imperative that permits variation within a "horizon of the taken for granted."[2]

Gay and *lesbi* Indonesians have received little academic attention not only because they do not fit within an ethnolocalized spatial scale, but because no discourse appears to correlate with their existence. My analysis departs from most of the literature on sexuality and nationalism in that I ask how the state can shape sexual subject positions that it neither incites as normative nor calls into being through oppression, what Foucault termed a reverse discourse (Foucault 1978). In the case of *gay* and *lesbi* Indonesians, sexuality—what might appear to be the most intimate, personal, prepublic domain of life—is configured through state discourse, but not in an intentional manner or as a form of oppositional consciousness (Sandoval 1991). In Indonesia "the state's powers are manifest less through coercive force or economic interventions than in a quieter percolation through schools, village meeting halls, minor bureaucratic offices, churches, and the like" (Keane 1997:39). It is these indirect "percolations" of national discourse that *gay* and *lesbi* Indonesians transform through their sexual subjectivities.

To further illuminate how sexuality and nation intersect in *gay* and *lesbi* subjectivities, it is necessary to specify the most relevant elements of national discourse. Though the Pancasila or Five Principles of the state, first set out during Sukarno's rule, have been central (Morfit 1981; Ramage 1995), these principles are relatively abstract. For the New Order state (and the regimes following it), two of the most significant elements of national discourse that concretize Pancasila's principles of unity, morality, and justice have been the archipelago concept (*wawasan nusantara*) and the family principle (*azas kekeluargaan*).

In previous chapters I foreshadowed the influence of these elements of national discourse—from the notion of "archipelago style" to the dynamics of *gay* and *lesbi* "heterosexual" marriages. One could conduct a thought experiment in which the *gay* and *lesbi* subject positions had formed under a different set of circumstances. What would these subject positions have looked like had they developed under Sukarno's Old Order government, which was in power from independence in 1945 until the mid-1960s? During this period Sukarno attempted to build nationalism through a much more antagonistic relationship to the world outside Indonesia. National belonging was articulated not so much in terms of paternalist development but as an oppositional national identity. In such a context Indonesians might have even produced ethnolocalized homosexualities. Yet this did not happen: the *gay* and *lesbi* subject positions came into being under the New Order's hegemony. How has this contingent conjunction shaped what it means to be *gay* or *lesbi*?

THE ARCHIPELAGO CONCEPT

> I used [the term "archipelago"] only once, and that was to designate, via the title of Solzhenitsyn's work, the carceral archipelago: the way in which a form of punitive system is physically dispersed yet at the same time covers the entirety of a society.
>
> —Michel Foucault, "Questions on Geography"

Throughout the period of anticolonial nationalism, intellectuals and political leaders struggled to define a social and political entity that would challenge Dutch rule. It was a breathtakingly new idea: "Indonesian nationalism, the European-derived idea that the diverse indigenous people of the territory then called Netherlands India constituted a single nation and had a right to independence and a state of their own, dates as a political movement only from the first or second decade of the twentieth century" (Liddle 1988:4). It was far from certain that the colonial entity the "Dutch East Indies" would be succeeded by an entity with identical boundaries, rather than a number of smaller states. It was a question of similitude and difference: what did the members of this far-flung archipelago share to counterbalance differences in ethnicity, language, religion, wealth, colonial experience, and culture? How was the new nation to integrate an imagined community of "broad, horizontal comradeship" (Anderson 1983), given the regional history of "deploying spatially defined imagery for the legitimacy of systems of political and spiritual authority" (Kuipers 1998:8–9)?[3] It is in this sense that the notion of "Indonesia" has been the greatest legacy of the colonial encounter, as territorial boundaries have been to many postcolonial nation-states. By converting the colonial concept of the "East Indies" into something authentic, the state reinterprets denizens of what was known as the "Malay Archipelago" (Wallace 1962) as citizens of an Indonesian archipelago. This is a question of recognition, but whereas national recognition in liberal multicultural democracies is usually assumed to be the recognition of difference (Povinelli 2002:17), from the beginning Indonesian national discourse also framed recognition in terms of similitude. During the final decades of colonial rule, the vision of a nation where difference would be the precondition for similitude—like islands are necessary for an archipelago—became increasingly codified. One important moment was the Kongres Pemuda or "Youth Meeting" of 1928. At this meeting, "an ethnically diverse, Dutch-educated native intelligentsia . . . renamed Malay (*bahasa Melayu*) as Indonesian (*bahasa Indonesia*), language of their nation-to-be. Their famous 'Oath of the Youth,' still repeated on its anniversary every year across the country, conferred public, formal recognition on the project of a unified people (*satu bangsa*), speaking one language (*satu bahasa*), in a single homeland (*satu nusa*)" (J. Errington 1998:52).

The use of *nusa* (island) for the unitary nation demonstrates the recursivity of what would become the archipelago concept: islands make up a national archipelago, but on a metalevel the nation is a single island in a global archipelago of nation-states. The term *nusantara* (archipelago) (which can be used as a colloquial term for Indonesia itself) combines *nusa* with *antara*, which means "between" in Indonesian but in the original Sanskrit means "other" (R. Jones 1973:93). It has been dated to copper inscriptions from 1305 (Avé 1989:230) but was not central to the anticolonial movement. The term *nusantara* appears to have been first used in its modern sense in the 1920s by several Dutch figures, including Brandes and E. F. Douwes Dekker (R. Jones 1973:94). It was then taken up by Ki Hadjar Dewantara, an important nationalist figure and founder of the Taman Siswa schools (Avé 1989:231), but appears nowhere in the 1945 constitution.[4] The archipelago concept become elaborated and implemented as a central element of state discourse only during the postcolonial era, in the context of an international dispute over maritime boundaries. At the First International Conference of the Law of the Sea, held in Geneva in December 1957, the Indonesian state argued that its borders were not limited to a certain distance from the coast of each island, as was the international norm (and as Indonesia had inherited from the colonial state), but should include all of the waters "within" the archipelago (see figs. 7–1 and 7–2).[5] Indonesia's request was granted, and the Second International Conference in 1960 recognized the notion of an "archipelagic state" and with it the archipelago concept. The archipelago concept took its final form only in March 1973,[6] and the map of the nation showing the archipelago concept was formally introduced on May 2, 1984, at the height of the New Order.[7]

Since the 1970s the archipelago concept has been promulgated by the state—particularly the military—as a *cultural* concept wherein similitude encompasses difference. It is a way to think of oneself in simultaneously ethnolocalized and national terms—for instance, as both Makassarese and Indonesian, or both Sundanese and Indonesian. A core element of this project has been to extend the archipelago concept backward in time and claim it as "indigenous." In so doing, this discourse attempts to forge a citizen-subject whose selfhood is keyed to *national* culture as much as ethnolocalized culture. Thus Mochtar Kusumaatmadja, foreign affairs minister from 1978 to 1988, claimed "it would not be exaggerating to say that it is [through the archipelago concept] . . . that the effort or the journey of the Indonesian nation towards *rediscovering* its own subjectivity has been carried out" (1982:25, emphasis added). General Benny Moerdani, one of the most powerful figures of the New Order, claimed that the archipelago concept could be found not only in the 686 oath of King Syailendra of the Sumatra-based Sriwiyayan empire, but in the fifteenth-century "palapa oath" of Gajah Mada, a renowned chief minister of the Java-based Majapahit empire (Moerdani 1986:35–36). It is unclear to which islands Gajah Mada referred. The relevant line of this oath is as follows (in Javanese): *Lamun huwus kalah Nusantara/Insun amukti palapa, lamun kalah* (Once I have subdued the Nusantara, only then will I rest) (Sudibyo 1991; see also Avé 1989:230; R. Jones 1973:93–94).

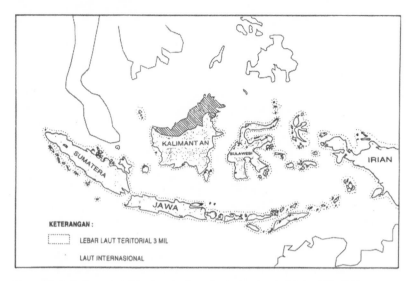

Figure 7–1. Indonesia's borders before the invention of the archipelago concept, as inherited from a 1939 colonial law. From Lembaga Ketahanan Nasional (1995:16).

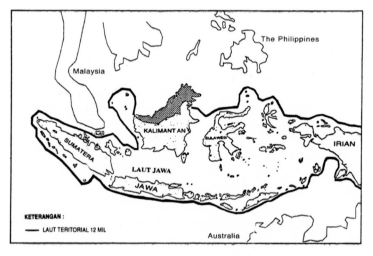

Figure 7–2. Indonesia's borders after the invention of the archipelago concept in December 1957. Lembaga Ketahanan Nasional (1995:17).

Through the efforts of state bureaucracies and officials, including not only Kusumaatmadja and Moerdani but Lieutenant General Ali Moertopo, one of the most powerful figures of the New Order, "the notion of archipelagic culture (*kebudayaan nusantara*) has served as a central attribute of the unified nation, as one of the pivotal notions that has enabled the positing of the national subject's continuity across History" (Acciaioli 2001:12). In this understanding, *negara* (state) and *nusantara* (archipelago) come together to define Indonesian uniqueness—what Sukarno had in 1959 already identified as the "national personality" (*kepribadian bangsa*; Bourchier 1997:157). Within what the national anthem terms "our lands and waters" (*tanah air kita*), Indonesians supposedly inherit a "single vision" (*pandangan satu*) from their ancestors (Moerdani 1986:36); Indonesia is understood to be a single culture in which similitude trumps difference, a unified culture that will allow Indonesians to selectively accept or reject global influences. Thus Indonesia's postcolonial future, where the archipelago concept will be the "bridge" incorporating the global within the national, can be described as the *zaman nusantara* (archipelagic era) (Rustam 1986:78). Frequently, official writings on the archipelago concept conclude it is a *cara pandang bangsa Indonesia*; literally, a national style of seeing (Sudibyo 1991:2).

Foucault (1978) identified the concept of an archipelago in repressive terms. Yet his understanding of power as productive and "capillary"—distributed in mundane practices as much as official ideologies—suggests that the notion of archipelagic culture can be vulnerable to transformation. Troubling notions of similitude and difference, the archipelago concept can also be used to problematize received understandings of exterior and interior. State ideology is never without its contradictions. The archipelago concept implies that all regions have equal status, but the obvious political and economic superiority of Java (indeed, of Jakarta, the capital) recalls colonial and precolonial modes of sovereignty, when the ruler's palace was the "axis of the world" (Anderson 1990:41). However, one of the best-known models for sovereignty and national belonging in postcolonial Indonesia does not invoke a core and periphery. It is *Taman Mini*, the "Beautiful Indonesian Park in Miniature," brainchild of Soeharto's wife following a visit to Disneyland, with its cultural pavilions for each province, surrounding a central lake with tiny islands mapping the archipelago. This park has attracted attention (e.g., Pemberton 1994) because it demonstrates how the state deploys difference. The archipelago concept not only tolerates but demands difference as the raw material the nation incorporates into "unity." By ethnolocalizing this difference, the state claims it as authentic, asli, prior to the colonial encounter and the postcolonial state.

IDENTITY DIAGRAM

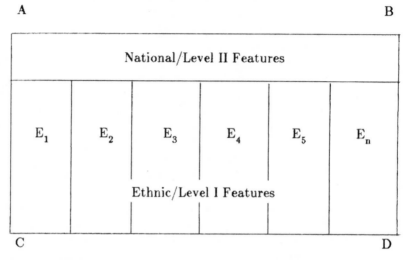

Figure 7–3. The nation subsumes the ethnolocal. Abas (1987:149).

The archipelago concept is easily visualized as a conceptual line drawn around Indonesia's islands. It also appears in schematic representations such as the "identity diagram," which appears in a work on language policy with the explanation that "The rectangle ABCD encloses all features that comprise national as well as ethnic identities and identifies them as a socio-cultural and political unity" (Abas 1987:149; fig. 7–3). By refracting difference through the archipelago concept, the state acquires legitimacy. The state can be taken to represent the similitude that difference needs to be legible as such: the "*wawasan nusantara* envisages, in both abstract and material form, the unification of the archipelagic nation-state as a total organism . . . stressing unity above decentralization" (van Langenberg 1990:124; see also Fletcher 1994). As the national motto states, *Bhinneka Tunggal Ika*, unity *in* diversity, one *over* many. Similitude has been the modality of the postcolonial state's authoritarianism, but also of a distinct and, for many Indonesians, deeply felt sense of nationalism. While Indonesians are no more likely to accept uncritically the archipelago concept than all U.S. citizens accept the idea of the melting pot, the archipelago concept is hegemonic: backed by state power, it dominates "common sense" and helps define the bounds of acceptable discussion. For instance, it shapes notions of "tradition" and "local autonomy" characterizing contemporary politics of indigenous rights in Indonesia, with their focus on recognition (Li 2003). That the Indonesian state's hegemony is never stable or complete does not nullify its power: it creates space for improvisation and transformation—for dubbing—of which the *gay* and *lesbi* subject positions are signal examples.

THE FAMILY PRINCIPLE

> The history of political ideas begins, in fact, with the assump-
> tion that kinship in blood is the sole possible ground of com-
> munity in political functions . . . but the family here spoken
> of is not exactly the family as understood by a modern.
> —Henry Maine, *Ancient Law*

Postcolonial states typically justify their sovereignty by claiming an or-
ganic link to their citizenry that the colonial power did not possess, even
as they take up virtually unchanged the physical boundaries of that regime.
Foucault was speaking of Europe when he claimed that historically "[the
family] disappears as the model of government, except for a certain number of residual themes of a religious or moral nature" (1991:99); the trope
of the family remains central to many modern governmentalities. Nationalism has been a "normalizing process that imagined modern collectivities
as ethnically homogeneous and inherently masculinist entities [and] depended on the foundational construction of constitutive outsides" (Bunzl
2004:13). In the Austrian context Bunzl analyzes, "homosexuals thus became central players in the social drama of modernity. Constituted as always already outside the margins of respectability, their abjection gave
coherence to the fiction of German nationness" (13). In the Indonesian
case we do not find homophile movements going back a hundred years,
nor do we find an explicit focus upon homosexuality as a social ill. Yet
while *gay* and *lesbi* Indonesians were not "constituted" per se by the Indonesian state, they are very much a "constitutive outside," the implicit if
rarely acknowledged failure of kinship and thus the nation itself.

Just as postcolonial states take up colonial boundaries, so this trope of
the family typically indigenizes a notion of the middle-class nuclear family
characteristic of colonial sensibilities (Chatterjee 1993; Stoler 2002b).
Historically, marriage and family life in what is now called "Indonesia"
involved relations between social groups, not just a bride and groom; as
a result "the rhetoric of emotions and personal experience associated with
marital and sexual relations can be a potent idiom for talking about the
self in the context of social groups, categories and relations" (Kuipers
1998:44). The idea that "familyness" (*kekeluargaan*; derived from *keluarga*, "family") is fundamental to being Indonesian dates back to the early

period of nationalism (Bourchier 1997) and "found its first institutional expression in the 1920s in the establishment of the Taman Siswa national educational movement [founded by Ki Hadjar Dewantara, which set] forth for the first time the idea that the internal order of an organization should be sustained by familial bonds, [providing] a clear model for the form of future Indonesian organizations" (Shiraishi 1997:82; see also K. Dewantara 1959:10–16). Thus Ki Hadjar Dewantara played an important role in establishing both the archipelago concept and the family principle. Alongside Dewantara, other key early nationalist figures such as Sukarno, Hatta, and Supomo helped articulate the family principle as central to what being "Indonesian" meant (Reeve 1985). Like the archipelago concept, the family principle came into its own as a postcolonial trope: "After Indonesian independence, the family ideology was used in educational practice in a different way: all Indonesians became part of a family in which the Indonesian government was the parent and the student-citizens were the children" (Kuipers 1998:137).

By the Old Order's end, "sexuality had become, in multiple ways, a primary idiom through which national identity was articulated, intra-national divisions were stated or smoothed, and international conflicts were defined and waged" (Dwyer 2000:38). However, it was during the New Order that the family principle (*azas kekeluargaan*) came to the fore as a principle of governance: "There is no question that the remarkable staying power of [the New Order] . . . depended in large measure on its ability to insert itself deep within the domestic sphere throughout Indonesian society" (S. Brenner 1998:226; see also Chapman 1996). This concept "has a powerful and pervasive ideological presence in modern Indonesia. It is enshrined in the 1945 constitution, and the family language is inseparable from the political language of Indonesia's New Order" (Shiraishi 1997:81). It was during the New Order that the idea of Indonesia as a familial state (*negara kekeluargaan*) was first articulated by state officials (Bourchier 1997:170). The family principle was inculcated through the public education system, where "school lessons linguistically construct a single model of the family" (Shiraishi 1997:131). As a result, "the traditional family is now merely customary while the Indonesian family is an effect of the nation, deriving its legitimacy and its form from outside itself" (Siegel 1998:87). At issue is thus not just state paternalism (*bapakisme*) or the "state momism" discussed in chapter 4, but the heteronormativity that links these together to produce the modern family as foundational unit of the nation.

Family planning has been central to the promulgation of this heteronormative family principle. In June 1970, at the outset of his rule, Soeharto established the National Family Planning Coordinating Board (Badan Koodinasi Keluarga Berencana Nasional, BKKBN). From its beginnings family planning was used to distinguish the New Order from its predecessor: it "signaled the reversal of the strong pro-natal policy it had inherited from the previous government, which had regarded contraception almost as criminal" (BKKBN 1999:5). In contrast to the pronatalist stance of the Old Order (Dwyer 2000:36), now interpreted as irresponsible, the New Order would control and manage families, and it would be the modernity and prosperity of these families, not their mere number, that would constitute progress. As Soeharto declared in 1993, "Indonesian families should be the place for nation-building" (BKKBN 1999:26). Thus, "The family planning program can be seen as part of a project of redefinition of Indonesian political culture, where the mass of the people are becoming receptive to the right claimed by the state to intervene in civil society, as well as in political life. This is an important part of forging the new society embodied in the New Order's vision of *kekeluargaan*, with the state embodying paternalistic authority" (Robinson 1989:30–31).

Key to the success of family planning has been disseminating the notion of normative (*normal*) sexuality. Persons who comply with the Family Planning program are known as "acceptors" (*akseptor*); accepting the "transfer of responsibility" for family planning from the state to individual helps make them *normal* (Warwick 1986:455). It is primarily through defining the *normal*, rather than the deviant, that the Indonesian state has linked sexuality and nation (Dwyer 2000:28). Sexuality and nation are to come together in a particular kind of heteronormative family: male head of household, wife who might work but always puts her role as wife and mother first, and two children. This family came to symbolize the stability and integrity of the social order.

As discussed in chapter 4, this is a sexuality formed through notions of choice and love. It can be shaped by globalizing discourses—Valentine's Day, for instance, has become a popular celebration of *normal* sexuality—but is seen as originating in Indonesia. While literally clothed in the language of tradition (see fig. 7–6), its authenticity comes from its link to the nation: "The goal of preserving national unity, fought and won by the youth of the 1920s, continues to this day as the overarching goal of the country's life as a nation—an end anchored on the nurturing of the family as the strong foundation of society" (BKKBN 1999:20).

This is the paradox of Indonesian postcoloniality: "Authenticity does not accrue but, on the contrary, must be built in as a unique quality that will survive through time, in spite of time" (Pemberton 1994:159). To not follow Family Planning is tantamount to disavowing national belonging; marginalized social groups, such as ethnic Chinese, can thus be presented as resistant to Family Planning (Departemen Dalam Negeri 1974:37; see also Butt 2001). When, for instance, a *gay* man in Makassar said one reason he married a woman was "because in Indonesian culture (*budaya*

Indonesia) the family is a joy of its own," the notion of "Indonesian culture" he deployed is not outside state discourse. Through the "spectacle" of Family Planning, "the Indonesian state at once offers a compelling version of nationalism and sexuality and positions itself as the primary author of national representation. By staging these spectacles, the state works to instill a regime where people monitor themselves and their sexual practices to accommodate to public displays of sexual 'normalcy'" (Dwyer 2000:41).

By the 1980s the family principle had become a primary mode through which the New Order state articulated its notion of development: the nuclear family, not the citizen in isolation, was construed as the smallest unit of the nation (Suryakusuma 1996:95–97). The ideal citizen response to everything from regional separatism to HIV education was *secara kekeluargaan*, "family style" (among other things, this implies settling disputes without resorting to the law): "The family . . . bears a heavy burden in the transformation of Indonesia's population into 'modern' citizens of the nation-state" (S. Brenner 1998:228). This concept of the family is not representational but normative; it has been "aimed not at accurately representing the diverse social entities that we call families but at presenting a model that all families are supposed to emulate, directed toward the furthering of goals that always exceed the boundaries of the family itself" (S. Brenner 1998:228).

When the Indonesian state declares that the family is the smallest unit of the nation, it has a specific kind of family in mind, with particular gender and class characteristics: the ideal citizen family is not a "traditional" extended family but the modern, heterosexual, paternalistic nuclear family (figs. 7-4, 7-5), the middle-class family of consumerism (see chapter 4). In many understandings worldwide, the middle class "occupies a precarious position along two continua" (Liechty 2003:7)—between poor and rich, on the one hand, and tradition and modernity, on the other. For the Indonesian case I would add a third continuum: the middle class occupies a national space, between local and global. *Gay* and *lesbi* Indonesians lie at the intersection of these three continua and are shaped by the notions of choice found in dominant ideologies of the middle class.

The family principle has a strong temporal element. Families are actively built through the efforts of their members and the state; they are cause and product of national development. They are both foundational element and microcosm of the nation, a domestic Taman Mini: like that theme park, the ideal nuclear family is to be a "perfectly cultural representation" of Indonesia (Pemberton 1994:153): "In the ideologies of the New Order, the family/household is not considered to be autonomous in any way; it is merely a fraction of a national whole, a unit that has no indepen-

Figure 7–4. The "traditional" family. *BKKBN* (1988:24).

Figure 7–5. The "modern" family. *BKKBN* (1988:5).

dent meaning or existence apart from the nation-state" (S. Brenner 1998:238). Heterosexuality animates the family principle; in postcolonial Indonesia, men and women are to choose heterosexual marriage based on love.[8] Through this choice they make the families that are the building blocks of the nation, and through this choice they also make themselves into proper, authentic citizens who will be recognized by the nation: "[In Indonesia] sexuality and gender may be reified as essential, non-negotiable attributes of national identity" (Dwyer 2000:27).

THE ARCHIPELAGO CHILD

> On February 4, 1997, a healthy baby . . . was born in a small village in the province of West Nusa Tenggara. His birth marked him as the 200 millionth Indonesian citizen and was celebrated as a special occasion. . . . The President awarded him a special name, Wahyu Nusantaraaji, which literally means "a valuable revelation to [the archipelago]."
> —National Family Planning Coordinating Board

Little Wahyu Nusantaraaji was certainly unaware of his name's significance on that fateful day in 1997, but the naming of this archipelago child reveals how an articulation between the archipelago concept and the family principle is built into, indeed is defining of, Indonesian postcolonial governmentality. The intersection of the archipelago concept and the family principle is illustrated by the well-known map of Indonesia in which each province is essentialized in terms of a single "tradition," signified through clothing on a *heterosexual* couple (fig. 7–6; see also Rutherford 1996:584). Heterosexuality, usually placed at the bottom of such maps, constitutes ethnolocalized "diversity"; the archipelago concept (typically

BHINNEKA TUNGGAL IKA

Figure 7–6. Heterosexual and ethnolocalized couples constituting the nation. Courtesy of Danilyn Rutherford.

at the top), "unity." Together they literally bracket the national motto of "unity in diversity."

The archipelago concept and the family principle intersect even in lower-level official discourse. I recall attending an evening neighborhood Independence Day celebration in 2000 in Makassar; as is typical, a residential street was blocked off and filled with chairs, with a stage at one end. A banner behind the stage read "different but always one" (*beda tetap satu*). On this evening a local official spoke to the crowd, emphasizing that "if you have a problem, go to a local leader; don't go to the mass media or to outsiders. We should solve our problems family style (*secara kekeluargaan*). Even though we were from different ethnicities (*suku*) and religions, we are all one people (*bangsa*)."

The archipelago concept and the family principle are aesthetic forms and political structures—indeed, they aestheticize the political—and crucially, their intersection is predicated upon the conflation of "heterosexuality" and "choice." The growth of the individuals within the family—and the growth of the family as a unit—*is* national development, not just a metaphor for it. Since the New Order, development has been central to Indonesian governmentality; Soeharto termed himself the "father of development" (*bapak pembangunan*). It was under this discourse of heterosexualized development that the *gay* and *lesbi* subject positions took form, and while this discourse has been partially discredited in the wake of Soeharto's fall, no pretender to the throne—reform, civil society, human rights, or regional autonomy—has completely dissociated itself from its assumptions. Development has been linked to the archipelago concept since 1973, when Decree No. IV of the People's Consultative Assembly (MPR) stated that the archipelago concept was to be "the concept that forms the basis of Indonesia's national development," one that "gives life to national development in all its aspects—political, educational, social, cultural, and that of defense" (Kusumaatmadja 1982:12, 25). Another example of the archipelago concept and family principle's intersection can be seen in that

> in each provincial museum [there is] an area set aside as the Ruang Nusantara— the nusantara (archipelago) room, or gallery—where visual comparisons are made between local artifacts and those from elsewhere in Indonesia. The nusantara room might contain, for example, swords or wedding costumes from each province in the archipelago . . . with the implication that, for all its variations, Indonesia is one. . . . One of the most widely used kinds of nusantara gallery displays [is] *sets of male and female dolls dressed in wedding garments of each province*—a custom also seen in places like Jakarta's Taman Mini amusement park. (Taylor 1994:79–80; emphasis added)

These archipelago rooms illustrate how the archipelago concept and the family principle intersect in national discourse: heterosexuality brings together ethnolocalized "tradition" and modern choice; it turns diversity into unity, reproducing national belonging. Throughout its career, the concept of the Indonesian nation has been constructed in terms of a "collective ethical agent" which, through instrumental rationality, creates forms of organization that make the modern Indonesian nation-state possible (Cheah 2003:256). What has largely escaped scholarly attention is how this collective ethical agent, and its form of organization, are founded in heteronormativity.

ARCHIPELAGIC SELFHOOD

To my knowledge Wahyu Nusantaraaji is the only acknowledged archipelago child. Yet *gay* and *lesbi* Indonesians are also children of the archipelago—dubbing elements of national discourse with global discourses of homosexual desire. Without the archipelago concept and the family principle, the *gay* and *lesbi* subject positions would not have taken the forms they have. For example, as the archipelago concept shapes a sense of national subjectivity, the family principle shapes a sense that "heterosexual" marriage is the precondition to being a successful citizen. The choice most *gay* and *lesbi* Indonesians make to marry illustrates how the *gay* and *lesbi* subject positions are archipelagic—not predicated on a singular selfhood that coheres across time and space, but capable of movement through different "islands" of life that do not need to resolve into one. The archipelago concept thus shares some elements with notions of "double consciousness" like the "Black Atlantic" that "call the very desire to be centered into question" (Gilroy 1993b:190). When in 1987 the magazine *Tempo* inadvertently termed the then-new *gay* zine *GAYa Nusantara* "*gaya hidup nusantara*," not "archipelago style" but "archipelago lifestyle," this mishearing reflected how the archipelago concept was understood to apply to individual citizen lives.[9]

The choice to marry indicates how the state's archipelago concept and family principle are "dubbed" in *gay* and *lesbi* life. For most *gay* and *lesbi* Indonesians "heterosexual" marriage is assumed, and the beliefs of those who do not wish to marry make no sense, nor did my own claims that I would never marry a woman: why would you want to hurt your parents by not marrying? How will you think of yourself as an adult, as complete? For most *gay* and *lesbi* Indonesians, a multiply narrativized *gay* self or *lesbi* self can be a married, procreating self, even when marriage is to some extent a dreaded event. When a *gay* man turns to his lover in bed and tells him to marry, he is not confused about who he "really" is, nor is he internalizing homophobia or denying reality. He is expressing and perpetuating a subjectivity best thought of as archipelagic, rather than cosmopolitan, diasporic, or hybrid. The idea of a *gay* man and *lesbi* woman marrying each other is so rare because of the way these subjectivities straddle a contradiction—not between "tradition" and "modernity," but between two contradictory state rhetorics, the archipelago concept and the family principle. The first makes possible a subjectivity where the self does not have to be the same in all contexts. This renders thinkable a *gay* or *lesbi* self who is also "heterosexually" married. But the family principle constructs marriage as not only an alliance between families, but a totalizing conjugal relationship providing love, meaning, and purpose as well as sex, children, and a household—uniting the multifarious domains of modern life and engendering national recognition.

My discussion of *gay* and *lesbi* sociality in earlier chapters demonstrates how these Indonesians are the truest children of the archipelago: their senses of sexual selfhood are irreducible to ethnolocality. While those calling themselves *gay* or *lesbi* may think of themselves in ethnolocalized terms—as Bugis, Javanese, and so on—with regard to any number of domains of life, from kinship to religion to illness and health, in regard to their sexualities they think of themselves as *gay* and *lesbi* Indonesians. In some cases this link to national discourse is explicit, as when *gay* men speak of *gay* identity cards or of working together as *gotong royong*, a term for mutual help promulgated by the state (Bowen 1986), *lesbi* women speak of having "no place" in Indonesia, or both name groups with terms derived from *GAYa*. For an entertainment event, *gay* men will sometimes create a "welcoming line of multi-ethnic 'women' of Indonesia in native costumes" (Howard 1996:297). The link to national discourse is also implicit in the sense that the *gay* and *lesbi* worlds are distributed across Indonesia, and that *gay*ness and *lesbi*ness are never learned from "tradition" or local knowledge. In the shadow of rhetorics of national belonging, *gay* men and *lesbi* women engage in dubbing culture, troubling the borders between similitude and difference, East and West, asli and dubbing, living apparently foreign subjectivities through reconfiguring state discourse and transforming Western concepts of homosexuality.

As noted in chapter 2, persons inhabit multiple subject positions, and those subject positions need not have isomorphic spatial scales. Persons modify subject positions as they inhabit them—subjectivities always exceed the bounds of the subject positions they instantiate—but within horizons of intelligibility. A gay man in the United States can be gay in different ways, but it is unlikely he believes the concept "gay" is unique to Iowa, or to Boston: improvisation usually takes place within the subject position's spatial scale. Since subject positions can be structured by multiple spatial scales, there is no reason that *gay* and *lesbi* could not be ethnolocalized. Thus it is all the more astounding that the ethnographic materials presented in this book offer not a single unambiguous case of someone understanding themselves as, say, *gay* Javanese or *lesbi* Balinese. For over thirty years persons of the archipelago have been inhabiting these subject positions across multiple lines of difference: class, generation, region, urban versus rural, religion. Yet a powerful similitude, a sense of national subjectivity, links these persons, making all the more salient the failure to attain national belonging, authenticity, and recognition.

The dominant logic of the Western gay and lesbian subject positions originates in "confessional" metaphors, taken up by sexology and psychology since the mid-nineteenth century, that assume an interior self is the origin of subjectivity (Foucault 1978). This self's authenticity is contingent upon similitude: one is to be the same sexual person in all domains of life. One is to "come out," first by coming out to oneself, then to one's parents, workplace, and so on. This sense of expansion through time was codified in the mid-twentieth century by psychologists like Erik Erikson—whose fifth stage of self-development, "subjectivity versus role diffusion," valorizes a unitary subjectivity that does not vary with social context—and specifically by psychological models of "Homosexual Identity Formation," sometimes known as "HIF" models. One review of HIF models emphasized that "although 'coming out' begins when individuals define themselves to themselves as homosexual, lesbians and gay males typically report an increased desire over time to disclose their homosexual identity to at least some members of an expanding series of audiences. Thus, coming out, or identity disclosure, takes place at a number of levels: to self, to other homosexuals, to heterosexual friends and family, to co-workers, and to the public at large" (Troiden 1988:36).

The origin of this "desire over time to disclose" is treated as a presocial, universal need: "to the extent that people routinely present themselves as homosexual in most or all social settings, their homosexual identities are realized" (Troiden 1988:41). In this interpretation, to say one is gay or lesbian only to certain people, in certain places, or at certain times, means one's self-development is incomplete. Millions of gay and lesbian Westerners live their lives through this dominant ontology of selfhood. This is not a totalizing discourse; there are, for instance, many men and women in the West who have same-gender sex but do not term themselves gay or lesbian, and there are many men and women in the West who term themselves gay or lesbian yet engage in "heterosexual" sex. But in terms of the dominant discourse, such persons are seen as atypical, self-denying ("they're really bisexual"), even abnormal. This is the power of the confessional discourse of homosexuality, which not only appears in social scientific literature but is produced by gay men and lesbians themselves, as in the following excerpt from a self-help text:

> Coming out essentially means letting other people know that we are gay. . . . It takes a lot of effort to hide who you are . . . in the long run staying in the closet makes you feel guilty, ashamed, and unhappy. If you have to hide facets of your life, you will never be able to live freely. (Ford 1996:67–68)

These models of Western homosexual subjectivity share a lack of attention to the implicit theory of selfhood that undergirds them:

> The Western conception of the person as a bounded, unique, more or less integrated motivational and cognitive universe, a dynamic center of awareness, emotion, judgment, and action organized into a distinctive whole and set contrastively both against other such wholes and against its social and natural background, is, however incorrigible it may seem to us, a rather peculiar idea within the context of the world's cultures. (C. Geertz 1983:59)

One of the central projects of queer theory has been to denaturalize and destabilize this dominant discourse (e.g., Butler 1990; Sedgwick 1991), but often without reference to sexuality outside the West. Indeed, much of the concern with non-Westerners terming themselves "gay" or "lesbian" originates in a fear that such nomenclature inevitably brings the dominant Western discourse of homosexuality in its wake. Through concepts like "dubbing culture," I hope to indicate how such Western discourses of homosexuality are reworked in the Indonesian context, not through "tradition" but through rhetorics of national belonging. *Gay* and *lesbi* subjectivities tend to be "archipelagic"—a more ethnographically and theoretically precise specification of multiplicity than the rather obfuscating term "fluidity." To Westerners the most striking example of this archipelagic self might be that many *gay* men and *lesbi* women marry "heterosexually," do not see this as inconsistent with their subjectivities, and assume that Western gay men and lesbians do the same. When, for instance, *gay* men imagine a better future, it usually takes the form of a *gay* world that is more socially accepted, with more places, bigger events, and more *gay* men in it. Yet few *gay* men outside of activist organizations desire a *gay* world in which *gay* men do not normatively marry women.

This is not a schizophrenic or split subjectivity in the Western sense; a closer analogue would be the metaphor of the self as actor playing different roles (a metaphor *gay* men and *lesbi* women sometimes use). In the West it is easy to imagine how someone could be a teacher and an administrator, a soccer coach and office worker, or a mother and a mountain-climber. It is more difficult for a Westerner to imagine someone being "homosexual" and "heterosexual" at the same time. However, most *gay* men and *lesbi* women consider themselves "open" in reference to the *gay* or *lesbi* world, with no necessary relation to other aspects of life. As one *gay* man put it: "I read the situation first. If it's open (*buka*), I'm open. If it's closed (*tutup*), I'm closed. What's good is: don't be open right away." Another *gay* man once mused that "in most cases I don't think it's right to say 'closed' (*tertutup*; the most common term); it's more correct to say 'closing oneself' (*menutup diri*). *Tertutup* means anywhere at all they're closed, like they can't accept their situation or they are closed to everyone without exception. *Menutup diri* means that it depends on the location or environment." This grammatical distinction highlights a pervasive sense that what makes *gay* or *lesbi* subjectivity authentic is not uniformity over all domains of life, but participation in the *gay* or *lesbi* world—an island of life that does not necessarily have implications for other islands of life.

Such subjectivities are the kind of homosexuality that dominant Western frameworks see as immature or inauthentic. They are often labeled "situational," as if sexuality (like all domains of life) is not always contextual; the expectation is that sexuality be confessed everywhere. But *gay* and *lesbi* subjectivities are archipelagic in that their authenticity does not require renouncing other subjectivities. One *gay* man noted that since marrying "my perspective [*wawasan*] has grown, and I've been able to compare things with my married *gay* friends about what our lives will be like in the future, how to get ready for that, to find a solution for living in this Indonesia" [*hidup di Indonesia ini*]. To be *gay* and *lesbi*, one opens

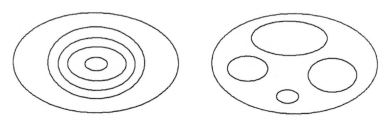

Figure 7–7. Confessional self, archipelagic self.

oneself to the *gay* or *lesbi* world, but for most *gay* and *lesbi* Indonesians there is no sense that one should ideally open oneself to the world in general. This is why for so many *gay* and *lesbi* Indonesians the desire to marry "heterosexually" does not contradict a sense of being *gay* or *lesbi* and is not understood as bisexuality. The idea of multiple, fractal, or "dividual" subjectivities can be shaped by "traditional" discourses as well as those of the nation-state, and exists in many parts of the Asia/Pacific region (e.g., Strathern 1988:268–274; 1992:125; Shore 1982:41, 133–141). However, the ethnographic data support the conclusion that the particular form of multiplicity in *gay* and *lesbi* lives has been formed by dubbing Western notions of homosexual selfhood with national discourse, as exemplified by the archipelago concept (fig. 7–7).

It appears that in *gay* and *lesbi* lives the archipelago concept is triply recursive: "worlds" of life make up the self, which is one "island" in a national *gay* or *lesbi* archipelago, which is one "island" in a global gay and lesbian archipelago. On all these levels the archipelago concept permits a nuanced grid of similitude and difference in comparison to confessional and continental discourses, which tend toward binarism. For instance, *gay* and *lesbi* Indonesians consistently insist that they are "the same" as gay and lesbian Westerners, yet they are also quite cognizant of difference—they do not see themselves as derivative of Western homosexuality, even though it is frequently images and narratives of Western homosexuality that they "dub" from the first time they begin to occupy the *gay* or *lesbi* subject position. They believe that gay and lesbian Westerners (and gay men and lesbians elsewhere in the "Third World," such as Latin America) share a set of desires and practices and inhabit analogous places. Frequently during fieldwork I would ask my *gay* and *lesbi* interlocutors if they had questions about the West. I received queries ranging from "Do gay bars really exist?" to "Have you met Leonardo DiCaprio?," but just as often they responded politely that "I feel I already know everything about your life." One *gay* man phrased this as "We're the same [*sama*], just separated; there is no difference" (*perbedaan*): another said, "It's the same style, *gay* men here and there" (*sama aja gayanya, gay-gay di sini dengan sana*).

Gay and *lesbi* Indonesians are, in my experience, always aware that the terms *gay* and *lesbi* have analogues outside Indonesia, though the degree to which they feel they have knowledge about these analogues varies. For *gay* and *lesbi* Indonesians, the West tends to be an unknown and strange place, both attractive and threatening. "California," for instance, is some-place (a region? a town?) in or near America: "Is it bigger than the city of Surabaya?" I was once asked; "Is it near Hollywood?" Yet with regard to being *gay* or *lesbi* the West is, at a fundamental level, familiar. When *gay* Indonesians talk about possible differences between the lives of gay Westerners and their own, comparisons are almost always drawn along an axis of openness and closedness. To wit, it is a sense that the West is more opened (*terbuka*), which denotes social acceptance and political rights. It is imagined in utopian terms: there must be lots of tempat ngebers that are busy all night long, ubiquitous *gay* discos and cafes, and a general ease in finding sexual and romantic partners. It is usually as-sumed that these gay Westerners have relationships with other men marked by romance and sexual variety.

Nevertheless, *gay* men tend to assume that gay Westerners marry women. A few have learned from tourists (or, more rarely, mass media) that this is not so, but even such reports may not sway their minds. For instance, Ikbal's discovery that I did not plan on marrying was a source of unending consternation. One night at *Texas* he informed me that "I may be living in the big city, but at heart I'm still a village boy. I know I'm influenced by a lot of foreign concepts, but what I do is receive those things that are good and the other things I just ignore." When I asked: "What do you take and what do you reject?" he replied: "I'll use you as an example. You are very friendly and good. So excuse me for saying so, but what I reject is you saying that you're never going to marry. I reject this Western thing where you say something is not possible when you haven't even made an effort. I reject the idea that *gay* people don't marry and have children. How can you say it's not possible for you when you haven't tried?"

One difference between *gay* men and *lesbi* women is that *lesbi* women more often believe that the West is a worse place than Indonesia. This appears to be a product of the violence (domestic and otherwise) experi-enced by Indonesian women, combined with Hollywood images of the West as a place of unbridled violence, and occasional mass media report-age on homophobic violence. As one *lesbi* woman put it: "It's better here than in America, right? Because there the antigay people are stronger than here." In its November 1997 premiere issue, the *lesbi* zine *MitraS* ran the following commentary:

There is definitely no place for G [*gay*] & L [*lesbi*] people to act as freely as those who live on the Western half of the globe. Go ahead and dream about it! But that doesn't mean that G & L people in the Western nations are always more lucky than we who are quiet in Indonesia. "Anti" groups appear along with the increased activities of G & L groups. . . . What's more, the actions of who are "anti" can even take the form of violence towards a person who has made themselves known as G or L. . . . We in Indonesia feel like were are emasculated, that our freedom to move is very limited; however, the reaction from groups in society is not yet too harsh; it's still at the degree of a "phobia." So which is better? It depends on the opinion of each [*lesbi*].

Yet none of these speculations about the West implies a radical alterity—it is a matter of degree not kind, "opened" or "closed," not Other. A *gay* man from Surabaya once emphasized that "here people are less open. Well, in here [*di sini*] they are opened, but out there [*di luar*] they are not." This *gay* man was speaking to me in a disco, wearing women's clothes and makeup for a playback competition. Yet we were having a conversation about the United States and Indonesia, and the deictic terms "in here" and "out there" referred not just to the walls of the disco, but to the boundaries of a *gay* world understood as an archipelago of places within the Indonesian nation.

For my *gay* and *lesbi* interlocutors, gay and lesbian Westerners are distant but present, conceptually near even if they had never met one before myself. The structure of imagination is analogous to the way an Indonesian at one end of the archipelago imagines Indonesians at the other end of the archipelago. I have never heard anyone speak of the possibility that an ETP like bissu or warok might be found in the West, but it is self-evident that gay and lesbian Westerners exist and are linked to *gay* and *lesbi* Indonesians in a grid of similitude and difference for which I can think of no better moniker than "archipelagic."

The relationship between *gay* and *lesbi* Indonesians and national discourse is one of resonances, borrowings, and transformations: as noted earlier, only occasionally does it become the topic of direct commentary. It is thus quite different from the "Queer Nation" movement in the United States, an ironic, camp-inflected mimicry of nationalism (Berlant and Freeman 1993). That *gay* and *lesbi* subjectivities are complexly imbricated with state discourse does not make them experience-distant: they are deeply felt senses of selfhood, founded in rhetorics of the nation, that do not supplant ethnolocalized subjectivities but interact with them in an additive manner (after all, the valorization of pluralism is central to the state's self-presentation as an archipelagic container of diversity). The state stands as inadvertent idiom for *gay* or *lesbi* subjectivities. For this reason the proper parallel is not Queer Nation, but how Western gay, lesbian, bisexual, and transgender subject positions are normatively structured by the idea that sexuality is a core element of self-identity that must be confessed and integrated into all domains of life to be ontologically valid—but this indebtedness to nineteenth-century psychoanalytic thought does not mean that such Westerners support or even know of psychoanalysis.

Just as a minority of *gay* and *lesbi* Indonesians plan on never marrying, so there are those who see archipelagic selfhood as painful, undesirable, or inauthentic. Donny was a relatively wealthy *gay* man living in Surabaya. When I asked him if *gay* men could become *normal*, he replied, "It depends on your wishes. I choose the middle road. Not *biseks* [i.e., thinking of himself as bisexual], but the road of moderation between sex and my career." For Donny, "my career is proof that I'm normal" (*karir saya bukti bahwa saya orang normal*). He felt that his career was "an escape to forget . . . sex? No, not sex. Scratch that from your notes. It's to forget a beautiful dream . . . that cannot be achieved. This is our life here."

I will take seriously Donny's request to scratch the idea of "escape" from my notes. His discomfort with archipelagic selfhood is not a simple function of class; persons with similar sentiments can be found among working class *gay* men and *lesbi* women, and many wealthy Indonesians see no conflict between their subjectivities and "heterosexual" marriage. However, the view of the world expressed by Donny and others shares a key feature with the majority of *gay* and *lesbi* Indonesians who embrace archipelagic subjectivities: a concern with the performance of good and successful deeds—from one's "career" to everyday acts of kindness. These deeds, known as *prestasi*, are crucial to *gay* and *lesbi* subjectivities. The importance of prestasi indicates how, as Donny intimates, being *normal* is about more than heterosexuality: it is about a kind of personhood-as-career where "success" carries momentous implications for recognition and belonging.

SEXUALITY AND NATION

> I am a regular Indonesian
> Who works for the Indonesian people
> In an Indonesian style [*dengan cara Indonesia*]
> —Ki Hajar Dewantara

The "style" of *gay* and *lesbi* life demonstrates how sexual citizenship (see Evans 1993) is key to the economic and political workings of the postcolonial Indonesian state. *Gay* and *lesbi* Indonesians reconfigure state hegemony in a manner the state never intended. *Gay* and *lesbi* are the clearest cases of truly national subject positions, irreducible to ethnolocality, and moreover synthesizing East and West in a manner consistent with long-standing tropes of the "modern Indonesian" (Frederick 1997).

Yet this very irreducibility to ethnolocality marks the *gay* and *lesbi* subject positions as failures: exceeding the state's own discourse of national belonging, they can never have the "traditional" diversity that represents the raw material to be unified by the archipelago concept. However, while *gay* and *lesbi* Indonesians are marginal to the body politic, in one sense their subject positions are a kind of distillation of national discourse, an ultimate achievement of the national project. In another sense, their presence challenges the state's own mode of governmentality. The *gay* and *lesbi* subject positions do not participate in the ethnolocalized logic of territoriality: they do not hope one day to have an island of their own because they belong to the archipelago. These subject positions are places where the state's own tactics of recognition and belonging are revealed by their absence; they symptomatize the contradictions of the postcolonial state. These national subject positions reveal the mechanics of how the state requires the production of ethnolocalized identities. The *gay* and *lesbi* subject positions are supreme but unanticipated examples of the postcolonial state's efforts to carry out the five consequential words of Article 32 of the 1945 Constitution, still in effect—"The government shall advance Indonesian national culture" (*Pemerintah memajukan kebudayaan nasional Indonesia*)—a goal that for the state is "a crucial aspect of its nation building" (Acciaioli 1997:289; see also F. Ali 1997; Hooker and Dick 1993). At the same time, they implicitly critique the postcolonial state's self-representation as arbiter of tradition, authenticity, modernity, and belonging.

In the Dutch East Indies, racial categories defined a colonial governmentality "concerned above all with disabling old forms of life by systematically breaking down their conditions, and with constructing in their place new conditions so as to enable—indeed, so as to oblige—new forms of life to come into being" (Scott 1995:193). The mixed-race person blurred the boundary between colonizer and native, raising the specter of a "metamorphosis" that would destabilize the racial logic of colonial rule (Stoler 2002b:6). Because Dutch colonial discourse assumed that reproduction (and thus miscegenation) was heterosexual, homosexuality received little attention: while not desirable, it was assumed not to produce mixed-race children (Stoler 1995:96). Like the borders of the nation, this understanding of sexuality was taken from colonial into postcolonial discourse. Proper sexuality is central to acting in what Dewantara—the person credited with bringing the term *nusantara* into nationalist discourse—terms an "Indonesian style." It is the substitution of choice and love for arrangement. Choice implies the possibility of failed choice; with this substitution, homosexuality becomes thinkable as something that constitutes persons and reflects on them (rather than on the bad arrangements of a family whose child divorces the spouse selected for them). This postcolonial context shapes how *gay* and *lesbi* Indonesians think of their subjectivities as modern: clearly not passed down through tradition, dubbing transnational discourses of homosexuality, and having a national scope, but in a failed way. They are not recognized. They are "of" the archipelago, yet their style does not belong. Lyotard notes:

> In the Introduction to [Kant's] third Critique, the dispersion of the genres of discourse is . . . dramatized to the point that the problem posed is that of finding "passages" (Uebergange) between these heterogeneous genres. . . . This object could only be a symbol. Let's say, an archipelago. Each genre of discourse would be like an island; the faculty of judgment would be, at least in part, like an admiral or like a provisioner of ships who would launch expeditions from one island to the next. . . . This interventionist force has no object, and does not have its own island, but it requires a milieu—this would be the sea. (1988:130–131)

For the Indonesian state, the archipelago metaphor addresses the problem of dispersion within the nation—difference—in a world where globalization appears ubiquitous, even banal. *Gay* and *lesbi* Indonesians rework this archipelago metaphor and in so doing forge "genres," styles, that invoke the national and transnational. The dominant imagining of the Western life course is as a race course; either "each man is an island" or not being able to stand alone makes you a "dependent." You start at one place and move forward in time and space to the finish line. For *gay* and *lesbi* Indonesians, we could say figuratively that the course is more like a sailing course, tacking back and forth among landing points widely dispersed in space-time, and the self is an archipelago. But even this is insufficient. For *gay* and *lesbi* Indonesians, the self is not that which moves from island to island; it is the water itself, lapping up on multiple shores at the same time. After all, the etymology of both "archipelago" and "nusantara" refers not to a set of islands, but to the water between them. It is this sense of the self as the thing between the "islands," the water lapping on the shore, that explains how *gay* and *lesbi* Indonesians feel linked to distant but familiar Others across the globe. It is a style of selfhood forged through dubbing the discursive resources at hand within a horizon of power.

Nikolas Rose has noted how "Third Way" political theory in the West increasingly understands the politics of behavior in terms of "the values, beliefs, and sentiments thought to underpin the techniques of responsible self-government and the management of one's obligations to others" (2000:1399). The postcolonial Indonesian state appears to have anticipated the West in this regard. Ever since the New Order's rise, national belonging has been defined in terms of not just status but the performance of good deeds. What the state terms "national discipline" is an ethical practice, a development-in-miniature where the citizen prospers through good deeds (prestasi), of which the nuclear family is one of the most significant. As one married *gay* man put it: "It's a prestasi if we're married; it means we have responsibilities. We are no longer like a child, but an adult. . . . People who have a family are listened to, they receive a greater share [of respect] compared to a child."

Throughout my fieldwork, discussions of good deeds were a common theme among *gay* and *lesbi* Indonesians (and also warias). Again and again *gay* and *lesbi* Indonesians would speak about the possibility for social acceptance by saying "it comes back to us." It was assumed that if they behaved well and contributed to the social good, they would be more recognized. One of the most ubiquitous phrases I encountered in all three of my primary field sites was that of wanting to be "accepted by society" (*diterima oleh masyarakat*). As one *gay* man put it, "We have to do better than society."

By implication, the social nonrecognition of *gay* and *lesbi* sexuality indexes a failing on the part of *gay* and *lesbi* Indonesians themselves. One *gay* man in Bali described how happy he was to have learned where *gay* men hung out at night: "But I still wasn't satisfied, in the sense that I thought 'Is this all?' Just going to Puputan and hanging out, it didn't seem to have any meaning. I thought that gay people could have some positive contributions too, some 'value plus' [*nilai plus*]." Sex is never counted as a prestasi, and both my *gay* and *lesbi* interlocutors often expressed frustration that society, to the degree it was aware of them at all, saw them as interested "only" in sex. Even if unsure what this acceptance would entail, it was a deeply and consistently expressed aspiration. The notion of "society" invoked here and elsewhere by *gay* and *lesbi* Indonesians *never* in my fieldwork referred to ethnolocalized groupings. It always indexed a public culture (*masyarakat luas, masyarakat umum*) understood in national terms. One *gay* man defined society as "a group living together, needing each other, building a single life, helping each other [*saling tolong menolong*]." Prestasi bring meaning to sociality: "What's important," a *gay* man once explained, "is that our activities are good and don't shame our families." *Gay* and *lesbi* Indonesians would castigate each other for only caring about throwing parties, or stealing each other's girlfriends or boyfriends, or gossiping, rather than doing something "positive" (*positip*).

One of the clearest illustrations of the importance *gay* and *lesbi* Indonesians place on the dialectic between good deeds and belonging can be found in the informally produced magazines or "zines" that they have been creating since 1982 (Boellstorff 2004c). In these zines we find a recurrent trope: the idea that love can be the ultimate good deed demonstrating that *gay* and *lesbi* Indonesians are worthy of national inclusion. In these zines, *gay* Indonesians assume that prestasi must be visible to society to have these effects of inclusion. However, since it is difficult to speak positively of same-sex love in Indonesia, love fails as a prestasi. Belonging is deferred, and tropes of separation permeate *gay* zines as a result.

The link between love and nation often appears explicitly in zines; one of many examples is the short story *"Selingkuh,"* a term that among *gay* men refers to having sex with a man other than one's boyfriend (see chapter 4). The story appears in the zine *GAYa Nusantara* ("archipelago style," the same name as the group in Surabaya that has published this zine since 1987). In this story Adam and Sam are lovers who each, unbeknownst to the other, take out a personal ad in *GAYa Nusantara* to find a new sex partner. When Sam gets a reply he is excited:

Yess! Sekali lagi Sam bersorak-sorak bergembira, bergembira semua, sudah bebas negri kita, untuk s' lamaamanya. . . . Aduh, sampe keterusan nyanyi-nyanyi lagu perjuangan . . .[10]

Yess! Once again Sam shouted with happiness, everything was happy, our nation is now free, for all time. . . . Oh my, to the point that I accidentally sing a song of the struggle . . .

When Sam's joy leads him to sing a song from the anticolonial struggle, he breaks character to address the zine reader directly. When Adam receives *his* reply and is preparing for his blind date, he showers and dresses himself "carefully and in the shortest possible time (like the Proclamation) [*kayak proklamasi aja*]."[11] *Proklamasi* refers to the famously short (two-sentence) Declaration of Independence read by Sukarno on August 17, 1945, Indonesia's Independence Day. These are ironic and joking references to the nation, but the joke's bite comes from their appearance in a zine that, like all zines, regularly contains writing that employs nationalist discourse. Of course, it turns out that Adam and Sam have unknowingly chosen each other's personal ads; when they learn this, they celebrate their renewed love with a night of raucous sex. This story's author is from Ponorogo, the region of Java where "traditional" homosexual relations between warok actors and their gemblak understudies originate (see chapter 2), yet there is no mention of this "tradition"; *gay* love and *gay* belonging are national matters.

Heterosexist logics of national recognition can make nonnormative sexualities and genders into not only perversions but subversions, threats to national authenticity (Bunzl 2004). As Peter Jackson notes in the case of Thailand, homosexuality can be seen to represent more of a danger to national society than transgenderism, since transgenderism can be made to fit within a heterosexist logic where those who desire men must be effeminate and those who desire women must be masculine (Jackson 1999b:238). Homosexuality can also be seen as more threatening than transgenderism due to the widespread Southeast Asian assumption that inner states should match exterior bodily presentations (S. Errington 1989:76). Warias, who identify themselves as men with women's souls, properly display this inner mismatch in their cross-dressing, as do the lesser-known tombois. In contrast, *gay* men and ceweks have a "desire for the same," but this is not clearly exteriorized; they can appear *normal*. The cultural expectation that exterior presentation should match inner state or belief has been politicized before; during the Soeharto years one of the most successful ways to create fear of a by-then nonexistent communist movement was to describe it as an "organization without shape" (*organisasi tanpa bentuk*); that is, a collectivity whose exterior did not match its interior, just as it was supposed that individual communists were failing to exteriorize their political beliefs. With their difficult-to-read sexualities, *gay* men and effeminate *lesbi* women can be interpreted as possessing desire "without shape." Such a desire without shape appears inauthentic. As noted in earlier chapters, the concept of *asli* (authenticity) has been important to how the Indonesian state defines its legitimacy. It is the ultimate criterion for belonging; what belongs to Indonesia and is deserving of recognition is that which is authentic. It is a filter for responding to forces of globalization; through authenticity it will be possible to know what is compatible with being Indonesian. In 1952 Mohammad Hatta, first vice-president of Indonesia, emphasized that "the location of our homeland as an archipelago . . . has always led us to mix a lot with the foreigners calling here. . . . We can enrich our culture by making use of foreign cultures without forgetting the basis of our own" (Hatta 1970:287–288).

Gay and *lesbi* Indonesians talk about notions of authenticity quite frequently, as when joking about gender. They also talk in negative terms about people who are hypocrites, using terms like *munafik, hipokrit,* or *palsu*. In so doing they reflect how "the growing popularity of words to describe hypocrisy . . . is . . . significant. All these words imply betrayal of a single Real reality" (Anderson 1990:151). I have often encountered *gay* men using terms like *munafik* in everyday speech to speak about sexual duplicity—*gay* men who have a boyfriend but then also carry on affairs with other men. In more reflective contexts like interviews, *gay* men speak not only in terms of relationships, but of desire, as in the case of the *gay* man from Surabaya who said in chapter 4 that "We can't be hypocrites: if a man likes a man that means he's *gay*." A third use of terms like *munafik* in more reflective contexts indexes movement between the *gay* and *normal* worlds, as when a *gay* man in Bali spoke of *gay* men who would make fun of effeminacy at work to keep themselves above suspicion as "hypocrites." In a discussion with a group of *gay* men in Surabaya, one man noted how "I feel I'm munafik, that I'm sinning, because in the everyday world [*dunia umum*] it's like I'm a regular man, but in my [*gay*] world my asli self is totally visible." A *gay* interlocutor from Makassar also explicitly brought together hypocrisy and authenticity when he said that "some people say I'm a hypocrite because I'm married, but that's not true. I know who I am; I'm clear about myself. And even though I'm married, I identify [*mengidentifikasi diri*] as an authentic gay [*gay asli*]."

Indonesian postcolonial discourse takes ethnolocalized aspects of subjectivity like "Javanese" as self-evidently authentic, the diversity that is both precondition for national belonging and its product. In contrast, *gay* and *lesbi* subjectivities are a dub for which there is no authentic original. They are self-evidently *not* ethnolocalized, a distinction they share, uncomfortably, with the postcolonial state. In state discourse it is the archipelago concept that mediates ethnolocalized authenticity and the danger of national hypocrisy; it is through this self-same concept, as well as the family principle, that *gay* and *lesbi* Indonesians reconfigure ostensibly Western concepts of sexuality. *Gay* men and *lesbi* women dub nationalist discourse and in so doing dub the foreign "gay" and "lesbian" into *gay* and *lesbi*, into a set of identifications, sexual practices, and social contexts they feel to be authentically Indonesian. They give lie to the "common misperception" that "whatever is not recognizably local or is obviously borrowed—the institution of the Presidency, say, or Garuda Indonesia Airways—is foreign, specifically Western, and therefore by definition not part of Indonesian culture" (Liddle 1988:6). On the margins of local, national, and transnational rhetorics of selfhood, *gay* and *lesbi* Indonesians live their lives archipelago style.

CHAPTER EIGHT

The *Gay* Archipelago

TRANSLATING SELFHOOD

In the proceeding chapters I have investigated how the *gay* and *lesbi* subject positions—licensed by no tradition, marketed by no corporation, and supported by no official—are taken up on the margins of society by thousands, if not millions, of Indonesians. I have emphasized how the national, not ethnolocalized, character of these subject positions has important consequences for *gay* and *lesbi* lives and also indicates how an anthropology of similitude can contribute to understanding intersections of globalization and postcoloniality. The concepts "*gay*" and "*lesbi*" are certainly shaped by globalizing processes, but the *nation* is the spatial scale and cultural-political-economic form through which *gay* and *lesbi* are experienced as social facts.

As noted earlier, this does not mean that *gay* and *lesbi* are not shaped by other spatial scales (ethnolocalized, global, regional) with regard to other aspects of their lives, nor does it mean that ethnolocalized (or globalized) *gay* and *lesbi* subject positions could not appear in the future. It means that to date and from their inception, these subject positions are lived "archipelago style." For two reasons neither I nor those interlocutors with whom I have spoken about the subject believe ethnolocalized *gay* or *lesbi* subject positions will emerge in the immediate future. First, the cultural dimensions of current moves toward regional autonomy have been predominantly expressed in a heteronormative language of revitalizing tradition that excludes concepts like *gay* and *lesbi*. Second, since subject positions are shaped by the historical circumstances during which they first took form, and since the *gay* and *lesbi* subject positions were formed during the New Order era, it seems likely they will retain national spatial scales for some time.

What we find in Indonesia is a *gay* archipelago and a *lesbi* archipelago: noncontiguous fields of social relations stretching across a national stage, and a predominant sense that one's *gay*-ness or *lesbi*-ness is one island in an archipelagic self. The relationship between nationalism and difference is thus more complex than the clear black lines of modern maps suggest (Gupta 1992).

I have also emphasized the importance of mass media to the consolidation of *gay* and *lesbi* subjectivities. Fragmentary mentionings of Western homosexuality frequently appear as the means by which *gay* and *lesbi* Indonesians come to know of themselves as such. *Gay and lesbi* subjectivities emerge as a kind of reading practice of the West. This impact of mass mediated coverage of Western homosexuality is particularly interesting because the resulting subjectivities are *national*, not transnational per se. This is why I find the notion of "dubbing culture" useful: it indexes forms of language reterritorialization that trouble dominant definitions of translation. Being *gay* and Indonesian is like hearing Tom Cruise "speak Indonesian" through the magic of dubbing. It is self-evidently inauthentic—out of cultural joint—yet socially efficacious. Somehow, you the Indonesian listener can understand what Tom Cruise is "saying"; somehow, *gay* and *lesbi* Indonesians "belong." The process of transforming messages from "outside" Indonesia is not unique to *gay* and *lesbi* Indonesians; youth culture, for instance, environmental movements, or Islamic and Christian communities of various kinds do this too. But what makes the case of *gay* and *lesbi* Indonesians special is the lack of institutional or corporate powers that intentionally contribute to the translocation. Misunderstandings that a "Gay International" contributes significantly to subjectivities like *gay* and *lesbi* reflect the assumption that such organized forces are necessary for "globalization" (Massad 2002). The phenomenon of "dubbing culture" indicates this not need be the case.

Feminist and postcolonial analyses have highlighted how Western understandings of translation posit a "strong generative" original and "weaker and derivative" product that encodes hierarchies of male-female or colonizer-colonized (Simon 1996:1; see also Niranjana 1992:1). Some of these analyses employ an idea of "translational culture" for how "newness enters the world" (Bhabha 1994:212; see also Chakrabarty 2000:17; Spivak 2000). This is a view of translation as metaphor, but also a literal "mode of translation" that through "localization" creates unforeseen possibilities (Rafael 1988:xviii, 15). These analyses often understand translation to be the production of completed texts: "in creating coherent and transparent texts and subjects, translation participates—across a range of discourses—in the fixing of colonized cultures" (Niranjana 1992:3). But if, as Niranjana notes, translation is interpellation, then what happens in dubbing? With this translational form, no coherent or transparent text or subject appears: the original and its "translation" are held together, side by side, without any unification or even the hope for such unification.

If "translational culture" can be construed in terms of *les belles infidèles*, the unfaithful woman, then "dubbing culture" is queer. Dubbing appears nonprocreative; it places two things alongside each other without clearly giving birth to something new. A power relation exists: few Indonesian films, for instance, get dubbed into English, and most Westerners do not lip-synch Indonesian popular music. It is not a free-for-all where anything gets put together with anything. But neither is it a rigid system where Western domination determines postcolonial reality. The life-worlds of *gay* and *lesbi* Indonesians indicate a more contingent inequality—queering translational theories of culture, indicating how unexpected selfhoods can be dubbed from hegemonies that might otherwise appear total, and globalizations that might otherwise appear seamless and beyond question.

The two greatest conceptual barriers to understanding *gay* and *lesbi* subjectivities are the rush to "tradition" as an explanatory principle, and the assumption that culture is by default local. These barriers are rooted in a theory of knowledge predicated on difference. The "archipelago style" of *gay* and *lesbi* life forces a consideration of how grids of similitude and difference are bound up with processes of globalization, and so must be included in the act of social analysis. Doing so reveals how *gay* and *lesbi* Indonesians do not fit the "Gay Planet" trope of immanent similitude or the "McGay" trope of unbridgeable difference. They cannot symbolize globalization's triumph, nor can they fill a queer "savage slot" that seeks an Other to "constitute the West as we know it" (Trouillot 1991:18). They chart a third, archipelagic path between similitude and difference, one that resists conflating difference with distance: others may be near at hand while one may share a bond of similitude with those on "islands" far away. Never have I heard a *gay* or *lesbi* Indonesian say they were Western or wished to become Western; nor have I heard a *gay* or *lesbi* Indonesian say they were completely distinct from gay and lesbian Westerners. The question is by what rubrics these Indonesians experience mediations of similitude and difference. I suggest that the answer lies in reconfigurations of national and global discourses productively glossed as "dubbing."

A kind of dubbing culture has always been central to the Indonesian national project. Key to the transformation of the "Dutch East Indies" to "Indonesia" was the transformation of "Malay" into "Indonesian." By the beginning of the twentieth century, Malay had become not just the language of trade and administration, but a means by which information from outside the Indies entered the archipelago: it "began to bring to the Indies the literatures and the events of the world and of one's neighbors. . . . Somewhat abruptly, via the medium of the lingua franca, most places in the world began to be felt in the Indies" (Siegel 1997:18–19). It is in the latter national context that the *gay* and *lesbi* subject positions, with their entailment of global connectivity, have taken form. Whereas warias understand their subjectivity as national (Boellstorff 2004b), *gay* and *lesbi* Indonesians *think the transnational through the national*: the waria subject position took form through a colonial "Malay archipelago" while the

TABLE 8–1.
Apparent isomorphisms.

Sexuality	ETPs (*bissu, warok*)	*waria*	gay
Spatial scale	local	national	global
Temporality	indigenous (way back then)	modern (then)	postmodern (now and future)
Political economy	precolonial	colonial	postcolonial
Language	Javanese, Balinese, Makassarese, etc.	Malay	Indonesian

gay and *lesbi* subject positions took form through a postcolonial national archipelago.

Given the waria subject position's origin in this colonial encounter, and the *gay* (and *lesbi*) subject position's origin in the postcolonial state, one can draw a parallel between language ideology and regimes of sexual subjectivity: "waria" is to "*gay*" as "Malay" is to "Indonesian." It might appear that a developmental path exists (table 8–1).

What such a developmentalist interpretation misses is how *gay* (and *lesbi*) Indonesians see themselves in national, not global, terms. Its neat narrative of displacement elides how, for instance, the waria subject position does not appear to be in the process of being replaced by the *gay* subject position. Through the notion of "dubbing culture," I hope to have set forth an ethnographically grounded theoretical framework for considering how, recalling Bhabha, newness enters an apparently already globalized world through conjunctural processes that are shaped by power relations but not just the "translation" of them. Dubbing neither seeks nor rejects the authentic; it lies alongside the authentic, opening up new possibilities for reconfiguration. It is not "meta" but "para"; it operates not through claiming causal hierarchy, but through a cultural logic of juxtaposition.

TRAVELING ARCHIPELAGOES

Because so few *gay* and *lesbi* Indonesians travel outside Indonesia, and as a result the globalizing forces that make the *gay* and *lesbi* subject positions possible are reconfigured through national discourse, I have emphasized neither other non-Western queer subject positions nor international travel. I have worked to construct an ethnographic corpus and theoretical architecture that reflect *gay* and *lesbi* lifeworlds, even while drawing upon

Western intellectual debates. Yet this book has been inspired by, and can be placed in the context of, a growing literature on persons outside the West who use terms "derived" from "gay" and "lesbian."[1]

A few *gay* men and *lesbi* women are able to travel to the West—because they are from a wealthy family and go for education, pleasure, or to visit relatives; because they are working-class and obtain work on a cruise ship or elsewhere; or because they have a Western partner who brings them to the West for a visit or longer-term residence. My *gay* and *lesbi* interlocutors who were able to visit the West speak of confounded expectations. Some return to Indonesia telling stories of amazing social acceptance and community: bars, discos, feminist groups, saunas, bookstores. Udin, a *gay* man in Surabaya who had lived for a few months in Melbourne, recalled these differences in terms of social acceptance, using terms common to state rhetoric like *wawasan* and *gotong royong* (Bowen 1986), and the archipelagic idea of a distributed set of places:

> The most striking difference was really the social acceptance [*penerimaan masyarakat*]. . . . I realize that it's not the case that in all Western nations, America or Australia, their people can accept them as if it's nothing, no, it's not like that, but there are certain locations where the general public already knows "this is the place [*tempat*] so we can expect that," yes? . . . People's perspective [*wawasan*] is wider. . . . Here, maybe because were accustomed to mutual aid [*gotong royong*], people ask about all our affairs, "What what what? Where are you going? Where have you come from?" . . . So, it probably just depends on culture.

However, many of my *gay* and *lesbi* interlocutors who had traveled outside Indonesia returned feeling that the West is a worse place to live. Made, from Bali, had a lover who brought him to see the lover's Western Australian hometown:

> Before, I used to think that gay life in the West was easy: open and free. I thought gay people didn't pay attention to gossip from society or anything. And that the government acknowledged their existence, and so on. But it turned out that my thinking was completely wrong, and I had to turn it around 180 degrees. For instance, I got invited to Western Australia. Well, it turned out that gays there were very closed, especially in the small town where my lover worked. There were no other openly gay people there, and because my lover is a teacher, he had to be closed too. So I thought, "Well, apparently it's just the same as here in Bali!" It was a learning experience for me, homework for me; I realized that I had to explain to my friends back in Bali that gay life in the West was like that.

Nira, a *lesbi* woman originally from northern Sumatra, had lived in Bali for many years and met Western lesbians:

My most recent relationship lasted five years. It was with an American woman: she went to Amherst and is from a wealthy family. We lived together here in Bali for five years, and she took me to America with her once: we were there for a little over a year, on the East Coast. I liked Provincetown and North Carolina. But I didn't really like America. All we did was sit around with her friends, talking in their houses over coffee, their voices so loud and the TV blaring all the time. I didn't like it; I was bored! It's hard to get me to leave Indonesia; I'm very proud of Indonesia, a fanatic for Indonesia you could say.

Some *gay* and *lesbi* Indonesians who never leave Indonesia are able to meet gay and lesbian Westerners, but this can be difficult, since few Indonesians speak English, and Western tourists tend not to spend long periods of time in the urban centers where the *gay* and *lesbi* worlds are most extensive. When it does happen it is often at sites like shopping malls, where it is sometimes possible to meet a Western tourist or expatriate by "playing eyes." It is usually gay expatriate Westerners (and the occasional gay Western anthropologist), not gay tourists, who sometimes go to *tempat ngebers*. The concentration of tourists in Bali makes it a special case; *gay* Indonesians sometimes go to Bali for the purpose of trying to meet a gay Westerner, regardless of language barriers. Because of their more limited mobility, socializing between *lesbi* women and Western lesbians tends to be limited to upper-class urban contexts or the tourist industry in Bali. For Ita in northern Bali, contacts with Western lesbians were a never-ending source of fascination:

> I meet lots of Western *lesbi* women here at the restaurant. I can tell by the way they look, or they ask: "I see you have a ring. How long have you been married?" I just tell them, "I'm not married; this is from my girlfriend." They're usually very nice to me. Some of them have had problems with their families too; I even met one, from Sweden I think, who'd been thrown out of her family because she was *lesbi*. Isn't it funny that there are no other words for *lesbi* women, how *lesbi* women have the same name the world over. I've met tourists from everywhere, from Italy, from Switzerland, and no matter where they're from, they look it up in their dictionaries and it's always the same: lesbian.

While travel outside Indonesia is a rare theme in the lives of *gay* and *lesbi* Indonesians, internal migration and travel (in search of work, to visit relatives, or for pleasure) is much more common, as it is for Indonesians generally. For many *gay* and *lesbi* Indonesians, travel within the nation provides an opportunity to encounter and reflect upon a sense that being *gay* or *lesbi* is national. When *gay* and *lesbi* Indonesians move from one part of Indonesia to another, they expect to find *gay* men and *lesbi* women there, and particularly for the case of *gay* men moving to cities, suspect where they may be found. For instance, Udin had traveled not only from

Surabaya to Melbourne, but to another island in the early 1990s, to one of the early *gay* and *lesbi* Congresses. The trip confirmed his sense that being *gay* was part of a national style, and his reflections on the experience were once again peppered with terms common to state rhetoric like *wawasan* and *menyatukan* (unify):

> UDIN: When I got there I saw lots of people who had lots of perspective [*banyak wawasan*], had a high level of perspective [*wawasan yang tinggi*] . . . people who had concepts and knowledge, yet some of them were unwilling [*malu*] to be called "*gay*" [in public].
>
> TB: So when you met these people from across Indonesia, did you think they were similar or different to you?
>
> UDIN: In principle they were the same [*sama*] . . . there were a few differences I guess, but they were in a personal style [*secara pribadi*], not in terms of group style [*secara kelompok*]. . . . All the same [*sama semua*] . . . we get the influences of the West . . . and, what's the word for it, unify [*menyatukan*] them, and in the end develop openness within the *gay* community.

THE POLITICS AND ETHICS OF BELONGING

The Indonesian nation-state is predicated on heterosexuality, on the *normal*, and thus on the denial of queerness. By taking *gay* and *lesbi* subjectivities seriously, we "queer" the Indonesian nation-state, illuminating the foundational moment of sexual exclusion that naturalizes itself as the traditional and authentic.

The question of belonging is central to the experience of being *gay* or *lesbi*. These concepts are self-evidently not from tradition, family, or ethnolocality; yet they are experienced as both intimate aspects of selfhood and national phenomena. The most enduring Western stereotype regarding homosexuality and transgenderism in Indonesia (and Southeast Asia more generally) is that these regions are "tolerant." Although it is true that there have been—and in some cases, still are—socially recognized roles for male-to-female transgenders as well as widespread acceptance of secretive homosexual behavior, transgenderism and homosexuality are hardly valorized in contemporary Indonesian society. Although homosexuality and transgenderism usually escape official comment, if directly asked, most religious and state authorities swiftly condemn transgenderism and homosexuality as sinful and incompatible with "Indonesian tradition."

It proves helpful to develop a distinction between heterosexism (the belief that heterosexuality is superior to other sexualities) and homophobia (a psychologized fear or hatred of nonnormative sexualities). While heterosexism and homophobia often co-occur, this need not always be the case, and in Indonesia historically heterosexism has not implied homophobia. This lack of "gay-bashing" has often led non-Indonesians to misrecognize "Indonesian culture" as "tolerant" of homosexuality. Since the late 1990s there have been a few cases of unprecedented violence toward *gay* men when they stake a claim to the public sphere. While such "political homophobia" is disturbing (Boellstorff 2004d), it remains exceptional, and for most *gay* and *lesbi* Indonesians their oppression takes the form of a lack of recognition (which for some includes a pressure to marry "heterosexually" when they do not wish to do so). For instance, when *gay* men speak of wishing to be "accepted by society," they usually hope not that the social pressure to marry would disappear, but that they would not be the target of shaming gossip and could carry out their same-gender affairs in the *gay* world undisturbed.

Gay and *lesbi* Indonesians are aware they do not fit into dominant cultural norms; even if they marry "heterosexually," their "desire for the same" is not recognized as authentic. But when these Indonesians speak of wishing to be accepted by society in everyday conversation or more formal contexts like zines, "Balinese culture" or "tradition" is not the entity from which they seek acceptance. Nor is it Westerners or other Southeast Asians. Rather, it is a public culture conceived as national. Yet rarely is this a desire for recognition as understood by Western queer rights movements, and rarely does it take the form of a political movement. Since *gay* and *lesbi* Indonesians rework Western concepts of homosexuality through the lens of state discourse, their existence begs the question of politics and belonging.

In "The Politics of Recognition," Charles Taylor notes that the contemporary "demand for recognition" in the West presupposes a notion of authenticity: "We might speak of an individualized identity, one that is particular to me, and that I discover in myself" (1994:28). This is the confessional discourse of a selfhood that begins "in myself," gaining authenticity through exteriorization and recognition. The Western metaphor of "coming out" draws upon this confessional discourse. In the West, many treat politicization as the final realization of "coming out" and thus the ultimate form of homosexuality (notwithstanding grudging acknowledgment of "men who have sex with men," lesbian continua, and other figures of the incompletely recognized sexual minority). Politicization is interpreted as doing for the community what "coming out" does for the individual: assert a claim to rights, achieve a continuity between domains of life, secure an ongoing sense of self. By the late 1980s this conception of politicization was appearing in guises like Adam's frequently cited "five elements of modern homosexuality," which included "Exclusive homosexuality, now possible for both partners, has become an alternative path to conventional family norms" (1987:6)—not an element to which all *gay* and *lesbi* Indonesians would subscribe. This view of politicization as coming-out-writ-large is common in Western analyses of "global homosexualities":

> In over fifty countries around the globe, persons with homoerotic inclinations are "coming out" publicly, organizing movements for recognition and human rights, and, by doing so, challenging the authority of the traditional family, religious doctrine, and state power. (Likosky 1992:xv)

> There are impressive parallels in the names of organizations: many countries have known "gay liberation fronts," "revolutionary leagues," and so on, indicating that movements follow more or less comparable paths, pass through the same phases, and draw names from other social and political movements with which there is some resemblance in terms of ideology, goals, or methods of resistance. (Adam, Duyvendak, and Krouwel 1999:369–370)

However, the amount of recognizably activist activities undertaken by *gay* and *lesbi* Indonesians has been irregular and quite peripheral to the *gay* and *lesbi* worlds. The first *gay* organization, Lambda Indonesia, announced its existence to the world in March 1981. The first nationwide congress of *gay* organizations took place in Kaliurang (near Yogyakarta) from December 10 to 12, 1993, and further congresses were held in 1995 and 1997, each with around fifty participants.[2] Yet in the mid-1990s the total amount of activism among *gay* men seems to have decreased: long before the post-Soeharto rise of political Islam, *gay* men involved in organizations complained how most *gay* men were interested only in entertainment events. Beginning about 2002 there has been an increasing amount of activist work among *gay* men (appearing on television, for instance, or participating in national conferences), but such activities remain exceptional.[3]

Lesbi women have also engaged in organizational work since the 1980s, though their greater confinement to the domestic sphere and general exclusion from HIV prevention funding have made this work difficult. In Bali and Makassar, for instance, tombois have worked to build a greater sense of community. In the early 2000s a *lesbi* group in Jakarta inaugurated a website and listserv that generated sustained discussion and several events in the city. A tomboi group formed in Makassar in 2000 succeeded in obtaining funding from foreign donors for HIV prevention work among tombois. *Lesbi* women engaged in organizational work share with their *gay* counterparts a frustration with those uninterested in activism. In 1994 one woman expressed this frustration in a zine article entitled "GTM" (*Gerakan Tutup Mulut* or the "Closed Mouth Movement"):

It feels like of all peoples in the world, the people who like the Closed Mouth Movement more than anyone else are lesbians. . . . Indonesian lesbians are like red, newborn babies. . . . In truth we have already been born into the world, but in the same manner as a new-born baby, so we still have not done anything. Not yet a few words, much less speaking, only shrill crying! . . . Compared with lesbians in the West, who we can say have moved to adulthood, who can shout about their situation to demand attention, we are still far behind.[4]

The overall situation, then, is as follows: Indonesia has over two hundred million citizens, yet there are only a handful of *gay* or *lesbi* groups that could be glossed as "organizations" even in an informal sense; most of them exist for only two or three years before disbanding. Given that most such "organizations" have between two and ten active members, I estimate that from the 1980s to the early 2000s there were never more than one hundred *gay* and *lesbi* Indonesians at any one time who participated in activism in the Western sense of the term. Languages of politicization sometimes appear—as when, soon after the fall of Soeharto in 1998, letters to the zine *GAYa Nusantara* began calling for an "Indonesian *Gay* Party" or "Pink Triangle Party,"[5] or when *gay* activists in the city of Yogyakarta have held rights protests covered by the local newspaper. However, such incidents remain relatively small and ephemeral islands in the *gay* and *lesbi* archipelagoes. Unilinear narratives of a global movement are troubled further by the fact that gay men and lesbian women in other Southeast Asian nations, notably the Philippines and Thailand, do engage in recognizably political activities—gay pride marches, protests directed at government bureaucracies, letters in the mass media, demands for legal reforms.[6] Additionally, there is a long history of activism by ordinary Indonesians in spheres ranging from religion to the environment and women's rights. How are we to explain the "failure" of Indonesian *gay* and *lesbi* politics, and what does this tell us about a *gay* and *lesbi* politics of recognition?

Taylor highlights how the Western politics of recognition depends on the belief that selfhood is at stake: "The thesis is that our identity is partly shaped by recognition or its absence, often by the *mis*recognition of others, and so a person or group of people can suffer real damage, real distortion, if the people or society around them mirror back to them a confining or demeaning or contemptible picture of themselves" (Taylor 1994:25).

One of the greatest paradoxes of the *gay* and *lesbi* subject positions is that while they have a national spatial scale and draw upon national discourses, their cultural logics do not seem to demand the link between meaningful selfhood and political recognition that Taylor identifies as so important in the West. Yet a desire to be accepted by society is a recurring theme in *gay* and *lesbi* narratives. It is part of the *gaya* or style of being *gay* or *lesbi*, recalling Foucault's notion of a "style of life" as "a mode of ethical elaboration" (Halperin 1995:72). There appears to be an implicit equation of societal acceptance and homosexual love: *gay* and *lesbi* Indonesians "desire the same" and desire that the nation love them. It is largely an unfulfillable desire, so that a separation from national society is assumed to be the inevitable consequence of being *gay* or *lesbi*, even though these are "national" ways of being (see Boellstorff 2004c).

It is significant that *gay* and *lesbi* Indonesians speak so often of a desire to be recognized by society (*masyarakat*) and so rarely of a desire to be recognized by the government (*pemerintah*): the link between *gay* and *lesbi* subjectivities and national discourse is not that of Western ideas of a "queer nation." As an "out" Western gay man, I would sometimes describe the idea of gay rights to my *gay* interlocutors, who often reacted with shock: why would someone want to be known as *gay* in all domains of one's life? Why would you want to do that to your parents, to your spouse, children, and coworkers? What possible benefit would this bring? Do you get a raise at your job? To be "open" usually implies participating in the *gay* world, not to trouble the boundaries of that world by becoming more accepted in the *normal* world. The idea of activism makes an archipelagic life largely untenable. For example, Amin, a *gay* man in Surabaya, was taken aback when he learned that Dédé Oetomo openly shared a home with his male lover: "if two *gay* men live together, that's too much." One *gay* man in Makassar saw activism as a kind of improper borrowing:

> We don't need to say—excuse me for saying this—like GAYa Nusantara, that we're a "*gay* group" and stuff like that. In my own opinion, we don't need to open ourselves [*membuka diri*] too much, unless society itself makes comments. We don't need to proclaim ourselves [*memproklamasi diri*]. We have a tendency to imitate the West too much. Between us and the West there are great differences [*beda sekali*]. . . . In the West, I feel that the openness is great. For instance, in regard to parents. There, if the parents know that their child is *gay*, it's no problem, because it's regarded as their private affair. Here, it can't be like that. Here, even if the parents know, they'll do anything to get the child to marry, they'll do anything so that the child will not become *gay*. So the biggest difference is social acceptance [*penerimaan masyarkat*]. . . . For instance, in the West, you can kiss your boyfriend in public, right? But here, that's very opposed. Society will not like it.

When talking about the belief in much of the West that in Asia homosexuality is tolerated, another *gay* man replied:

> In Indonesia, it's the worst. *Gays* do not have any protection. . . . It's true that you can have sex with anyone here. But it has to be done secretly. . . . Here in

Indonesia, if someone's boss finds out they are *gay*, they can be fired for no reason. . . . If I imagine that happening to myself, I'd think: I have rights as a *gay* person; why am I fired from my job? I haven't bothered anyone! It's my personal business.

In both of these cases, reflections on the idea of activism lead to an emphasis on *difference* rather than similarity. When comparing Indonesia and the West, *gay* and *lesbi* Indonesians usually imagine recognition as the primary axis of difference. They tend not to think that gay and lesbian Westerners engage in different kinds of sexual acts, or lead radically different lives (for instance, they often assume that gay and lesbian Westerners mostly marry "heterosexually" as they do). Where they imagine difference is in the idea that gay and lesbian Westerners are more recognized by society: they can kiss in public, for instance. Increasingly, *gay* and *lesbi* Indonesians contemplate fragmentary news that there is something like "marriage" between gay men or lesbian women in the West—particularly since Holland, the former colonial power, became in 2001 the first nation to permit same-gender marriages. Given the importance of "heterosexual" marriage in *gay* and *lesbi* lives and its explicit conflation with proper citizenship in postcolonial Indonesia, this interest is understandable.

Yet the idea of recognition for same-gender relationships is dangerous as well as enticing, because of the clear threat it poses to a *gay* or *lesbi* world kept distinct from the *normal* world. In the West, claims to cultural citizenship are articulated through a language of the visible: *identity* allows the state and civil society to *identify* claimants to equality. For the Western queer subject, being "out" is a prerequisite to a progressive politics. But for many *gay* men and *lesbi* women, visibility would jeopardize important boundaries between islands of their archipelagic subjectivities.

Rather than label *gay* and *lesbi* Indonesians as self-hating or backward, the details of their own self-understandings might offer clues. Over and over again these Indonesians emphasize acts rather than statuses: the idea that one can become *gay* or *lesbi* through "addiction," or the idea that good deeds lead to acceptance. Alongside a politics of recognition, this suggests the possibility of an ethics of recognition. In chapter 2, I discussed how my understanding of subject positions draws from Foucault's later work on modes of subjectivation and technologies of the self—"The most neglected side of Foucault's work, and perhaps now the most important for anthropology" (Knauft 1996:164). Perhaps *gay* and *lesbi* Indonesians evince an ethics of recognition that construes belonging in terms of a "care for the self" rather than a concern with the image of self mirrored back by society.

Such a perspective might reveal acts of resistance that otherwise might not be seen as political—for instance, the entertainment events that *gay* men often organize. A more extended example: in northern Bali, Tuti and Ita, the *lesbi* couple who ran a restaurant, recalled how they met Esthi. This twenty-one-year-old woman had come from a village many miles inland to the tourist zone in search of work, but soon fell in love with Karlina, a *lesbi* friend of Tuti and Ita. Tuti managed to employ Esthi at her souvenir shop, and at the time I met them Esthi and Karlina had been lovers for over two years. News of Esthi's relationship eventually made it back to her parents, who called her back to the village with the excuse that there was a Hindu family ceremony she needed to attend. When Esthi arrived she was confronted by her parents, and her mother threatened to commit suicide: "If you go back and then you hear later that I've killed myself, you'll know it's because of what you've done." Esthi's parents also threatened to kick her out of the family, saying, "If you leave here and go back to Karlina, we will not consider you our child any more and you can never come back."

Esthi fled her village in a panic and returned to Karlina and her friends at the restaurant. Soon her father, together with several uncles and male cousins, came looking for her, but upon arriving they were greeted by Tuti and Tuti's older sister, who had come to accept that Tuti was *lesbi*. Tuti and her sister sat down with Esthi's father and "explained what it meant to be *lesbi*, that *lesbi* women weren't bad people." Esthi's father seemed to accept Tuti's argument and returned with his relatives to the village to explain the situation to Esthi's mother. A few days after this encounter, Tuti was still pleased with the outcome: "We don't know what will happen, but we're hoping Esthi's mother will understand eventually. Part of the problem is that they live out in the village; they don't get to see gay and lesbian tourists like people do here. So it's just something with which they have no experience; that's half the problem."

This example of Esthi and Karlina's relationship illustrates how an ethics of recognition does not stand outside social context. In comments as applicable to Indonesia as the West, Taylor notes that "it is not surprising that in the culture of authenticity, relationships are seen as the key loci of self-discovery and self-affirmation. Love relationships are not just important because of the general emphasis in modern culture on the fulfillments of ordinary needs. They are also crucial because they are the crucibles of inwardly generated identity" (Taylor 1994:36). Recognition, authenticity, and sexuality are fused in this understanding of belonging—an understanding that, like the nation-state form itself, underlies the constitution of the Indonesian subject.

Figure 8–1. Outside Ngurah Rai airport, Bali. Courtesy of Jane H. Patten.

POSTLUDE

Through "dubbing culture," *gay* and *lesbi* Indonesians come to sexual subjectivities that challenge common understandings of globalization. Whenever exiting the airport in Bali during my fieldwork, I would pass by the sign shown in figure 8–1. Like elsewhere in Asia, Indonesians have proven capable of relocalizing McDonald's in a way that furthers its corporate goals, but also reworks "fast food" to new ends (J. Watson 1998). This sign would always remind me how, while many aspects of *gay* and *lesbi* Indonesians' lives are unique, others reflect broad patterns of culture and globalization.

I have referred to the *gay* and *lesbi* subject positions as the greatest success stories of Soeharto's New Order—the greatest examples of subject positions irreducible to ethnolocality—albeit success stories the state never intended to facilitate into being. In doing so, I draw from these subject positions the insight that a new Indonesia need not rest on obliterating or revitalizing the past, but realizing that the past is never as set in stone as it makes itself out to be. *Gay* and *lesbi* Indonesians show their fellow citizens that it is possible to imagine a new kind of national belonging where difference stands no longer as raw "diversity" to be ground into national "unity," but glittering islands of possibility in an archipelago of tolerance and justice.

Books seem to be worlds in themselves, but like any text they demand painful choices as to what will be included and what will be left out. As this book closes I am haunted by all I have left unsaid, all the islands of the *gay* archipelago not visited: stories that remain ensconced within my fieldnotes and my memory. Yet one story in particular comes to mind as I reflect on "dubbing culture" and the paths by which *gay* and *lesbi* Indonesians find meaning, community, and love. The paths by which *gay* and *lesbi* Indonesians insist they belong.

Setting: Makassar. *Place*: the vast athletic field where *gay* men play volleyball in the afternoons. *Time*: April 15, 1998, four o'clock. I remember.

I remember standing in the field; there are dark clouds to the east, but no one seems to mind. There are hundreds of people on the field, mostly young men. At the north end of the field several games of soccer are underway; to the south the basketball courts are a frenzy of motion and chatter. I am with about twenty-five *gay* men, an island of the *gay* world between soccer and basketball. The *gay* men are playing volleyball twelve at a time, six on each team. Everyone else sits and talks along the sidelines. One of the *gay* men misses a shot and lets out an ear-piercing shriek. A *gay* man sitting with me remarks, "Wherever we are, we're visible." Visible and yet not visible, I think to myself: many of these *gay* men will go home to their wives and children. This is one of many islands of the *gay* archipelago; its lines of connection, binding together lives and loves, invisible to the *normal* world.

I remember how, many games later, the setting sun is shining red on the underbellies of the clouds and the evening call to prayer booms from the great mosque just down the road. It starts to rain and the athletic field is all motion to its edges. Several *gay* men get on a minibus with me; some of the many *gay* men who have taken care of me though my years in Indonesia, teaching me more than any book can say. I remember the streets of Makassar rushing by in the rain and the fading sun's glow; the dash to the front door of my little house. We are inside and making tea and turning on the television: it's "Word Quiz," a popular game show. I remark there's a similar show in the United States, and they say "It's like there are no new ideas here—we just use ideas from the West." But the statement carries no tone of chagrin; it is the way things are in this world, and obvious that "using" an idea means making it into one's own style.

I remember that a couple of hours later the visitors have left and Irwan, one of the two *gay* men living with me, has come home from a conference on "Fighting AIDS from the Bugis and Makassarese Religious and Cultural Perspective," sponsored by the provincial Department of Health. As a member of a local AIDS organization he was invited to attend. I sit down to drink tea before dinner with him. Unlike most folks in town, these government officials know terms like *homoseks* and *gay*, and Irwan is worried that tomorrow the conference will turn into a platform for saying that being *gay* is not compatible with being Indonesian—"Indonesian," he says, not "Bugis" or "Makassarese," even though that's what the conference is ostensibly about. Irwan says he wants to give people at the conference a different perspective (*wawasan*).

I remember how, after a few moments, Irwan gave me, offhand, a definition of culture and belonging as simple and powerful as any I've ever heard. I remember how he looked down at his steaming tea and said: "Culture is something that is created by humans and then believed. There are people who have created '*gay*' here in Indonesia and believe in what they have created. So *gay* is part of Indonesian culture."

Notes

1. Tombois often called themselves *lesbi* during my fieldwork; see also Prawira-kusumah and Ramadhan (1988:19–20).

2. *Lesbi* sometimes refers to masculine and feminine women and sometimes only to feminine women. *Lesbian* has been part of the Indonesian language since at least the early 1980s. The widespread preference for *lesbi* over *lesbian* is probably because in the Indonesian language *-an* is a common suffix that typically derives nouns from verbs, such as *makanan* "food" from *makan* "eat" (Sneddon 1996:30–31). *Lesbian* thus feels like a compounded term, particularly because it is three syllables long, rather than Indonesian's typical two-syllable root word structure.

3. Here, as throughout this book, I do not italicize "gay" when referring to non-Indonesians.

4. The pioneering works by anthropologists on "Indonesia" emphasize mass media (Heider 1991) or history (Siegel 1997) rather than ethnography.

5. I owe this phrase to Stephan Helmreich.

6. See, for instance, Joseph Massad's (2002) essay concerning what he terms the "Gay International" in the Arab world. While Massad's attention to unequal global power relations and the problematic nature of human rights discourse is salutary, his implicit theory of globalization, participation in the stereotype that homosexuals are upper class (362, 372–373), and assumption that the apparent "movement" of "gay" is always brute mechanical transfer (383) all follow the McGay trope that "gay" is irredeemably Western (382). Given the resonance between "Gay International" and "Communist International," the former term could be seen to suggest a global gay menace by participating in the McCarthyist stereotype that homosexuals recruit.

7. Concerns of similitude and difference are not limited to postcolonial and queer theory; they have been one of the animating concerns of anthropology (from the "psychic unity of mankind" to "cultural relativism") and also of Southeast Asian studies, under the figure of "continuity and change" (Benda 1972; Smail 1961).

8. See also, inter alia, Anagnost (1997); Bowen (1997); S. Brenner (1998); Cohen (1995, 1998); Ivy (1995); Kahn (1993); Mills (1995); Ram and Jolly (1998); Stivens (1998); Tanabe and Keyes (2002); Tsing (1993).

9. The irony is that postmodernism is associated not with elitism but with effacing the distinction between high and low culture (compare "modernist" Mondrian to "postmodernist" Warhol, or "modernist" Schönberg to "postmodernist" Glass).

CHAPTER TWO
HISTORICAL TEMPTATIONS

1. Homosexuality appears in the Dutch colonial penal code (*Wetboek van Strafecht*), Article 292 (which remains Article 292 in the Indonesian penal code), but is oriented toward sexual assault and sex below the age of consent. This law was apparently never enforced before the late 1930s. Dutch civil law was derived from the Napoleonic Code, which gave little emphasis to homosexuality. In comparison, British common law was significantly more disapproving of homosexuality, still visible in the harsher legal regimes of former British colonies like Malaysia and Singapore. The lack of attention to homosexuality in the Dutch East Indies is particularly surprising given the relatively large number of military prosecutions for homosexual behavior in nineteenth-century Holland itself; one discharged navy officer claimed to have had sex with forty-one Indonesians during a two-and-a-half-year stint in the colony (Hekma 1991:283).

2. Halilintar Lathief, comments at the National Conference on Male Sexual Health, Puncak, Indonesia, September 6, 2004.

3. Some bissus dress androgynously only for ritual purposes and otherwise appear as *normal* men, complete with wife and children: "[E]ven a 'normal' married man seems to be capable of being a bissu as long as he merely conducts himself half as man and half as woman during the ritual" (Chabot 1996[1950]:194). See also Hamonic (1975:125); Lathief (2004:58); Mattulada (1974).

4. See Wilson (1999); *Tiras* no. 16, thn 1, 18 May 1995, special insert p. H.

5. They were also a favorite subject of colonial ethnographers; see, e.g., the summary provided in Karsch-Haack (1911:188–215).

6. This narrative is apparently taken in full from an article published in the newspaper *Persamaan* on Monday, February 13, 1939. It is summarized in Budiman (1979:111–113). Amen Budiman was a historian based in Semarang (Central Java) who wrote on Indonesian homosexuality and transgenderism (Budiman 1979, 1982). Budiman claimed to have discovered this narrative in *Pimpinan Islam* (1940), Mohammad 'Ali Alhamidy, pp. 60–61, publisher unknown, but I have been unable to locate this text. The version here is taken from Alhamidy (1951:47–48).

7. Ulrich Kratz, personal communication, October 5, 2004.

8. See Kratz (1978). My analysis is based on Budiman's edited and Indonesianized version of the narrative (the original was in a mixture of Javanese and Indonesian), but I am here interested in the broad outlines of Sucipto's life, not a close linguistic analysis. I will use Budiman's modernized spelling of "Sucipto's" name.

9. A city in Java.

10. By 1940 enough arrests had taken place that a sample of one hundred arrested men could be used for a study on homosexual prostitution and disease (Simons 1940).

11. See Gouda (1995: chaps. 4 and 5).

12. Sucipto's biography was discovered in Overbecks's papers. Ulrich Kratz, personal communication, October 5, 2004.

CHAPTER THREE
DUBBING CULTURE

1. *Oxford English Dictionary,* second ed., vol. 4.

2. This phrase references Oetomo (1997).

3. Homosexuality was removed as a psychological disorder in January 1982 in Indonesia.

4. "*Aku Menemukan Kepribadianku Sebagai Seorang Homosex,*" Anda, no. 44 (July 1980):26, 30.

5. The inside title was: "This is a real shock—the first time in Indonesia: Girl [*cewek*] married with a girl. The marriage ceremony attended by the parents and 120 guests."

6. Reported in *Gaya Hidup Ceria,* no. 1 (8/82). The Western magazine in question was not named.

7. *Report on Lesbians in Indonesia,* p. 2.

8. See Heider (1991) and Sen (1994) for detailed historical and contemporary accounts of Indonesian cinema (both works were published before the rise of private television in Indonesia). Heider notes that between 1945 and 1990 the number of films produced yearly in Indonesia ranged from zero (in 1946 and 1947, for instance) to over one hundred in 1977 and 1989 (19).

9. *Popular* (May 1997):33. Despite an illustrious history of film production and a number of directors producing serious films (Heider 1991; Sen 1994) "the 1980s saw the near-collapse of the domestic film industry" (Hefner 1997:94) due to competition from Hollywood and other exporters, coupled with the New Order's stifling censorship policies. During the 1990s domestic production was dominated by soft-porn films targeting lower-class audiences. For example, of the twenty-seven films produced in Indonesia in 1996 that received nationwide distribution, only one had a theme other than sex (*Popular* [May 1997]).

10. E.g. *Nusa,* March 6, 1998.

11. *Popular* (March 1996):53.

12. *Nusa,* March 18, 1998.

13. *Bali Post,* March 1, 1998, p. 8.

14. On March 15, 1998, the Balinese newspaper *Nusa* ran a two-page exposé on *lesbi* life composed of ten articles. While much of the coverage was sensationalistic, several articles called for greater social acceptance of *lesbi* women.

15. For instance, in 1997 *Popular* magazine sent a reporter to cover the Gay/ Lesbian Mardi Gras in Sydney; he related tales of hanging out in gay bars and meeting a lesbian couple as well as the lesbian executive director of the event (April 1997:44, 48–50). International events like the Gay Games are covered, as are same-sex rights and domestic partner legislation in Europe, the United States, and South Africa. See, e.g., "Homoseks Marriage: An Example of Moral Pluralism" [*Perkawinan Homoseks: Contoh Pluralisme Moral*], *Kompas,* June 12, 1996. See chapter 9.

16. Imported programs come from around the world, with many favorites from India, Latin America, and Japan. To my knowledge, however, *gay* and *lesbi* seem to be formed exclusively with reference to programs originally in English and originating above all from the United States, as these examples indicate.

17. For instance, many print media carried articles on Doug Savant, the actor playing the gay character Matt Fielding in *Melrose Place* (e.g., *Bintang*, May 28, 1997).

18. Examples of significant interviews with Oetomo appear in *Jakarta Jakarta*, May 22–28, 1993; *Popular* (July 1995); and *Matra* (August 1999).

19. "Tayangan yang Menjadi Buah Bibir," *Talk Show*.

20. *Kompas*, June 25, 1997. This comes from a *pojok* or "corner column": "the essence of the pojok is biting, anonymous comment on the latest news. . . . The art of pojok writing is one of allusion, innuendo, sarcasm, and mock surprise" (Anderson 1990:142–143).

21. In the wake of these protests, RCTI and SCTV "cleaned up" their shows, which in RCTI's case included firing Debra Yatim in favor of a less controversial moderator.

22. *Nusa*, November 28, 1997.

23. Since about 2003 there have appeared some soft-porn taboids such as *X-Pos* that speak openly about homosexuality (and all forms of nonmarital heterosexuality), using images of Western bodies found on the Internet. Around this time some male sex workers also began advertising their services (barely concealed as "massage") in tabloids like *Memorandum*. Fundamentalist Islamic groups have protested such publications on occasion; an event held by *X-Pos* in Central Java in 2004 was raided by an Islamic group that made threats and burned all the copies of *X-Pos* they found but did not injure anyone. Should such more explicit mass media images and texts persist and expand, they will undoubtedly shape how *gay* and *lesbi* Indonesians come to their sexual subjectivities.

24. See, inter alia, Anderson (1983), J. Errington (1998), Maier (1993), Siegel (1997), Sneddon (2003).

25. The five private stations at the time were RCTI, SCTV, TPI, Anteve, and Indosiar. The number is increasing. Estimates of the proportion of shows originating outside of Indonesia range from two-thirds (Wahyuni 2000:116) from the United States to 50 percent from the United States and Europe combined (Groves 1996:42).

26. *Republika* (Jakarta), May 2, 1996. RCTI was not only the first private television station to go national (in 1995), but the first to begin broadcasting, in 1989. Even the government television station TVRI was introduced only in the late 1970s (Lindsay 1997:117, 113).

27. As does *negotiate*; these subjectivities are not negotiated in the sense that Maira (1999) speaks of an "identity dub" among South Asian Americans in the New York club scene.

28. Here I use *articulation* in its English sense. The term originally entered social theory through Marx, but *Gliederung* has only the first of the two meanings noted above. The root word, *Gleid*, means "limb" or "joint" but can also mean "penis" *(männliches Glied)*. Surely there is great potential in a psychoanalytic treatment that links the moment of speech to erection.

29. Lydia Liu notes that in studying how "a word, category, or discourse 'travels' from one language to another," we must "account for the vehicle of translation" and address "the condition of translation" itself (1995:20–21, 26), a con-

cern with a long history in anthropology as well (Asad 1986; Streck and Maranhão 2003).

CHAPTER FOUR
ISLANDS OF DESIRE

1. For instance, in 1951 Alhamidy spoke of sex between women as "usually done *suka sama suka*, not by force" (1951:48).

2. With regard to *gay* men in Jakarta, Howard notes they "hold a distinctive conception of homosexuality as a social product rather than as a feature of an internal, biological[ly] based sexual orientation" (1996:109).

3. In Howard's primary sample of fifty-one *gay* men in Jakarta, "22 . . . described becoming aware of their gay identities" after having been seduced (Howard 1996:133).

4. See S. Wieringa (1999a:218). This is also the driving force in *Menguak Duniaku*, where at one point three women vie for Hen and even initiate sexual contact (Prawirakusumah and Ramadhan 1988:33, see also 36, 118–119, 121). Even as one of these women ends her relationship, she speaks of her desire and Hen's tomboi desire as the same (159).

5. This appears to be the case even in the 1930s' southern Sumatra incident described in chapter 3.

6. The identity/behavior binarism originated in nineteenth-century notions of acquired (situational, circumstantial) versus innate (congenital) homosexuality (see Bleys 1995).

7. Historically, only in cases of physical or mental disability, or of high-status women unable to find suitable husbands, is there any evidence of an honorable way to avoid marriage (Florida 1996; S. Errington 1989).

8. For instance, Barth (1993), Jones (1994), Hoskins (1998), Niehof (2003).

9. "Very often the first conflicts and disappointments [between parents and children who had been given a 'modern' education] centered around the choice of a wife. . . . In such communities marriage did not merely represent the union of boy and girl, but a further extension of all kinds of family relationships. . . . It is thus not altogether surprising that in the literature of the young Indonesian generation, which began to appear in this atmosphere of conflict between modern and traditional Indonesian culture, the conflict, in all its aspects, was a major theme" (Alisjahbana 1966:30–31; see also Hatley and Blackburn 2000).

10. See also Rodgers (1995:3). This link between postcolonial self and nation is not unique to Indonesia: frequently in postcolonial literature "an individual's story represents that of an entire collectivity by narrating a return to the roots of identity (both individual and collective) and the birth of political consciousness" (Hayes 2000:13).

11. *GAYa Nusantara* 102 (2003):5.

12. Heteronormativity, of course, has been a key element of nationalist discourse since its beginnings (Eder, Hall, and Hekma 1999; Mosse 1985) and has played a role in debates over definitions of proper citizenship in Euro-America (Beriss 1996, Berlant 1997; Borneman 1992; Duggan and Hunter 1995; Parker

et al. 1992; Warner 1999). In contemporary postcolonial societies, debates over national belonging can take forms that incorporate, in various ways, these European origins of heteronormative nationalist ideology (Garcia 1996; Heng and Devan 1995; Jackson 1997, 1999; Lancaster 1995; Lumsden 1996; Manalansan 2003; Mankekar 1999; McLelland 2000; D. Murray 1996, Parker 1999; Sang 2003; Schein 1996).

13. In one sample, 89% of sixty-two unmarried core interlocutors planned on marrying women.

14. Though I knew of no cases personally, interlocutors in more than one field site spoke of cases where a tomboi and waria married each other, with the tomboi wife becoming pregnant in some instances.

15. "Javanese women are generally more deeply committed than men to the social and economic welfare of the family and therefore rarely overstep the marital boundaries. They are tolerant of their husbands' irregularities because men are considered to be by nature irresponsible. Their sexual promiscuity is called being nakal (naughty), which is the same term applied to disobedient or unruly children, there being no connotation of adult misdemeanor; and they are expected to be nakal both during their bachelorhood and after marriage. When a woman is young, her injured pride makes her angry upon discovery of her husband's infidelity, but, as she grows older and there are children, she is more concerned with the loss of money that might otherwise be spent in the family's interests" (H. Geertz 1961:131). See also Brenner (1998:149–157) and Suryakusuma (1996).

CHAPTER FIVE
GEOGRAPHIES OF BELONGING

1. Because most gay and lesbi Indonesians come to their sexual subjectivities with little face-to-face interaction, it is possible to be gay or lesbi without contact with the gay or lesbi worlds, leading a celibate life or having sex with normal men or women. Letters to newspapers identifying the writer as a gay or lesbi person who has never met another indicate that such Indonesians exist. I have no way of estimating how many gay and lesbi Indonesians live separate from the gay and lesbi worlds.

2. I draw from two interlinked traditions in my analysis of these ethnographic materials. The first is the work of feminist and queer geographers who have emphasized how gender and sexuality are produced through spatial relationships (Bell and Valentine 1995; Ingram, Bouthillette, and Retter 1997; Massey 1994). Second, I draw on the work of thinkers who examine how the "practices of everyday life" shape how space is "directly lived through its associated images and symbols" (Lefebvre 1991:39; also Bourdieu 1977; N. Brenner 1998, 1999, 2000).

3. Gay men and lesbi women began using the Internet in significant numbers around 1995, but the first online editions of magazines, gay chat groups, and other computer-based activities did not begin until mid-1998. The effect of the Internet on gay and lesbi subjectivities is still uncertain but sure to increase. Internet use adds new class and educational barriers to the gay and lesbi worlds,

since one must know how to use a computer and be able to access it with some degree of privacy.

4. Tunjungan Plaza is to my knowledge the only mall in Indonesia that has, for certain periods of time, had stores that sold condoms and sex toys (Kroeger 2000:121).

5. Sabang is in Indonesia's extreme northwestern corner (in the province of Aceh) while Merauke is in the extreme southeastern corner (in the province of Papua [formerly Irian Jaya]). Ironically, both of these provinces currently have strong separatist movements.

6. "Several [*gay* Indonesians in Jakarta] told me of their 'discovery' of the idea of homosexuality after reading an article on homosexuality in the women's magazine *Sarinah* in 1981" (Howard 1996:254).

CHAPTER SIX
PRACTICES OF SELF, TESTS OF FAITH

1. The notion of "style" has appeared in other contexts with regard to the conjuncture of nonnormative genders and sexualities; for instance, Tonga (Besnier 2002) and the Philippines (Johnson 1997). For further discussion of citizenship as performative, see, e.g., Kuipers (2003).

2. *Lesbi* women refer to these masculine and feminine genderings with a variety of terms. A few know the English terms "butch" and "femme," but more often they employ paired sets of terms from standard Indonesian vocabulary: *masculin* versus *feminin*, *kelakian* (maleness) versus *kewanitaan* (femaleness), *cowok* (boy) versus *cewek* (girl; see Blackwood 1999), *gaya laki-laki* (male style) versus *gaya perempuan* (female style), and the Javanese terms *sentul* (masculine) versus *kantil* (feminine). In Makassar and other parts of Indonesia, feminine *lesbi* women can be termed *lines*; this is a *gay* language transformation of *lesbi* that also sometimes refers to *lesbi* women in general.

3. For instance, in a television commercial shown nationally in 2000, a mother comments on her favorite brand of laundry detergent as her young daughter is shown walking home from school, wearing a school uniform and also a Muslim headscarf. As the little girl runs home, getting dirt and chocolate ice cream on her headscarf, the mother opines "my girl is a real tomboi."

4. The only case to my knowledge of an ethnolocalized term for tomboi is Bugis *calalai'*, but in urban southern Sulawesi at least this term does not appear to be in common use. Most of my tomboi interlocutors there did not know of this term and used "hunter" and/or "tomboi" to describe themselves.

5. Two *ngondhek* men in a sexual relationship may be jokingly referred to as *lesbi* by other *gay* men, even though many *gay* men know that *lesbi* relationships are usually between tombois and ceweks.

6. Ngondhek (sometimes spelled ngondek) appears to be the best-known term (see Howard 1996:301). There are a range of other terms for male effeminacy with varying degrees of national circulation, including *mégol* (mostly in South Sulawesi), *kewanitaan* (an abstract noun derived from *wanita*, "woman"), *kriting* (curly), *lémbéng* (mostly in Java), and *feminin*.

7. See Butler (1993); Foucault (1978); Halperin (1995); Sedgwick (1991).

8. Published in *GAYa Nusantara* 51 (August 1997).

CHAPTER SEVEN
THE POSTCOLONIAL STATE AND *GAY* AND *LESBI* SUBJECTIVITIES

1. I develop my theory of hegemony in dialogue with Birmingham School theorists like Stuart Hall despite the fact that some anthropologists believe that such theorists (and many anthropologists) have strayed too far from Gramsci's understanding of hegemony (Crehan 2002; Kurtz 1996).

2. This recalls Bourdieu's concept of habitus: "Because the subjective necessity and self-evidence of the commonsense world are validated by the objective consensus on the sense of the world, what is essential *goes without saying because it comes without saying*" (Bourdieu 1977:167, emphasis in original).

3. "Spatial metaphors, both implicit and explicit, form a pervasive mode of organizing consciousness in [Island Southeast Asia]" (S. Errington 1989:13).

4. Proyek Penelitian Keagamaan (1984:5).

5. The usual formula, the Indonesians argued, would result in over ten thousand miles of border due to the number of islands within Indonesia. See Kusumaatmadja (1982); Proyek Penelitian Keagamaan (1984:5). This declaration that Indonesia was an archipelagic state is known as the "Djuanda Declaration" after the name of the prime minister at the time (Proyek Penelitian Keagamaan [1984:5]).

6. Proyek Penelitian Keagamaan (1984:8).

7. Centre for Strategic and International Studies (1991:17–18).

8. There is an extensive literature on the relationship between the postcolonial state and marriage in Indonesia, as well as the sexism of the family principle. See, for instance, Blackburn and Bessell (1997); Hatley (1997); Sears (1996); Sen (1998); Suryakusuma (1996); Tiwon (1996).

9. Tempo no. 36, thn. 17, November 7, 1987:105.

10. *GAYa Nusantara* 83:28–29 (2001).

11. *GAYa Nusantara* 83:29 (2001).

CHAPTER EIGHT
THE *GAY* ARCHIPELAGO

1. Some key works in this literature I have not yet cited include Donham (1998), Elliston (1999), Sinnott (2004), B. Tan (1999), M. Tan (1995).

2. The first national congress (*kongres nasional*) for the nationalist movement was also held in Yogyakarta, in 1908, the first "to include all levels of society" regardless of ethnicity or religion (K. Dewantara 1950:10).

3. In this history of activism, the figure of Dédé Oetomo looms paramount. This raises fascinating questions about the relationship between individuals and social formations, a difficult topic for anthropology, with its focus on the transindividual. Oetomo's activist orientation reflects his association with gay and les-

bian organizations at Cornell in the United States while a doctoral student. He has also cultivated connections with gay and lesbian activists worldwide since attending the International Gay Association Conference in Wina, Austria, in July 1983, linkages further strengthened by HIV/AIDS work. Oetomo's decades of activism, fluency in English, and international connections make him not only one of best-known *gay* men in Indonesia but one of the most atypical (Oetomo is also both openly atheist and ethnic Chinese).

4. *GAYa LEStari* (July 1994).

5. *GAYa Nusantara* 57:10 (1998); 58:8 (1998).

6. See, inter alia, Jackson (1997); Manalansan (1995); Morris (1997); Thongthiraj (1996).

Works Cited

Abas, Husen. 1987. *Indonesian as a Unifying Language of Wider Communication: A Historical and Sociolinguistic Perspective*. Canberra: RSPAS Publishing.

Abdullah, Hamid. 1985. *Manusia Bugis Makassar: Suatu Tinjauan Historis Terhadap Pola Tingkah Laku dan Pandangan Hidup Manusia Bugis Makassar* [The Bugis Makassar People: A Historic Perspective Regarding the Behavior and Worldview of the Bugis Makassar People]. Jakarta: Inti Idaya Press.

Abelove, Henry. 1992. "Some Speculations on the History of 'Sexual Intercourse' during the 'Long Eighteenth Century' in England." Pp. 335–342 in *Nationalisms and Sexualities*, Andrew Parker et al., eds. New York: Routledge.

Acciaioli, Greg. 1997. "What's in a Name? Appropriating Idioms in the South Sulawesi Rice Intensification Program." Pp. 288–320 in *Imagining Indonesia: Cultural Politics and Political Culture*, Jim Schiller and Barbara Martin-Schiller, eds. Athens: Ohio University Press.

———. 2001. "'Archipelagic Culture' as an Exclusionary Government Discourse in Indonesia." *Asia Pacific Journal of Anthropology* 2(1):1–23.

Adam, Barry. 1987. *The Rise of a Lesbian and Gay Movement*. Boston: G. K. Hall.

Adam, Barry D., Jan Willem Duyvendak, and André Krouwel. 1999. *The Global Emergence of Gay and Lesbian Politics: National Imprints of a Worldwide Movement*. Philadelphia: Temple University Press.

Agamben, Giorgio. 1998. *Homo Sacer: Sovereign Power and Bare Life*. Translated by Daniel Heller-Roazen. Stanford: Stanford University Press.

———. 1999. *The Man without Content*. Stanford: Stanford University Press.

Agha, Asif. 1998. "Stereotypes and Registers of Honorific Language." *Language in Society* 27(2):151–193.

Ahearn, Laura M. 2001. *Invitations to Love: Literacy, Love Letters, and Social Change in Nepal*. Ann Arbor: University of Michigan Press.

Alhamidy, Mohammad (Md.) 'Ali. 1951. *Islam dan Perkawinan* [Islam and Marriage]. Jakarta: Penerbit Al Ma'arif.

Ali, Fachry. 1997. "Sharing a Room with Other Nonstate Cultures: The Problem of Indonesia's Kebudayaan Bernegara." Pp. 186–197 in *Imagining Indonesia: Cultural Politics and Political Culture*, Jim Schiller and Barbara Martin-Schiller, eds. Athens: Ohio University Press.

Ali, Novel. 1997. "Sulih Suara Dorong Keretakan Komunikasi Keluarga" [Dubbing Breaks Family Communication]. Pp. 338–346 in *Bercinta Dengan Televisi: Ilusi, Impresi, dan Imaji Sebuah Kotak Ajaib* [In Love with Television: Illusions, Impressions, and Images from a Magical Box], Deddy Mulyana and Idi Subandy Ibrahim, eds. Bandung: PT Remaja Rosdakarya.

Alisjahbana, Sutan Takdir. 1966. *Indonesia: Social and Cultural Revolution*. Kuala Lumpur: Oxford University Press.

Althusser, Louis. 1971. "Ideology and Ideological State Apparatuses (Notes towards an Investigation)." Pp. 121–173 in *Lenin and Philosophy and Other Essays*, Ben Brewster, trans. New York: Monthly Review Press.

Altman, Dennis. 2001. *Global Sex*. Chicago: University of Chicago Press.

Anagnost, Ann. 1997. *National Past-Times: Narrative, Representations, and Power in Modern China*. Durham: Duke University Press.

Andaya, Leonard. 2000. "The Bissu: Study of a Third Gender in Indonesia." Pp. 27–46 in *Other Pasts: Women, Gender, and History in Early Modern Southeast Asia*, Barbara W. Andaya, ed. Honolulu: University of Hawaii Press.

Anderson, Benedict R. O'G. 1983. *Imagined Communities: Reflections on the Origins and Spread of Nationalism*. London: Verso.

———. 1990. *Language and Power: Exploring Political Cultures in Indonesia*. Ithaca: Cornell University Press.

———. 1996. " 'Bullshit!' S/he Said: The Happy, Modern, Sexy Indonesian Married Woman as Transsexual." Pp. 270–294 in *Fantasizing the Feminine in Indonesia*, Laurie Sears, ed. Durham: Duke University Press.

———. 2001. "Dari Tjentini Sampai GAYa Nusantara" [From Tjentini to GAYa Nusantara]. Pp. xi–xxvii in *Memberi Suara pada yang Bisu* [Giving Voice to the Voiceless], by Dédé Oetomo. Yogyakarta: Galang Press.

Appadurai, Arjun. 1996. *Modernity at Large: Cultural Dimensions of Globalization*. Minneapolis: University of Minnesota Press.

Ary, R. M. 1987. *Gay: Dunia Ganjil Kaum Homofil* [Gay: The Queer World of Homophiles]. Jakarta: Pustaka Utama Grafiti.

Asad, Talal. 1986. "The Concept of Cultural Translation in British Social Anthropology." Pp. 141–164 in *Writing Culture: The Poetics and Politics of Ethnography*, James Clifford and George E. Marcus, eds. Berkeley: University of California Press.

Aspinall, Edward, and Greg Fealy. 2003. "Introduction: Decentralisation, Democratisation and the Rise of the Local." Pp. 1–11 in *Local Power and Politics in Indonesia: Decentralisation and Democratisation*, Edward Aspinall and Greg Fealy, eds. Singapore: Institute of Southeast Asian Studies.

Avé, Jan B. 1989. " 'Indonesia,' 'Insulinde,' and 'Nusantara': Dotting the I's and Crossing the T." *Bijdragen tot de taal-, land- en volkenkunde* 145:220–234.

Badan Koodinasi Keluarga Berencana Nasional (BKKBN). 1988. *Keluarga Bertanggung Jawab: Modul Pendidikan KB [Keluarga Berencana] Bagi Generasi Muda* [Responsible Families: A Family Planning Module for the Young Generation]. Jakarta: Badan Koodinasi Keluarga Berencana Nasional.

———. 1999. *Change amidst Continuity: The Family Planning Movement of Indonesia*. Jakarta: Badan Koodinasi Keluarga Berencana Nasional.

Bakhtin, Mikhail Mikhailovich. 1981. *The Dialogic Imagination: Four Essays*, Michael Holquist, ed., Caryl Emerson and Michael Holquist, trans. Austin: University of Texas Press.

Barth, Fredrik. 1993. *Balinese Worlds*. Chicago: University of Chicago Press.

Bell, David, and Gill Valentine. 1995. *Mapping Desire: Geographies of Sexualities*. New York: Routledge.

Benda, Harry Jindrich. 1966. "The Pattern of Administrative Reforms in the Closing Years of Dutch Rule in Indonesia." *Journal of Asian Studies* 25(4): 589–605.

———. 1972. *Continuity and Change in Southeast Asia*. New Haven: Yale University Southeast Asia Series.

Benedict, Ruth. 1932. "Configurations of Culture in North America." *American Anthropologist* 34(1):1–27.

Benjamin, Walter. 1955. *Illuminations: Essays and Reflections*. Hannah Arendt, ed.; Harry Zohn, trans. New York: Schocken Books.

Beriss, David. 1996. "Introduction: 'If You're Gay and Irish, Your Parents Must Be English.'" *Identities* 2(3):189–196.

Berlant, Lauren. 1997. *The Queen of America Goes to Washington City: Essays on Sex and Citizenship*. Durham: Duke University Press.

Berlant, Lauren, and Elizabeth Freeman. 1993. "Queer Nationality." Pp. 193–229 in *Fear of a Queer Planet: Queer Politics and Social Theory*, Michael Warner, ed. Minneapolis: University of Minnesota Press.

Besnier, Nico. 2002. "Transgenderism, Locality, and the Miss Galaxy Beauty Pageant in Tonga." *American Ethnologist* 29:534–566.

Bhabha, Homi. 1994. *The Location of Culture*. New York: Routledge.

Bijkerk, J. C. 1988. *Selamat Berpisah: Sampai Berjumpa di Saat yang Lebih Baik* [Goodbye: Until We Meet in a Better Time]. Jakarta: Penerbit Djambatan.

Blackburn, Susan, and Sharon Bessell. 1997. "Marriageable Age: Political Debates on Early Marriage in Twentieth-Century Indonesia." *Indonesia* 63:107–142.

Blackwood, Evelyn. 1999. "Tombois in West Sumatra: Constructing Masculinity and Erotic Desire." Pp. 181–205 in *Female Desires: Same-Sex Relations and Transgender Practices across Cultures*, Evelyn Blackwood and Saskia E. Wieringa, eds. New York: Columbia University Press.

Blackwood, Evelyn, and Saskia E. Wieringa. 1999. "Sapphic Shadows: Challenging the Silence in the Study of Sexuality." Pp. 39–66 in *Female Desires: Same-Sex Relations and Transgender Practices across Cultures*, Evelyn Blackwood and Saskia E. Wieringa, eds. New York: Columbia University Press.

Bleys, Rudi. 1995. *The Geography of Perversion: Male-to-Male Sexual Behavior Outside the West and the Ethnographic Imagination, 1750–1918*. New York: New York University Press.

Boellstorff, Tom. 1999. "The Perfect Path: Gay Men, Marriage, Indonesia." *GLQ: A Journal of Gay and Lesbian Studies* 5(4):475–510.

———. 2002. "Ethnolocality." *Asia Pacific Journal of Anthropology* 3(1):24–48.

———. 2004a. "Authentic, of Course!": Gay Language in Indonesia and Cultures of Belonging. Pp. 181–210 in *Speaking in Queer Tongues: Globalization and Gay Language*, edited by William L. Leap and Tom Boellstorff. Urbana: University of Illinois Press.

———. 2004b. "Playing Back the Nation: Waria, Indonesian Transvestites." *Cultural Anthropology* 19(2):159–195.

———. 2004c. "Zines and Zones of Desire: Mass Mediated Love, National Romance, and Sexual Citizenship in Gay Indonesia." *Journal of Asian Studies* 63(2):367–402.

Boellstorff, Tom. 2005. "Between Religion and Desire: Being Muslim and *Gay* in INdonesia." *American Anthropologist* 107(4).

———. 2004d. "The Emergence of Political Homophobia in Indonesia: Masculinity and National Belonging." *Ethnos* 69(4):465–486.

———. 2004e. "Gay Language and Indonesia: Registering Belonging." *Journal of Linguistic Anthropology* 14(2):248–268.

Borneman, John. 1992. *Belonging in the Two Berlins: Kin, State, Nation.* Cambridge: Cambridge University Press.

Bourchier, David. 1997. "Totalitarianism and the 'National Personality': Recent Controversy about the Philosophical Basis for the Indonesian State." Pp. 157–185 in *Imagining Indonesia: Cultural Politics and Political Culture*, Jim Schiller and Barbara Martin-Schiller, eds. Athens: Ohio University Press.

Bourdieu, Pierre. 1977. *Outline of a Theory of Practice.* Cambridge: Cambridge University Press.

Bowen, John R. 1986. "On the Political Construction of Tradition: Gotong Royong in Indonesia." *Journal of Asian Studies* 45(3):545–561.

———. 1995. "The Forms Culture Takes: A State-of-the-field Essay on the Anthropology of Southeast Asia." *Journal of Asian Studies* 54(4):1047–1078.

———. 1997. "Modern Intentions: Reshaping Subjectivities in an Indonesian Muslim Society." Pp. 157–181 in *Islam in an Era of Nation-States: Politics and Religious Renewal in Muslim Southeast Asia*, Robert W. Hefner and Patricia Horvatich, eds. Honolulu: University of Hawaii Press.

Braidotti, Rosi. 1997. "Revisiting Male Thanatica." Pp. 214–222 in *Feminism Meets Queer Theory*, Elizabeth Weed and Naomi Schor, eds. Bloomington: Indiana University Press.

Breckenridge, Carol. 1995. *Consuming Modernity: Public Culture in a South Asian World.* Minneapolis: University of Minnesota Press.

Breman, Jan. 1982. "The Village on Java and the Early Colonial State." *Journal of Peasant Studies* 9(4):189–240.

Brenner, Neil. 1998. "Between Fixity and Motion: Accumulation, Territorial Organization, and the Historical Geography of Spatial Scales." *Environment and Planning D: Society and Space* 16(4):459–481.

———. 1999. "Beyond State-Centrism? Space, Territoriality, and Geographical Scale in Globalization Studies." *Theory and Society* 28(1):39–78.

———. 2000. "The Urban Question as a Scale Question: Reflections on Henri Lefebvre, Urban Theory, and the Politics of Scale." *International Journal of Urban and Regional Research* 24(2):361–378.

Brenner, Suzanne April. 1996. "Reconstructing Self and Society: Javanese Muslim Women and 'the Veil.'" *American Ethnologist* 23(4):673–697.

———. 1998. *The Domestication of Desire: Women, Wealth, and Modernity in Java.* Princeton: Princeton University Press.

Budiman, Amen. 1979. *Lelaki Perindu Lelaki: Sebuah Tinjauan Sejarah dan Psikologi Tentang Homoseks dan Masyarakat Homoseks di Indonesia* [Men Who Yearn for Men: A Historical and Psychological Perspective on Homosexuality and Homosexual Culture in Indonesia]. Semarang: Tanjung Sari.

———, ed. 1992. *Jalan Hidupku: Autobiografi Seorang Gay Priyayi Jawa Awal Abad XX* [Path of My Life: The Autobiography of a Gay Javanese Nobleman from the Early Twentieth Century]. Jakarta: Apresiasi Gay Jakarta.

Bunzl, Matti. 2004. *Symptoms of Modernity: Jews and Queers in Late-Twentieth-Century Vienna.* Berkeley: University of California Press.

Butler, Judith. 1990. *Gender Trouble.* New York: Routledge.

———. 1993. *Bodies That Matter: On the Discursive Limits of "Sex."* New York: Routledge.

———. 1997. *The Psychic Life of Power: Theories in Subjection.* Stanford: Stanford University Press.

Butt, Leslie. 2001. "KB Kills: Political Violence, Birth Control, and the Baliem Valley Dani." *Asia Pacific Journal of Anthropology* 2(1):63–86.

Castells, Manuel. 1997. *The Information Age: Economy, Society, and Culture. Volume 2: The Power of Identity.* Boston: Blackwell.

Centre for Strategic and International Studies. 1991. *Kliping tentang Wawasan Nusantara* [Clippings about the Archipelago Concept]. Jakarta: Centre for Strategic and International Studies.

Chabot, Hendrik Theodorus. 1996 [1950]. *Kinship, Status, and Gender in South Celebes.* Leiden: KITLV Press.

Chakrabarty, Dipesh. 2000. *Provincializing Europe: Postcolonial Thought and Historical Difference.* Princeton: Princeton University Press.

———. 2002. *Habitations of Modernity: Essays in the Wake of Subaltern Studies.* With a foreword by Homi K. Bhabha. Chicago: University of Chicago Press.

Chamberlain, Lori. 2000. "Gender and the Metaphorics of Translation." Pp. 314–329 in *The Translation Studies Reader,* Lawrence Venuti, ed. London: Routledge.

Chapman, Rebecca Jane. 1996. *The Significance of Family Planning for Women in Indonesia.* Melbourne: Monash Asia Institute.

Chatterjee, Partha. 1986. *Nationalist Thought and the Colonial World: A Derivative Discourse.* Minneapolis: University of Minnesota Press.

———. 1993. *The Nation and Its Fragments: Colonial and Postcolonial Histories.* Princeton: Princeton University Press.

Chauncey, George. 1994. *Gay New York: Gender, Urban Culture, and the Making of the Gay Male World, 1890–1940.* New York: BasicBooks.

Cheah, Pheng. 2003. *Spectral Nationality: Passages of Freedom from Kant to Postcolonial Literatures of Liberation.* New York: Columbia University Press.

Clifford, James. 1988. *The Predicament of Culture: Twentieth-Century Ethnography, Literature and Art.* Cambridge, MA: Harvard University Press.

Clifford, James, and George Marcus, eds. 1986. *Writing Culture: The Poetics and Politics of Ethnography.* Berkeley: University of California Press.

Cohen, Lawrence. 1995. "The Pleasures of Castration: The Postoperative Status of Hijras, Jankhas, and Academics." Pp. 276–304 in *Sexual Nature/Sexual Culture,* P. R. Abramson and S. D. Pinkerton, eds. Chicago: University of Chicago Press.

———. 1998. *No Aging in India: Alzheimer's, the Bad Family, and Other Modern Things.* Berkeley: University of California Press.

Cohn, Bernard S. 1996. *Colonialism and Its Forms of Knowledge: The British in India.* Princeton: Princeton University Press.

Collier, Jane F. 1988. *Marriage and Inequality in Classless Societies.* Stanford: Stanford University Press.

Collier, Jane F. 1997. *From Duty to Desire: Remaking Families in a Spanish Village*. Princeton: Princeton University Press.

Collier, Jane F, Bill Maurer, and Lilana Suárez-Navaz. 1995. "Sanctioned Identities: Legal Constructions of Modern Personhood." *Identities* 2(1/2):1–27.

Collier, Jane F., Michelle Z. Rosaldo, and Sylvia Yanagisako. 1997. "Is There a Family? New Anthropological Views." Pp. 71–81 in *The Gender/Sexuality Reader: Culture, History, Political Economy*, Roger N. Lancaster and Michaela di Leonardo, eds. New York: Routledge.

Comaroff, Jean, and John Comaroff. 1991. *Of Revelation and Revolution: Christianity, Colonialism, and Consciousness in South Africa*. Chicago: University of Chicago Press.

Cott, Nancy F. 2000. *Public Vows: A History of Marriage and the Nation*. Cambridge, MA: Harvard University Press.

Crehan, Kate. 2002. *Gramsci, Culture, and Anthropology*. Berkeley: University of California Press.

Das, Veena. 2000. "The Making of Modernity: Gender and Time in Indian Cinema." Pp. 166–188 in *Questions of Modernity*, Timothy Mitchell, ed. Minneapolis: University of Minnesota Press.

de Certeau, M. 1984. *The Practice of Everyday Life*. Steven Rendall, trans. Berkeley: University of California Press.

Deleuze, Gilles, and Felix Guattari. 1987. *A Thousand Plateaus: Capitalism and Schizophrenia*. Translation and foreword by Brian Massumi. Minneapolis: University of Minnesota Press.

Departemen Dalam Negeri. 1974. *Rencana Pembangunan Tahap Ke-II (Repelita II)*, Tahun Pertama (1974/1975) [Second Development Plan, Year One]. Jakarta: Departemen Dalam Negeri, Republik Indonesia.

Derrida, Jacques. 1996. *Archive Fever: A Freudian Impression*. Translated by Eric Prenowitz. Chicago: University of Chicago Press.

Dewantara, Bambang Sokawati. 1989. *Ki Hajar Dewantara, Ayahku* [Ki Hajar Dewantara, My Father]. Jakarta: Pustaka Sinar Harapan.

Dewantara, Ki Hadjar. 1950. *Dari Kebangunan Nasional Sampai Proklamasi Kemerdekaan* [From National Development to the Proclamation of Independence]. Yogyakarta: N. V. Usaha Penerbitan Indonesia.

———. 1959. *Demokrasi dan Leiderschap* [Democracy and Leadership]. Yogyakarta: Madjelis Luhur Taman Siswa Jogjakarta.

Dick, Howard W. 1985. "The Rise of a Middle Class and the Changing Concept of Equity in Indonesia: An Interpretation." *Indonesia* 39:71–92.

———. 1990. "Further Reflections on the Middle Class." Pp. 63–70 in *The Politics of Middle Class Indonesia*, Kenneth Young, and Richard Tanter, eds. Clayton, Australia: Monash University Press.

Donham, Donald L. 1998. Freeing South Africa: The "Modernization" of Male-male Sexuality in Soweto. *Cultural Anthropology* 13(1):3–21.

Duggan, Lisa, and Nan D. Hunter. 1995. *Sex Wars: Sexual Dissent and Political Culture*. London: Routledge.

Dwyer, Leslie K. 2000. "Spectacular Sexuality: Nationalism, Development and the Politics of Family Planning in Indonesia." Pp. 25–62 in *Gender Ironies of Nationalism: Sexing the Nation*, Tamar Mayer, ed. London: Routledge.

Echols, John, and Hassan Shadily. 1989. *Kamus Indonesia Inggris: An Indonesian-English Dictionary.* 3rd ed. Jakarta: Gramedia Pustaka Utama.

Eder, Franz X., Lesley A. Hall, and Gert Hekma, eds. 1999. *Sexual Cultures in Europe: National Histories.* Manchester: Manchester University Press.

Elliston, Deborah A. 1995. "Erotic Anthropology: 'Ritualized Homosexuality' in Melanesia and Beyond." *American Ethnologist* 22(4):848–867.

———. 1999. "Negotiating Transnational Sexual Economics: Female Mahu and Same-Sex Sexuality in 'Tahiti and Her Islands.'" Pp. 230–252 in *Female Desires: Same-Sex Relations and Transgender Practices across Cultures*, Evelyn Blackwood and Saskia E. Wieringa, eds. New York: Columbia University Press.

Engels, Frederick. 1972. [1884]. *The Origin of the Family, Private Property, and the State.* New York: International Publishers.

Errington, J. Joseph. 1998. *Shifting Languages: Interaction and Identity in Javanese Indonesia.* Cambridge: Cambridge University Press.

———. 2000. "Indonesian('s) Authority." Pp. 205–228 in *Regimes of Language: Ideologies, Polities and Identities*, ed. Paul V. Kroskrity. Santa Fe: School of American Research Press.

Errington, Shelly. 1989. *Meaning and Power in a Southeast Asian Realm.* Princeton: Princeton University Press.

———. 1990. "Recasting Sex, Gender, and Power: A Theoretical and Regional Overview." Pp. 1–58 in *Power and Difference: Gender in Island Southeast Asia*, Shelly Errington and Jane Monnig Atkinson, eds. Stanford: Stanford University Press.

Evans, David T. 1993. *Sexual Citizenship: The Material Construction of Sexualities.* New York: Routledge.

Faderman, Lillian. 1992. "The Return of Butch and Femme: A Phenomenon in Lesbian Sexuality of the 1980s and 1990s." *Journal of the History of Sexuality* 2(4):578–598.

Faisal. 2003. "Aku Menjadi Waria di Tanah Perantauan" [I Became Waria Abroad]. *GAYa Nusantara* 110:37–40.

Ferguson, James. 1999. *Expectations of Modernity: Myths and Meanings of Urban Life on the Zambian Copperbelt.* Berkeley: University of California Press.

Fishman, Joshua A. 1978. "The Indonesian Language Planning Experience: What Does It Teach Us?" Pp. 333–339 in *Spectrum: Essays Presented to Sutan Takdir Alisjahbana on His Seventieth Birthday*, S. Udin, ed. Jakarta: Dian Rakyat.

Fletcher, Helen F. 1994. "The Archipelagic State and the Full Recognition of Indonesian National Independence." *Indonesian Quarterly* 22(2):103–113.

Florida, Nancy K. 1996. "Sex Wars: Writing Gender Relations in Nineteenth-Century Java." Pp. 207–224 in *Fantasizing the Feminine Indonesia*, Laurie Sears, ed. Durham: Duke University Press.

Ford, Michael Thomas. 1996. *The World Out There: Becoming Part of the Lesbian and Gay Community.* New York: The New Press.

Foucault, Michel. 1970. *The Order of Things: An Archeology of the Human Sciences*. New York: Vintage Books.

———. 1978. *The History of Sexuality, Vol. 1: An Introduction*. Translated by Robert Hurley. New York: Vintage Books.

———. 1980. "Questions on Geography." Pp. 63–77 in *Power/Knowledge: Selected Interviews and Other Writings, 1972–1977*, Colin Gordon, ed. New York: Pantheon.

———. 1985. *The History of Sexuality, Vol. 2: The Use of Pleasure*. Translated by Robert Hurley. New York: Vintage Books.

———. 1991. "Governmentality." Pp. 87–104 in *The Foucault Effect: Studies in Governmentality*, Graham Burchell, Colin Gordon, and Peter Miller, eds. London: Harvester/Wheatsheaf.

Frederick, William H. 1997. "Dreams of Freedom, Moments of Despair: Armijn Pane and the Imagining of Modern Indonesian Culture." Pp. 54–89 in *Imagining Indonesia: Cultural Politics and Political Culture*, Jim Schiller and Barbara Martin-Schiller, eds. Athens: Ohio University Press.

Freeman, Elizabeth. 2002. *The Wedding Complex: Forms of Belonging in Modern American Culture*. Durham: Duke University Press.

Friedman, Thomas. 2000. *The Lexus and the Olive Tree: Understanding Globalization*. New York: A. A. Knopf.

Furnivall, J. C. 1944. *Netherlands India*. Cambridge: Cambridge University Press.

Gal, Susan. 1998. "Multiplicity and Contention among Language Ideologies: A Commentary." Pp. 317–331 in *Language Ideologies: Practice and Theory*, Bambi B. Schieffelin, Kathryn A. Woolard, and Paul V. Kroskrity, eds. New York: Oxford University Press.

Gal, Susan, and Judith Irvine. 1995. "The Boundaries of Language and Disciplines: How Ideologies Construct Difference." *Social Research* 62(4):967–1001.

Garcia, J. Neil C. 1996. *Philippine Gay Culture, The Last 30 Years: Binabai to Bakla, Silahis to MSM*. Diliman, Quezon City: University of the Philippines Press.

Gaudio, Rudolf P. 1994. "Sounding Gay: Pitch Properties in the Speech of Gay and Straight Men." *American Speech* 69(1):30–57.

Gayatri, B.J.D. 1996. "Indonesian Lesbians Writing Their Own Script: Issues of Feminism and Sexuality." Pp. 86–97 in *From Amazon to Zami: Towards a Global Lesbian Feminism*, Monika Reinfelder, ed. London: Cassell.

Gays in Indonesia Collective. 1984. *Gays in Indonesia: Selected Articles from the Print Media*. Fitzroy, Australia: Sybylla Press.

Geertz, Clifford. 1960. *The Religion of Java*. Glencoe, IL: Free Press.

———. 1973. "The Impact of the Concept of Culture on the Concept of Man." Pp. 33–54 in *The Interpretation of Cultures*. New York: Basic Books.

———. 1983. "From the Native's Point of View: On the Nature of Anthropological Understanding." Pp. 55–72 in *Local Knowledge: Further Essays in Interpretive Anthropology*. New York: Basic Books.

———. 1990. " 'Popular Art' and the Javanese Tradition." *Indonesia* 50:77–94.

Geertz, Hildred. 1961. *The Javanese Family: A Study of Kinship and Socialization*. New York: Free Press of Glencoe.

————. 1963. "Indonesian Cultures and Communities." Pp. 24–96 in *Indonesia*, Ruth McVey, ed. New Haven: HRAF Press.

Gibson, Thomas. 2000. "Islam and the Spirit Cults in New Order Indonesia: Global Flows vs. Local Knowledge." *Indonesia* 69:41–70.

Gibson-Graham, J. K. 1996. *The End of Capitalism (as We Knew It): A Feminist Critique of Political Economy*. Cambridge, MA: Blackwell.

Gilroy, Paul. 1993a. "Nationalism, History, and Ethnic Absolutism." Pp. 63–74 in his *Small Acts: Thoughts on the Politics of Black Cultures*. London: Serpent's Tail.

————. 1993b. *The Black Atlantic: Modernity and Double Consciousness*. Cambridge, MA: Harvard University Press.

Goffman, Irving. 1971. *Relations in Public*. New York: Harper & Row.

Gouda, Frances. 1995. *Dutch Culture Overseas: Colonial Practice in the Netherlands Indies, 1900–1942*. Amsterdam: Amsterdam University Press.

Graham, Sharyn. 2001. "Negotiating Gender: Calalai' in Bugis Society." *Intersections: Gender, History, and Culture in the Asian Context*, issue 6. http://www.sshe.murdoch.edu.au/intersections/issue6/graham.html, accessed September 23, 2001.

————. 2003. "Hunters, Wedding Mothers, and Transgendered Priests: Conceptualising Gender among Bugis in South Sulawesi, Indonesia." Ph.D. dissertation, Departments of Anthropology and Asian Studies, University of Western Australia.

Gramsci, Antonio. 1971. *Selections from the Prison Notebooks*. Quintin Hoare and Geoffrey Nowell-Smith, trans and eds. New York: International Publishers.

Groeneboer, Kees. 1998. *Gateway to the West: The Dutch Language in Colonial Indonesia, 1600–1950. A History of Language Policy*. Amsterdam: Amsterdam University Press.

Groves, Don. 1996. "Exhibition Still Modest in Indonesia." *Variety* 363 (11):42–44.

Gupta, Akhil. 1992. "The Song of the Nonaligned World: Transnational Identities, Late Capitalism, and the Reinscription of Space." *Cultural Anthropology* 7(1):63–79.

————. 1998. *Postcolonial Developments: Agriculture in the Making of Modern India*. Durham: Duke University Press.

Gupta, Akhil, and James Ferguson. 1997. "Discipline and Practice: 'The Field' as Site, Method, and Location in Anthropology." Pp. 1–46 in *Anthropological Locations: Boundaries and Grounds of a Field Science*, Akhil Gupta and James Ferguson, eds. Berkeley: University of California Press.

Halberstam, Judith. 1998. *Female Masculinity*. Durham: Duke University Press.

Hall, Stuart. 1988a. "The Toad in the Garden: Thatcherism among the Theorists." Pp. 35–57 in *Marxism and the Interpretation of Culture*, Cary Nelson and Lawrence Grossberg, eds. Urbana: University of Illinois Press.

————. 1988b. "Gramsci and Us." Pp. 161–173 in his *The Hard Road to Renewal: Thatcherism and the Crisis of the Left*. London: Verso.

————. 1996. "When Was 'The Post-Colonial'? Thinking at the Limit." Pp. 242–260 in *The Post-Colonial Question: Common Skies, Divided Horizons*, Ian Chambers and Lidia Curti, eds. London: Routledge.

Halley, Janet E. 1994. "Sexual Orientation and the Politics of Biology: A Critique of the Argument from Immutability." *Stanford Law Review* 46(3):503–568.

Halperin, David M. 1995. *Saint Foucault: Towards a Gay Hagiography.* New York: Oxford University Press.

———. 2002. *How to Do the History of Homosexuality.* Chicago: University of Chicago Press.

Hamonic, Gilbert. 1975. "Travestissement et Bisexualité Chez les 'Bissu' du Pays Bugis" [Transvestitism and Bisexuality among the "Bissu" of Bugis Country]. *Archipel* 10:121–134.

Hamzah, Aminah P. 1978. *Bissu dan Peralatannya* [Bissu and Their Tools]. Ujung Pandang: Proyek Pengembangan Permuseuman Sulawesi Selatan.

Hardjomartono, Soejono. 1961. "Rejog, Warok dan Gemblakan di Ponorogo: Tritunggal Jang Tak Dapat Pipisah-pisahkan" [Rejog, Warok, and Gemblakan in Ponorogo: Three Things That Cannot Be Separated]. *Brosur Adat Istiadat dan Tjeritera Rakyat* [Brochure of Tradition and Folk Stories] 6:12–30. Jakarta: Department of Culture.

Hardt, Michael, and Antonio Negri. 2001. *Empire.* Cambridge, MA: Harvard University Press.

Harootunian, Harry. 2002. *History's Disquiet: Modernity, Cultural Practice, and the Question of Everyday Life.* New York: Columbia University Press.

Harvey, David. 1989. *The Condition of Postmodernity: An Enquiry into the Origins of Cultural Change.* Cambridge: Basil Blackwell.

———. 2000. *Spaces of Hope.* Berkeley: University of California Press.

Hatley, Barbara. 1997. "Nation, 'Tradition,' and Constructions of the Feminine in Modern Indonesian Literature." Pp. 90–120 in *Imagining Indonesia: Cultural Politics and Political Culture*, Jim Schiller and Barbara Martin-Schiller, eds. Athens: Ohio University Press.

Hatley, Barbara, and Susan Blackburn. 2000. "Representations of Women's Roles in Household and Society in Indonesian Women's Writing of the 1930s." Pp. 45–67 in *Women and Households in Indonesia: Cultural Notions and Social Practices*, Juliette Koning et al., eds. Richmond, Surrey: Curzon Press.

Hatta, Mohammad. 1970. "Take the Core of Foreign Culture and Throw Away the Peel." Pp. 286–291 in *Indonesian Political Thinking 1945–1965*, Herbert Feith and Lance Castles, eds. Ithaca: Cornell University Press.

Hayes, Jarrod. 2000. *Queer Nations: Marginal Sexualities in the Maghreb.* Chicago: University of Chicago Press.

Hebdige, Dick. 1979. *Subculture: The Meaning of Style.* London: Methuen.

Hefner, Robert W. 1997. "Print Islam: Mass Media and Ideological Rivalries among Indoneisan Muslims." *Indonesia* 64:77–104.

Heider, Karl G. 1991. *Indonesian Cinema: National Culture on Screen.* Honolulu: University of Hawaii Press.

Hekma, Gert. 1991. "Homosexual Behavior in the Nineteenth-Century Dutch Army." *Journal of the History of Sexuality* 2(2):266–288.

Helmreich, Stefan. 1998. *Silicon Second Nature: Culturing Artificial Life in a Digital World.* Berkeley: University of California Press.

Heng, Geraldine, and Janadas Devan. 1995. "State Fatherhood: The Politics of Nationalism, Sexuality, and Race in Singapore." Pp. 195–215 in *Bewitching*

Women, Pious Men: Gender and Body Politics in Southeast Asia, Aihwa Ong and Michael G. Peletz, eds. Berkeley: University of California Press.

Herlinatiens. 2003. *Garis Tepi Seorang Lesbian*. Introduction by Saskia E. Wieringa. Yogyakarta: Galang Press.

Hervey, Sándor. 1992. "Registering Registers." *Lingua* 86(2–3):189–206.

Hill, Hal. 1996. *The Indonesian Economy since 1966: Southeast Asia's Emerging Giant*. Cambridge: Cambridge University Press.

Hooker, Virginia Matheson, and Howard Dick. 1993. "Introduction." Pp. 1–23 in *Culture and Society in New Order Indonesia*, Virginia Matheson Hooker, ed. Oxford: Oxford University Press.

Hoskins, Janet. 1998. *Biographical Objects: How Things Tell the Stories of People's Lives*. New York: Routledge.

Howard, Richard Stephen. 1996. "Falling into the Gay World: Manhood, Marriage, and Family in Indonesia." Ph.D. dissertation, University of Illinois at Urbana-Champaign.

Hull, Terence H. 2002. "The Marriage Revolution in Indonesia." Paper presented at the Annual Meeting of the Population Association of America, Atlanta, 9–11 May.

Idrus, Nurul Ilmi. 2003. "To Take Each Other: Bugis Practices of Gender, Sexuality, and Marriage." Ph.D. dissertation, Department of Anthropology, Research School of Pacific and Asian Studies, Australian National University.

Indonesian Gay Society. 1999. "Gay Gay Gay." *New Jaka-Jaka* 6:15–16.

Ingram, Gordon Brent. 1997. "Marginality and the Landscapes of Erotic Alien(n)ations." Pp. 27–52 in *Queers in Space: Communities, Public Places, Sites of Resistance*, Gordon Brent Ingram, Anne-Marie Bouthillette, and Yolanda Retter, eds. Seattle: Bay Press.

Ingram, Gordon Brent, Anne-Marie Bouthillette, and Yolanda Retter, eds. 1997. *Queers in Space: Communities, Public Places, Sites of Resistance*. Seattle: Bay Press.

Ivy, Marilyn. 1995. *Discourses of the Vanishing: Modernity, Phantasm, Japan*. Chicago: University of Chicago Press.

Jackson, Peter A. 1997. "*Kathoey*><Gay><Man: The Historical Emergence of Gay Male Identity in Thailand." Pp. 166–190 in *Sites of Desire, Economies of Pleasure: Sexualities in Asia and the Pacific*, Lenore Manderson and Margaret Jolly, eds. Chicago: University of Chicago Press.

———. 1999a. "An American Death in Bangkok: The Murder of Darrell Berrigan and the Hybrid Origins of Gay Identity in 1960s Thailand." *GLQ: A Journal of Gay and Lesbian Studies* 5(3):361–411.

———. 1999b. "Tolerant but Unaccepting: The Myth of a Thai 'Gay Paradise.'" Pp. 226–242 in *Genders and Sexualities in Modern Thailand*, Peter A. Jackson and Nerida M. Cook, eds. Chiang Mai: Silkworm Books.

———. 2003. "Performative Genders, Perverse Desires: A Bio-History of Thailand's Same-Sex and Transgender Cultures." *Intersections: Gender, History and Culture in the Asian Context*, issue 9. http://www.sshe.murdoch.edu.au/intersections/issue9/jackson.html, accessed October 12, 2003.

———. 2004. "Gay Adaptation, Tom-Dee Resistance, and Kathoey Indifference: Thailand's Gender/Sex Minorities and the Episodic Allure of Queer English."

Pp. 202–230 in *Speaking in Queer Tongues: Globalization and Gay Language*, William L. Leap and Tom Boellstorff, eds. Urbana: University of Illinois Press.

Jameson, Fredric. 1991. *Postmodernism, or the Cultural Logic of Late Capitalism*. Durham: Duke University Press.

Johnson, Mark. 1997. *Beauty and Power: Transgendering and Cultural Transformation in the Southern Philippines*. Oxford: Berg.

Jones, Gavin W. 1994. *Marriage and Divorce in Islamic South-East Asia*. Kuala Lumpur: Oxford University Press.

Jones, Russell. 1973. "Earl, Logan, and Indonesia." *Archipel* 6:93–118.

Josselin de Jong, J P.B. de. 1977. "The Malay Archipelago as a Field of Ethnological Study." Pp. 164–182 in *Structural Anthropology in the Netherlands: A Reader*, P.E. de Josselin de Jong, ed. The Hague: Martinus Nijhoff.

Kahn, Joel S. 1993. *Constituting the Minangkabau: Peasants, Culture, and Modernity in Colonial Indonesia*. Providence: Berg.

Karsch-Haack, Ferdinand. 1911. *Das Gleichgeschlectliche Leben der Naturvolker* [The Same-Sex Life of Tribal Peoples]. Munich: Ernst Reinhardt.

Kartini, Putri. 2003. *Suara Perih Perempuan: Lesbian dan Kawin Bule* [The Pained Voice of a Woman: Lesbian and Married to a White Man]. Yoygakarta: Galang Press.

Keane, Webb. 1997. "Knowing One's Place: National Language and the Idea of the Local in Eastern Indonesia." *Cultural Anthropology* 12(1):37–63.

———. 2003. "Public Speaking: On Indonesian as the Language of the Nation." *Public Culture* 15(3):503–530.

Keeler, Ward. 1983. "Shame and Stage Fright in Java." *Ethos* 11(3):152–165.

Kennedy, Elizabeth Lapovsky, and Madeline D. Davis. 1993. *Boots of Leather, Slippers of Gold: The History of a Lesbian Community*. New York: Routledge.

Kessler, Suzanne J., and Wendy McKenna. 1985. *Gender: An Ethnomethodological Approach*. Chicago: University of Chicago Press.

Knauft, Bruce M. 1996. *Genealogies for the Present in Cultural Anthropology*. New York: Routledge.

Kompas. 1997. "Presiden Resmi Minta DPR Bicarakan Lagi RUU Penyiaran" [The President Formally Asks the Parliament to Further Discuss the Broadcasting Law]. July 25, 1997. http://www.kompas.com/9707/25/hiburan/mint.htm, accessed April 9, 1998.

Kratz, E. U. 1978. "Djalan Sempoerna: Eine Frühe indonesische Autobiographie" [The Perfect Path: An Early Indonesian Biography]. Pp. 340–356 in *Spectrum: Essays Presented to Sutan Takdir Alisjahbana on His Seventieth Birthday*, S. Udin, ed. Jakarta: Dian Rakyat.

Kroeger, Karen. 2000. "Risk, Boundary Making, and the Social Order: Understanding the Social Construction of AIDS and Sexuality in Indonesia." Ph.D. dissertation, Department of Anthropology, Washington University, St. Louis.

Kuipers, Joel C. 1998. *Language, Identity, and Marginality in Indonesia: The Changing Nature of Ritual Speech on the Island of Sumba*. Cambridge: Cambridge University Press.

———. 2003. "Citizens as Spectators: Citizenship as a Communicative Practice on the Eastern Indonesian Island of Sumba." Pp. 162–191 in *Cultural Citizen-*

ship in Island Southeast Asia: Nation and Belonging in the Hinterlands, Renato Rosaldo, ed. Berkeley: University of California Press.

Kulick, Don. 1998. *Travesti: Sex, Gender, and Culture among Brazilian Transgendered Prostitutes*. Chicago: University of Chicago Press.

Kurtz, Donald V. 1996. "Hegemony and Anthropology: Gramsci, Exegeses, Reinterpretations." *Critique of Anthropology* 16(2):103–135.

Kusumaatmadja, Mochtar. 1982. "The Concept of the Indonesian Archipelago." *Indonesian Quarterly* 10(4):12–26.

Lancaster, Roger N. 1995. "That We Should All Turn Queer? Homosexual Stigma in the Making of Manhood and the Breaking of a Revolution in Nicaragua." Pp. 135–156 in *Conceiving Sexuality: Approaches to Sex Research in a Postmodern World*. R. G. Parker and J. H. Gagnon, eds. New York: Routledge.

Lathief, Halilintar. 2004. *Bissu: Pergulatan dan Peranannya di Masyarakat Bugis* [Bissus: Their Struggle and Role in Bugis Society]. Depok, Indonesia: Desantara.

Leach, Edmund R. 1964. *Political Systems of Highland Burma: A Study of Kachin Social Structure*. Boston: Beacon Press.

Leap, William L. 1999. "Introduction." Pp. 1–21 in *Public Sex, Gay Space*, William L. Leap, ed. New York: Columbia University Press.

Lefebvre, Henri. 1991. *The Production of Space*. Translated by Donald Nicholson-Smith. Oxford: Blackwell.

Lembaga Ketahanan Nasional. 1995. *Wawasan Nusantara* [The Archipelago Concept]. Jakarta: Balai Pustaka.

Leong, Lawrence. 1995. "Space and Place in Gay Singapore: Implications for AIDS Prevention and Control." *The Act* 12:4–5.

Lev, Daniel S. 1990. "Intermediate Classes and Change in Indonesia: Some Initial Reflections." Pp. 25–43 in *The Politics of Middle Class Indonesia*, Kenneth Young, and Richard Tanter, eds. Clayton, Australia: Monash University Press.

Lewin, Ellen. 1991. "Writing Lesbian and Gay Culture: What the Natives Have to Say for Themselves." *American Ethnologist* 18(4):786–792.

Li, Tania Murray. 2003. "*Masyarakat Adat*, Difference, and the Limits of Recognition in Indonesia's Forest Zone." Pp. 380–406 in *Race, Nature, and the Politics of Difference*, Donald S. Moore, Jake Kosek and Anand Pandian, eds. Durham: Duke University Press.

Liddle, R. William. 1988. "The National Political Culture and the New Order." *Prisma* 46:4–20.

Liechty, Mark. 2003. *Suitably Modern: Making Middle-Class Culture in a New Consumer Society*. Princeton: Princeton University Press.

Likosky, Stephan. 1992. "Introduction." Pp. xv–xviii in *Coming Out: An Anthology of International Gay and Lesbian Writings*, Stephan Likosky, ed. New York: Pantheon.

Lindsay, Jennifer. 1997. "Making Waves: Private Radio and Local Identities in Indonesia." *Indonesia* 64:105–124.

———. 2005. "Speaking the Truth: Speech on Television in New Order Indonesia." In *The History of Translation in Indonesia and Malaysia*, Henri Chambert-Loir, ed. Paris: EFEO-Archipel.

Lindsey, Timothy. 1997. *The Romance of K'tut Tantri and Indonesia: Text and Scripts, History and Identity*. Kuala Lumpur: Oxford University Press.

Liu, Lydia H. 1995. *Translingual Practice: Literature, National Culture, and Translated Modernity—China, 1900–1937.* Stanford: Stanford University Press.

———, ed. 1999. *Tokens of Exchange: the Problem of Translation in Global Circulations.* Durham: Duke University Press.

Lumsden, Ian. 1996. *Machos, Maricones, and Gays: Cuba and Homosexuality.* Philadelphia: Temple University Press.

Lyotard, Jean-François. 1984. *The Postmodern Condition: A Report on Knowledge.* Translation by Geoff Bennington and Brian Massumi; foreword by Fredric Jameson. Minneapolis: University of Minnesota Press.

———. 1988. *The Differend: Phrases in Dispute.* Minneapolis: University of Minnesota Press.

Macpherson, C. B. 1962. *The Political Theory of Possessive Individualism: Hobbes to Locke.* Oxford: Oxford University Press.

Maengkom, Freddy Wawea. 1997. *Apakah Orang-orang Wawea Itu* [Who Are the Wawea]? Jakarta: Libro Sannyasi.

Mahmood, Saba. 2001. "Feminist Theory, Embodiment, and the Docile Agent: Some Reflections on the Egyptian Islamic Revival." *Cultural Anthropology* 16(2):202–236.

Maier, Hendrik Menko Jan. 1993. "From Heteroglossia to Polyglossia: The Creation of Malay and Dutch in the Indies." *Indonesia* 56:37–65.

Maine, Henry. 1916 [1861]. *Ancient Law.* London: John Murray.

Maira, Sunaina. 1999. "Identity Dub: The Paradoxes of an Indian American Youth Subculture (New York Mix)." *Cultural Anthropology* 14(1):29–60.

Malinowski, Bronislaw. 1922. *Argonauts of the Western Pacific.* New York: E. P. Dutton & Co.

Mamdani, Mahmood. 1996. *Citizen and Subject: Contemporary Africa and the Legacy of Late Colonialism.* Princeton: Princeton University Press.

Manalansan, Martin F. 1995. "In the Shadows of Stonewall: Examining Gay Transnational Politics and the Diasporic Dilemma." *GLQ: A Journal of Gay and Lesbian Studies* 2(4):425–438.

———. 2003. *Global Divas: Filipino Gay Men in the Diaspora.* Durham: Duke University Press.

Mankekar, Purnima. 1999. *Screening Culture, Viewing Politics: An Ethnography of Television, Womanhood, and Nation in Postcolonial India.* Durham: Duke University Press.

Marcus, George. 1995. "Ethnography in/of the World System: The Emergence of Multi-sited Ethnography." *Annual Review of Anthropology* 24:95–117.

Massad, Joseph. 2002. "Re-Orienting Desire: The Gay International and the Arab World." *Public Culture* 14(2):361–385.

Massey, Doreen. 1994. *Space, Place, and Gender.* Cambridge: Polity Press.

Mattulada. 1974. *Bugis-Makassar: Manusia dan Kebudayaannya* [Bugis-Makassar: The People and Their Culture]. Jakarta: Jurusan Antropologi, Fakultas Sastra Universitas Indonesia.

McBeth, John. 1997. "Technical Problems: Suharto Bends Constitution by Returning Broadcast Bill." *Far Eastern Economic Review* 160(36):24.

McLelland, Mark J. 2000. *Male Homosexuality in Modern Japan: Cultural Myths and Social Realities*. Richmond, Surrey: Curzon Press.

Mead, Margaret. 1980. *Sex and Temperament in Three Primitive Societies*. New York: Morrow Quill Paperbacks.

Millar, Susan B. 1983. "On Interpreting Gender in Bugis Society." *American Ethnologist* 10:477–493.

Mills, Mary Beth. 1995. "Attack of the Widow Ghosts: Gender, Death, and Modernity in Northeast Thailand." Pp. 244–273 in *Bewitching Women, Pious Men: Gender and Body Politics in Southeast Asia*, Aihwa Ong and Michael G. Peletz, eds. Berkeley: University of California Press.

Mintz, Sidney W. 1998. "Swallowing Modernity." Pp. 183–202 in *Golden Arches East: McDonald's in East Asia*, James L. Watson, ed. Stanford: Stanford University Press.

Mintz, Sidney W., and Richard Price. 1976. *The Birth of African-American Culture: An Anthropological Perspective*. Boston: Beacon Press.

Moerdani, L. B. 1986. "Hikmah Kebangkitan Nasional dalam Kerangka Mewujudkan Ketahanan Nasional" [The Power of National Awakening in the Framework of Establishing National Endurance]. Pp. 32–53 in *Wawasan Kebangsaan, Ketahanan Nasional dan Wawasan Nusantara* [Concept of the People, National Endurance, and the Archipelago Concept]. Yogyakarta: Lembaga Pengkajian Kebudayaan Sarjana Wiyata Tamansiswa.

Morfit, Michael. 1981. *Pancasila: The Indonesian State Ideology According to the New Order Government*. *Asian Survey* 21(8):838–851.

Morris, Rosalind C. 1995. "All Made Up: Performance Theory and the New Anthropology of Sex and Gender." *Annual Review of Anthropology* 24:567–592.

———. 1997. "Educating Desire: Thailand, Transnationalism, and Transgression." *Social Text* 15(3/4):53–79.

———. 2000. *In the Place of Origins: Modernity and Its Mediums in Northern Thailand*. Durham: Duke University Press.

Mosse, George L. 1985. *Nationalism and Sexuality: Respectability and Abnormal Sexuality in Modern Europe*. New York: Howard Fertig.

Murray, Alison. 1999. "Let Them Take Ecstasy: Class and Jakarta Lesbians." Pp. 139–156 in *Female Desires: Same-Sex Relations and Transgender Practices across Cultures*, Evelyn Blackwood and Saskia E. Wieringa, eds. New York: Columbia University Press.

Murray, David. 1996. "Homosexuality, Society, and the State: An Ethnography of Sublime Resistance in Martinique." *Identities* 2(3):249–272.

Murray, Stephen O. 1992. "Austronesian Gender-Defined Homosexuality: Introduction." Pp. 151–170 in *Oceanic Homosexualities*, Stephen O. Murray, ed. New York: Garland Publishing.

Nagazumi, Akira. 1978. "The Word 'Indonesia': The Growth of Its Political Connotation." *Indonesia Circle* 17:28–34.

Nagengast, Carole. 1994. "Violence, Terror, and the Crisis of the State." *Annual Review of Anthropology* 23:109–136.

Niehof, Anke. 2003. "Women and the Social Context of Fertility under the New Order." Pp. 163–184 in *Two Is Enough: Family Planning in Indonesia under the New Order, 1968–1998*, Anke Niehof and Firman Lubis, eds. Leiden: KITLV Press.

Niranjana, Tejaswini. 1992. *Siting Translation: History, Post-structuralism, and the Colonial Context.* Berkeley: University of California Press.

Oetomo, Dédé. 1996a. "Gender and Sexual Orientation in Indonesia." Pp. 259–269 in *Fantasizing the Feminine in Indonesia*, Laurie Sears, ed. Durham: Duke University Press.

———. 1996b. "Bahasa Indonesia dan Kelas Menengah Indonesia" [Indonesian and the Indonesian Middle Class]. Pp. 195–212 in *Bahasa dan Kekuasaan* [Language and Power], Yudi Latif and Idi Subandy Ibrahim, eds. Bandung: Mizan.

———. 1997. "Ketika Sharon Stone Berbahasa Indonesia" [When Sharon Stone Speaks Indonesian]. Pp. 333–337 in *Bercinta Dengan Televisi: Ilusi, Impresi, dan Imaji Sebuah Kotak Ajaib* [In Love with Television: Illusions, Impressions, and Images from a Magical Box], Deddy Mulyana and Idi Subandy Ibrahim, eds. Bandung: PT Remaja Rosdakarya.

———. 2000. "Masculinity in Indonesia: Genders, Sexualities, and Identities in a Changing Society." Pp. 46–59 in *Framing the Sexual Subject: The Politics of Gender, Sexuality, and Power*, Richard Parker, Regina Maria Barbosa, and Peter Aggleton, eds. Berkeley: University of California Press.

Ortner, Sherry, and Harriet Whitehead. 1981. "Introduction: Accounting for Sexual Meanings." Pp. 1–28 in *Sexual Meanings: The Cultural Construction of Gender and Sexuality*, Sherry Ortner and Harriet Whitehead, eds. Cambridge: Cambridge University Press.

Pandoyo, S. Toto. 1985. *Wawasan Nusantara dan Implementasinya Dalam UUD 1945 Serta Pembangunan Nasional* [The Archipelago Concept and Its Implementation in the 1945 Constitution and National Development]. Jakarta: Penerbit Rineka Cipta.

Parker, Andrew, et al. 1992. *Nationalisms and Sexualities.* New York: Routledge.

Parker, Richard. 1999. *Beneath the Equator: Cultures of Desire, Male Homosexuality, and Emerging Gay Communities in Brazil.* New York: Routledge.

Patterson, Thomas C. 2001. *A Social History of Anthropology in the United States.* Oxford: Berg.

Peacock, James L. 1968. *Rites of Modernization: Symbolic and Social Aspects of Indonesian Proletarian Drama.* Chicago: University of Chicago Press.

Peletz, Michael G. 1996. *Reason and Passion: Representations of Gender in a Malay Society.* Berkeley: University of California Press.

Pelras, Christian. 1996. *The Bugis.* Oxford: Blackwell.

Pemberton, John. 1994. *On the Subject of "Java."* Ithaca: Cornell University Press.

Petkovic, Josko. 1999. "Dédé Oetomo Talks on Reyog Ponorogo." *Intersections: Gender, History, and Culture in the Asian Context*, issue 2. http:// wwwsshe.murdoch.edu.au/ intersections/issue2/Oetomo.html, accessed March 15, 2000.

Philpott, Simon. 2000. *Rethinking Indonesia: Postcolonial Theory, Authoritarianism and Identity.* New York: St. Martin's Press.

Picard, Michel. 1996. *Bali: Cultural Tourism and Touristic Culture.* Singapore: Archipelago Press.

Pinches, Michael. 1999. "Cultural Relations, Class, and the New Rich of Asia." Pp. 1–55 in *Culture and Privilege in Capitalist Asia*, Michael Pinches, ed. London: Routledge.

Pinches, Michael, ed. 1999. *Culture and Privilege in Capitalist Asia*. London: Routledge.

Poerwadarminta, W.J.S. 1976. *Kamus Umum Bahasa Indonesia* [General Indonesian Dictionary]. Jakarta: Balai Pustaka.

Povinelli, Elizabeth A. 2001. "Radical Worlds: The Anthropology of Incommensurability and Inconceivability." *Annual Review of Anthropology* 30:319–334.

———. 2002. *The Cunning of Recognition: Indigenous Alterities and the Making of Australian Multiculturalism*. Durham: Duke University Press.

Prawirakusumah, R. Prie, and Ramadhan K. H. 1988. *Menguak Duniaku: Kisah Sejati Kelainan Seksual* [Revealing My World: A True Story of Sexual Deviance]. Jakarta: Pustaka Utama Grafiti.

Priaga, Lanang. 2003. *Menembus Kaum Gay Jakarta* [Penetrating the World of Gay Jakarta]. Jakarta: Abdi Tandur.

Proschan, Frank. 2002. "Eunuch Mandarins, Soldats Mamzelles, Effeminate Boys, and Graceless Women: French Colonial Constructions of Vietnamese Genders." *GLQ: A Journal of Gay and Lesbian Studies* 8(4):435–467.

Proyek Penelitian Keagamaan. 1984. *Penerapan Wawasan Nusantara dalam Pembinaan Kehidupan Beragama (Pokok Pokok Pikiran)* [The Application of the Archipelago Concept in Building Religious Life (Key Concepts)]. Jakarta: Badan Penelitian dan Pengembangan Agama, Departemen Agama Republik Indonesia.

Rabinow, Paul. 1986. "Representations Are Social Facts: Modernity and Post-Modernity in Anthropology." Pp. 234–261 in *Writing Culture: The Poetics and Politics of Ethnography*, James Clifford and George E. Marcus, eds. Berkeley: University of California Press.

Rafael, Vicente L. 1988. *Contracting Colonialism: Translation and Christian Conversion in Tagalog Society under Early Spanish Rule*. Ithaca: Cornell University Press.

Ram, Kalpana, and Margaret Jolly, eds. 1998. *Maternities and Modernities: Colonial and Postcolonial Experiences in the Asia Pacific*. New York: Cambridge University Press.

Ramage, Douglas E. 1995. *Politics in Indonesia: Democracy, Islam, and the Ideology of Tolerance*. London: Routledge.

Ratri, M., ed. 2000. *Lines: Kumpulan Cerita Perempuan di Garis Pinggir* [Lesbians: Collected Stories of Women on the Margins]. Jakarta: Millennium.

Redfield, Robert. 1955. *The Little Community: Viewpoints for the Study of a Human Whole*. Chicago: University of Chicago Press.

Reeve, David. 1985. *Golkar of Indonesia: An Alternative to the Party System*. Singapore: Oxford University Press.

Reid, Anthony. 1988. *Southeast Asia in the Age of Commerce 1450–1680, Vol. 1: The Lands below the Winds*. New Haven: Yale University Press.

Republika. 1996. "Stasiun TV Menyambut" [TV Stations Reply], May 2, 1996. http://www.hamline.edu/apakabar/basisdata/1996/05/02/0041.html, accessed April 10, 1998.

Rhodius, Hans, and John Darling. 1980. *Walter Spies and Balinese Art.* Zutphen, Netherlands: Terra.

Ricklefs, Merle C. 1998. *The Seen and Unseen Worlds In Java, 1726–1749: History, Literature and Islam in the Court of Pakubuwana II.* Honolulu: University of Hawaii Press.

Robinson, Kathryn. 1989. "Choosing Contraception: Cultural Change and the Indonesian Family Planning Programme." Pp. 21–38 in *Creating Indonesian Cultures,* Paul Alexander, ed. Sydney: Oceania Publications.

———. 1998. "Love and Sex in an Indonesian Mining Town." Pp. 63–86 in *Gender and Power in Affluent Asia,* Krishna Sen and Maila Stivens, eds. London: Routledge.

Robison, Richard. 1996. "The Middle Class and the Bourgeoisie in Indonesia." Pp. 79–104 in *The New Rich in Asia: Mobile Phones, McDonalds and Middle-Class Revolution,* Richard Robison and David S. G. Goodman, eds. London: Routledge.

Rodgers, Susan. 1991. "Imagining Tradition, Imagining Modernity: A Southern Batak Novel from the 1920s." *Bijdragen tot de Taal-Land-en Volkenkunde* 147:273–297.

———. 1995. *Telling Lives, Telling History: Autobiography and Historical Imagination in Modern Indonesia.* Berkeley: University of California Press.

Rofel, Lisa. 1999. *Other Modernities: Gendered Yearnings in China after Socialism.* Berkeley: University of California Press.

Rosaldo, Michelle Z. 1980. "The Use and Abuse of Anthropology: Reflections on Feminism and Cross-Cultural Understanding." *Signs: Journal of Women in Culture and Society* 5(3):389–417.

Rose, Nikolas. 2000. "Community, Citizenship, and the Third Way." *American Behavioral Scientist* 43(9):1395–1411.

Rubin, Gayle. 1975. "The Traffic in Women: Notes on the 'Political Economy' of Sex." Pp. 157–210 in *Toward an Anthropology of Women,* Rayna R. Reiter, ed. New York: Monthly Review Press.

———. 1984. "Thinking Sex: Notes for a Radical Theory of the Politics of Sexuality." Pp. 267–319 in *Pleasure and Danger,* Carole S. Vance, ed. London: Routledge & Kegan Paul.

Rumsey, Alan. 1990. "Wording, Meaning, and Linguistic Ideology." *American Anthropologist* 92(2):346–361.

Rustam, Soepardjo. 1986. "Pemantapan Ideologi Pancasila: Suatu Deskripsi Historis" [The Stabilization of the Pancasila Ideology: A Historical Description]. Pp. 54–81 in *Wawasan Kebangsaan, Ketahanan Nasional dan Wawasan Nusantara* [The National Concept, National Endurance, and the Archipelago Concept], Lembaga Pengkajian Kebudayaan Sarjana Wiyata Tamansiswa, ed. Yogyakarta: Lembaga Pengkajian Kebudayaan Sarjana Wiyata Tamansiswa.

Rutherford, Danilyn. 1996. "Of Birds and Gifts: Reviving Tradition on an Indonesian Frontier." *Cultural Anthropology* 11(4):577–616.

———. 2003a. "Ethnography without Culture? Modernity and Marginality in the Anthropology of Indonesia." *Reviews in Anthropology* 32:91–108.

———. 2003b. *Raiding the Land of the Foreigners: The Limits of the Nation on an Indonesian Frontier.* Princeton: Princeton University Press.

Ryanto, Tony. 1998. "Indonesia Biz Resilient." *Variety* 373(3):42.

Salim, Peter, and Yenny Salim. 1991. *Kamus Bahasa Indonesia Kontemporer* [Dictionary of Contemporary Indonesian]. Jakarta: Modern English Press.

Sánchez-Eppler, Benigno, and Cindy Patton. 2000. "Introduction: With a Passport Out of Eden." Pp. 1–14 in *Queer Diasporas*, Benigno Sánchez-Eppler and Cindy Patton, eds. Durham: Duke University Press.

Sandoval, Chela. 1991. "U.S. Third World Feminism: The Theory and Method of Oppositional Consciousness in the Postmodern World." *Genders* 10:1–24.

Sang, Tze-Ian D. 2003. *The Emerging Lesbian: Female Same-Sex Desire in Modern China*. Chicago: University of Chicago Press.

Schein, Louisa. 1996. "The Other Goes to Market: The State, the Nation, and Unruliness in Contemporary China." *Identities* 2(3):197–222.

———. 1999. "Performing Modernity." *Cultural Anthropology* 14(3):361–395.

Scott, David. 1995. "Colonial Governmentality." *Social Text* 43:191–220.

Sears, Laurie. 1996. "Fragile Identities: Deconstructing Women and Indonesia." Pp. 1–46 in *Fantasizing the Feminine in Indonesia*, Laurie Sears, ed. Durham: Duke University Press.

Sedgwick, Eve Kosofsky. 1991. *Epistemology of the Closet*. London: Harvester/Wheatsheaf.

Sen, Krishna. 1994. *Indonesian Cinema: Framing the New Order*. London: Zed Press.

———. 1998. "Indonesian Women at Work: Reframing the Subject." Pp. 35–62 in *Gender and Power in Affluent Asia*, Krishna Sen and Maila Stivens, eds. London: Routledge.

Shields, Rob. 1997. "Spatial Stress and Resistance: Social Meanings of Spatialization." Pp. 186–202 in *Space and Social Theory: Interpreting Modernity and Postmodernity*, Georges Benko and Ulf Strohmayer, eds. Oxford: Blackwell.

Shiraishi, Saya S. 1997. *Young Heroes: The Indonesian Family in Politics*. Ithaca: Cornell Southeast Asia Program.

Shohat, Ella. 1992. "Notes on the 'Post-Colonial.'" *Social Text* 31/32:99–113.

Shore, Bradd. 1982. *Sala'ilua: A Samoan Mystery*. New York: Columbia University Press.

Siegel, James T. 1969. *The Rope of God*. Berkeley: University of California Press.

———. 1986. *Solo in the New Order: Language and Hierarchy in an Indonesian City*. Princeton: Princeton University Press.

———. 1997. *Fetish, Recognition, Revolution*. Princeton: Princeton University Press.

———. 1998. *A New Criminal Type in Jakarta: Counter-Revolution Today*. Durham: Duke University Press.

———. 2002. "The Idea of Indonesia Continues: The Middle Class Ignores Aceh." *Archipel* 64:199–229.

Silverman, Kaja. 1983. *The Subject of Semiotics*. New York: Oxford University Press.

Silverstein, Michael. 1993. "Metapragmatic Discourse and Metapragmatic Function." Pp. 33–58 in *Reflexive Language: Reported Speech and Metapragmatics*, J. A. Lucy, ed. Cambridge: Cambridge University Press.

Simon, Sherry. 1996. *Gender in Translation: Cultural Identity and the Politics of Transmission*. London: Routledge.

Simons, R.D.G. 1939. "Indrukken over de Prostitutie en de Homosexueele Prostitutie, en over het Voorkomen van Geslachtszieken in Ned Oost-Indie" [Impressions Concerning Prostitution and Homosexual Prostitution, and Concerning the Appearance of Venereal Disease in the Netherlands East Indies]. *Nederlandsch Tijdschrift voor Geneeskunde* [Netherlands Periodical for Medicine] 83(47):5574–5579.

———. 1940. "Homosexualiteit en Geslachtsziekten" [Homosexuality and Venereal Disease]. *Geneeskundig Tijdschrift voor Nederlandsch-Indie* [Medical Periodical for the Netherlands Indies] 80(42):2478–2487.

Sinnott, Megan J. 2004. *Toms and Dees: Transgender Identity and Female Same-Sex Relationships in Thailand*. Honolulu: University of Hawaii Press.

Sirk, U. 1975. "On Old Buginese and Basa Bissu." *Archipel* 10:225–237.

Smail, John R. W. 1961. "On the Possibility of an Autonomous History of Modern Southeast Asia." *Journal of Southeast Asian History* 2(2):72–102.

Sneddon, James N. 1996. *Indonesian: A Comprehensive Grammar*. London: Routledge.

———. 2003. *The Indonesian Language: Its History and Role in Modern Society*. Sydney: University of New South Wales Press.

Soeharto. 1997. Indonesian Presidential Directive R.09/jo/VII/1997. Jakarta, Indonesia.

Solzhentsyn, Aleksandr I. 1973. *The Gulag Archipelago, 1918–1956: An Experiment in Literary Investigation*, Thomas P. Whitney, trans. New York: Harper & Row.

Spivak, Gayatri Chakravorty. 2000. "The Politics of Translation." Pp. 397–416 in *The Translation Studies Reader*, Lawrence Venuti, ed. London: Routledge.

Spyer, Patricia. 1996. "Diversity with a Difference: Adat and the New Order in Aru (Eastern Indonesia)." *Cultural Anthropology* 11(1):25–50.

———. 2000. *The Memory of Trade: Modernity's Entanglements on an Eastern Indonesian Island*. Durham: Duke University Press.

Steedly, Mary Margaret. 1999. "The State of Culture Theory in the Anthropology of Southeast Asia." *Annual Review of Anthropology* 28:431–54.

———. 2000. "Modernity and the Memory Artist: The Work of Imagination in Highland Sumatra, 1947–1995." *Comparative Studies in Society and History* 42(4):811–846.

Steiner, George. 1998. *After Babel: Aspects of Language and Translation*. 3rd ed. London: Oxford University Press.

Stivens, Maila. 1996. *Matriliny and Modernity: Sexual Politics and Social Change in Rural Malaysia*. St. Leonards: Allen & Unwin.

———. 1998. "Theorizing Gender, Power, and Modernity in Affluent Asia." Pp. 1–34 in *Gender and Power in Affluent Asia*, Krishna Sen and Maila Stivens, eds. London: Routledge.

Stoler, Ann Laura. 1995. *Race and the Education of Desire: Foucault's History of Sexuality and the Colonial Order of Things*. Durham: Duke University Press.

———. 2002a. "Colonial Archives and the Arts of Governance." *Archival Science* 2:87–109.

————. 2002b. *Carnal Knowledge and Imperial Power: Race and the Intimate in Colonial Rule.* Berkeley: University of California Press.

Strathern, Marilyn. 1988. *The Gender of the Gift: Problems with Women and Problems with Society in Melanesia.* Berkeley: University of California Press.

————. 1992. *Reproducing the Future: Anthropology, Kinship, and the New Reproductive Technologies.* New York: Routledge.

————. 1996. "Cutting the Network." *Journal of the Royal Anthropological Institute* 2:517–535.

Streck, Bernhard, and Tullio Maranhão, eds. 2003. *Translation and Ethnography: The Anthropological Challenge of Intercultural Understanding.* Tucson: University of Arizona Press.

Suara Pembuaran Daily. 1996. "Kalangan DPR: Alih Suara di TV Sebaiknya Tunggu UU Penyiaran" [The Parliamentary Group: Television Voice Experts Had Best Wait for the Broadcasting Laws]. May 3, 1996. http://www.hamline.edu/apakabar/basisdata/1996/05/03/0046.html, accessed April 10, 1998.

Sudibyo, Parmono. 1991. *Implementasi Wawasan Nusantara dalam Mengembangkan Rasa Cinta Tanah Air, Mempertebal Semangat Kebangsaan, dan Rasa Kesetiakawanan Sosial* [The Implementation of the Archipelago Concept in Fostering Love for the Homeland, Strong Nationalism, and Social Solidarity]. Jakarta: Markas Besar Angkatan Bersenjata, Republik Indonesia, Lembaga Pertahanan Nasional.

Suryakusuma, Julia I. 1996. "The State and Sexuality in New Order Indonesia." Pp. 92–119 in *Fantasizing the Feminine in Indonesia*, Laurie Sears, ed. Durham: Duke University Press.

Syahmin, A. K. 1988. *Beberapa Perkembangan dan Masalah Hukum Laut Internasional* [Some Developments and Problems in International Maritime Law]. Bandung: Penerbit Binacipta.

Tan, Beng Hui. 1999. "Women's Sexuality and the Discourse on Asian Values: Cross-Dressing in Malaysia." Pp. 281–307 in *Female Desires: Same-Sex Relations and Transgender Practices across Cultures*, Evelyn Blackwood and Saskia E. Wieringa, eds. New York: Columbia University Press.

Tan, Michael. 1995. "From Bakla to Gay: Shifting Gender Identities and Sexual Behaviors in the Phillippines." Pp. 85–96 in *Conceiving Sexuality: Approaches to Sex Research in a Postmodern World*. R. G. Parker and J. H. Gagnon, eds. New York: Routledge.

Tanabe, Shigeharu, and Charles F. Keyes. 2002. *Cultural Crisis and Social Memory: Modernity and Identity in Thailand and Laos.* Honolulu: University of Hawai'i Press.

Taylor, Charles. 1994. "The Politics of Recognition." Pp. 25–73 in *Multiculturalism: Examining the Politics of Recognition*, Amy Gutmann, ed. Princeton: Princeton University Press.

Taylor, Paul Michael. 1994. "The Nusantara Concept of Culture: Local Traditions and National Identity as Expressed in Indonesia's Museums." Pp. 71–90 in *Fragile Traditions: Indonesian Art in Jeopardy*, Paul Michael Taylor, ed. Honolulu: University of Hawaii Press.

Thongthiraj, Took Took. 1996. "Toward a Struggle against Invisibility: Love between Women in Thailand." Pp. 163–174 in *Asian American Sexualities: Di-*

mensions of the Gay and Lesbian Experience, Russell Leong, ed. New York: Routledge.

Tiwon, Sylvia. 1996. "Models and Maniacs: Articulating the Female in Indonesia." Pp. 47–70 in *Fantasizing the Feminine in Indonesia*, Laurie Sears, ed. Durham: Duke University Press.

Troiden, Richard R. 1988. *Gay and Lesbian Identity: A Sociological Analysis.* Dix Hills, NY: General Hall.

Trouillot, Michel-Rolph. 1991. "Anthropology and the Savage Slot: The Poetics and Politics of Otherness." Pp. 17–44 in *Recapturing Anthropology: Working in the Present*, Richard G. Fox, ed. Santa Fe: School of American Research Press.

Tsing, Anna Lowenhaupt. 1993. *In the Realm of the Diamond Queen: Marginality in an Out-of-the-Way Place.* Princeton: Princeton University Press.

Tylor, Edward Burnett. 1958. *Primitive Culture, Volume 1: The Origins of Culture.* New York: Harper and Row.

Utomo, Iwu Dwisetyani. 2002. "Sexual Values and Early Experiences among Young People in Jakarta." Pp. 207–227 in *Coming of Age in South and Southeast Asia: Youth, Courtship, and Sexuality*, Lenore Manderson and Pranee Liamputtong, eds. Richmond, Surrey: Curzon Press.

van der Kroef, Justus M. 1992. "Transvestitism and the Religious Hermaphrodite in Indonesia." Pp. 89–97 in *Asian Homosexuality*, Wayne R. Dynes and Stephen Donaldson, eds. New York: Garland Publishing.

Van Doorn, Jacques. 1983. *A Divided Society: Segmentation and Mediation in Late-Colonial Indonesia.* Rotterdam: CASP.

van Langenberg, Michael. 1990. "The New Order State: Language, Ideology, Hegemony." Pp. 120–137 in *State and Civil Society in Indonesia*, Arief Budiman, ed. Clayton, Australia: Monash University Press.

Vickers, Adrian. 1989. *Bali: A Paradise Created.* Hong Kong: Periplus Editions.

———. 1996. "Modernity and Being *Moderen*: An Introduction." Pp. 1–36 in *Being Modern in Bali: Image and Change*, Adrian Vickers, ed. New Haven: Yale University Southeast Asia Series.

Volosinov, V. N. 1973. *Marxism and the Philosophy of Language.* Ladislaw Matejka and I. R. Titunik, trans. Cambridge, MA: Harvard University Press.

Wachirianto, Iwan. 1991.*Gemblakan dalam Perspektif Sosiologis* [Gemblakan from a Sociological Perspective]. Surabaya: FISIP Airlangga.

Wahyuni, Hermin Indah. 2000. *Televisi dan Intervensi Negara: Konteks Politik Kebijakan Publik Industri Penyiaran Televisi* [Television and State Intervention: The Political Context of Public Policy for the Television Broadcasting Industry]. Yogyakarta: Penerbit Media Pressindo.

Wallace, Alfred Russel. 1962 [1869]. *The Malay Archipelago.* New York: Dover Publications.

Warner, Michael. 1999. *The Trouble with Normal: Sex, Politics, and the Ethics of Queer Life.* Cambridge, MA: Harvard University Press.

Warren, Carol. 1993. *Adat and Dinas: Balinese Communities in the Indonesian State.* Oxford: Oxford University Press.

Warwick, Donald P. 1986. "The Indonesian Family Planning Program: Government Influence and Client Choice." *Population and Development Review* 12(3):453–490.

Waters, Malcolm. 1995. *Globalization*. London: Routledge.

Watson, C. W. 2000. *Of Self and Nation: Autobiography and the Representation of Modern Indonesia*. Honolulu: University of Hawaii Press.

Watson, James L., ed. 1998. *Golden Arches East: McDonald's in East Asia*. Stanford: Stanford University Press.

Weber, Helmut. 1994. "The Indonesian Concept of Development and Its Impact on the Process of Social Transformation." Pp. 194–210 in *Continuity, Change, and Aspirations: Social and Cultural Life in Minahasa, Indonesia*, Helmut Buchholt and Ulrich Mai, eds. Singapore: Institute of Southeast Asian Studies.

Weston, Kath. 1993. "Lesbian/Gay Studies in the House of Anthropology." *Annual Review of Anthropology* 22:339–367.

———. 1995. "Forever Is a Long Time: Romancing the Real in Gay Kinship Ideologies." Pp. 87–110 in *Naturalizing Power: Essays in Feminist Cultural Analysis*. Sylvia Yanagisako and Carol Delaney, eds. New York: Routledge.

White, Hayden. 1978. *Tropics of Discourse: Essays in Cultural Criticism*. Baltimore: Johns Hopkins University Press.

Wieringa, Edwin. 2003. "Writing Love: Expressing Nearness and Dearness in Malay-Language Love Letters." *Indonesia and the Malay World* 31(91): 317–338.

Wieringa, Saskia E. 1999a. "Desiring Bodies or Defiant Cultures: Butch-Femme Lesbians in Jakarta and Lima." Pp. 206–229 in *Female Desires: Same-Sex Relations and Transgender Practices across Cultures*, Evelyn Blackwood and Saskia E. Wieringa, eds. New York: Columbia University Press.

———. 1999b. "Sexual Metaphors in the Change from Sukarno's Old Order to Suharto's New Order in Indonesia." *Review of Indonesian and Malaysian Affairs* 32:143–178.

———. 2000. "Communism and Women's Same-Sex Practices in Post-Suharto Indonesia." *Culture, Health, and Sexuality* 2(4):441–457.

———. 2002. *Sexual Politics in Indonesia*. New York: Palgrave Macmillan.

Wilson, Ian Douglas. 1999. "Reog Ponorogo: Spirituality, Sexuality, and Power in a Javanese Performance Tradition." *Intersections: Gender, History, and Culture in the Asian Context*, issue 2. http://wwwsshe.murdoch.edu.au/intersections/issue2/ Warok.html, accessed March 15, 2000.

Winch, Peter. 1958. *The Idea of a Social Science and Its Relation to Philosophy*. New York: Humanities Press.

Winters, Jeffrey A. 1996. *Power in Motion: Capital Mobility and the Indonesian State*. Ithaca: Cornell University Press.

Yanagisako, Sylvia, and Carol Delaney. 1995. "Introduction." Pp. 1–19 in *Naturalizing Power: Essays in Feminist Cultural Analysis*, Sylvia Yanagisako, and Carol Delaney, eds. New York: Routledge.

Young, Robert J. C. 1995. *Colonial Desire: Hybridity in Theory, Culture, and Race*. London: Routledge.

Zaretsky, Eli. 1976. *Capitalism, the Family, and Personal Life*. New York: Harper & Row.

Index